Front End Drupal

Front End Drupal
Designing, Theming, Scripting

Emma Jane Hogbin
Konstantin Käfer

PRENTICE
HALL

Upper Saddle River, NJ • Boston • Indianapolis • San Francisco
New York • Toronto • Montreal • London • Munich • Paris • Madrid
Capetown • Sydney • Tokyo • Singapore • Mexico City

Many of the designations used by manufacturers and sellers to distinguish their products are claimed as trademarks. Where those designations appear in this book, and the publisher was aware of a trademark claim, the designations have been printed with initial capital letters or in all capitals.

The authors and publisher have taken care in the preparation of this book, but make no expressed or implied warranty of any kind and assume no responsibility for errors or omissions. No liability is assumed for incidental or consequential damages in connection with or arising out of the use of the information or programs contained herein.

The publisher offers excellent discounts on this book when ordered in quantity for bulk purchases or special sales, which may include electronic versions and/or custom covers and content particular to your business, training goals, marketing focus, and branding interests. For more information, please contact:

U.S. Corporate and Government Sales
(800) 382-3419
corpsales@pearsontechgroup.com

For sales outside the United States please contact:

International Sales
international@pearsoned.com

Visit us on the Web: informit.com/ph

Library of Congress Cataloging-in-Publication Data

Hogbin, Emma Jane.

Front end Drupal : designing, theming, scripting / Emma Jane Hogbin and Konstantin Käfer.

p.   cm.

Includes index.

ISBN 978-0-13-713669-8 (pbk. : alk. paper) 1. Drupal (Computer file) 2. Web sites-Design-Computer programs. 3. Web site development. I. Käfer, Konstantin. II. Title.

TK5105.8885.D78H65 2009

006.7'6—dc22

2009002636

ISBN-13: 978-0-13-713669-8
ISBN-10:   0-13-713669-2

Text printed in the United States on recycled paper at R.R. Donnelley in Crawfordsville, IN.
First printing, April 2009

Editor-in-Chief
Mark Taub

Executive Editor
Debra Williams Cauley

Development Editor
Songlin Qiu

Managing Editor
John Fuller

Project Editor
Anna Popick

Copy Editor
Jill Hobbs

Indexer
Michael Loo

Proofreader
Linda Begley

Technical Reviewers
Károly Négyesi
Bernie Monette
Lynda Chiotti
Caroline Hill
R.G. Daniel

Cover Designer
Chuti Prasertsith

Composition
Gloria Schurick

Graphics
Tammy Graham
Laura Robbins

Contents

Foreword

At DrupalCon Barcelona in 2007, while giving my regular "State of Drupal" presentation, I remarked that during my hour-long session, four new Drupal sites would be launched. I went on to suggest that three of those four sites would be ugly. A year later, at DrupalCon Szeged in Hungary, those four new sites per hour had grown to seven and Drupal 6 had been released, making it easier to create great-looking Web sites. Still, even now, Drupal faces a common problem on the Web—the relative lack of new, high quality themes.

Front End Drupal tackles that problem directly and is designed to help both experienced designers and rank novices get an understanding of how Drupal theming works. From using contributed "starter themes," to customizing templates to modify the markup used in Drupal's output, to using jQuery and JavaScript to enhance the user experience, *Front End Drupal* clearly charts a path to theming mastery. In fact, I'll be the first to admit that I learned a lot from this book.

The Drupal community has created a remarkable platform that powers sites of all sizes and descriptions, all around the world. Together, we've crafted a robust, extensible content-management system that illustrates some of the key values in our community: flexibility and utility, innovation and openness. But Drupal has always been a developer's platform, even with the many designers in our ranks. It's about time those designers had a great book. In fact, this book is valuable not just to the designers we have, but to the designers we want—the thousands who have never worked with Drupal.

The thing is that creating a Drupal theme isn't always easy. It's a crosscutting experience that requires a lot of diverse skills and utilizes expertise in XHTML, CSS, JavaScript, and PHP, all within the context of Drupal. Doing a Drupal theme right can be challenging, but it is also exciting and incredibly rewarding. A survey I conducted in 2008 listed "Finding skilled Drupal designers" as the number one entry on the list of the "Top five most difficult things," as reported by both expert and novice users. We need to do more to find new themers, as well as encourage and support the ones we already have.

I'm excited that Emma Jane and Konstantin recognized that and authored this book. It fills an important need in the Drupal ecosystem and will bring a new attention to design in Drupal. Since I've mostly focused on the "back end," it's nice to see the "front end" get more and more attention. For Drupal to succeed, we need books like this. We need the skills it teaches and we need the people it attracts. We need the new themes those people will create and the new suggestions and improvements they bring to our project.

Dries Buytaert
Drupal founder and project lead

Preface

Drupal is an open-source content management system software package that is free to download, modify, and use. It has been implemented by thousands of people around the world and is used by millions of people daily as the basis for discussion Web sites, community portals, corporate intranets, e-commerce Web sites, vanity Web sites, resource directories, image galleries, podcasts, and more! By choosing to use Drupal, you are accessing not only an award-winning Web platform, but also its vibrant community.

This book will teach you how to customize how Drupal looks. Applying new designs is very easy—the code that controls how Drupal *works* is separated from the code that controls how Drupal *looks*. The design part of Drupal is referred to as the theme layer—and that's what this book is all about. Individual designs are referred to as "themes" and the people who create and implement them are referred to as "themers." By the time you reach the end of this book, you will have the tools to customize the experience for your content managers, Web site visitors, and Drupal administrators.

The book assumes you are familiar with how Drupal works and that you have been an administrator of a Drupal Web site. It would help if you are comfortable with Web site design and development, but these concepts will be explained for those who have only a limited experience with them. More specifically, this book will use code snippets written in HTML, CSS, PHP, and JavaScript.

Chapter 1

This chapter covers the basics of Web page design. It will help you to prepare your information so that it will slide easily into a Drupal Web site. You will learn how to describe content and its organization; structure page layouts so that all of your interface components fit sanely onto your Web pages; and implement a work flow that works for your Drupal team.

Chapter 2

With the basics of Web design under your belt, it is time to prepare your workstation for Drupal theming. In this chapter, you will learn about Drupal terminology and theming strategies as well as must-have modules and browser tools. Chapter 2 also includes language references for each of the machine languages used in creating a Drupal theme.

Chapter 3

You will now move on to learning the basic anatomy of a Drupal theme. In Chapter 3, you will learn how to find and install a premade Drupal theme. You will also learn the anatomy of a Drupal theme and discover how to use Starter Themes to reduce your development time. Tips are included on how to convert themes from WordPress, Joomla!, and Drupal 5.x.

Chapter 4

The overall structure of pages in Drupal is defined by the page template. In this chapter, you will learn how to customize every part of this template—from using sitewide page variables and menus, to changing page templates based on the section you are currently in. Information on print-friendly templates and mobile devices is also included in this chapter.

Chapter 5

It's time to get to the guts of your Web site—so in Chapter 5, you will learn how to customize your Web site content, including individual nodes and teaser summaries. This chapter also describes the most appropriate image module to use for your Web site. Examples of output are provided to help you make the best decision for your content.

Chapter 6

The most commonly overlooked area in Drupal theme design is content editing forms. In this chapter, you will learn simple tips and tricks to make your forms more usable and will get a gentle introduction to altering forms with the Form API. Techniques described in this chapter will help you to enhance the usability of your content editing forms.

Chapter 7

If you are running a community site, this chapter is a must—it includes information on how to theme user profiles, community comments, and user-generated content. Additional information is provided on creating private, member-only sections to your Web site.

Chapter 8

In this chapter, which covers administrative interfaces, you will learn how to make the administration of Drupal a little bit easier. Techniques include creating custom administrative interfaces, adding task-based navigation, creating administrative menus, and customizing your Web site's error messages.

Chapter 9

In this chapter, you will acquire the JavaScript skills required for writing truly stunning, portable, and flexible components for your theme. Basic concepts or advanced object orientation—there's certainly something you'll learn in this chapter.

Chapter 10

An introduction to jQuery, the JavaScript library that ships with Drupal, will bring you up to speed with today's most prevalent JavaScript library. You'll also learn how jQuery is used in Drupal, how you can create stunning animations, and how you can implement AJAX callbacks to the server.

Chapter 11

In this chapter, you will learn how to apply your newfound JavaScript and jQuery knowledge to a Drupal Web site. By creating a horizontal scroller component, you'll learn step by step how to architect a highly flexible and reusable JavaScript widget. Additional information in this chapter includes server-side JavaScript integration and an excursion into the vast supply of ready-made jQuery plugins.

Appendices

Information on how to install Drupal and contributed modules is included in Appendix A. Appendix B contains the code samples that are referenced in the JavaScript chapters. These code samples can also be downloaded from the book's Web site.

Acknowledgments

Emma wishes to thank her mum, Maryann Thomas, for making sure Emma didn't die of scurvy while writing the book. Thanks also to Kim Werker, for trusting me with CrochetMe; Steven Champeon, for his endless patience and insistence that Web sites be built properly; and Bernie Monette, for introducing me to fountain pens and teaching me how to spell "awkward." Thanks to all my reviewers and my production team at Pearson, and especially to Lynda Chiotti, who also provided an ear as I worked through my first Real Book with a Big-Time Publisher. The Drupal Documentation Team provided the empathy and the encouragement I needed to get things done—thanks! And finally thanks to LugRadio Live, for inviting me to speak at their conference and inadvertently introducing me to Debra Williams Cauley, the best acquisitions editor an author could hope for!

Konstantin first and foremost wants to thank his parents, Gertrud and Friedrich, for enabling him to dive into computer technology at a time when home computers weren't as common as they are today and for their tremendous support at all times. Thanks to NowPublic Technologies, which helped and supported me while writing this book. Thanks also to Károly Négyesi, also known as "chx," for the unbelievable work he has done and is still doing for the Drupal community; to Steven Wittens, for his inspiration and creativity; and to Susanne Weigel, for teaching me how to create mind maps. Finally, thanks to Debra Williams Cauley for bearing with missed deadlines and for poking me when I was procrastinating too much.

Thanks also to the following businesses who graciously allowed us to capture images from their Web sites: Trillium Healing Arts Centre, Toilet Birthdays, The Ginger Press, CrochetMe (Interweave), CSS Zen Garden, Ubuntu Screencasts, Memory Garden Retreats, and Hear the North.

About the Authors

Emma Jane Hogbin has been working as a Web developer since 1996, helping individuals and organizations to realize both their own potential and the potential of their online presence. She creates systems that enable her clients to succeed—by using her infectious enthusiasm and ability to explain concepts without using technical jargon that puts even the greatest technophobes at ease. Passionate about helping people to acquire knowledge, Emma volunteers with the Drupal and Ubuntu documentation teams. She is well known in the Drupal community not only for her technical knowledge, but also for her engaging and humorous means of bringing Drupal to a wider audience—such as the Drupal socks and their GPLed pattern. Through her consulting company HICK Tech, and at conferences around the world, Emma has inspired people to overcome fear, uncertainty, and doubt and to tackle problems head-on. She is known as "emmajane" on drupal.org and chronicles her adventures at `http://www.emmajane.net`.

Konstantin Käfer started his adventures into Web development in 1999. In high school, he led the Web development and school Web site class for several years. While still in high school, he also participated in Google's Summer of Code 2006, doing usability enhancements for the Drupal project. In the Drupal community, he is widely known for his JavaScript skills. Konstantin has been a speaker at several DrupalCons and other Open Source conferences. He is currently studying IT Systems at the Hasso Plattner Institute Engineering in Potsdam, Germany. He also works as a consultant for NowPublic, a large citizen journalism Web site based on Drupal. He can be found blogging on `http://kkaefer.com` about design, Web development, and Drupal.

Chapter 1

Web Page Design

To start your adventure of becoming a Drupal themer, you must first understand how all of the Drupal components fit together to become a whole Web site. This chapter will be useful to everyone who works on the team responsible for building a Drupal Web site, including graphic designers, content managers, and, of course, Drupal themers. It contains important information that will help team members to talk about how Drupal can be manipulated into storing and displaying content for your Web site. This chapter could have easily been named "Thinking Like Drupal" because it has all the ingredients you will need to convert your brain to Drupal's way of thinking.

In this chapter you will learn about each of the steps needed to build a Web site with Drupal. You will learn how to describe content so that you can build useful content types. You will learn about lists of content so that you can build perfect entry points into your content. You will also learn about layout and available space on your Web pages so that you can build appropriate page templates. This chapter also includes a few remarks on the computer languages needed to build a Drupal theme—although this is not a "coding" book, you will gain more from it if you are familiar with Web construction languages. Finally, we will explore the steps required to build a Drupal site, including the work flow that occurs during this process.

Describing Content

This section is intended to help you identify each of the pieces of content that you will store (and possibly display) in your Web site. Later, you will combine these pieces of content into the lists of content that visitors will use to navigate your site. Finally, you will integrate your content into the design of the whole page. This progression may seem awkward, or tedious, or too time-consuming at first. Please do not skip this part of the book! In this code-free chapter, you will learn how to think like Drupal—matching your brain to Drupal's way of storing and retrieving content. This process will allow you to easily identify and "theme" every part of every page in your Web site.

> **Description before design**
> Before you begin the design process for your Drupal site, be sure to define exactly what your site will do when it is working properly. Having a clear description of how your site works will help you make the right decisions when you are building your Web site and implementing the theme for your design.

Each page on a Web site has several components. If you strip away all of the context from a Web page, you are left with just the barebones content. For example, if you removed the navigation elements, the branding and search tool from the Web site in Figure 1.1, you would be left with content (the inset image).

FIGURE 1.1   Content in the Trillium Healing Arts Centre Web site.

On any given page, Drupal will combine several elements to create the page you see—one of which might be content. The flow chart in Figure 1.2 shows the same information that is displayed in the Web site in Figure 1.1, but in terms of the hierarchy of each page component. On the left side of the diagram are all of the elements that are displayed, but are not content. On the right side of the diagram you see several stories, each of which has its own components. In this part of the chapter, we focus on the structure of the content (the right side of the diagram).

Displaying Content

When designing your Web site's page layout, you must consider how content will be displayed on each page. The decisions you make at this point may affect the way you build your content types later on. Adding more fields to your content type allows you to have greater control over how the information is displayed. For example, the front page of your Web site may have a simple list of titles, each of which leads to a full story; alternatively, you may have a more complicated list, where the link to each story contains a title, an icon, and a short "teaser" of the full story. You can create a content type with specialized fields for any flavor of content you need to display on your site—even toilet birthdays! Figure 1.3 shows a Web page that displays a list of several toilets whose birthdays have been identified. (Yup, flip the tank lid off your toilet and look for a date stamp. That is its birthday!)

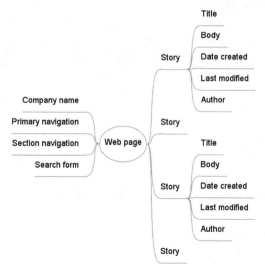

FIGURE 1.2   The page components displayed in the Trillium Healing Arts Centre Web page.

FIGURE 1.3 The front page of the Toilet Birthdays Web site displays ten toilets with a pager at the bottom to view previously added toilets.

The decisions you make about how your content should be displayed in the final Web site allow you to confirm that you are collecting the correct granularity of data for each of your content types. Each content field can be displayed as a separate item in the theme layer. In subsequent chapters, you will learn how to hide individual content fields on summary pages, and how to hide fields to create private data.

To begin the process of describing the content, start with a list for each different kind of content displayed within your Web site. You may want to ask yourself the following kinds of questions:

- Does this content have a corresponding image?
- Are there categories for this content (and do the categories have icons)?
- Is the author's name displayed with the content?
- Should the creation date or last-updated date be displayed?
- Is this a date-based event that will be displayed in a calendar?
- Are there video and audio files associated with this content?
- Can people leave their comments on this content?

Content Types and Content Fields

In Drupal terminology, "story" and "blog" refer to very specific types of content. Each type of content is distinguished by its content type name. For example, your Web site might have the following types of content: Story, Blog, Image, and Event. Each of these types of content would have its own template that content authors would use to create and edit new content. Although it is tempting to think of content types as "types of Web pages," resist this temptation! When you create a new unit of content (for example, a new "Story"), Drupal uses the term "node" to refer to that content. A single Web page that is displayed in a Web browser may contain several nodes along with other page components (see Figure 1.2).

> **Origins of the word "node"**
> Computer scientists define "node" as an abstract unit that contains either data or a link to more nodes. They adopted the term from the world of botany, where the definition and analogy are much easier to understand. In botany, a "node" is the point where a leaf is attached to the stem of the plant. The leaves on a tree are like the units of content stored in your database. You can think of the sections in your Web site as branches on a tree.

Drupal stores the data for each content node in several tables in the database. When a specific unit of content is requested, Drupal collects all relevant information from each of the database tables to produce a snapshot of the content for display. When you are building themes, you may choose to display all, or only some, of the information Drupal has collected for you.

Before building your new Drupal Web site, you must carefully examine the content that will be entered into the Web site. Look closely for similarities in the structure of your content to find all necessary fields for each of your content types. Perhaps your content can be contained within a simple "Story" content type, which allows you to enter only the title and a "body" of information. With this content type, however, you will be limited to sorting information based on the date the story was created, or last updated, and its title. For example, if you are storing a library of books you have read in your Drupal Web site, you may also want to list the books according to the name of the author, the year of the book's publication, the date when you read the book, and perhaps your quality rating for the book. Unfortunately, the content type Story, without modification, does not permit sorting books based on these fields. As such, it would not be a suitable content type to store information about the books you have read.

> **Changing from one content type to another**
> There is no way to easily convert your information from one content type to another content type once you have created a node. You must choose the best content type each time you want to add new information to your Web site. You can, however, customize your content types to include new form fields at any time.

Visualize the data entry form you will use to enter your content into your Web site. Your content must have a title and perhaps a longer description (Figure 1.4). Drupal includes its own information for each piece of content added to your Web site as well. These fields include the date on which the content was created and the author of the content.

If your Web site is very simple, you may be able to enter all new content with one of the two default content types: Story, which displays all new entries on the front page of the Web site, or Page, which is not displayed on the front page by default. Additional content types provided in Drupal's core include Blog, Book, Comment, Forum, and Poll. If your content has a different structure than these default content types, you may need to create your own content types to store information—you will learn how to do this in the next chapter. Figure 1.5 shows an example of a more complicated Web form that contains several additional content fields.

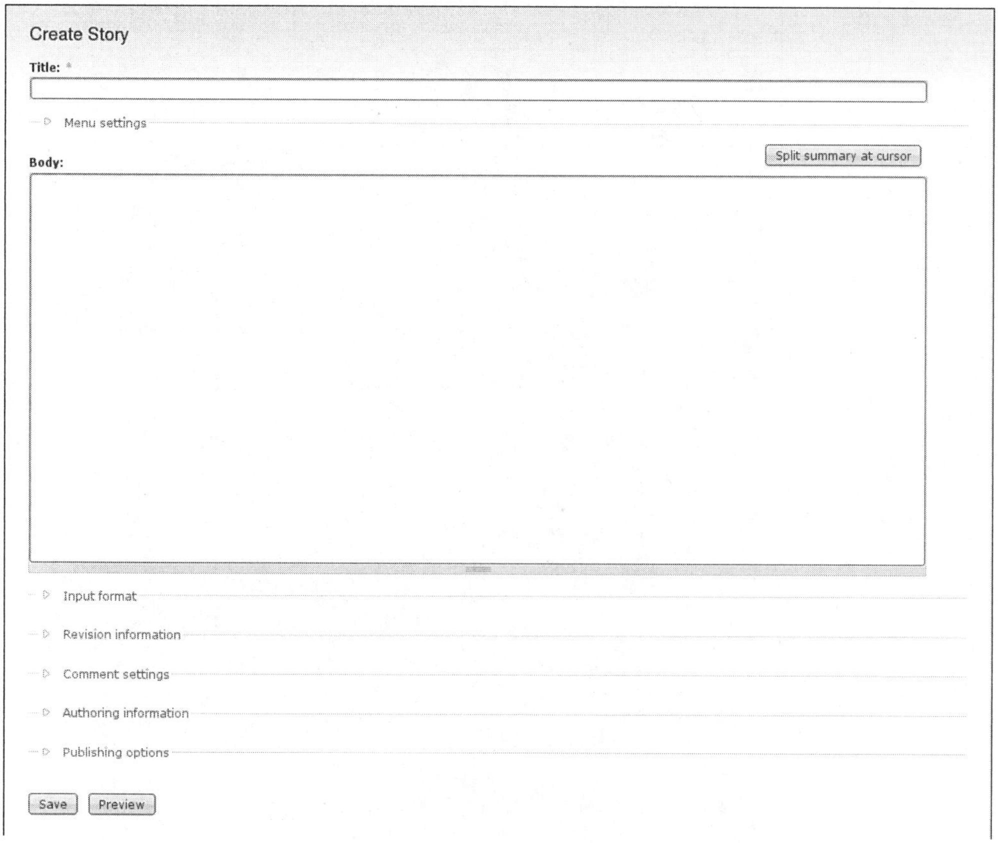

FIGURE 1.4 The form used to create a new instance of the content type "Story."

In the form shown in Figure 1.5, the content fields include information about the toilet and about the human who took the photo of the toilet. Having each of these fields remain separate from the others means the content can be sorted according to any of these fields; also, each of the fields can be hidden or displayed, as appropriate. When you keep the birthdays separate from the description of the toilet, and you apply a little extra scripting, Drupal is able to send birthday greetings to Web site contributors on the appropriate dates. This is possible only because the birthday is kept as a separate content field.

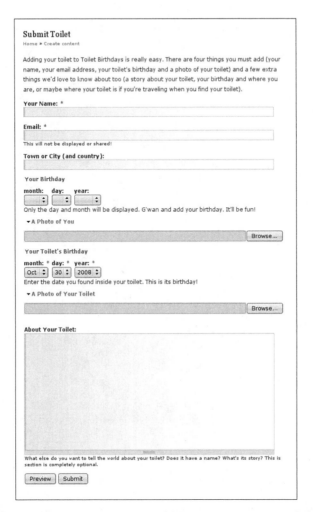

FIGURE 1.5 The form used to create a new instance of the custom content type "Toilet" on the Web site http://www.toiletbirthdays.com.

Organizing Lists of Content

Content can be organized in a lot of different ways. In this section, we look at how Web site visitors navigate through content. This process is not the same as considering where the navigation areas appear on the page. Your content must be sorted in a way that your Web site visitors recognize. By understanding how you want to arrange lists of content on your site, you will be better equipped to choose the most appropriate tools to build these lists.

The rest of this section describes common ways to sort content. Each of these examples has a different implementation pattern in Drupal. Read through these examples and make a few notes on which ones you think best match the content for your Web site. It is possible that you will implement more than one of these options.

Chronological Organization

Most Web site visitors are highly familiar with the chronological form of content organization, as it is commonly seen in blogs and calendars. In a blog, the units of content (blog entries) are sorted from most recent to oldest. Visitors to the Web site must navigate through the history of the Web site to find each unit of content. When using the Blog Module, Drupal displays new entries on the front page of the Web site by default (see Figure 1.6).

A variation on this sort of chronological organization is a display calendar. This format is most appropriate when listing upcoming events (Figure 1.7). It may also be appropriate to show an archive of stories if the information is date specific (for example, a Web site that reports on community events). Think about how people will access and use the list of content. Consider how many events will be added as well. In some instances it will be appropriate to use a full display calendar as well as a quick summary organized as a bullet list of the next ten events.

FIGURE 1.6 A blog is a series of short entries sorted by reverse chronological order.

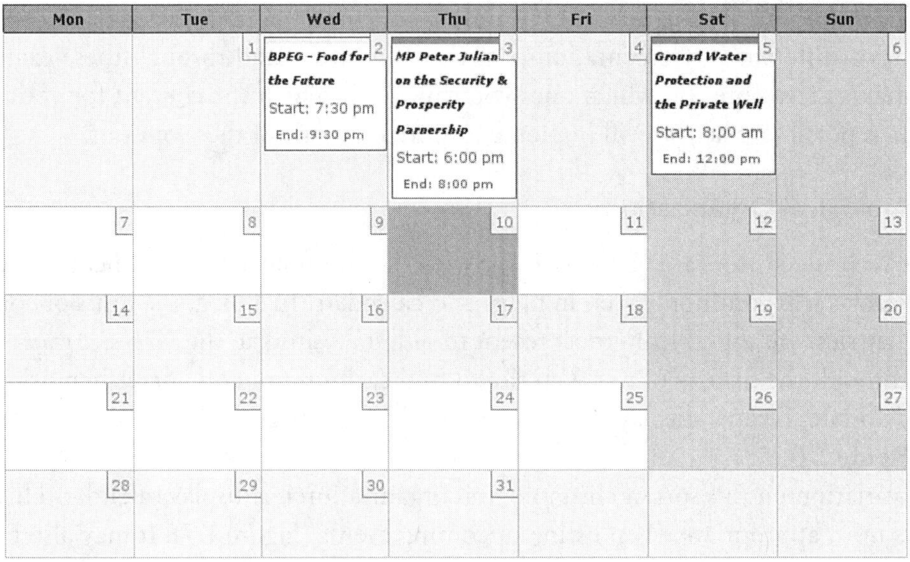

Mon	Tue	Wed	Thu	Fri	Sat	Sun
1	2 *BPEG - Food for the Future* Start: 7:30 pm End: 9:30 pm	3 *MP Peter Julian on the Security & Prosperity Parnership* Start: 6:00 pm End: 8:00 pm	4	5 *Ground Water Protection and the Private Well* Start: 8:00 am End: 12:00 pm	6	
7	8	9	10	11	12	13
14	15	16	17	18	19	20
21	22	23	24	25	26	27
28	29	30	31			

FIGURE 1.7 Upcoming events displayed as a calendar.

Linear Organization

Novels have a beginning, a middle, and an end. Authors create stories and assume they will be experienced in a linear way. Similarly, your Web site may have sections that ought to be read from start to finish, just like a book. For example, linear organization is appropriate for instructions and documentation, where you build on the knowledge that was obtained in a previous section, or where there is a logical progression of ideas from start to finish (Figure 1.8).

Topical Organization

If your content is sorted hierarchically into sections and subsections, visitors to your site will be able to browse through each of the different categories to find information that is of interest to them (Figure 1.9). Within Drupal, you may choose to implement a controlled vocabulary with pre-determined categories, or you can opt to use "free tagging" and allow categories to be entered when the content is created. Both approaches have merits. A controlled vocabulary generates a rigorous system that is predictable for both content editors and Web site visitors. Free tagging, by comparison, is often more appropriate for community-generated content where thousands of users may enter slightly different types of content into your Web site.

Naturopathic Medicine

Naturopathy is a natural, comprehensive approach to preventing illness,
improving health, and treating disease. Naturopathic doctors believe in the
body's innate capacity for self-healing, and seek to address and remove the
cause of illness. The cause of disease may lie in the physical, mental, emotional
or spiritual plane, and each of these areas is taken into consideration when
developing a treatment plan. The whole person is addressed, rather than a
single symptom. Often a physical symptom is an expression of an underlying
mental, emotional or spiritual conflict that needs to be brought to the surface to
restore balance to the whole.

- Naturopathic Therapies
- Principles of Naturopathic Healing
- Principles of Naturopathic Medicine

Naturopathic Therapies ›

Printer-friendly version

FIGURE 1.8 A section of content with built-in navigation. Pages within the group are listed below the introductory paragraph.

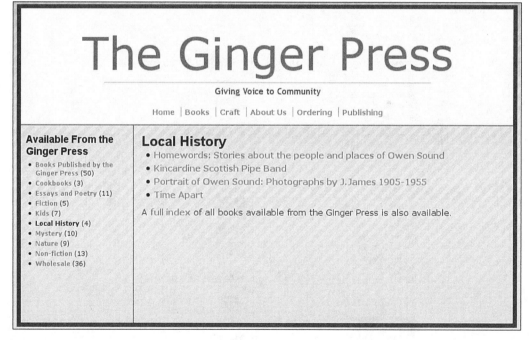

FIGURE 1.9 On this book shop's Web site, the content is sorted by category.

Alphabetical organization works best when users know the exact name of the thing they are looking for. This is especially true with very long lists of content. The word "the" is perhaps the biggest enemy to alphabetical organization. Although your Web site visitors may know exactly what they are looking for, "the" can end up putting the content in an unexpected spot in machine-sorted lists of content. If possible, try to limit alphabetical lists of content to a single display page. In other words, avoid paginated lists of alphabetical content. This approach will allow users to more easily scan the full list of options to find what they are looking for.

Popularity-Based Organization

Many social networking sites feature popularity-based content organization for their front pages. For example, Digg (http://www.digg.com) features this type of content sorting. CrochetMe (http://www.crochetme.com), the social networking site for crocheters shown in Figure 1.10, uses popularity to rank content on its Patterns page. An FAQ, or set of help pages, may also be ordered according to how often the content is requested.

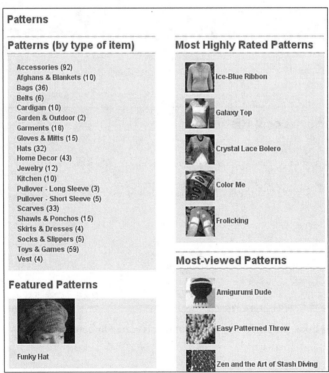

FIGURE 1.10 CrochetMe groups and displays its content by popularity.

Task-Based Organization

From the very beginning of your Drupal installation, you will be working with task-based organization. Your Web site might include tasks such as adding new content, moderating comments, searching or filtering the content, and viewing recently updated content. Figure 1.11 shows the task-based menu that Drupal provides to help organize these actions. You may also have a set of tasks that are available to different roles within your team of authenticated users.

Task-based organization is appropriate for the presentation and navigation of action-oriented pages as opposed to content-oriented pages. You will need to decide how related tasks are grouped and how they are ordered within that group. You will also need to decide how to integrate the tasks into the page. In some cases, tasks may be available from a menu option (for example, Create Content); in other cases, tasks may be presented as tabs on a page (for example, Edit This Page). The administration area of Drupal allows you to build scenarios of related tasks. For example, selecting "Create Content" from the Drupal navigation menu presents you with a new page with the different kinds of content you can add to your Web site; it also reveals an extended menu in the navigation area on the left side of Figure 1.11.

Now that you know what your content looks like and how it will be organized, you can start to think about the layout of your Web pages.

FIGURE 1.11 This list shows administrative tasks that can be performed. It includes a subset of tasks to Create Content, where the administrator can choose from a list of different types of content to add to the Web site.

Page Design and Layout

Armed with your detailed description of each content type and the structure for your lists of content, you are ready to start filling in the gaps of your Web site's page template. Around the outer edges of the content, you will need to fill in navigation areas, logos, and maybe even spaces for ads. Common interface components are listed in this section, though your own site may have additional requirements that go beyond this list.

At this stage you should sketch out what your Web site will look like, including all of the elements that will be displayed on the page. You might use a graphic design tool such as Illustrator, Photoshop, or the GiMP to accomplish this step, or you may want to start with paper and a pencil.

Fill in as much detail as possible to give yourself a good sense of how crowded your pages will be. Your sketches may influence the number of columns on your site and identify other technical constraints. Depending on the size of your Web site, you may have several different templates. Combine multiple layouts into a single template and note where options differ for each of your content types. If you are using a graphics program, consider creating digital page mock-ups; if you are working manually, sketch out your ideas onto separate sheets of paper.

> **Administrative templates**
> The most common problem encountered during this step of Web site design is creating too narrow a column for the content. Although your Web page might not have any large data tables, Drupal's administrative interface uses tables that are quite wide. Consider using an administrative theme that has a very wide content area to accommodate these administrative tables if your main site uses a narrow content area.

Interface Components

When you are designing your template, you must consider several issues in addition to the content, navigation area, and logo. Even if your site will initially use a very basic layout, it is a good idea to think ahead, and allow for additional components to be added in the future. For example, if you plan to add a calendar to your Web site, set aside a space for that element in your design template now. A little forethought at the design stage will help your Web site grow with elegance.

Outlined in this section are several examples of interface components that your site might have in the future.

> **Make space**
> Be sure to add more than enough regions into your template. You may not need them all now, but you will probably need them as your site grows. For example, will there be a time when you might want three columns of information in your footer instead of just one?

All Web sites have some kind of identifying mark that tells you which Web site you are visiting. It might consist of an image-based logo, a line of plain text, or a combination of the two. Generally this information appears at the top of your Web site. You may also want to include a value proposition or slogan as part of your site name. Visitors arriving from a search engine will be able to use this statement to quickly identify if they have arrived at a page that is useful to them.

If you know visitors will be able to search your Web site, remember to include the search interface as part of your page layout. You may wish to include the input box and activation button; alternatively, you might have just a button that leads to an advanced search page.

Many of today's Web sites include advertising. Whether you are soliciting ads from specific companies or using an ad service that places advertisements on your Web site automatically, you may need to consider at some point how you will display ads. Perhaps you will end up designating different areas on your page for different levels, and different kinds, of advertising. For example, you might make a distinction between text-based ads and graphical ads. Even if you do not plan to rely on advertising as a source of revenue, you may need to recognize sponsors. For example, your content may highlight large events with corporate sponsors, or your organization may need to acknowledge that it has received funding from a specific agency for a specific project. Consider each of these interface components as you design your Web site templates.

Regions

When you created your template, you probably identified several regions on your Web pages. The largest area was likely reserved for content, whereas other, smaller areas contained interface components. These regions may display the same page elements throughout the site (for example, the logo); alternatively, the content of each region may change from page to page (for example, subnavigation). When you are creating your Drupal theme, you will be able to place special markers to identify these regions in each of your templates. Some of the more extensible premade Drupal designs have as many as 12 different regions! This sort of organization gives a lot more flexibility than merely choosing between a two- or three-column layout.

> **Fixed or fluid?**
> In a fixed-design site, the total width of the page never changes. Thus you will always have exactly the same amount of space to lay out your content. In a fluid-design site, the total width of the page depends on how wide (or narrow) the visitor's browser is. Given the choice, many print-based designers will select a fixed-width design. If this description applies to you, consider using two variations on your theme: a fixed-width design for the public Web site and a fluid design for the administrative area.

In subsequent chapters, you will learn how to convert your Web page design into a full Drupal theme. You will be able to define as many regions as your site needs. Even if your Web site is a simple two-column layout, you will be able to decide if the narrow column appears on the left or the right side of the page. Figure 1.12 displays Drupal's Zen theme—by default, there are eight available regions in this theme.

FIGURE 1.12 The Zen theme-building theme comes with eight different regions; they are represented by thick black bars.

In addition to the basic layout of the Web site, Drupal allows you to create custom templates for each of the pages on your Web site. CrochetMe.com uses a custom template for its front page (Figure 1.13) to divide the main content area into five separate regions, increasing the number of regions to eight in total (Figure 1.14). The eighth region is the logo found at the upper-left corner of the page.

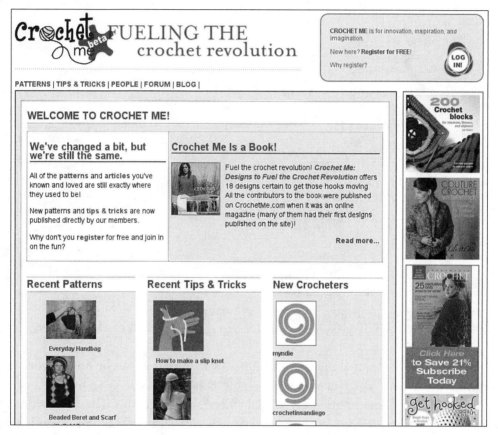

FIGURE 1.13 The CrochetMe Web site uses several techniques to show a complex grid layout on its front page.

Design Resources

If you are a developer who is intimidated by graphic design, you will find that a lot of excellent templates are readily available that can be easily adapted to suit your needs. For their part, experienced designers who are new to Drupal can use these templates to get a sense of what is possible beyond the basic themes that Drupal

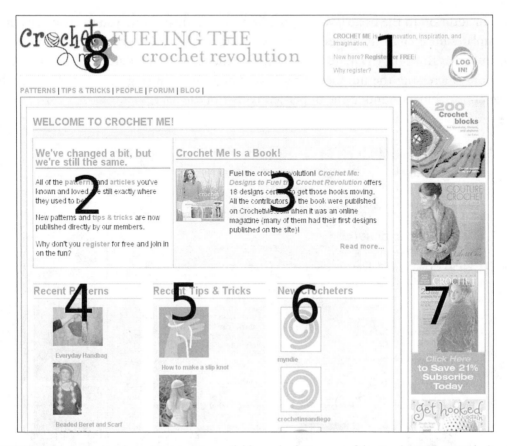

FIGURE 1.14   In total, eight regions are now available on the front page of the CrochetMe.com Web site.

provides by default. Drupal.org lists a number of themes that can be downloaded and customized (`http://drupal.org/project/Themes`) to suit your project's needs. To see each of these themes on a real Web site, visit the Theme Garden at `http://www.themegarden.org/drupal6/`. Of course, the Web and its design inspirations are much larger resources than the limited set of information found on the main Drupal Web site.

Copyright
The designs listed in this section are not necessarily free to modify and use. Many of the templates are licensed under the Creative Commons or the General Public License (GPL), and can be used if appropriate credit is given to the original designer. Please be sure to respect the terms of the individually licensed designs.

The CSS Zen Garden (`http://www.csszengarden.com`) is an excellent design resource. The content of each page is identical but the page has been restyled by applying a unique Cascading Style Sheet (CSS) prepared by an expert designer. Figure 1.15 shows a summary of the designs available in this unique theme browser. CSS Zen Garden shows you exactly how easy it ought to be to apply a new theme to your Drupal site. You will be able to achieve a nearly instantaneous visual overhaul of this Web site by changing only the style sheet that is applied to the underlying HTML. If the CSS Zen Garden can perform such a dramatic transformation with only a style sheet, imagine what you will be able to do by combining this capability with Drupal's powerful theme system.

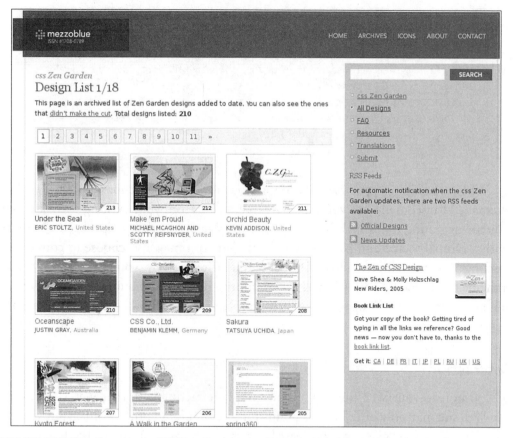

FIGURE 1.15 Each theme in the CSS Zen Garden uses the same underlying HTML markup. The visual design is overhauled by changing only the Cascading Style Sheet.

If you need more ideas, even more template sites are available on the Internet. Scan through these resources for inspiration, or use the templates as a starting point for developing your own Drupal theme. The Open Web Design (`http://www.openweb-design.org`) and Open Source Web Design (`http://www.oswd.org`) sites provide a wide range of sample layouts. From these sites, you can download a package containing HTML, CSS, and image files. These files must then be converted into a Drupal theme; this conversion is described later in the book. The Open Source Web Design (OSWD) site also has an excellent "See Designs in Use" section where you can see how the OSWD templates have been modified and implemented on real Web sites (`http://www.oswd.org/links`).

> **Photos**
> By changing only the photo used in a design, you can change the whole feel of a Web site. If you decide to include photos of people as part of your site, make sure you have their permission. High-quality photos with appropriate model release can be purchased for very little money from stock photography Web sites. If you are using your own photos of people, be sure your models sign a release form. A sample form is available from the following URL: `http://www.istockphoto.com/docs/languages/english/modelrelease.pdf`.

When developing your page design and layout, you may choose to start with a premade Drupal theme, or you may have a template from your existing Web site that you are migrating to Drupal. If you are new to Drupal, the easiest approach is to start with a Drupal theme and customize it as needed. You may also choose to convert an existing Web site template into a Drupal theme. Alternatively, you may want to create a theme from scratch. You will find useful information throughout this book on creating and customizing Drupal themes. The fundamentals of how to create a theme are covered in Chapter 3.

Interaction

The visitors to your Web site will be constantly interacting with that Web site. A simple Web site may only offer links as points for interaction; in other words, your visitors may be able to view pages and navigate between them, but not much else. In contrast, in a community Web site, where visitors are able to interact and enhance Web site content, you will need to consider more fully how visitors and community members interact with your Web site.

As part of this process, you need to think about the tools your Web site visitors are using to capture and consume the content on your Web site. To accommodate their needs, your interaction plan may include developing a printer-friendly version of your pages, a high- and low-bandwidth template, and a public/private theme for your site. If your Web site is updated regularly, and you are providing an RSS feed for your content, you will also need to consider the attributes for this feed. Will you publish the whole story or merely a content summary?

Your Web site should never prevent people from accessing public content. Consideration should also be given to people who will use adaptive technology to access your site. In most cases it makes good business sense to accommodate their special needs, but in some cases you are also required by law to provide your content in an accessible manner. For more information on creating accessible Web sites, read the free online resource, "Dive into Accessibility," by Mark Pilgrim; it is available from `http://www.diveintoaccessibility.org`.

User Satisfaction

Your Web site must be able to communicate to its visitors all aspects of the tasks it is capable of performing as well as the content that is available to be consumed. Your visitors must have a clear understanding of what everything on the screen means before taking action. This means visitors must have a clear sense of what they will be revealing or accomplishing before they perform a task. By using both images and language, you can combine content and style to produce a pleasing experience for your Web site visitors.

Every screen in your Web site represents a decision point. Each time a user performs an action, that individual will have a certain idea of the desired outcome based on the information you have provided on each page. Based on this action, the screen will change and the user's objectives will be either met or not met. Either way, the screen will have entered a new state. Based on the new state, Web site visitors may be able to confirm whether they have successfully completed the original task. Based on the feedback received, Web site visitors will then be able to proceed with a new task from the current screen or else may need to modify the original set of actions if the first attempt at the task failed. You must ensure the choices on every page are clear and complete.

Make sure your presentation and feedback are always clear. Look at your design carefully and assess whether it is easy to see how to initiate an action and what will happen once the action has been started. To achieve success within your Web site, visitors must be able to name the task they want to accomplish, perform the task, and then verify the task has been successfully achieved. All three components are critical elements in achieving user satisfaction.

Guided Tasks

Tasks should require as few steps as possible to complete. People like finishing things, so why not make it easier for your Web site visitors to be happy? Wherever possible, you should provide clear instructions on how users can perform the discrete tasks that are relevant to them. Limiting each task to a single screen allows people to complete the steps at their leisure. Sometimes, however, you may need to guide your Web site visitors through a specific series of tasks. Perhaps the most common of these sequences is the navigation of a payment gateway. If you know you cannot avoid a multistep process, consider adding the following features:

- Remove unnecessary links and content from the page template.
- Remove navigation bars, tab rows, and locational breadcrumbs, leaving behind only the links, actions, and buttons related to the task at hand.
- Add a progress bar to show users where they are in the sequence of tasks they are working through.
- Maintain branding images and the overall site style.

Make it clear how to proceed from one page to the next. Prevent errors by clearly marking your expectations for the user at every point of interaction (especially on required fields). Where you cannot *prevent* errors, provide useful error messages and a way forward through the correction—never force a visitor to use the browser's back button to fix a mistake.

Code

In Web page design, two or three factors typically affect how your page looks: (X)HTML, CSS, and sometimes JavaScript. Drupal is a database-driven Web site that uses the scripting language PHP to output the markup that is rendered by Web browsers. Keep in mind that XHTML, CSS, and JavaScript are separate languages that work in concert to provide your site visitors with a beautiful and engaging experience. The more you can separate these three languages in your mind, the easier it will be for you to create an effective Drupal theme. To do so, you will need to determine what is controlling the appearance of the element you want to change. It is easier to perform this diagnostic test when you are used to making distinctions among the underlying languages that control the content's appearance on the screen.

Separating Form, Function, and Behavior

XHTML is the structural language that describes each of the elements displayed on a page. Its job is not to format the information, but simply to describe the information: "This is a paragraph." "That is an image." This structural language also describes specific areas on the page: "This is the navigation area." "This is the content area."

To change the visual appearance of items on a page, you will need to alter their styles using CSS descriptors. Information contained in a CSS file may include anything from font sizes and colors to the background images used in certain areas of the page.

JavaScript enhances interaction within the page. Using JavaScript, you can control simple animations to morph page elements from one state to another. You can also make areas on your site appear or disappear with the click of a mouse button. In addition, you can use JavaScript to save changes to your database without having the Web site visitor change pages.

Although you do not necessarily need to be an expert in each of these three languages, the more you know about them, the more easily you will be able to customize how Drupal looks.

> **Reduce, reuse, recycle**
> When creating your HTML markup, use the correct elements for headings and lists. Check the markup Drupal uses by default. Where it makes sense to do so, emulate this markup. Maintaining this type of consistency will make it easier to reuse the styles you have created and to ensure uniformity in your page-specific designs.

XHTML

Drupal can produce sites that use valid XHTML markup (Strict or Transitional). While you may need to adjust some of the markup that is created by third-party modules, the Drupal core outputs valid XHTML. Also, although you might have created a perfect Web site, your content managers may enter content that is not perfect XHTML. Fortunately Drupal can perform additional tests on data entered by your content editors through its input filters.

A full introduction to XHTML is beyond the scope of this book, but many excellent resources are available online. A good place to start is the Opera Web Standards Curriculum (http://www.opera.com/wsc).

Cascading Style Sheets

The most powerful language in styling Drupal is the style sheet language known as Cascading Style Sheets. Throughout this book you will see examples of CSS. In general, styles are applied from an external style sheet through a combination of selectors, properties, and values.

A full introduction to CSS is beyond the scope of this book, but many excellent resources are available online. A good place to start is the W3 Schools' CSS Tutorial (`http://www.w3schools.com/css`).

Scripting Languages

There are two additional scripting languages you will encounter at various points in this book. JavaScript is a client-side scripting language. Web sites that allow you to interact with the interface in real time are using JavaScript. For example, a drag-and-drop function uses JavaScript to engineer the movement of an object within the page. In many cases, it is possible to completely avoid JavaScript and still have the site display exactly the content you want in exactly the way you want. If you want to alter the behavior of a page, however, you may need to learn a bit more about this scripting language. Fortunately, sophisticated libraries are available that will allow you to write complicated behaviors quickly and with relative ease.

To create a Drupal template, you will also need to know a little bit of the scripting language PHP. This server-side language is never visible on the Web site, but rather is rendered by the Web server. When you use the PHP function, "print", the PHP script will create a page that is built from one or a combination of the three previously described languages (XHTML, CSS, or JavaScript), which are in turn rendered by the browser for everyone to see. As a consequence, you can use PHP to completely hide content from Web site visitors. Unlike the other scripting languages, PHP produces hidden content that is truly hidden!

Interaction with JavaScript

JavaScript interactions can be useful and fun for your Web site visitors. Imagine being able to build a conference schedule by dragging sessions into the appropriate time slot or by sliding images into a gallery. Or how about using a fancy fade on an important message to draw the user's eye to the information? Drupal now offers modules that allow you to accomplish the following tasks:

- Dynamically add new content to a page
- Edit rich text (allowing your content editors to update text, without having to know HTML)
- Create simple Web animations for error messages
- Enable drag-and-drop interaction with content

If you are new to theming, these ideas might seem like impossible tasks. But take heart: JavaScript has come a long way, and many function-rich libraries are now available. In some cases you do not need to know any JavaScript to add this functionality to your Web site. Later in this book, you will find everything you need to know to get up and running with JavaScript. We will also show you how to use existing JavaScript libraries, such as jQuery, so that you do not have to build everything from scratch!

Work Flow

Drupal sites are typically built through a collaboration between a programmer, a designer, and a content manager. Sometimes, however, these roles are combined into a single person. Perhaps you theme Drupal on a full-time basis but are also responsible for a little bit of design, or maybe you handle module programming and data entry in addition to your theme creation work. Identifying each of the tasks that needs to be completed will help you to carry out those functions in the right order. Each project may have a slightly different list of tasks, and identifying the kind of project will help you to carry out these tasks in the appropriate order. For example, is it more important to prototype functionality first, or does the site need to look "right" before the client (or your Web users) starts using it?

Write down all of the tasks you need to accomplish before launching the site. In a second list, put the tasks in order of what needs to happen first, what needs to happen right before launch, and what all the in-between steps are. If you have multiple people working on the project, put each team member's name beside a task. This list may also help you to develop the project timeline (especially if all tasks by one person need to be completed before the next team members' can start their tasks).

The following tasks must be completed in order:

1. Identify content, and content types, that will be contained in the Web site.
2. Identify and record the way the Web site will be used (flowcharts).
3. Design the structure of the Web site (wireframes).

4. Add design elements to the wireframes to make beautiful templates for each unique part of your Web site.

5. Install Drupal.

6. Install and configure Drupal modules—where necessary, complete additional programming and module development.

7. Convert the design into HTML.

8. Create a Drupal theme (including template files).

9. Add content and create user accounts.

10. Launch the Web site.

There are, of course, many more possible roles than the ones outlined here. For example, you will be performing quality assurance (QA) at each stage of the development process. You may also be collaborating with an information architect, copy editors, sound and video technicians, translators, and more! Outline each of the tasks that will be performed by your team members. Ask the people on your team at which points they would like to be included in the project. An information architect, for example, might want to be involved with the planning stages, but less involved during the programming stages.

As a team, take the time to look at a Drupal Web site together. It is important to have the shared experience of understanding how Drupal works and where it must be customized to meet the needs of your Web site. Encourage each member of the team to talk about his or her role and how it is integrated with the work of the other team members.

Working with Designers

You may have both a graphic designer and an interaction designer on your team. The designer's role is to create an elegant and usable design. Graphic designers make Web sites look pretty; interaction designers need to create a usable interface. Although the interaction designer will be involved in all aspects of the building of a Web site to ensure the whole system is appropriate for its users, a graphic designer may only focus only on the visual aesthetics of the site.

To carry the graphic designer's work forward into your other promotional material, you should ask this person to complete a style guide that specifies the fonts, colors, and graphics used in the creation of the Web site. Consider storing this information within the site itself. Depending on the size of the site and the number of users, the key information might take the form of a private section or simply an unpublished page. Your interaction designer, however, will be working throughout the entire development process to evaluate and improve the user experience within the Web site. This process includes customizing help messages, determining the flow between sections, and deciding when it is most appropriate to use fancy enhancements.

Working with Programmers

If you are having custom modules developed, you need to make sure your programmer and your designer are aware of the additional elements that will be exposed by the new programming. Perhaps the design will need to be adjusted to accommodate new content. Or perhaps the programming will need to be adjusted to accommodate the graphic and interaction design. Even if your programmer says, "Drupal can't look like that," that does not mean the programmer is right! Perhaps it is true that Drupal has never looked like your design before—but this may be because everyone else has been lacking imagination. This whole book is dedicated to helping you make Drupal look exactly the way you want!

If you are creating new modules, be sure your team has a clear understanding of each screen that will be built. Your programmers and designers must understand how the new functionality is integrated into the Web site as a whole. What seems like a minor change to the graphic design may, in fact, have a huge impact on the programming; conversely, what seems like a trivial programming change may have a huge impact on the interaction or graphic design. Maintain a shared workspace where all team members can see how all of the components fit together. The information provided in this workspace should include both a text description of how Web site visitors will interact with the module (including information about role- or permission-dependent tasks) and mockups of each screen the module creates.

Working with Clients

Although it is possible you are your own client, it is more likely you will be designing Web sites for other people, too. One of the major reasons to choose Drupal as a platform is the fact that it can make client relations go a lot easier: "Want your site to use pirate-speak on September 19? No problem! Drupal has a module to do exactly that."

Unfortunately, even the best, most rational clients can be affected by feature creep. Make sure you have a list of deliverables in writing before you start. If you are lucky enough to have the best client in the whole world, you might be tempted to deliver more than the client wanted. Don't be tempted! Stick to your list and instead deliver the project ahead of time and under budget.

Sometimes what the client wants has nothing to do with the words the client uses to describe the end result. This disconnect can affect which modules you choose to use and how you store the data.

Working with Site Visitors

The great thing about the Internet is that nothing is permanent (ignoring, of course, those sites that allow you to view old versions of pages, such as The Way Back Machine on archive.org). Working with your Web site visitors to make tiny adjustments to your interface on a regular basis can help you to create a loyal fan base because it is involved in the development of the Web site. You may even choose to apply the open-source development philosophy of "Release early. Release often. Listen to your customers." Massive changes to a user interface suddenly will be more disruptive than a series of small changes that happen on a regular basis. Each of these changes might be small (for example, improving the navigation for a specific set of tasks, offering new tools, fixing the display for specific browsers), but their collective impact on your visitors may be huge.

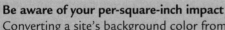

Be aware of your per-square-inch impact
Converting a site's background color from green to pink, with no other changes, will still feel like a major change. Even if is relatively minor to change one color to another in a CSS file, you may be implementing a change that has a very large visual impact on the overall design of your Web site.

If you are working with an online community that has a forum, you might want to add a forum topic for Web site suggestions. Alternatively, you might decide to include a category in your contact form for Web site feedback. Such an invitation to give feedback may be open to the entire community or just to a trusted subset of community members who represent a range of technical skills and operating system/browser combinations. Reporting on computer error messages entails use of a skill set better known as "bug reporting" within the technical community. You may need to work with your site visitors to develop their ability to report useful bugs. Do solicit their opinions, and do act on the advice you are given.

Summary

Drupal is extremely flexible; it is a framework that you can manipulate in many ways. The more you know about your options, the less your Web site will look like every other Web site. This chapter introduced some of the key elements associated with the creation of Drupal-based sites:

- Elements on a page
- Lists of content
- Page design and layout
- Interaction
- Markup
- Work flow

This chapter covered the basic toolkit you will need to design Drupal sites. Use this chapter as a reference as you work through the rest of the book. When you develop an idea for your content types, consider how it will be viewed on the site to determine the best way to theme or to control the display of the content. Being able to describe the feature and its function within the site will help you choose the right way to apply your design to it.

Chapter 2

The Themers' Toolkit

Throughout this book you will learn how to configure Drupal from the administration area and how to build template files using scripting and markup languages. You have already made the commitment to working with the Drupal framework. *Framework* is a term that is often tossed around by developers, designers, and software pundits. Of course, you know what a framework is, but stopping to think about the definition will help to set the tone for much of this chapter. According to Wikipedia, a framework is "a basic conceptual structure used to solve or address complex issues." This chapter introduces the tools you need to build Web sites within the Drupal framework.

In this chapter, you will learn about the basics of a Drupal theme, must-have modules, and browser-based tools. You will learn how to create a custom content type with the CCK module. You will learn step-by-step how to create a mini portfolio Web site. The chapter also includes a brief section where you can find more information about the computer languages that are used in the Drupal theming system. The tools highlighted in this section are essential to the sane development and deployment of a Drupal theme. Taking the time to set up your system with the appropriate toolkit will save you hours—if not days—in development time.

A Gentle Introduction

In Drupal, a *theme* is the final step in the process of building a Web page for display. It converts the data from PHP objects and arrays into HTML markup and CSS style definitions. Working at the theme layer you have the ultimate and final control over how a page is displayed. Once a theme is created, it may be applied with the simple click of a button. If you have ever used a downloaded theme, you know how impressive and instantaneous the process is to flip from your current theme to one that you downloaded and unpacked only a few moments ago.

Many changes can be made to Drupal from the administration area. Nevertheless, building and customizing themes require comfort with at least three computer languages: PHP, HTML, and CSS. Knowing a little bit of XML and JavaScript also helps. Chapters 9 to 11 include an extensive primer on using JavaScript in Drupal. Throughout this book, you will learn how to use the PHPTemplate theming engine to build and modify Drupal themes. By far the most popular engine, PHPTemplate offers many starter templates to choose from. Most of the online documentation also refers to this template engine.

Building a Page for Display

A single Web page that is built by Drupal and is viewed in your Web browser is a combination of data and formatting information. Drupal takes several steps to prepare a page for viewing in a Web browser:

1. It retrieves information from the database. Although pages can be saved (or "cached"), information retrieved from the database is "dynamic" or changeable for each page requested.

2. It checks the retrieved data against relevant output filters. This step may include the conversion of URLs into clickable links and line breaks into new paragraphs.

3. It inserts the information into each of the relevant templates provided by Drupal core, contributed modules, and your theme. This includes combining many small templates into an overall page template.

4. It displays the formatted page in the Web browser.

Drupal provides generic templates for every type of information that will be displayed in your Web site. If you have not created your own template, Drupal will use one of its own. Using the theming system, you can customize each of the default templates to adjust how data is displayed in your Web site.

Directory Structure

Drupal allows you to run different Web sites from a single instance of Drupal files on your Web server. You could, for example, run two Web sites example.com and mysite.org from the same code base, with each site having its own database. To create multiple sites, you simply create a subfolder within the Drupal folder sites. These site folders must have the same name as the domain names they represent. For example, the domain name example.com would have a folder named sites/example. com. Each of your site-specific folders will contain a file named settings.php as well as a subdirectory to hold site-specific modules and site-specific themes. If you would like a module or theme to be available to all sites, use the folders sites/all/modules and sites/all/themes, respectively. Do not place downloaded modules and themes into the Drupal core directories. Keeping the Drupal core pristine will make it easier to perform security updates.

Paths

Drupal places information it needs into the URL for each page you view. This information is referred to as the "Drupal path." These paths are in no way related to the directory structure of Drupal files; however, every "page" in Drupal has a distinct path. For example, http://example.com/node/1337 has the path node/1337. These paths instruct the Drupal module Path about which information needs to be compiled to display each page. The Path module allows you to create an alias for each page. For example, you might want to create an alias for node/1337 so that site visitors may request the same content from the URL http://example.com/free-kittens. When you are working with Drupal page templates in Chapter 4, it will be important to know if you are looking at a Drupal path or at the alias of a path. More information is provided in Chapter 4 on how to tell the difference between the two.

Theming Strategies

Many different strategies may be used to prepare templates for Drupal. The best approach for your Web site will depend on how you need to display the data, how much the display of data needs to be altered from the default templates provided by

Drupal, and what the technical abilities of the person who will be maintaining the theme for your Web site are. Programming logic, structure of information, and the visual style of the displayed page are separated into different types of files in your theme's directory. The Drupal database does not "think" about how the content will be displayed; it merely stores user-submitted data.

Best Practices

Throughout this book you will learn how to theme Drupal by separating each task into different types of files within your theme's directory. These tasks are distinguished as follows:

- Definitions, including regions and style sheet file names, are placed into a `.info` file.
- Logic and "decision making" are placed into a `template.php` file.
- HTML markup is placed into template files ending with `.tpl.php`. This extension is pronounced "tipple-fip."
- Style definitions are placed into Cascading Style Sheet files.

This separation of tasks into files is a "best practice" that is relevant to the PHPTemplate theme engine and will be used throughout this book. Different theming engines may use different file naming conventions. Of course, there are exceptions to this organization: Sometimes it makes sense to include a bit of markup in your logic file, and sometimes it is essential to test for certain conditions before displaying marked-up data (for example, testing whether a variable is set).

Alternative Strategies

A variety of alternative strategies have been described online. They offer good ideas that are completely appropriate for some cases. You may choose to incorporate some of these ideas into your own themes; however, this book focuses on the best practices mentioned previously.

Palantir offered a full description of its theming strategy for one of its Web sites at `http://www.palantir.net/blog/graycor-drupal-theming-works`. Its theming strategy optimizes for changes to CCK content types from the Web interface. The company themes as much as possible at the field level in the file `template.php` instead of at the node level in individual `tpl.php` files. This approach allows Palantir's clients to easily change the order of the fields from within the Web-based GUI without needing FTP access to the server and without requiring knowledge of how to change a template file. Although the fields can be themed in individual `tpl.php` files, this strategy keeps the theme directory free of clutter. It might also improve performance, because Drupal does not have to open many small template files to build a single page. With the theme registry's caching system in Drupal 6, however, it is unlikely this technique will offer a significant improvement in terms of performance.

A second, completely different strategy is to use the module ConTemplate. This module allows you to rearrange content by adding PHP snippets in the Web interface to rearrange content before it reaches the theming stage. This approach allows ConTemplate to change search indexing and RSS feeds; however, any other theming should be performed at the theme level. To accomplish these pre-theme changes, ConTemplate stores theme-like PHP snippets in the database and uses the PHP function `eval` to convert the theme instructions into the pages that are viewed in a Web browser. This method of processing theme instructions is slower than if you were to use PHPTemplate as described earlier.

Text files associated with themes can be easily placed into a version control system such as CVS, Subversion, or Bazaar. By contrast, ConTemplate stores its snippets in the database; as a consequence, you cannot keep incremental snapshots of your changes. ConTemplate's snippets are not stored within the database in the same way that versions of a node are stored in the table `node_revisions`. This means you cannot "undo" changes that you make. You can also potentially wreck your Web site if the PHP is faulty.

If you know you need to alter search indexing and RSS feeds, you can find out more about ConTemplate from its project Web site (`http://drupal.org/project/contemplate`).

> **Working with text files**
> ConTemplate can be configured to read its theme snippets from text files instead of the database. This strategy requires copying and pasting template information from the Web site into files that reside on your server. By working only with the theme's template files, you can accomplish the same thing but without having to set your preferences from within the administration area of the Web site first.

Over time you will undoubtedly develop your own strategies. Nevertheless, using techniques that are promoted within the Drupal core will make it easier to upgrade your work over time. The techniques described throughout this book are aligned with the recommended approach to theming Drupal (with a few exceptions that are noted as such).

Now that you have learned the components that make up a Drupal theme, it is time to prepare the toolkit you will use for the rest of this book, and indeed as a Drupal themer!

Drupal Terminology

Newcomers to Drupal quickly realize there is a whole vocabulary that is specific to the development and maintenance of Drupal. In this section you will be introduced to a few of the terms that are used throughout this book.

Node

Each time you create a new unit of content in Drupal, you are really creating a new *node*. A node can be a simple page with text and images on it, but it could also be a completely customized content type that you have created to store your entomological collection of bug photographs. A node refers to a single instance of content, whereas a *content type* (sometimes called a "node type") refers to a specific data structure that is used for a series of nodes. By default, there are two content types enabled: "Page" and "Story." Drupal offers some basic ways of navigating through the nodes, but with the Views module (one of the must-have modules described later in this chapter) you may create whatever navigation scheme is appropriate for your Web site.

Figure 2.1 shows some of the properties of a node, including the metadata, settings, and version-controlled content. Modules may add additional properties to nodes in the database. In Figure 2.1, the comment module has added two fields to the settings for the node, and the taxonomy module has added "tags" to the version-controlled content. Using the CCK module you will learn how to add even more fields to your content. CCK fields use a different storage structure within the database.

Users, Roles, and Permissions

Two kinds of users are distinguished for a Drupal Web site: (1) users who have created an account on the Web site and are logged in (authenticated users) and (2) users who have not taken these steps (anonymous users). Having only two types of users is very limiting for large Web sites that are maintained by several kinds of content authors and comment moderators. For this reason, Drupal has a role-based permission system to accommodate the permission granularity required to maintain complex Web sites.

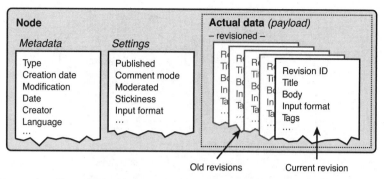

FIGURE 2.1 Properties of a node, including metadata, settings, and version-controlled content.

The first user account has a role of its own
One very special authenticated user is identified by Drupal: The first user that creates an account in any Drupal Web site has ultimate power and can carry out any task in that Web site. This account, which is referred to as user/1, must be used when performing security updates.

Creating a new role is a trivial task: Just navigate to the Administer, User management, Roles page and submit your new role title in the form that appears. Once an appropriate name has been created, you may alter the permissions for this role by navigating to Administer, User management, Permissions. For example, you might create a new role called "Editor" and then allow this role to "upload files" and "access user profiles."

Figure 2.2 displays several permissions in the form of a Venn diagram. In this figure, the role named Administrator has all permissions of the role Editor plus two additional permissions. Anonymous users have permission only to search the site, view content, and post comments. A Web site visitor who is using an authenticated account may also post comments without the consent of an administrator. Account holders may be assigned multiple roles. For example, if the user has the roles Editor and Authenticated User, that individual may "administer users" and "post comments."

Blocks and Regions

The Drupal page is divided into markup, the content of the page, and the regions for the page. Regions may contain zero, one, or more blocks. A block may contain a navigation menu, a random image, a list of recent comments, or anything else that you

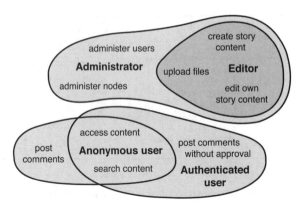

FIGURE 2.2 Sample roles and their permissions displayed as a Venn diagram.

might need. Blocks are typically defined by modules, but you can also create your own custom blocks. Each block must be placed into a region before it will become visible on the Web site. As the Web site developer, you may control the order in which multiple blocks appear in the same region. You may also decide to limit the visibility for certain blocks to specific pages or to specific roles.

Many modules provide their own blocks. For this reason, each time you enable a new module, you should check whether new blocks are now available. To ensure the blocks are visible to the appropriate user roles, you may need to adjust the permissions defined by the new module.

Blocks can be dynamic, or they can contain static information that does not change from page to page. One dynamic block is the "Who's online" block provided by the module `user.module`. This block presents a list of Web site users who have been active on the Web site within the last few minutes. You can also create context-sensitive blocks—for example, an "Author information" block containing further information about the user who created the currently displayed node.

To create a custom block, navigate to Administer, Site building, Blocks. Select the link to "Add block." Custom blocks need not be limited to just displaying text. You may also use PHP and place virtually any content into the block—for example, a search form or a Flash video.

Categories, Taxonomy, Vocabularies, and Terms

Humans seem to have an insatiable need to classify things. We build libraries with books sorted by topic, we use Latin naming conventions to sort plants and animals into families, and we use categories to sort our blog posts. This science of naming and classifying things is known as taxonomy. Within Drupal, the term *taxonomy* refers to any form of organization based on categories and classification. A taxonomy typically has a hierarchical structure, like a family tree—there are terms at the top of the tree structure that are relevant to many things, but as you descend the structure the terms become narrower and apply to a smaller subset of the items being described. In Drupal, you are not required to create a hierarchy of your taxonomy terms. Figure 2.3 shows three different kinds of relationships that taxonomy terms (categories) may have: no hierarchy, a single hierarchy, and multiple hierarchies. Notice that only the second and third diagrams are similar to a "family tree," with fewer items appearing at the top and many items found at the bottom of the "tree."

Within your Web site, you may have several unrelated topics that you want to assign to categories. For example, your blog categories may be separate from your

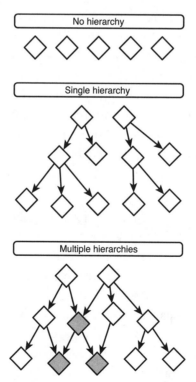

FIGURE 2.3 Taxonomy terms may have no hierarchy, a single hierarchy, or multiple hierarchies.

recipe categories. In this case you will create a new "vocabulary" for each of the discrete topics in the Web site. You must have at least one vocabulary if you want to use the taxonomy system. Within each vocabulary, however, you may have as many terms as you like. In Figure 2.3, the diamonds represent terms included as part of one vocabulary.

Parent Items and Weight

In the administration system, the terms *parent item* and *weight* often remain hidden, because Drupal uses a drag-and-drop interface to rearrange items. Nevertheless, there are some screens where you will need to understand their meanings.

Both taxonomy and menus may rely on hierarchies for their organization. When items are organized within a hierarchical sorting system, Drupal uses the term "parent item" to define which taxonomy term or menu item is closer to the top of the "family tree." When you are placing an item into a menu, for example, you must decide under which "parent" the specific menu item should be placed.

The "weight" of an item refers to the order of the item relative to all other items in that group. With the Drupal core, the metaphor is that "Heavy items sink." As a Canadian writing this chapter in winter, I find that weather temperatures that dip into negative degrees Celsius do not feel "light," so I have provided an alternative metaphor: The weight is a little bit like a timeline. Zero is the present; a large negative value is in the past (and will appear on the far left side of a list of items that are read from left to right, or at the top of a list that is read from top to bottom); and a large positive value is in the future (and will appear on the far right side of a list of items that are read from left to right, or at the bottom of a list of items that are read from top to bottom).

Menu

A menu consists of three entities: the menu tree, the menu items, and the menu item links. Menus are typically added to the page via blocks. The menu module provides a block for every menu, and blocks can be enabled by navigating to Administer, Site building, Blocks. Menu items are located within a menu tree and contain exactly one menu item link. They have properties indicating whether the menu item is a leaf, an expanded menu item, or a collapsed menu item. Additionally, a menu item can also be in the "active trail," which means that the page currently being rendered is a child of the menu item (or the menu item itself). Figure 2.4 shows a menu and each of its components. The lines drawn around each section outline the parts of a menu.

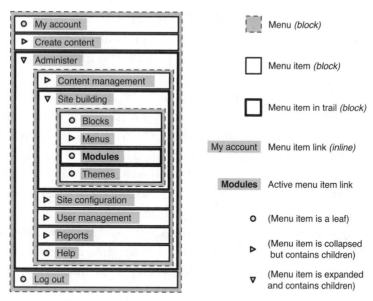

FIGURE 2.4 A menu can be placed into a Web site through a block. Menu items may be either a leaf (no subsections), a collapsed menu item (with hidden subsections), or an expanded menu item (with visible subsections).

Pagers

No, not the thing you strap to your hip when you're "on call." A *pager* is a collection of links that breaks a very long list of nodes or comments into smaller sections. Each page contains the same number of items. For example, a list of 100 items with 10 items per page would yield 10 pages of results. Pagers typically have links for "next" and "previous" pages as well. Figure 2.5 shows a pager.

Hooks and Naming Conventions

Drupal's extensibility is based on the naming conventions used for its functions; these conventions are referred to as *hooks*. Modules contain a selection of those hooks to

FIGURE 2.5 A pager allows you to navigate through a very long list of items.

change content generated or provided by other modules, to add in the hook's own handling functions, or to register menu items, theme functions, and so on. Understanding their origins removes some of the mystery of how Drupal makes its magic happen in the file `template.php`.

For example, when Drupal creates a menu, it "asks" each module if it has any items it would like to add to the menu tree by looking for functions with a special naming convention. If there is a function that matches the naming convention, Drupal will perform the function and retrieve the relevant data. Hooks are always named using the format `<module name>_<hook name>`. You will see these naming conventions many times in your theme development. Part of the function name is customized to match your theme name, while other parts will remain the same.

These conventions are the reason you must name your functions carefully in the file `template.php`. Throughout this book, you will see naming patterns for many theme-related functions, including a series of functions that begin with `theme_` as well as the `preprocess` functions.

Must-Have Modules

There are three contributed modules that you will need to include in your theming toolkit:

- Content Creation Kit (CCK) module: used to extend the basic content type additional field.
- Views module: used to create lists of content.
- Devel module: includes the Themer Info module, which allows you to identify the Drupal characteristics necessary to theme any item displayed in a Drupal Web site.

Information on how to download and install contributed modules appears in Appendix A.

Content Creation Kit (CCK) Module

This section describes how to create new content types. The example walks you through the creation of a content type to store a "portfolio" of your Web design work. This content type was chosen because it contains many different *field* types that can be applied to a wide range of *content* types. These content types could be news stories, movie or music reviews, community events such as conference sessions, or products in an online store. If you are working on a specific challenge within your own Web site, you should change the example immediately to suit your needs.

At its most basic, a unit of Drupal content is a node that contains only a terse description (a title) and text-based content (the body). Additional metadata for this node is also stored—namely, the content author; the date the metadata was first submitted to the database; the date it was last updated; whether comments are allowed; and whether the node should appear on the front page of the Web site. To extend this basic content type, you must first know which additional information you will need to store. Refer back to the preparation work you did in Chapter 1 and look at each of the different content types you defined for your Web site. As part of this exercise, you also defined the fields that make up each content type. You will need to use the properties of these fields when you create your custom content type. Specifically, you will need to know the following information for each content type that you create:

- The properties of each field (for example, will data be captured best as a terse text description, or will you need to use a controlled vocabulary and preset the options in a selection list)
- The grouping of individual fields within the content type, especially for long forms and complicated content types
- The privacy settings for each field
- Optional fields versus required fields
- The default settings for each of comments, and work flow settings

With this information in hand, you are ready to create new types of content, and their associated input forms, in your Web site.

Installing CCK and Related Modules

If you have not already installed the Content Creation Kit, you should do so now. Appendix A contains instructions on how to install the necessary modules. In this section, you will make a sample portfolio Web site. It will include text fields, a selection list, and an image field. You will need the following additional modules to create this content type:

- cck (http://drupal.org/project/cck)
- date (http://drupal.org/project/date)
- filefield (http://drupal.org/project/filefield)

- `imagefield` (http://drupal.org/project/imagefield)
- `token` (http://drupal.org/project/token)

With these five modules you will be able to make a wide range of content types. For additional field types, visit the CCK category on the Drupal Web site at http://drupal.org/project/Modules/category/88. Additional modules can be downloaded and enabled if you need a field specifically for computed fields (PHP snippets), numbers, embedded media (video and audio), or node and user references. More information is available from the main CCK project page at http://drupal.org/project/cck.

Once the modules have been downloaded and placed into your site's module directory, you will need to enable them from Drupal's module administration area. Note that the names of the projects you downloaded in the previous step will not be an exact match to the module names you need to install in the next step. Navigate to Administer, Site building, Modules and enable each of the following modules:

- Content (listed under CCK)
- FileField (listed under CCK)
- ImageField (listed under CCK)
- Option Widgets (listed under CCK)
- Text (listed under CCK)
- Date (listed under Date/Time)

The Token module will also be enabled, as it is required by the FileField module. The Date API and Date Timezone modules are required by the Date module and will be installed as well. You are now ready to create a custom content type.

Creating a Custom Content Type

Content in Drupal almost always has a title (a short description for linking) and a body (a large field for the actual content). When you create a new content type, you will have these two fields to start, but you may add as many other fields as you need for your content type. The following example creates a new content type to store information about your "portfolio" of work. If you have a specific content type defined and ready to use, you should change the suggested values to match your own content type.

To create the shell for your new content type, you must complete the following steps:

1. Navigate to Administer, Content management, Content types, Add content type. You will be presented with a screen for the metadata for this content type.

2. Fill in the Name, Type, and Description for your new content type in the "Add content type" form as shown in Figure 2.6. Use values that are appropriate for your custom content type.

3. Click on "Submission Form Settings" to reveal the related options.

4. Change the "Title field label" to "Project name" and the "Body field label" to "About this project." You may close this fieldset when you have finished altering the fields by clicking "Submission Form Settings" a second time.

5. Click on "Workflow settings" to reveal the related options.

6. Adjust the defaults as appropriate for the following settings: Published; Promoted to front page; Sticky at top of lists; and/or Create new revision.

FIGURE 2.6 Content types have both metadata and associated fields. This information includes the name of the content type, form labels, and the default settings for work flow and comments for each new node.

7. Click on "Comments settings" to reveal the related options.

8. Set comments to "Disabled" for this content type. If you are working with your own content type and do want to have comments enabled, you may set the default settings now.

9. Scroll to the bottom and click "Save content type."

You will be returned to the summary of all content types after successfully creating your new content type. The next step is to extend the content type by adding new content fields.

Adding Fields

When a content type is first created, it contains only two fields in which to store data. You may "extend" your content type by adding more fields for specific types of data. Having discrete places in your Web form to enter data ensures that information will be complete, correct, retrievable, and sortable by field. When you add a new field to your content type, the content editing forms are automatically updated to show these new fields.

> **Extending existing content types**
> You may add content fields to both core and contributed content types. For example, if you want to extend the content type Page to include images, you could use the instructions included in this section, even though Page is provided by Drupal core. This same idea applies to contributed modules that offer their own content types. For example, you could add a field for "Photographer" to the content type provided by the Image module.

Your new portfolio content type will use several additional fields:

- Text descriptions of the project, including fill-in-the-blank text fields (both single-line and multiple-line "text areas")
- Web links and email addresses
- Selection lists
- Project start and end dates
- Text and binary file attachments (including screenshot images)

The processes for creating all field types use approximately the same steps. While creating your own fields, you should read the forms carefully for each field type and choose the options best suited to your needs. As an example, the following steps are required to create a new field that will allow content authors to upload and attach an image using the module `imagefield`:

1. From the list of Content types, click the "add field" link next to the content type you would like to customize. In this case you will click the link next to "Portfolio."

2. Enter the Field name (machine-readable) and the Label (human-readable).

3. Select the field type from the drop-down list. The options may not be immediately obvious. Here are a few hints: if you would like to add an Option Widget (which includes radio buttons, check boxes, and drop-down lists), choose "Text." If you would like to add an image field, choose "File."

4. Scroll to the bottom of the screen and click "Continue" to finish customizing your new field.

5. On the next screen, the Field name, Label, and Type will be fixed. Choose the Widget type for your field. Figure 2.7 shows the screen to add an image field. In this case, the Widget type is "Image." You could also attach a "File" if you

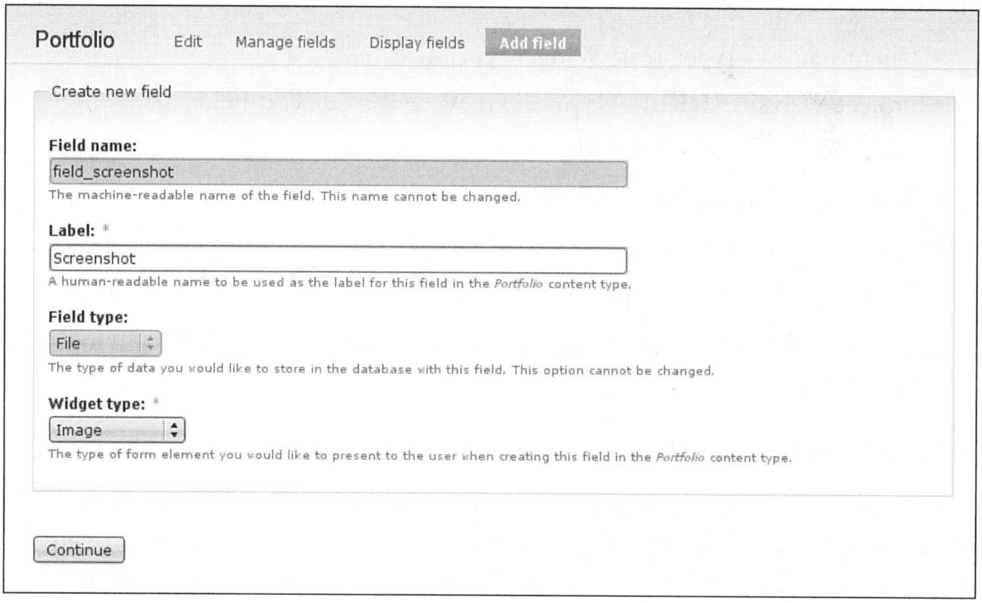

Portfolio   Edit   Manage fields   Display fields   Add field

Create new field

Field name:

field_screenshot

The machine-readable name of the field. This name cannot be changed.

Label: *

Screenshot

A human-readable name to be used as the label for this field in the *Portfolio* content type.

Field type:

File

The type of data you would like to store in the database with this field. This option cannot be changed.

Widget type: *

Image

The type of form element you would like to present to the user when creating this field in the *Portfolio* content type.

Continue

FIGURE 2.7 To add a field to your content type, you move through a series of screens to set the default options for the field type you have selected.

wanted to include the written documentation you supplied with the project. Scroll to the bottom of the screen and click "Continue."

6. On the final screen, you will see the options for the field type you have selected. Choose the best options for your field type.

7. Repeat these steps for each new field. You may change the order of the fields at any time. Fields can also be added after you have started creating content using this content type.

> **More images**
> Using the ImageField module, you may attach as many images as you would like to your content type. The Image Attach module allows only one image per node. The Image Assist module does not link images directly to a node (although you can display an uploaded image within the body of the node). For more information about how to choose the best image module for your needs, refer to Chapter 5.

The following list gives suggested field types for the portfolio content type example. Once each of these fields has been added, the summary of your portfolio content type will look like Figure 2.8.

- Client name—Type: Text; Widget type: Text field
- Project Web site (URL)—Type: Text; Widget type: Text field
- Screenshot—Type: File; Widget type: Image
- Start date—Type: Date; Widget type: Select list
- End date—Type: Text; Widget type: Select list
- Development tools—Type: Text; Widget type: Check boxes/radio buttons

You could also use Drupal's taxonomy system instead of having a CCK field to list your development tools.

Fields: Order, Display, and Groups

At this point, you are ready to arrange the form fields for your new content type. You may also choose to adjust the display for each of the fields and bring similar fields together into groups so the form is easier to complete. The settings for the order, display, and groupings can be configured from each of your content types. To use the instructions given in this section, you must first navigate to Administer, Content

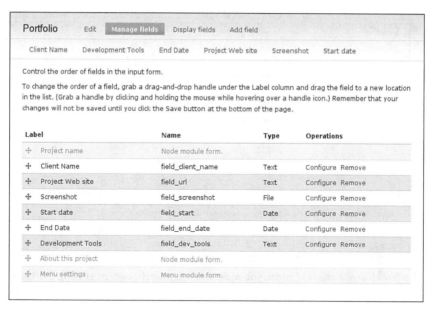

FIGURE 2.8 The portfolio content type has been created and is ready for use. Three core fields are present as well as six new custom fields.

management, Content types and then select "manage fields" beside the name of the content type to which you want to make adjustments.

Field Order

On the summary page for field management, you will see a screen that is similar to Figure 2.9. If you have JavaScript enabled, you will see a small crosshair beside each content field. To change the order of the fields, click the crosshair and drag the field to its new location. Once you have rearranged the fields, you must commit the changes to the database by clicking the button labeled "Save" at the bottom of the page (as shown in Figure 2.9).

Field Display

You may adjust the default display for each field by clicking the "Display fields" link at the top of the page. Each field type has different display settings that can be adjusted for the teaser and full node (see Figure 2.10). You may also choose to display the label beside the data when the content is viewed or decide to hide the label completely. The ability to make these minor adjustments from Drupal's administrative interface means a lot less work is required to create custom template files for each content type.

Label	Name	Type	Operations
✛ Project name	Node module form.		
✛ Client Name	field_client_name	Text	Configure Remove
✛ Project Web site*	field_url	Link	Configure Remove
✛ Screenshot	field_screenshot	Image	Configure Remove
✛ Start date	field_start	Date	Configure Remove
✛ End Date	field_end_date	Date	Configure Remove
✛ Development Tools	field_dev_tools	Text	Configure Remove
✛ About this project	Node module form.		
✛ Menu settings	Menu module form.		

* Changes made in this table will not be saved until the form is submitted.

Save

FIGURE 2.9 After changing the field order, you must commit your changes by clicking the "Save" button.

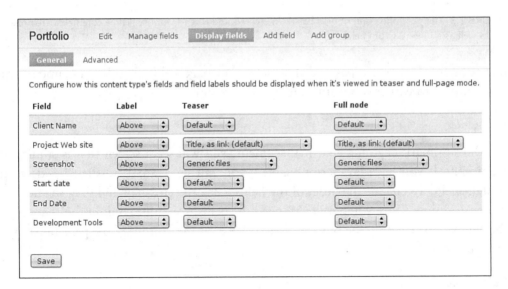

FIGURE 2.10 The display settings can be customized for the full node and teaser of each field type.

Field Groups

The CCK suite of tools includes the module Fieldgroup, which allows you to group content fields on the content editing screen. To enable this module, navigate to Administer, Site building, Modules. Scroll down to the CCK suite of modules and enable the Fieldgroup module. Scroll to the bottom and click "Save configuration."

Once the Fieldgroup module is enabled, you can create new groups by navigating to Administer, Content management, Content types and selecting the "manage fields" option next to the content type you wish to alter. At that point, you can add a new group by clicking the link "Add group" at the top of the page. You will be asked to complete a basic form with settings for your new field group, including the settings shown in Figure 2.11: the group's label, style (default visibility), help text (for editing content), and description.

The order of these groups may be adjusted in the same way as the order of individual fields. Figure 2.12 shows a field group integrated with individual fields. To add a field to a group, you must slide the field slightly to the right to show that the field belongs with that specific group. You may place only those fields you have created into a field group.

FIGURE 2.11 New groups have four settings that need to be configured: Label, Style, Help text, Description.

Label	Name	Type	Operations
✛ Project name	Node module form.		
✛ Client Name	field_client_name	Text	Configure Remove
✛ Start date	field_start	Date	Configure Remove
✛ End Date	field_end_date	Date	Configure Remove
✛ About this project	Node module form.		
✛ **Project information**	group_project_information		Configure Remove
✛ Project Web site	field_url	Link	Configure Remove
✛ Screenshot	field_screenshot	Image	Configure Remove
✛ Development Tools	field_dev_tools	Text	Configure Remove
✛ Menu settings	Menu module form.		

FIGURE 2.12 To add a field to a group, you must slide the field slightly to the right to show that the field belongs with that specific group.

Additional Settings

For each content type, you will need to adjust several settings. These include Attributions, Post Settings, and Permissions.

Attributions (Post Information)

The Attributions setting allows you to enable or disable the "submitted by Username on date" text when displaying content. If your content includes date-based information, such as a calendar of events, it is a good idea to remove the attributions because the "submitted on" information can be confusing if it is not themed to be very different from the date of the event. To adjust attribution settings, follow these steps:

1. Navigate to Administer, Site Building, Themes.
2. Choose the "Global settings" tab.
3. Adjust the display in the fieldset "Display post information on."
4. Scroll to the bottom of the screen and click "Save configuration."

Post Settings

The Post settings adjust the default length of the teaser text for all content types. This information acts as a global setting for all content types. Teasers are typically used in lists of content—for example, on the front page of your Web site or in a view of content. Navigate to Administer, Content management, Post settings and then adjust the following settings:

- Number of posts on main page
- Length of trimmed posts (in characters)
- Preview post (optional or required)

Permissions

You will also need to adjust the access permissions for the new content type, thereby determining who can view, edit, and create this content. Navigate to Administer, User management, Permissions. Under the "node" module, update the access control settings for the options: create portfolio content, delete portfolio content, and edit portfolio content. If you have enabled content permissions, you will also be able to adjust the permissions for each field type from this screen under the content_permissions module. When you are finished making changes, scroll to the bottom of the screen and click "Save permissions."

The portfolio content type is now ready for use.

Views Module

The second must-have contributed module is the Views module. The Content Creation Kit allows you to extend very simple forms into complex data types. The Views module, by comparison, completes the customization puzzle by allowing you to create your own unique lists of content. You can use this module to create anything from a simple list of recent comments to a complex photo gallery.

The Views module can be downloaded from the project page at http://drupal. org/project/views. Instructions for installing modules can be found in Appendix A. Additional help for the Views module is also available from the Advanced Help module. This module provides additional in-site instructions on how to use the Views module. Advanced Help can be downloaded from the project page at http://drupal. org/project/advanced_help.

There are three modules included in the Views project. To enable them, navigate to Administer, Site building, Modules and scroll down to the Views section. You will see the following modules listed:

- Views: used to create customized lists and queries from the Drupal database
- Views exporter: used to export multiple views at once
- Views UI: the Web-based administration tool used to create and edit customized views

To use Views, you will need to enable both the Views and Views UI modules. At this time you should also enable the Advanced Help module if you have downloaded it; it is listed under "Other" modules. It is highly recommended that you install the Advanced Help module.

> **Save server resources**
> Once you have created all of your views, you can disable the module Views UI. This module is needed only to build new views; it does not need to be enabled once your views are set. If you need to edit your views, you can enable the Views UI module any time to make the necessary changes.

Understanding Views

To reach the Views administration area, navigate to Administer, Site building, Views. Figure 2.13 shows the main configuration screen. This screen includes four tabs across the top (List, Add, Import, Tools), a link to the Getting Started tutorial (you must have Advanced Help enabled), a set of filters, and a series of views that are provided by default. (The Getting Started tutorial is a comprehensive guide to the use of Views— you should definitely read it.) The default views can be disabled, enabled, and altered, but never completely removed, because they are part of the Views module code. By contrast, all views that you create (referred to as "Normal" views) are stored in Drupal's database.

Begin by looking through the list of default views. Each view contains a summary of information about the view. Using the "archive" view as an example, you will see the following information:

- **Default:** the storage type for this view (one of: Normal, Default, Overridden)
- **Node view:** the type of view (Node, Comment, File, Node Revision, Term, or User)
- **Archive:** the machine-readable name of the view
- **Enable:** the view is currently disabled; click the link to enable this view

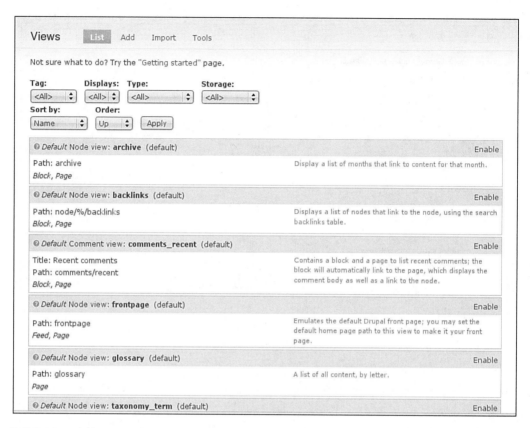

FIGURE 2.13 The Views administration area lists all views, both enabled and disabled. By default, no views are enabled.

- **Path:** archive: the URL for this view
- **Block, Page:** the displays for this view (Block, Page, or Feed)
- **Display a list of months that link to content for that month:** a summary of this view

To understand how views are built, take a look at the configuration screen for the "archive" view. You must first enable the view before configuring it.

1. Click the link "Enable" in the archive view summary.

2. An "Edit" link will appear. Click the "Edit" link to configure the archive view.

The Views configuration screen contains seven basic areas, as shown in Figure 2.14. More generally, the screen is divided into two sides: a navigation area on the left that

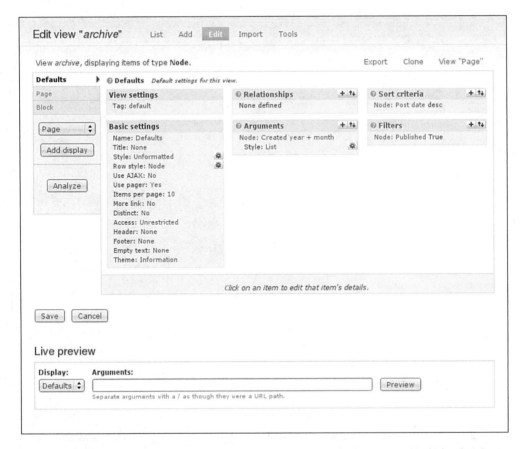

FIGURE 2.14 The Views configuration screen contains seven areas. The main screen includes the View settings, Basic settings, Relationships, Arguments, Sort criteria, and Filters. On the left of the screen is a display toggle that allows you to switch between the different types of views available.

allows you to switch between the types of views available (for example, Block, Page, and Feed) and the main configuration screen. The Views module uses JavaScript to hide and display components on the configuration screen. To edit an option, you click on the label, or text setting, of the component you would like to change. For example, if you wanted to change the number of items displayed on a default archive page, you would click the "10" next to the heading "Items per page" under the "Basic Settings" area.

The main screen includes six areas:

- **View settings** gives a brief description and tags that describe this view.
- **Basic settings** include the name of view, title to display, formatting options, and contextual information (header, footer, no results returned).

- **Relationships** specifies the linkages between items in this view and other things stored in the database (for example, the name of the author for a specific node).

- **Arguments** may change the list of content that is retrieved from the database based on the URL (most commonly used for categories).

- **Sort criteria** are used to define the order of appearance for nodes displayed in this view.

- **Filters** are a fixed set of rules that govern which content should be retrieved for this list.

At the bottom of the page is an option to preview the list of content that will be assembled for your view. This check will help you to ensure your configuration options are selecting exactly the content you want to display.

Creating a New View

Look through each of the default views provided by the Views module. Each shows you a different technique you can use for your own views:

- **taxonomy_term, backlinks,** and **glossary** show you how to use arguments.

- **glossary** shows you how to group nodes together (all nodes starting with "A", "B", "C", and so on) to create an index of your content.

- **comments_recent** shows you how to create relationships between nodes and their authors.

- **tracker** shows you how to make extensive use of filters.

From the main Views administration screen, choose the view that is closest to the type of view you would like to create. Click the link named "Clone" for that view. Complete each of the screens in the view creation wizard to create your customized view. If there is no match for the type of view you need to create, you may create one from scratch. You may add a new view with no preset values from any of the Views configuration pages by clicking on the "Add" tab at the top of the page.

Devel Module

The third must-have module is the Devel module, which contains a whole suite of incredibly useful tools, including a content generator to create random content to test your theme and a visual diagnostic tool, Theme developer, that allows you to dissect any part of your theme to reveal the underlying functions, templates, and variables in use at any point on the page. The project page for this module is found at `http://drupal.org/project/devel`.

The following modules are included in the Devel package:

- **Devel:** shortcuts and functions for developers
- **Devel generate:** generate sample users, nodes, and taxonomy terms
- **Devel node access:** block and page showing `node_access` records
- **Macro:** record and play back form submissions
- **Theme developer:** essential information for themers

Enable the Devel and Theme developer modules. You may enable other modules from this suite as well; however, only the Theme developer module will be used in this book.

Once the Theme developer module is enabled, you will see a new tool in the lower-left former of your Drupal Web site. This small gray widget, which is shown in Figure 2.15, allows you to toggle the display of the Drupal Themer Information window. Once the Themer info window has been opened, you can move your mouse around the screen and choose which part of the page you would like more information about.

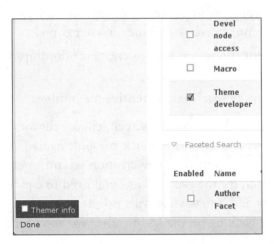

FIGURE 2.15 The Themer info widget appears on the lower-left corner of your Web site. Clicking it toggles the display of the Drupal Themer Information window.

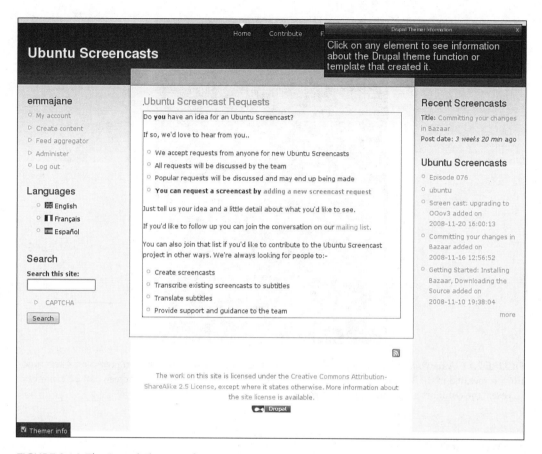

FIGURE 2.16 The Drupal Themer Information window (Themer info) allows you to obtain more information about any part of the page.

In Figure 2.16, the square surrounds the node displayed on the front page of a Web site. When you click beside the title of the node, the Themer info window reveals information about the templates used and preprocess functions that can be used to theme this portion of the page, as shown in Figure 2.17.

The Devel module will be used throughout this book to reveal information about the components of the page you are theming.

FIGURE 2.17 After you click on any part of the page, information about the theming templates and functions is revealed in the Themer info window. The "Array" bar at the bottom of the screen can be expanded to reveal the contents of the node object variable.

Browser Tools

In addition to installing Drupal's tools, you are well advised to install a range of browser-based, life-saving tools.

Firebug

Firebug is a Web browser plugin available for Firefox. Using this tool, you can easily get information about any page element, including its location in the page and styles that have been applied. For more information about Firebug, and to install it on your machine, visit the project's Web page at `http://www.getfirebug.com`. Once you have installed Firebug, you have access to a powerful diagnostic tool that offers the following features:

- Ability to identify and locate any HTML element on the page by right-clicking on the element and choosing "Inspect element"

- Ability to edit CSS properties and attributes to test possible enhancements immediately
- Visual display of width, padding, and margins for every page element
- A JavaScript debugger that allows you to pause your scripts
- A DOM inspector

Figure 2.18 shows the element inspector. From this screen, you can easily change just the relevant part of the style sheet, or you can override one of the core styles or a module's styles with something of your own.

Internet Explorer 8 ships with its own suite of Developer Tools. To enable this toolbar, open the Tools menu of the Internet Explorer 8 toolbar, and choose "Developer Tools." Additional information is available from `http://msdn.microsoft.com/en-us/library/cc848894(VS.85).aspx`.

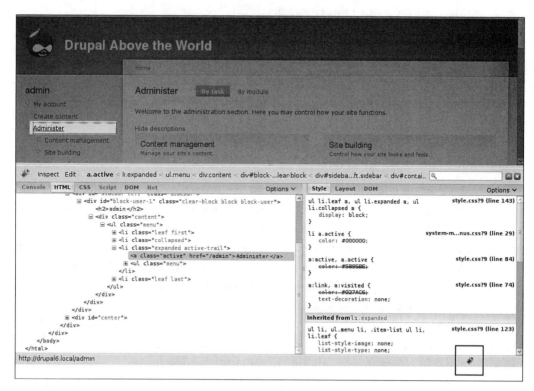

FIGURE 2.18 Firebug inspects the Administer link. You can also activate this console by clicking on the firebug in the lower-right corner of the browser.

The Web browser Opera also has a developer toolbar, named Opera Dragonfly. Additional information for this browser toolkit is available from `http://www.opera.com/dragonfly/`.

Web Developer's Toolbar

The Web Developer's Toolbar complements Firebug and is available for the browser Firefox. From viewing the path for each image on the page to validating your CSS, the Web Developer's Toolbar offers a shortcut for nearly everything. Some of its useful features are outlined here:

- Resize the browser window to any predefined size (a size of 800 × 600 pixels is provided by default).
- Validate the page using WAI and Section 508 tests.
- Check for broken links on this page.
- Validate the CSS and HTML for the page.
- Display line guides to determine whether page elements are aligned.

Figure 2.19 shows the Web Developer's Toolbar displayed along the top of the browser window. These options are also available in the Tools, Web developer menu. Additional information on the Web Developer's Toolbar is available from `http://chrispederick.com/work/web-developer/`.

Screen Shot and Testing Services

If you were to set up your own lab to test your Web site across multiple platforms and with multiple browsers, the process could prove quite expensive (and if you are currently relying on your friends as a test browser test environment, it is plausible they will eventually get bored of sending you screenshots). If you have a powerful-enough machine, you could also create virtual machines on your own desktop and install browsers on each of the different virtual machines. An alternative to these time- and resource-intensive testing approaches is to use an online browser testing service.

Two well-known and well-loved services are especially popular. Browser Cam (`http://www.browsercam.com`) is one of the longest-running browser testing services. It is highly customizable, highly configurable, and somewhat expensive if you need to test a Web site only occasionally. It also provides remote controllable machines, which are invaluable for testing interactive Web sites that use JavaScript and Flash.

FIGURE 2.19 The Web Developer Toolbar is integrated into the browser and provides quick access to a range of useful tools.

Fortunately, a free alternative is "good enough" for most testing purposes—Browsershots (http://www.browsershots.org). Browsershots doesn't have any glam to it, and you cannot change the screen resolution of the screenshots, but it will let you quickly identify potential problems in a range of Web browsers, as shown in Figure 2.20.

Choose only what you need
Browsershots has a daily maximum number of screenshots that you can have captured on your behalf. From the initial screen displayed in Figure 2.20, select only those browsers you need to test.

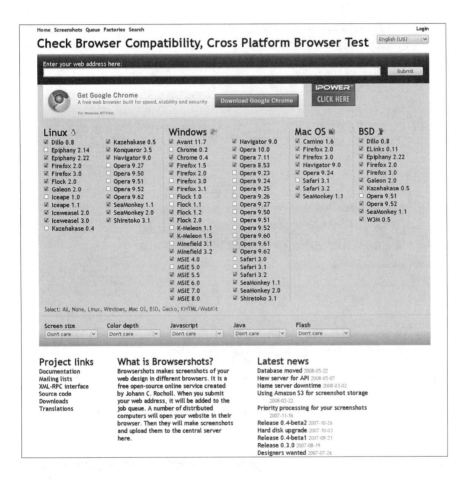

FIGURE 2.20 Browsershots allows you to view screenshots of your Web sites from a wide range of Web browsers.

After submitting your URL to Browsershots, you will need to wait several minutes to see your screen captures. The wait time depends on the number of requests ahead of you in the queue. By default, your screen captures remain available for 30 minutes after your initial request. You may extend this time if you would like. From the results page displayed in Figure 2.21, you may select an individual browser; alternatively, you may download all screen shots as a "zipped" archive.

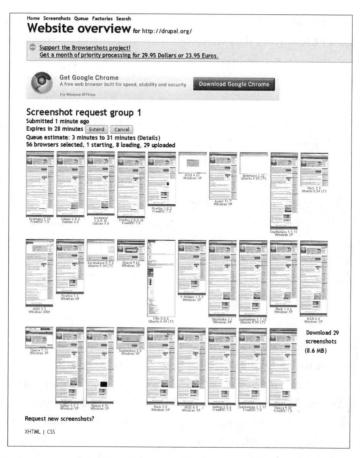

FIGURE 2.21 The results page of Browsershots includes a screen capture for each of your selected browsers and gives you the ability to download all screenshots simultaneously (lower-right corner).

Language References

Four machine languages are used in the creation and maintenance of a Drupal theme: PHP, XHTML, CSS, and JavaScript. Although you do not need to attain true mastery of each of these languages, theming Drupal is easier if you know enough about them to shuffle things around while still maintaining the integrity of how the machine language works. This book does not include a full reference for these languages, but rather assumes you understand the basics of each one. This section serves as a reminder of some of the excellent resources that are available online if you do need a quick reference for the code that appears in this book.

XHTML

The elements in XHTML are literally the building blocks for any page on the Web. If you are reading this book, chances are good you have dabbled with HTML or XHTML at some point. If you need a bit of a refresher, or if you want to know how to mark up a page the right way, head over to the Opera Web Standards Curriculum site (`http://www.opera.com/wsc`) and work through each of its lessons. It is important for you to use valid XHTML markup for your Drupal Web site. Failure to do so may result in pages that do not display correctly. The Web Developer's Toolbar includes a quick link to the W3C Markup Validation Service. You can also access this free online service directly at `http://validator.w3.org/`.

CSS

CSS brings visual excitement (or perhaps visual serenity) to your Web site. Fortunately, a lot of excellent tutorials explain how to work with Cascading Style Sheets. From designing for maximum browser compatibility to creating elegant expanding button-like backgrounds, the Web is rife with tutorials relevant to Drupal themers. A quick reference for all CSS selectors, properties, and values is available from the W3 Web site at `http://www.w3.org/TR/CSS2/cover.html#minitoc`. If you need a tutorial to remind you of the basics, visit the Opera Web Standards Curriculum (mentioned earlier) or visit the W3Schools Web site at `http://www.w3schools.com/css/`. As with XHTML, the CSS you write must be valid. The W3C offers a free online validation service at `http:jigsaw.w3.org/css-validator/`. For more information about designing with CSS and best practices, A List Apart provides dozens of articles on a wide range of CSS-related topics; visit its site at `http://www.alistapart.com/topics/code/css/`.

Grid-Based Frameworks

Whether you are a novice designer in need of all the help you can get or an experienced designer, one thing is certainly true: Grids make creating elegant designs easier. In a grid-based design process, your wireframes include a structured grid. Instead of sketching items "wherever," you place them based on columns that are already defined on the page. As an example, in Figure 2.22, a wireframe has been divided into 12 columns using the Grid 960 template system.

Grid-based design goes beyond a bunch of columns in a graphics editor; indeed, this approach has been extended into full CSS frameworks. These frameworks consist of a library of CSS files that allow you to easily develop a standards-compliant, browser-compatible, table-free layout. There are *many* frameworks available, including these options:

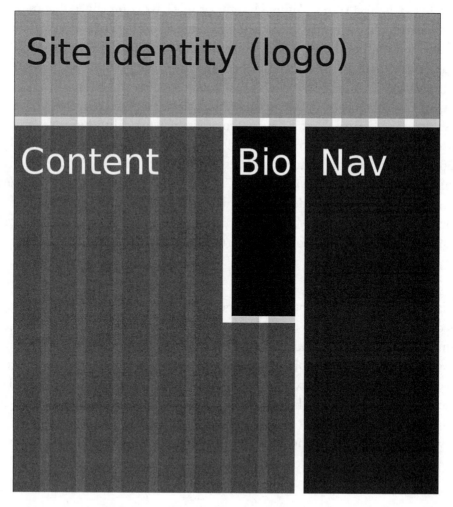

FIGURE 2.22 Using the 960 Grid System, the wireframe is divided into 6+2 columns for the content, 2 columns for the author information that "floats" next to the text, and 4 columns for the navigation.

- 960 Grid System (`http://960.gs/`)
- Blueprint CSS (`http://www.blueprintcss.org/`)
- YAML CSS Framework (`http://www.yaml.de/en/`)
- YUI Grids CSS (`http://developer.yahoo.com/yui/grids/`)

The Yahoo! User Interface (YUI) also comes with its own GUI to build a YUI. A full explanation of how to use the YUI grid framework is available at `http://developer.yahoo.com/yui/grids/` and the builder is available at `http://developer.yahoo.com/yui/grids/builder/`. Although some people have complained that frameworks are just bloated CSS files, they are actually quite useful for rapid development and save you from "reinventing the wheel." Among these frameworks are common CSS tools such as Eric Meyer's Reset CSS style sheet (`http://meyerweb.com/eric/tools/css/reset/`).

Several Drupal templates have been developed with a precise grid system in mind. For example, the Drupal themes Four Seasons, Framework, Hiroshige, Newswire, and Sky use the 960 Grid System to lay out the page. Its name comes from the fixed width of 960 pixels, which easily accommodates modern monitor screen resolutions with a minimum screen real estate of 1024×768 pixels. The 960 Grid System Web site (`http://www.960.gs`) includes a link to download template files. YAML for Drupal can be found at `http://www.yaml-fuer-drupal.de/de/download`. Blueprint is available at `http://drupal.org/project/blueprint`.

PHP

PHP is a server-side Web scripting language that is used to build Drupal and to make connections to your database to access the data for your Web site. The PHP online documentation is excellent; you can access it by visiting `http://www.php.net`. There are two search options available for this site. By default, the search field expects the name of a PHP function (for example, `array_merge`). If you need more general documentation, you must switch the drop-down menu to "online documentation" before submitting your search query.

If you are new to PHP and need the absolute basics, you will benefit from the CMS-agnostic tutorial, PHP 101. It is available at `http://devzone.zend.com/node/view/id/627`.

Drupal API

In addition to all of the PHP functions, Drupal has created its own functions. If you are searching for a function in the PHP documentation and cannot find it, you should remember to search the Drupal documentation as well! The API documentation is pulled from the source code of Drupal. It is written by developers, for developers, but you can read it, too. The Drupal API Web site (`http://api.drupal.org`) includes information on every single Drupal function available in the Drupal core. The search function allows you to search by function name and topic. Be sure you are reading the appropriate version of the documentation—look for the tabs for the Drupal 4.7, Drupal 5, Drupal 6, and Drupal 7 versions. You may also want to read the section on Default theme implementations (`http://api.drupal.org/api/group/themeable/6`); this page includes a full list of all theme-related functions in the Drupal core.

JavaScript

Chapters 9 to 11 of this book include a basic primer on JavaScript, the well-known client-side scripting language. If you find yourself yearning for more information, you can find it online. To increase the speed of development, Drupal uses a library of JavaScript functions known as jQuery. The online documentation for jQuery is excellent and includes tutorials on the basics of working with jQuery (`http://docs.jquery.com/Tutorials`). These tutorials include an introduction to jQuery, live examples of how jQuery works, and a special tutorial built for designers who want to add simple behaviors to their Web sites. This reference is tech-heavy—but then so is JavaScript.

Fortunately, not all online documentation takes the form of solid blocks of text in black and white. Nick La has written a beautiful primer on jQuery that shows you with circles and arrows what this technical language is all about. You can find it at jQuery Tutorial for Designers (`http://www.webdesignerwall.com/tutorials/jquery-tutorials-for-designers/`).

Maintaining Your System

There are two things that you absolutely must do to maintain your sanity: perform regular backups of your code and database (and restore from these files to ensure the integrity of your backups), and apply all relevant security patches that are released by the Drupal security team. An announcement mailing list can be found at `http://drupal.org/security`. These two statements may seem like the Murphy's Law of Web development ("If anything can go wrong, it will") to many people who have had their systems cracked into or who have overwritten an important file. If you are diligent about performing your backups and applying security patches, your hardware will never fail and your site will never be cracked. Beyond these two obvious steps to maintaining your system, there are two more tasks you should be aware of: scheduling Drupal's tasks and enforcing version control for your theme files.

Scheduling Tasks with Cron

If you are running the Drupal search function on your site, you must keep the search index updated. The task of updating the search index is performed only "as needed." That means if you do not request the index to be updated, your search results will never be up-to-date!

You can update the search index by navigating to Administer, Reports, Status report. Look for the section entitled "Cron maintenance tasks" and click the link to "run cron manually." Of course, it would be a time-consuming chore for you to click this link on a regular basis to keep your search index up-to-date. It is far more efficient to use a timer to tell Drupal how often the search index ought to be updated. This timer is referred as a "cron job," where "cron" is short for "chronograph" (which is a fancy word for a stopwatch or timing device). Unfortunately, this step cannot be accomplished within Drupal.

Luckily, many hosting providers will give you a Web-based administration tool to perform cron jobs. If this is the case, you may enter the following command into this tool:

your drupal address

```
45 * * * * /usr/bin/wget -O - -q http://example.com/cron.php
```

If the configuration tool allows you to set how frequently the timer is triggered, use only the following portion of the command:

```
/usr/bin/wget -O - -q http://example.com/cron.php
```

Revision Control

Regardless of whether you are working in an office as part of a multi-person team or alone at home with just your cat for company, you really ought to store your files in a version control system. This approach allows you to maintain a log of all changes that are made to your files and permits you to revert to a previously saved version of your file if necessary. Several different version control systems are available. The best one for you to use is the one you are motivated to use—a choice that may be dictated by the software selected by your officemates or by your clients. Commonly used version control systems include these packages:

- Concurrent Version System (CVS): `http://www.nongnu.org/cvs/`. Drupal is stored in this system.

- Subversion: `http://subversion.tigris.org/`. This is the most popular alternative to CVS.

- Bazaar: `http://bazaar-vcs.org`. This is an easy-to-use, distributed version control system.

While writing this book, the authors used all three of these version control systems: CVS to download Drupal and its contributed modules to ensure the code in the book was functional and accurate, and Subversion and Bazaar to store incremental versions of the book as it was written. An excellent overview of revision control and version control systems is available on Wikipedia at `http://en.wikipedia.org/wiki/Revision_control`.

Summary

This chapter covered a wide range of seemingly disparate topics:

- Drupal terminology
- Best practices for maintaining a Drupal theme
- Three must-have modules (CCK, Views, and Devel)
- Browser-based tools that help you identify page markup and diagnose errors
- Web references for the machine languages used to build Drupal
- System maintenance tips

You are now equipped to diagnose and repair (almost) any problem that you encounter in your theming adventures. You have also tricked out Drupal with the base modules you will need to make a wide range of Web sites. Additional modules will be recommended throughout the book. It is now time to take the first step in creating your own Drupal theme!

Chapter 3

Working with Drupal Themes

The actual creation of a Drupal theme is very simple. In this chapter you will learn the fundamentals. Following instructions blindly may end up feeling a bit like working through a "learn to draw" book you may have had as a child. Step 1: Draw a circle. Step 2: Add eyes, nose, mouth, and ears. Step 3: Add hair. Step 4: Apply your sketching skills to render the stick figure into a masterpiece that possesses depth and beauty and makes old men weep at a mere glance. Sound a bit like theming Drupal? Hang in there! This chapter will fill in many of the blanks between steps 3 and 4 from your old drawing book!

This chapter outlines the basics of finding, installing, and configuring a Drupal theme. You will learn how to create a lean Drupal theme from scratch to see the component parts—and also how to create a feature-rich subtheme from one of the many theme starter kits that are available for Drupal. The chapter wraps up with a brief look at how to convert older themes to Drupal 6, and how to convert themes from other content management systems to Drupal.

Finding Themes

The easiest way to theme your Drupal Web site is to start with a prebuilt theme that appeals to you. By swapping the banner image and changing the background color, you can transform a template with very little additional work.

In addition to the themes that ship with Drupal, premade Drupal themes can be found in many other places. A quick Web search for "Drupal themes" will turn up at least a few hundred thousand Web sites. The search results will range from free themes that may have been downloaded and implemented by lots of other Web sites to completely unique designs created by specialist-design companies. Depending on your time and budget, you may find any of these themes useful for your Web site.

> **Copyright**
> The designs listed in this section are not necessarily free to modify and use. Many of the templates are licensed under the Creative Commons and can be used if credit is given to the original designer. Please respect the terms of the individually licensed designs.

Generally the templates available from the Drupal Web site (`http://drupal.org/project/Themes`) and the Theme Garden (`http://www.themegarden.org`) are ready to be installed and used on your Web site. When you are selecting a theme, make sure you choose one that matches the version of Drupal you have installed. Themes that were created for Drupal 5 will not work with Drupal 6, for example. The list of themes on Drupal.org can be filtered based on the version of Drupal you are running. You must be logged into your Drupal.org account to use this filter.

> **Create a Drupal.org account**
> Many packages are available from Drupal.org. By creating an account, you can easily filter these packages for the version of Drupal you are using. Registration is free. To create a new account, go to `http://drupal.org/user/register`.

Figure 3.1 shows the Theme Garden—a preview site for the themes that can be downloaded from Drupal.org. There is not always a perfect match between the two lists, however, so be sure to check both sites for appealing designs.

FIGURE 3.1 The Drupal Theme Garden allows you to see how themes look on a real site with actual content. This is the Theme Garden styled using the Amadou theme.

The Drupal.org theme directory is set up a little differently (Figure 3.2). Each theme listed gives a summary of the theme, but not a full implementation of it. Details on the summary page for each theme include these items:

- A text description of the theme, including its features
- The version of the theme as well as its release date
- A screenshot giving a view of the "above the fold" view of the theme
- A link back to the project Web page for the theme (if one exists)

If you need new themes on a regular basis, take the time to find a theme directory that you like using. Each directory will have slightly different features. Themebot (http://www.themebot.com/website-templates/drupal-themes), for example, lists W3C compliance, indicates whether a design has a fixed or fluid width, and gives a full demo showing how content will be styled in blocks, sidebars, and the content area.

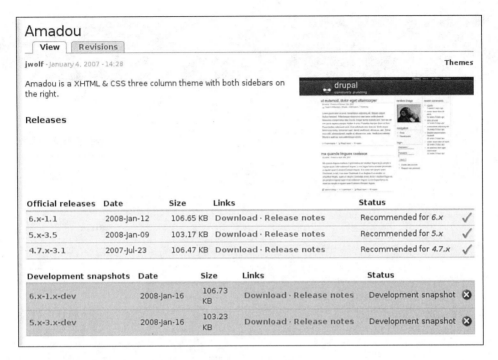

FIGURE 3.2 Drupal.org provides the same information for modules and themes as the Drupal Theme Garden. This is the project page for the Amadou theme.

Interface Components

When selecting a theme, it is important to consider the various page elements that you identified while working through the "Interface Components" section in Chapter 1. These features include how many columns the page contains, how the page expands into the available space (and how it contracts for narrower browser windows), which font sizes are used, and whether a search box has been integrated into the design. If you are trying to emulate an existing Web site design, you may want to skip ahead in this chapter and read the sections on how to convert a template into a Drupal theme.

Nearly everyone is drawn to color first and structure second. In some cases a design may be available in several different colors. The color may be controlled from within Drupal, or you may need to choose which colors you want to download the right theme. Designs can also be easily modified by altering the CSS style sheet and using the "Colorize" function within a graphics program such as GiMP or Photoshop. By altering the lightness and the hue of a color, you can convert a gray-scale design into a colored one. Conversely, you can switch a colored design to black and white by converting your graphics from RGB to gray-scale. You may find this ability especially useful if you are showcasing or selling products—a neutral interface will compete less with your content. A full tutorial on how to colorize a theme using the Color module is available at http://drupal.org/node/220789.

Refer back to the design decisions you made in Chapter 1 to help you choose a template with the appropriate number of regions for your content. If your design needs many small regions, take a moment to think about the content area: Should it be fluid and expand in wider display screens to give more visual importance to the content, or should it be fixed in size? In the Drupal Theme Garden you can resize your browser to see how the theme adjusts to different browser conditions.

If your site is a blog, and will only ever be a blog, chances are good you will be completely satisfied with a simple two-column design. By contrast, if you know your site will grow beyond its current wireframe within a short amount of time, you should consider using a template that can easily accommodate additional regions. Although many themes are limited to 4 or 5 regions, others have defined more than a dozen separate regions. If you do not need all the regions initially, be sure to check that the design collapses gracefully to suit your needs.

Develop a Library of Themes

It is very easy to apply a Drupal theme. If you see a number of themes you like, download them all! You can install each of the themes and test it with your own content before making a final decision on which theme to use. You may also want to keep a library of themes that you like, but aren't a perfect match for your current project. Be sure to store the themes in a way that makes it easy to retrieve exactly the right theme later on. Create a summary of the themes as well as a description of what you liked about the theme.

Zotero is an excellent design archiving tool. This Firefox extension allows you to take a snapshot of a Web page along with your notes (see Figure 3.3). Originally developed to help researchers collect, manage, and cite research sources, Zotero creates a library of Web pages on your computer for offline browsing. Additional features include the ability to take notes on a per-page basis, add tags to the page, and rename the page title. The ability to access and maintain the pages locally can prove very useful if you are in a meeting in a location that does not have an Internet connection. Zotero can be downloaded from http://www.zotero.org.

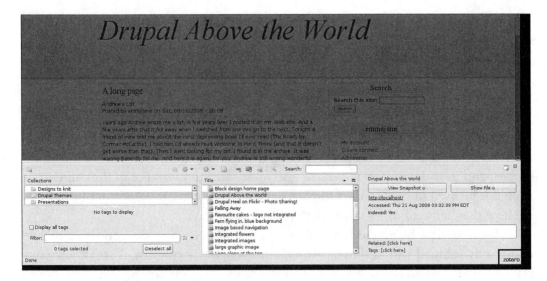

FIGURE 3.3 Zotero, a Firefox extension shown in the bottom of this screenshot, makes it easier to manage an offline gallery of themes. The tool integrates itself into Firefox and can be hidden or displayed using the "Zotero" icon in the lower-right corner of the browser.

Installing Drupal Themes

Once you've selected your theme, your next task is to install it.

Download and Unpack

Several files are included in a theme. These files will be packaged up and compressed to make it faster for you to download them. To prepare a new Drupal theme for use on your site, follow these steps:

1. Choose the right package for your Drupal installation. Themes that were designed for Drupal 5 cannot be used on a Drupal 6 Web site, for example.

2. Click the "download" button or link.

3. You will be prompted by your Web browser to save the file. Choose a location on your computer that you will remember—perhaps in your project folder for a specific Web site or on your desktop.

4. The browser may also ask you if you want to unpack the files. Go ahead and unpack the files if you are given the option to do so.

Look at the files inside the theme package. If a file named README or INSTALL present, be sure to read it. This kind of plain text file can be opened in any simple text editor.

Within the theme, there are several components, each of which must be placed into an appropriate home. The design elements are handled by style sheets; the graphics and the interactive behaviors are handled by JavaScript. The markup is handled by template files with the extension tpl.php. Logic, function calls, and variable assignments are handled exclusively by the file template.php. As a consequence, there should not be any markup in the template.php or any function calls in the individual tpl.php files. In your theme's folder, you will likely find the following files:

- An info file (themename.info)
- A page template (page.tpl.php)
- PHP functions that create new variables and alter the default variables provided by Drupal (template.php)
- A style sheet (themename.css or style.css)
- A screenshot (screenshot.png)

Although the only required file is the .info file, a theme won't be much of a design without at least one template file and a style sheet. The screenshot is provided to help you choose the right theme from the list of themes in the Drupal administration area; it is not used in the actual theme design.

Drupal ships with several default themes, which are stored in the themes directory. To distinguish your uploaded themes from the default ones, store your new themes in the sites folder. If you would like to make your theme available to all Web sites, upload the files to sites/all/themes/themename. If you would like your theme to be available to only one of your Web sites, upload it to sites/websiteurl.com/themes/themename. In both of these examples, "themename" will be the name of the folder on your computer that contains the theme. You may need to create a subdirectory named "themes" in the relevant "sites" folder.

Enable the New Theme

Once your theme is uploaded to your Web server, you will need to enable it in the Drupal administration area. Drupal provides an easy-to-use theme selection screen, as shown in Figure 3.4. This screen allows you to preview each of the themes (using a

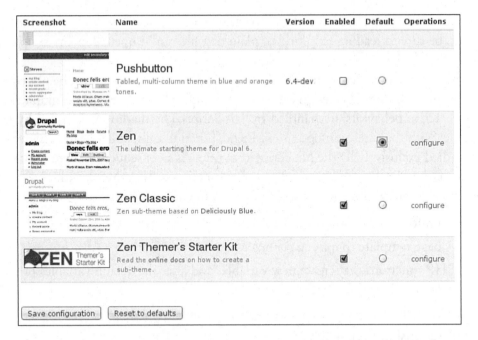

FIGURE 3.4 Use the Theme settings administration area to select the theme you want applied to your Web site. Multiple columns of information help you to enable the right theme for your Web site.

static screenshot created by the theme designer) and offers a link to additional configuration options that are available for the theme.

To enable the new theme, follow these steps:

1. Log into the Web site as the administrator.
2. Choose the "Administer" link from the navigation on the left (or "administration section" from the front page).
3. Choose "Themes" from the list of options on the main administration screen.
4. Scroll down to your new theme, select the check box to "Enable" the theme, and select the "Default" radio button to activate the theme.
5. Scroll to the bottom of the Web page and click "Save configuration."

Your new theme should now be applied sitewide!

Personal Themes

If your Web site is already live, you may want to enable your new theme privately to test its implementation before showing it to the rest of the world. To do so, you can use the "Personal Themes" feature of Drupal. It allows you to enable a theme that only you can view. Once the theme is working correctly as a personal theme, you can apply the theme to the entire Web site for everyone to use by following the instructions in the previous section.

If you are not the main administrator for the site (user/1), you will need to adjust the permissions so that you can use the Personal Theme feature.

1. From the Administration main page, navigate to the "Permissions" screen.
2. Scroll down to the "System" options and check the box for the appropriate role to "select different theme" as shown in Figure 3.5.
3. Scroll to the bottom of the Web page and click "Save permissions."

must have added administrator role first

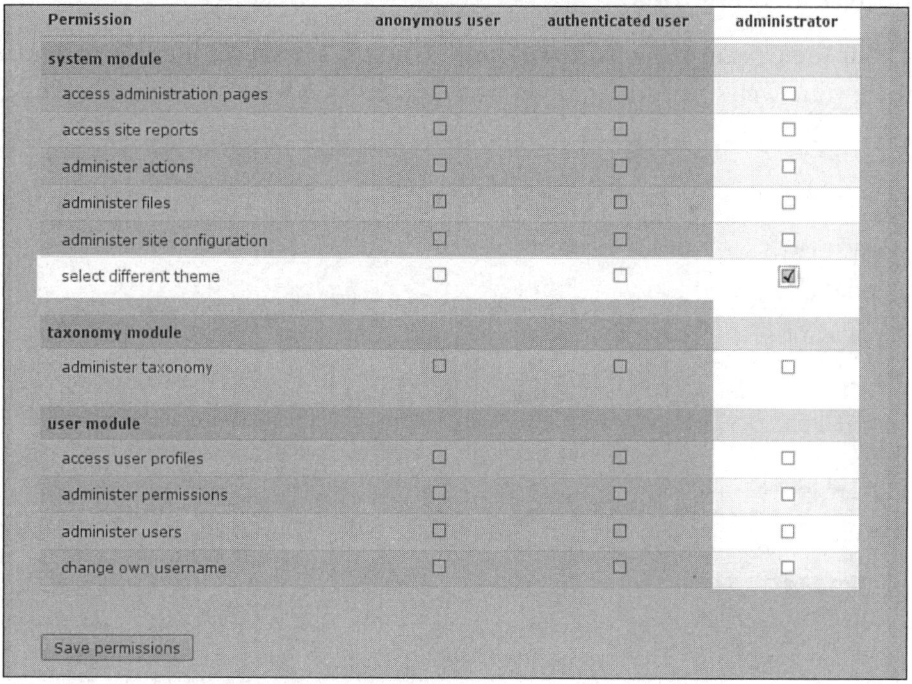

Permission	anonymous user	authenticated user	administrator
system module			
access administration pages	☐	☐	☐
access site reports	☐	☐	☐
administer actions	☐	☐	☐
administer files	☐	☐	☐
administer site configuration	☐	☐	☐
select different theme	☐	☐	☑
taxonomy module			
administer taxonomy	☐	☐	☐
user module			
access user profiles	☐	☐	☐
administer permissions	☐	☐	☐
administer users	☐	☐	☐
change own username	☐	☐	☐

Save permissions

FIGURE 3.5 Under the system module section, set the permissions for personal themes to test your theme before publishing it on your live Web site.

Once you have enabled your personal themes, you must configure the theme you would like to use for your account. To enable your personal theme:

1. In the Drupal navigation menu, navigate to "My account."
2. Click the "Edit" tab on your personal account.
3. Scroll down to the "Theme configuration" section as shown in Figure 3.6 and select the radio button next to your new theme.
4. Scroll to the bottom of the screen and click "Save."

Your new theme will now be enabled for only your account. When your theme has been completely customized and you know it is bug free, you may apply it to the entire site using the steps given in the previous section. If you have altered settings within the Drupal administrative section for your theme, you will need to reapply these changes when your theme is made public.

Administering Themes

Once your theme is installed, you will need to adjust several settings to customize the theme for your Web site. Although some of these settings were configured as part of the

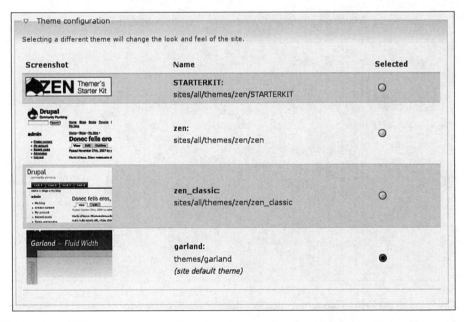

FIGURE 3.6 In the "Theme configuration" section of your account page, you can select a "personal theme" if you are a member of a role that has the correct permissions.

global theme when you first installed Drupal, there may be additional aspects of your theme that you need to customize. Theme-specific settings rely on variables within the theme's template files. If your theme does not use these variables, changes you make in the administration area will have no effect.

Global Settings

A single administration screen allows you to control the default display settings for your entire site, across all themes. The same screen is also provided on a per-theme basis and allows you to override any of the global settings. To access this configuration screen, click the "configure" link next to the theme name on the list of themes outlined in the previous section. To have these changes apply across all themes click the "Global settings" link near the top of the page as shown in Figure 3.7 before continuing.

FIGURE 3.7 Some theme settings can be applied across all current and future themes by using the Global settings screen.

Take a moment to scan through all of the configuration options to you. Toggle display allows you to turn off or on some of the sitewide variables:

- Logo
- Site name
- Site slogan
- Mission statement
- User pictures in posts
- User pictures in comments
- Search box
- Shortcut icon
- Primary links
- Secondary links

The site name, site slogan, and mission statement are text snippets that you wrote when you first installed Drupal. If you want to edit this text, you must navigate to Administer, Settings, Site Information.

In addition to changing the options listed previously, you can specify whether the ownership and time stamp information will be viewable on each of your pages. Each time a new content type is added to (or enabled on) your Drupal installation, you will need to return to this page to adjust its settings.

From the Global settings screen, you can change the sitewide logo. You may either choose a logo that has already been uploaded or upload a different logo through the Web-based interface. The shortcut icon (the `favicon.ico` file) can also be administered in the same way.

Theme-Specific Settings

Your theme can override the global settings defined in the previous section. You should also define the settings for your individual theme if your site is using different themes for the Administration pages and for the public Web site. In addition to the global settings, your theme may have additional settings to configure. Navigate to Administration, Site Building, Themes and click on the link "configure" next to your theme.

In the Zen theme, the following additional settings are available:

- Show block editing on hover
- Customizable breadcrumb separators
- Theme development settings

Different options may be available for your specific theme.

The Front Page

There are several ways to customize the front page of your Drupal Web site. Each technique must be themed in a different way. This section outlines the steps needed to implement each solution from the Web site administration area. Each section also includes the reference to a later chapter where the theming of this type of front page content is described in full.

Single "Welcome" Node

Some Web sites are very simple. They have a few pages of content, a contact page, perhaps a summary of upcoming workshops, and not much else. For this type of Web site, you should create a "home" or "welcome" page and assign it to the front page of the Web site using the following steps:

1. Click the "Create content" link from the Drupal-provided Navigation menu.
2. Choose the content type "Page."
3. Add a title and body for the page.
4. Scroll down to the "Publishing options." These options are hidden by default. You will need to click on the link to open the menu options.
5. Add a check mark beside "Promoted to front page."
6. Scroll to the bottom of the Web page and click "Save" to save your page.

This page should now appear as the front page of your Drupal Web site.

Another way to set the front page is to give Drupal a specific page to load within the Site information administration area. If you are working with an existing Drupal site and cannot figure out what is being displayed on the front page, check this option. Using only the core modules within Drupal, you can also configure this setting to have only one category of content be displayed on your front page. For example, you might want to highlight only those nodes that belong to the category "Front Page News."

To set the front page to a specific category, you will need to know the URL for the category you want to highlight.

1. Navigate to the category page which lists all nodes for that category.
2. Copy the query string for this page from your browser's address bar. It will be something like `taxonomy/term/113`.
3. Navigate to Administer, Site Configuration, Site information.
4. Scroll to the bottom of the page and copy your query string into the "Default front page" form field. Ensure you have only the query string and not the domain name of the Web site, as well.
5. Click "Save configuration."
6. Navigate to the front page of your Web site to confirm the changes have been applied correctly.

Content Teasers

At this point you may notice that only a partial summary of your content appears on the front page along with a "Read more" link, instead of the entire page. If you are happy with this format, excellent! What you are viewing is a list of "teasers" instead of the full node. The length of this text can be adjusted in the "Post settings" section of the administration area. To display the full node on the front page instead of a teaser, use the following steps:

1. Navigate to Administer, Content management, Post settings.
2. Change the "Number of posts on main page" to a number that is appropriate for your site (the default is 10).
3. Change the "Length of trimmed posts" to "Unlimited."
4. Scroll to the bottom of the screen and click "Save configuration."

To make your Web site load more quickly, Drupal stores the "teaser" as a separate field in the database. To make changes to your content retroactively, you will need to go back and re-save the items currently appearing on the front page. Navigate to the page you want to change, click the "Edit" tab, and re-save the page.

You can also force the teaser to split in a certain way by clicking the "Split summary at cursor" button; Figure 3.8 shows the results. Click the "Join summary" button to return to the default content editing configuration.

Chapter 5 provides more information on ways to style content teasers.

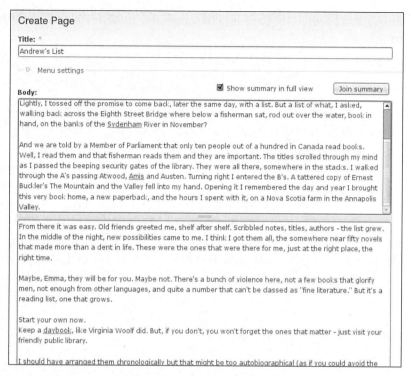

FIGURE 3.8 Use the "Split summary at cursor" button to create a visual break between the teaser of your story and the rest of the content. The resulting screen shows the teaser and remainder of the full content mode.

Several Nodes "Promoted to Front Page"

The default option for "Promoted to front page" can be set per content type. This option allows you to create a news-style front page that lists all new items of that content type by default. To set the default options for a specific type of content, you will need to set your preferences in the administration area for that content type.

1. Navigate to the administration page for a specific content type by following the path Administer, Content management, Content Types.

2. Click the "edit" link for the type of content you would like to modify. Drupal provides you with two content types: Page and Story. In Chapter 2, you also learned how to create your own content types. Choose the content type you wish to alter.

3. Scroll to "Workflow settings" and click the link to open the configuration menu.

4. Add a check mark beside "Promoted to front page."

5. Scroll to the bottom of the Web page and click "Save content type."

Any new items that are added from that content type will now be published to the front page by default. You may disable this option when you are creating or editing the page if you do not want those items to appear on the front page.

Anatomy of a Theme

Whether you are creating a theme from a basic HTML template or converting a theme from another Web-based content management system, the first step is always to convert your files to a simple Drupal theme. You can then add as much complexity as you like. In this section we examine the steps required to create a page template for a basic theme.

Naming and Initializing the Theme

Coming up with a name for your theme is perhaps the most difficult part of this set of instructions. The first Drupal theme you create can be created before finishing your morning's coffee and certainly will not require any kind of fancy skills that you will need to be wide awake to create and replicate. This new Drupal theme is affectionately named Bolg. (Yes, Bolg—the goblin chieftain and the son of Azog.) Adjust this theme name to suit your needs.

Use unique names
Your theme must have a name that is unique to Drupal. This restriction applies to the directory that holds your theme, not the human-readable theme name. It means you cannot use the same directory name as a module that is installed, or the name of a PHP function. If your theme name is already in use, your site may not function correctly, if at all.

The first thing Bolg needs is a home on your computer. Create a new folder for your theme files. Use the name of your theme—for example, "bolg." In the `bolg` directory, add a new text file that has the same name as your new theme directory and the suffix `.info`. For example, create a text file called `bolg.info` that resides in the directory named "bolg." This info file will contain information about your theme.

You will start with only the most basic information:

```
name = Theme Bolg

description = The theme of the goblin chieftain.

core = 6.x

engine = phptemplate
```

You should customize your .info file to give the name of your theme as well as a description of it. The core variable should match the DRUPAL_CORE_COMPATIBILITY defined in modules/system/system.module. This may be version 6.x or higher. Prior to this version, Drupal handled themes differently. The engine variable refers to the template engine that will be used to compile your theme. Use phptemplate for the engine variable. Although Drupal does support several template engines, by far the most common is phptemplate. If you have inherited a theme that is not using phptemplate, refer to the online documentation at http://drupal.org/node/176129 for more information.

Page Template

The next thing to do is create a simple page template for your Drupal theme. You will start with a very simple static XHTML file to learn the basics of theme building. More complicated XHTML templates can be used at this time if you already have an XHTML template created. The Bolg template is based on the XHTML 1.0 Strict template from the Web Standards Project. It can be downloaded from http://www.webstandards.org/learn/reference/templates/xhtml10t/. It contains the following XHTML:

```
<!DOCTYPE html PUBLIC "-//W3C//DTD XHTML 1.0 Strict//EN"

"http://www.w3.org/TR/xhtml1/DTD/xhtml1-strict.dtd">

<html xmlns="http://www.w3.org/1999/xhtml">

<head>

        <title>Conforming XHTML 1.0 Strict Template</title>

</head>

<body>


</body>

</html>
```

Paste this template into a new file named `page.tpl.php`. This file will serve as the basic framework for everything else; that is, you will drop variables into it.

If you are working from a rendered HTML page, you will need to remove the content from the page, leaving only the markup that surrounds your page template regions. You will also need to copy the associated images, CSS, and JavaScript into your theme's directory (and rename your `index.html` file to `page.tpl.php`).

> **Work with an HTML page**
> If you are converting your site from a Web-based content management system to Drupal, you may find it easier to work from a Web page that has been processed for display in a Web browser instead of the template source files. This processed page is also referred to as a "rendered" page. By using the output instead of the source files, you will be able to see exactly how the page ought to fit together by the time it reaches the Web browser.

In the file `page.tpl.php`, you will need to replace the text with the variables Drupal needs to deposit content into the right places. Here is a quick summary of the changes made to the Bolg template page:

- Replaced the contents of the `<title>` tag with Drupal's PHP variable `$head_title`
- Placed the variables `$head`, `$styles`, and `$scripts` into the `<head>` tag of the template
- Placed the page content, and its associated variables, into the `<body>` tag of the page
- Added the variable `$closure` to the bottom (this variable is used by modules such as Google Analytics)

The template now looks like this:

```
<!DOCTYPE html PUBLIC "-//W3C//DTD XHTML 1.0 Strict//EN"

"http://www.w3.org/TR/xhtml1/DTD/xhtml1-strict.dtd">

<html xmlns="http://www.w3.org/1999/xhtml">

<head>

        <title><?php print $head_title; ?></title>

        <?php print $head; ?>
```

```
        <?php print $styles; ?>
        <?php print $scripts; ?>
</head>
<body>
<?php print $title; ?>
<?php print $tabs; ?>
<?php print $help; ?>
<?php print $messages; ?>
<?php print $content; ?>
<?php print $feed_icons; ?>
<?php print $closure; ?>
</body>
</html>
```

In Chapter 4, you will learn how to expand this code into a complete template, including additional page variables and navigation. For now, it is useful to see the variables without having to wade through additional markup.

Including External CSS and JavaScript Files

If you are using external CSS and JavaScript files, you will need to update the file bolg.info. To identify your style sheet, use the stylesheets array in your .info file. It may contain values like these:

```
; Add style sheets for all media
stylesheets[all][]   = bolg.css
stylesheets[all][]   = navigation.css


; Add a style sheet for screen and projector media
stylesheets[screen, projector][] = projector.css


; Add a style sheet for print
stylesheets[print][] = print.css
```

If you have the file `style.css`, it will be automatically included in your page template only if no other style sheets are defined in your `.info` file. Additional information about including style sheets in a Drupal 6 theme is available at `http://drupal.org/node/171209`.

If you would like your JavaScript file to be automatically included, use the file name `script.js`. If you would like to include additional JavaScript files, you will need to update your `.info` file. Your theme's JavaScript files must reside in your theme's home directory. Off-site JavaScript files will not be included, as they represent a potential security threat to your site. In your theme's `.info` file, add the following line for each JavaScript file:

```
scripts[] = myscript.js
```

Regions

Regions can be placed throughout your template. First, however, they must be defined in the `.info` file for your theme; only then can the corresponding variable names be placed into your page template. You may have as many regions as you would like for each theme. Regions are defined by setting both the PHP variable name and a human-readable text name as follows:

```
regions[left] = Left sidebar

regions[right] = Right sidebar

regions[above_text] = Above content

regions[below_text] = Below content
```

Although three regions (`$left`, `$right`, and `$footer`) are available by default, they will appear only if you do not have any of your own regions defined. If you would like to use these defaults as well as your own regions, you must explicitly set the default regions in the same way as your new, custom regions.

Not all feet are the same

`$footer_message` is the snippet of text defined on the site information page; `$footer` is a region on the page where you can place blocks.

To place these region variables in the template, you may wish to add a conditional statement around the outside of each variable so that the container elements are printed only if the region is being used. This approach will allow you to collapse and expand your page as appropriate. The following snippet shows how the HTML markup that contains the variable $header is printed only if the variable is actually set.

```php
<?php if ($header) { ?>

  <div id="header">

    <?php print $header; ?>

  </div>
<?php } ?>
```

The Drupal convention is to print PHP inside HTML rather than to print HTML markup from PHP. In other words, you would use the sample markup above and **avoid** using the following format in your templates:

```php
print "<h2><a href=\"$node_url\" >$title</a></h2>";
```

Screenshot

If your theme has some basic colors, you may also want to include a screenshot at this point to give a visual cue as to its nature on the theme selection page. This "thumbnail" typically consists of a screenshot of the theme, although it could be any image that distinguishes your theme from the others installed on the Web site. The image should be approximately 150 pixels wide and included in the home directory for your theme. Update the .info file to include a reference to your thumbnail. This information should be included near the top of the file along with the theme name:

```
screen shot = screenshot.png
```

If you plan to distribute your theme to the wider Drupal community, you should follow the screenshot guidelines that are included in the Theming Handbook at http://drupal.org/node/11637. Broader guidelines for publicly distributed themes on Drupal.org are available at http://drupal.org/node/14208.

Starter Themes

It is a quick process to download a theme that matches your design and to customize it to meet your needs. Literally hundreds (if not thousands) of Drupal themes can be downloaded and used immediately; not surprisingly, the quality of these themes varies greatly. It is a distinct possibility that you will spend as much time adapting a downloaded theme to use each of Drupal's page variables as if you had created your own theme from scratch.

The alternative to working with mediocre themes is to begin with a Drupal starter theme that has an entire toolkit of Drupal-specific functions and customizations. Of course, if you need a little bit of design inspiration, there are certainly advantages in downloading a theme that is visually similar to your wireframes, and then rebuilding it using a starter kit. By taking this route, you get the advantage of working with a complete visual design (including banner images and icons) and a full suite of Drupal functions (including customized administrative links like those available in the Zen starter kit).

You do not need to rely exclusively on your imagination to create both the visual design and the code for a truly excellent theme. The default theme, Garland, has received a good scrub and can now be used as inspiration for your new theme. Several other starter kits are available as well. These kits, which typically have very little style, are intended to serve as a launching point for building your own unique Drupal theme. Each kit uses a CSS, table-free layout and has been tested in a variety of browsers. The documentation explaining how to implement each starter kit varies. Following are the sources for some popular starter kits:

- Zen: `http://drupal.org/project/zen`
- Genesis: `http://drupal.org/project/genesis`
- ATCK: `http://drupal.org/project/atck`
- Basic: `http://drupal.org/project/basic`
- Beginning: `http://drupal.org/project/beginning`
- Blueprint: `http://drupal.org/project/Blueprint`
- Clean: `http://drupal.org/project/clean`
- Flexible 2: `http://drupal.org/project/flexible`
- Foundation: `http://drupal.org/project/foundation`
- Framework: `http://drupal.org/project/framework`
- Hunchbaque: `http://drupal.org/project/hunchbaque`
- Tendu: `http://drupal.org/project/tendu`

An in-depth comparison of these starter kits is available at `http://drupalstaging.com/starter-themes/starter-theme-comparison.html`.

Zen

Touted as being "the ultimate starting theme for Drupal," the Zen starter kit provides an example of how to implement all of the basics. Its markup is clean and extensively documented. Whether you use it as a reference guide, pulling out the elements you need, or use the actual files as a base for your own theme, Zen will help you to produce cleaner themes, faster. Even a simple design is worthy of beginning with a starter kit like Zen. Although it is a simple template, the Web site shown in Figure 3.9 was built using the Zen starter kit. Going from a graphic file in GiMP to a deployed theme took less than a day—all because of Zen. The headaches of figuring out cross-browser, CSS-based design were completely eliminated.

FIGURE 3.9 The Memory Garden Retreats theme was built using the Zen starter kit in less than a day. Although this theme uses a simple Web template, its creation was virtually effortless thanks to the use of the easy-to-use starter kit.

You can download the Zen theme from `http://drupal.org/project/zen`. Unpackage the files and place the entire directory (and subdirectories) into the `themes` folder. The Zen package contains several themes, including a starter kit and Zen Classic. You can enable these themes by navigating to Administer, Site building, Themes. The Zen theme will help you to identify each area of a Drupal installation that can be customized and themed. Working with the Zen theme is much like working with the core of Drupal—you do not need to alter the main files. Instead, you create a subtheme that customizes every single element available in the main Zen theme (or perhaps retains some of the Zen's features).

Use the following steps to create a new subtheme named "Frodo:"

1. Create your own Zen subtheme by making a copy of the STARTERKIT folder within the `zen` folder.

2. Rename the folder to your new theme name; rename the `.info` file contained in the copied STARTERKIT folder to the same name as the folder it is contained in. For example, if you named your directory `frodo`, the corresponding `.info` file would be named `frodo.info`.

3. Copy the main CSS file from the `zen` folder into the `frodo` folder.

4. Copy the liquid, or fixed-width, CSS file from the main `zen` folder into the `frodo` folder.

5. Copy the print CSS file from the main `zen` folder into the `frodo` folder.

6. Edit the `frodo.info` file by changing the settings for the theme's name, description, and new CSS file names.

7. Edit the `template.php` and `theme-settings.php` files by changing all instances of STARTERKIT to your theme's name ("frodo," in this example).

8. Enable your new theme in Drupal's administrative Web interface by navigating to Administer, Site building, Themes.

9. Continue to adjust each of your new theme's settings and styles to suit your needs.

In addition to the Zen project, a series of default templates are available for many different core Drupal components. Most of these files correspond to specific modules and can be copied directly from your Drupal installation's core files. For example, three template files are available within the folder `modules/comment`: `comment-folder.tpl.php`, `comment-wrapper.tpl.php`, and `comment.tpl.php`. Throughout this book you will learn about these default templates and discover how to customize them to suit your needs.

Custom Theme Settings

The Zen theme takes advantage of the custom theme settings that are available in Drupal 6. When you use the Zen starter kit, you have at your fingertips a sample template that explains how to add even more custom settings to your theme. The Zen starter kit includes the following custom settings by default:

- Show block editing on hover
- Breadcrumb settings (including separators and pages on which to show/hide breadcrumb settings)
- Theme development settings (liquid versus fixed layout), and show borders around main layout elements to emulate wireframes

To view or alter these settings, navigate to Administer, Site building, Themes and select "configure" next to the relevant theme name (for example, Zen or Zen Classic). Figure 3.10 shows the settings page—it has a form with the global settings at the top as well as any theme-specific settings toward the bottom of the page. To add new settings to this page, you must alter the file named `theme-settings.php` in the relevant Zen theme directory. If you are using the starter kit, you already have a copy of this file in your theme's directory. Within this file you may add new items to your theme's setting by using the Form API.

If the sample settings in the Zen theme are not sufficient for you to create your own settings, read the Advanced Theme Settings tutorial at `http://drupal.org/node/177868`.

Customizing Banner Images

When working with starter kits, you may still want to download a theme, if only to use it for visual inspiration. Look for themes that inspire you not just through their photographs and icons, but also in terms of their color scheme, use of fonts, and layout.

FIGURE 3.10 By altering the file `theme-settings.php`, you can add new theme-specific settings to the theme's configuration screen. Shown here are the Global settings (top) and theme-specific settings (bottom) for the Zen theme.

Figure 3.11 shows that changing only the banner can make a great difference in the tone of the design.

To customize the banner for any theme requires only a few steps and rudimentary skills with a graphics editing program.

FIGURE 3.11 The same theme with two different banner images.

1. Create a backup of the current banner by copying the file to a new name (you will now have two identical banner images with different names).

2. Using a graphics program (such as GiMP or Photoshop), open the banner image provided by the theme (the one with the original file name).

3. Open the image you would like to use in your new banner. Copy and paste the image into the existing banner. You may need to enlarge or reduce the size of the new banner image so that it fits within the size constraints of the theme's original banner image.

4. Using the theme's original file name for the banner, save the new file. Your new banner image will now appear in the theme.

Migrating to Drupal 6

Many different content management systems (CMS) are available. Whether your experience is with another Web-based CMS or even an earlier version of Drupal, change in the systems you use—whether to a different system or to a different version of the same system—is inevitable. This section focuses on the process of evaluating a template with the goal of converting it to Drupal 6. The first step to migrating from one system to another is to carefully analyze both the current system and the new system, looking for similarities and differences between the two. If you are a visual thinker, you may even want to sketch a simple Web page and mark (in two different colors) the naming conventions employed by your current system and those used by Drupal.

Regardless of which system you are migrating from, a basic Drupal theme can be built from any template. If you are not a code monkey at heart, you may find it easier to work from a HTML page that is built by the CMS and its template, instead of using the content management system's template files. Review the first section of this chapter for more information on converting a flat HTML file to a Drupal theme.

Converting a Drupal 5.x Theme to a Drupal 6.x Theme

Drupal themes have changed radically from version 5 to version 6; however, there is no reason to change the design of page that is displayed to Web site visitors when you upgrade the theme from one version of Drupal to another. Keeping this point in mind, you should find it a relatively quick task to upgrade a theme with only a few minor changes to your current theme files. Work through the following checklist to create a Drupal 6 theme:

1. Create an information file for your theme. This file must have the same name as the directory that holds the theme's files and have the extension `.info`. It must contain the basic information about your theme, including its name, its description, the core version of Drupal the theme can be applied to, and the template engine.

2. Remove "region" definitions from your `template.php` file. List them in the `themeName.info` file, instead.

3. Confirm that the variables you have set in your template files match the current default variable names.

4. The `phptemplate_callback()` function has been replaced by individual `tpl.php` files. Remove relevant functions from the `template.php` file and place the themed markup into its corresponding `tpl.php` file. For example, the contents of `phptemplate_breadcrumb()` should be placed into the file `breadcrumb.tpl.php`.

5. Substitute the $layout variable in your template files for $body_classes. Update your CSS files according to the new classes defined. Classes can be used to identify front and internal pages, logged-in users and visitors, node ID and node type, and visible sidebars.

6. The $language variable is now an object. To update your theme, change this variable to $language->language.

7. jQuery version 1.2.3 is now included by default. Scripts can also be placed into a file named script.js for automatic inclusion in the main template for the site.

Keep your files organized
To keep your theme directories clean, place related tpl.php files into relevant subdirectories. If you have a lot of images, you may also want to put them into a subfolder.

WordPress

WordPress is a popular blogging tool that can be extended to create basic Web sites. Like Drupal, it has a rich developer and user community base and offers many plugins to extend the core framework. WordPress operates best when using a blog-style narrative to organize its pages.

Like Drupal 6, WordPress uses many smaller component files for its templates; however, the structure of a WordPress theme and the structure of a Drupal theme are quite different. To convert a WordPress theme to Drupal, you will need to combine some files and to split others into smaller components. WordPress will often use a function (ending with parentheses) to store the same kind of information that Drupal stores in a variable (starting with a dollar sign). These differences arise because of the rules created by the template engine used for each of the two systems.

A typical WordPress theme maps onto Drupal file names as shown in Table 3.1. A typical WordPress theme maps onto Drupal variable names as shown in Table 3.2.

Start with the following steps if you are given a WordPress template, but cannot easily install the blogging tool to confirm the output:

TABLE 3.1 WordPress and Drupal File Names

WordPress	Drupal
index.php	page.tpl.php
header.php	page.tpl.php (incorporated into)
footer.php	page.tpl.php (incorporated into)
404.php	GUI administration function
comments.php	comment.tpl.php
searchform.php	search-block-form.tpl.php and/or search-theme-form.tpl.php

1. Create a new folder with the name gollum.

2. Create a new .info file that describes your new theme. Be sure to include the name of your theme, a brief description, and the Drupal core version required by this theme. Use the WordPress theme screenshot for now. You may want to replace it later if there are significant enhancements made as part of the upgrade to Drupal.

3. Put a copy of the WordPress file index.php into the gollum directory and rename it page.tpl.php.

4. Throughout the new page.tpl.php file, replace the WordPress references to external files that describe structural components with their actual file contents. For example, replace get_header(); with the contents of the file header.php and get_footer(); with the contents of footer.php.

5. Copy the sidebar.php file into the new gollum directory and rename the file to block.tpl.php. In the new file page.tpl.php, replace get_sidebar(); with a variable representing the name of the region for this sidebar. Make sure this region is also defined in the theme's .info file (for example, gollum.info).

TABLE 3.2 WordPress and Drupal Variables

WordPress	Drupal
the_title();	$title;
the_content();	$content;
next_posts_link();	Handled by Drupal's pagination

6. Note the functions that were called from WordPress's `sidebar.php` file. These functions must be matched to blocks within Drupal. Additional information on blocks is available in Chapter 4. Once your Drupal theme is enabled, you will place these blocks into the appropriate region of your new template using the administration Web interface.

7. Move the contents of `index.php`, which relate to individual story items, into a new template file named `node.tpl.php`. This information may also be contained in the WordPress file `single.php`. Check both files to ensure you have migrated all of the WordPress theme components.

8. Check the WordPress file `functions.php` for additional theme information that may need to be migrated to Drupal either using a text-based `tpl.php` file or through Drupal's administration Web interface.

Joomla!

Joomla! is a Web-based content management system similar to Drupal. In direct comparisons against Drupal, advocates of Joomla! will often praise its document management system and calendaring options; by contrast, Drupal has more sophisticated user permissions and multiple-site management capabilities.

Joomla! at its most basic is similar to Drupal in its theme creation. It uses a single file to outline the structure of the page and calls in individual variables as needed to fill in the gaps.

Start with the following steps if you are given a Joomla! template. In this example, the new Drupal theme is named Bilbo. Adjust this theme name to suit your needs.

1. Create a new folder with the name `bilbo`.

2. Create a new `.info` file that describes your new theme. Be sure to include the name of your theme, a brief description, and the Drupal core version required by this theme. If your theme had a screenshot, include it for now. You may want to replace it later if there are significant enhancements made as part of the upgrade to Drupal.

3. Put a copy of the Joomla! file `index.php` into the `bilbo` directory and rename it `page.tpl.php`.

4. Replace references to `mosLoadModules()` in the `page.tpl.php` file with a variable representing the name of the region. Make sure this region is also defined in the theme's `.info` file (for example, `bilbo.info`).

5. Create the blocks within Drupal that will replace the output of the `mosLoad-Modules` functions in the old Joomla! Web site. Once your theme is enabled you will place these blocks into the appropriate region of your new template using Drupal's administration Web interface.

6. Move the contents of the Joomla! template file named `index.php`, which relate to individual story items, into a new Drupal template file named `node.tpl.php`.

7. Update Joomla!-specific variables to their Drupal equivalents (for example, the variable for the template directory becomes `$directory` in Drupal).

8. Move logic-based PHP scripting to the file `template.php`. Additional information on how to use `template.php` is included throughout each of the chapters of this book, including those focusing on page variables (Chapter 4) and content variables (Chapter 5).

The principles behind good design allow you to map functionality across different content management systems. Through careful examination of any theme, you should be able to map its essence into Drupal, even though the frameworks may differ significantly. If your specialty is Drupal and you are asked to convert a theme from another CMS, be sure to ask for the original theme files as well as the rendered HTML output for several pages (and with differing navigation depths). Converting an HTML page to a Drupal theme can be easier than trying to understand the construction of a theming system with which you have little or no experience.

Summary

Creating a simple Drupal theme can be very easy. When you are armed with the fundamentals of how to create a Drupal theme, it becomes much easier to make Drupal look however you want. In this chapter, we walked through the following tasks:

- Finding themes
- Installing prebuilt themes
- Customizing settings in the Web-based administration area
- Creating new themes
- Using starter kits to create new themes

- Adding new theme settings that can be customized from the theme administration screen

- Migrating other content management system themes to Drupal 6

This chapter has laid out the skeleton of a Drupal theme. Being organized and using good coding practices will allow you to easily move from simple layouts to the more complicated user interactions described later in this book.

## Chapter 4

The Drupal Page

Get out your crayons and your coloring book! In this chapter you will learn how to connect the dots and build context-sensitive page templates. The adventures in this chapter begin by dissecting how Drupal builds the pages that are delivered to your Web browser. You will then learn about sitewide variables so you can split your page templates into a clean HTML framework with Drupal-served data being injected into the right spots at the right times. Next, you will learn to draw "outside the lines" with custom page variables and page templates based on categories, page aliases, and content types. And for those who don't like to color at all, the chapter wraps up with information on creating print-friendly templates and building a mobile-friendly clone of your Web site. In this chapter you dive into the guts of a Drupal theme. Note that the code snippets included here require a basic understanding of PHP, CSS, and XHTML.

Elements of a Page

When you understand how Drupal builds its themes, it becomes very easy to achieve complicated tasks. A common question is, "I need to inject a block into the content of the front page—how do I do that?" This is not how Drupal thinks about

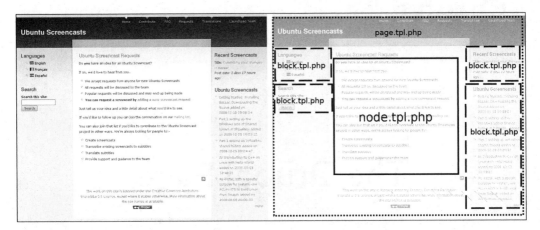

FIGURE 4.1 The Drupal page is customized by using many different templates.

this problem, so the answer seems very difficult. Instead of thinking about the page as it appears in the Web browser, you must think about each of the elements separately. Figure 4.1 illustrates how Drupal customizes a page with each of its template files.

The whole page is controlled by the template `page.tpl.php`. Within the whole page, several more template files are injected to customize each of the different components. These templates theme the output from various modules within Drupal. Block and node templates are shown in Figure 4.1. Each module that outputs content to the page will have its own templates, which you can in turn customize.

Dissecting a Theme

Most themes include a customization of the page, block, and node templates, which are the main building blocks that are used to construct the layout of a page. If you are working with a downloaded theme, look in your theme's directory for the following files:

- `page.tpl.php`
- `block.tpl.php`
- `node.tpl.php`

These three files are the building blocks that define the markup of your site. In-depth information on customizing `page.tpl.php` appears later in this chapter, and additional information on customizing `node.tpl.php` can be found in Chapter 5.

Here is another analogy for thinking about the Drupal page template: It is a little bit like a large parking garage with numbered spaces. The garage itself does not care which kind of car or truck or motorcycle is parked in each space; it merely houses the lines that show each of the areas where a vehicle might fit. The garage might have different colors for each of the levels to make it easier for people to remember which level they are parked on. The people who operate the garage may have rules about which space each person may park his or her vehicle. It is impossible to park your vehicle in two places at the same time in the parking garage.

In Drupal terminology, the page template defines regions (levels in the parking garage) where blocks may appear (assigned spaces for parked vehicles). A single block may not appear more than once in a page (cars may be parked in only one space at a time); however, this region can change location within the page template depending on the context (parking garages may have different colors for each level in the garage). Later in this chapter you will learn how to assign new blueprints to your "parking garage."

This analogy is not a perfect one, of course: In real life, a vehicle can park somewhere other than its assigned place. In contrast, blocks in Drupal may be assigned only one spot throughout the Web site. Nevertheless, the parking garage analogy is a helpful way to think about how the page template keeps order without being aware of the displayed content of a page.

In Chapter 3, you created with a basic page template that contained only Drupal output and a skeleton HTML framework. You will now start to build on these basics to create a more sophisticated page template.

Sitewide Page Variables

The variables available in the template file `page.tpl.php` are classified into several categories:

- **General utility variables** are used to build context-sensitive templates with directory names relevant to the path of the theme's location on the server.
- **Page metadata** includes page language, style and script tags relevant to the page, and body classes.
- **Site identity** takes the form of the site name, site slogan, site mission, and logo.

- **Navigation** includes items related to primary and secondary navigation, as well as search boxes.
- **Page content** includes the page title, dynamic help text and Drupal system messages, and tabs.
- **Footer and closing data** includes RSS feed icons, footer messages, and final markup from any modules ("closure").

Commonly used variables are identified in Figure 4.2, which depicts a fresh installation of Drupal, using the theme Garland.

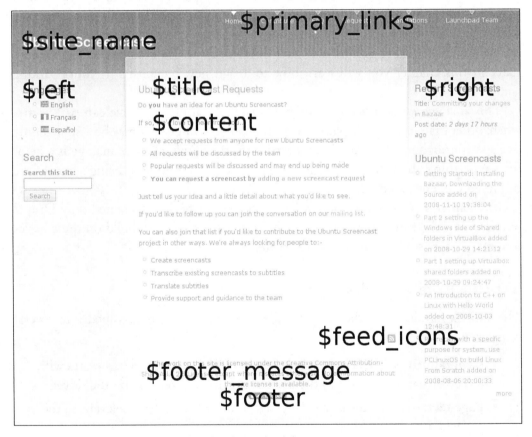

FIGURE 4.2 Common variables displayed in the Garland theme.

A complete list of page template variables is available from the Drupal directory `modules/system`, in the file `page.tpl.php`, which is also available online at `http://api.drupal.org/api/file/modules/system/page.tpl.php`.

General Utility Variables

The general utility variables represent a very basic toolkit with which you can customize your site's template based on the characteristics of the visitor. They include the following variables:

- Variables useful in linking to images and files within your site, such as `$base_path` (the base URL for the Drupal installation) and `$directory` (the base directory for this theme)
- `$is_front`, which reports if the current page is the front page of the site
- User status checks, including the test of whether the visitor is logged into the site (`$logged_in`) and whether the user has access to administration pages (`$is_admin`)

Page Metadata

The page metadata variables are used in the `<head>` tag of the page template. This set includes the following variables:

- An object containing the language the site is being displayed in. To print the text representation of the language to your template, use the following variable: `$language->language`.
- `$head_title`: A modified version of the page title containing the site name, for use in the `<title>` tag.
- `$head`: Metadata for metatags, keyword tags to be inserted into the `<head>` section.
- `$styles`: Style tags used to link all CSS files for the page.
- `$scripts`: Script tags used to load the JavaScript files and settings for the page.

In addition to this metadata, there is a wonderful variable that contains a set of conditions to help you style each page: `$body_classes`. The `$body_classes` variable includes the following information: the current layout (multiple columns, single column); whether the current visitor is an authenticated user; and the type of the node being displayed (for example, `node-type-book`). This variable includes only the names of the classes to be used by your style sheets. To use it in your theme, you must include the following PHP snippet:

```
<body class="<?php print $body_classes ?>">
```

Site Identity

The site identity information comprises a set of variables that outputs information about your site. You can alter the contents of and/or disable each of these variables in Drupal's administration area by navigating to Administer, Site configuration, Site information.

- `$front_page`: The URL of the front page. Use this variable instead of `$base_path` when linking to the front page. It includes the language domain or prefix.
- `$logo`: The path to the logo image, as defined in the theme.
- `$site_name`: The name of your Web site.

Two other variables can be set within the site identity section of the Drupal administration area:

- `$site_slogan`: The slogan of the site.
- `$mission`: The text of the site mission.

There is no rule that says you must use these last two variables for their intended purpose; in fact, you can use them to store any information you would like to display within your page template.

Page Content, Drupal Messages, and Help Text

Content is the most important part of your Web site. You must tell Drupal where to insert content into the page template! This is done with a simple variable, `$content`. You may place this variable anywhere in the template file `page.tpl.php`. From this simple variable, Drupal may present a single node, or a list of nodes, or whatever else Drupal may prepare as the "content" for any given page.

You must also print the title for this content using the variable `$title`. It is different than the variable `$head_title`, which includes the name of the Web site and is typically printed in the `<title>` tag for a page.

There are two modes for each node: view and edit. These modes can be accessed through the tabs that are displayed on each node. Within your page template, the variables $tabs (primary level of tabs) and $tabs2 (subnavigation available present in several administrative pages) are used to place links that access the "view" and "edit" modes for each node. The tab variables are typically printed between the $title and $content variables.

> **Breadcrumbs**
> Although there is a variable containing the breadcrumb path for each page, the breadcrumb trail is often incomplete. Many themes choose to display this variable only in the administrative section of the Web page.

Drupal communicates system messages to the user through the variable $messages. This variable may contain useful information that describes the successful submission of new content or content modifications, errors relating to a form submission, or messages within the administration system. Messages come in three flavors: *status, warning,* and *error.* Through your style sheet you can make these messages visually unique. Typical colors used for these messages are green for status messages, yellow for warning messages, and red for error messages. The messages are available as CSS classes and carry the corresponding name (for example, warning messages use the CSS selector .warning).

In addition to these system messages, Drupal will occasionally provide "help" text, which is made available through the variable $help. Both the help text and messages must be specified in your page template to ensure that the appropriate system messages are delivered to your Web site users.

Creating New Page Variables

In addition to using the variables that are provided by Drupal, you can create your own. Each time Drupal builds a page, it gathers the information it needs to display that page and makes sure the information is safe to display. This "preprocessing" is completed before the page is built using the template files. To keep your template files focused only on HTML output, you can insert any custom programming you need into the relevant preprocess function. Its output will be returned as a variable to the relevant tpl.php template file. Variables created in the preprocess functions are available only in the relevant template files (tpl.php).

> **Placing PHP snippets into templates**
> Throughout the rest of this chapter, you will be working with preprocess functions and creating new theme variables. The preprocess functions are always placed in your theme's `template.php` file. Theme variables are always placed in the relevant template file (for example, `page.tpl.php`).

Preprocess functions are named according to the template you want to "hook" your new variables to. Any module that has a template file can use the preprocess function. For example, the page, node, comment, and block types all have associated `.tpl.php` files; as a consequence, they can all be tied to a preprocess function. A full list of preprocess functions is available from the API documentation at `http://api.drupal.org/api/search/6/preprocess`. More information on creating additional template files is provided later in this chapter.

In the following example, you will add a new variable that can be used in the template `page.tpl.php`. Your imagination is the only limit on what these variables can contain! The Zen theme inserts additional, sophisticated body classes that allow you to create very specialized page customizations through CSS. The Garland theme uses a preprocess page function to hook into the color module. Later in this chapter, you will learn how to add new image banners based on which section of the Web site you are viewing.

In this example, we will add a new graphic to the page if the visitor is logged into the site but is not currently viewing the front page.

```
function bolg_preprocess_page (&$variables) {
    // Add a "go home" button to page.tpl.php

    if ($variables['logged_in'] == TRUE && $variables['is_front'] == FALSE) {
        $image_path = $variables['directory'] . "/images/go_home.jpg";
        $image_text = t("Go home!");
        $image = theme('image', $image_path, $image_text, $image_text);
        $variables['go_home'] = l($image, "<front>", array('html'=> TRUE));
    }
} // End of the preprocess_page function
```

In the file `page.tpl.php`, you can now place the new variable `$go_home` anywhere you would like the button to appear. Although the snippet could be simplified by hard-coding the HTML for the image, this method can be easily reused in many different themes and allows the text string to be translated for multilingual Web sites.

Modifying Page Variables

You may also choose to modify variables that have already been set by Drupal. The Zen theme uses this technique to remove the markup for an empty help message. The Newswire theme customizes page variables to modify the HTML for the content title depending on which page is being viewed; Newswire also customizes the logo that is displayed on the front page and the inner pages of the site. The Acquia Marina theme removes the markup for sidebars when they are not in use to create a clean, collapsible template layout. You can implement your own customizations as well.

To reset a variable, simply use the same variable name as an existing page variable. Do not unset unused variables, as this action may cause an ugly PHP error if the `page.tpl.php` file tries to print a variable that no longer exists. Instead, set the unused variable to a blank string:

```
function bolg_preprocess_page (&$variables) {
  // From the Zen theme
  // Don't display empty help from node_help().
  if ($variables['help'] == "<div class=\"help\"><p></p>\n</div>") {
    $variables['help'] = '';
  }
}
```

In addition to the techniques you will encounter later in this chapter, much can be gleaned from other themes. Download and examine a variety of themes to see how other people have customized their page templates by adding, and modifying, their template variables.

Navigation and Menus

Your page template includes two variables containing navigation menus that you can place anywhere you like in your Web page: `$primary_links` and `$secondary_links`. These variables contain items from the two Drupal menus of the same name—primary and secondary links. Drupal menus are collections of links to both on-site and off-site URLs.

To add new items to the menus, you can use one of two methods:

- To add a link to an existing node, navigate to the editing screen for the node and adjust its menu settings as in Figure 4.3.

- You may also use the menu administration system to add a page to the menu as shown in Figure 4.4 by navigating to Administer, Site building, Menus, Add item. This method allows you to add links to off-site URLs.

To add subsection menu items, you use the same technique described above, but change the "Parent item" to the menu item in which your new subsection ought to be included. For example, suppose you have a set of primary links containing "Mammal," "Amphibian," and "Reptile." To place "Kitten" as a subsection of "Mammal," you would set the "Parent item" to be "Mammal" when adding the menu information for the "Kitten" node.

> **More menus into your page template**
> The menu module provides a block for every menu, and blocks can be placed into any region on the site. To display a menu in a block, navigate to Administer, Site building, Blocks. Complete the on-screen instructions to add the menu to a Web site region. More information about creating custom, task-based menus appears in Chapter 8.

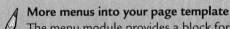

FIGURE 4.3 Adding a node to a menu from the node editing screen.

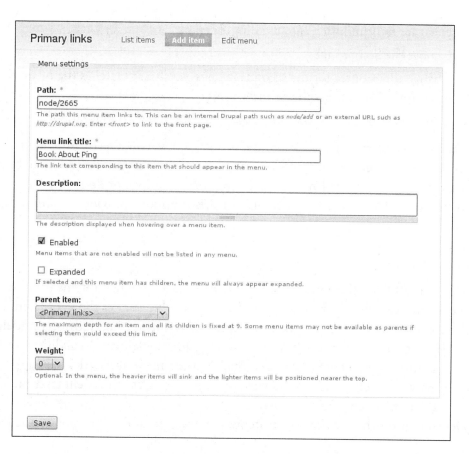

FIGURE 4.4 Adding a path to Primary links from the menu administration area.

Within the menu administration area, you can specify which menu is used for $primary_links and which menu is used for $secondary_links. By default, the variable $primary_links contains menu items from the menu "Primary links" and the variable $secondary_links contains items from the menu "Secondary links." To alter the menus that are used for these two navigation variables, navigate to Administer, Site building, Menus, Settings and adjust the settings as appropriate.

The variable $secondary_links can be configured in one of two ways: Either this menu can contain a second set of sitewide links for your site with "secondary" content (for example, legal notice, contact information), or you can configure $secondary_links to contain the relevant subsection navigation for your primary links. Use the following steps to change the default behavior:

1. Navigate to Administer, Site building, Menus.

2. Choose the Settings tab.

3. Change the "Source for the secondary links" so that it matches the menu that is set in the "Source for the primary links."

4. Scroll to the bottom of the Web page and click "Save configuration."

The page template variable `$secondary_links` now contains the subsection links that have been defined for each of the items in `$primary_links`. Referring to the previous example, "Kitten" will now be displayed in the output of `$secondary_links` when you select "Mammal" from the list of menu options provided by the variable `$primary_links`.

Theming Menus

A menu is built from three nested parts: the menu tree, the menu items (the "leaves" on the menu tree), and the menu item links. It is possible to alter the HTML for each of these components, although in most cases customizing the CSS for the default XHTML markup will be enough to make your menus look great. In addition to their basic structure, menus contain information about the menu leaves. For example, Figure 4.5 shows the active trail of the current page, Modules, and includes a menu of items that are collapsed, and expanded.

Depending on the type of menu items you want to alter, there are two relevant strategies:

- To alter the contents of the variables `$primary_links` and `$secondary_links`, use the page's preprocess function.

- To alter the markup for all menus, use theme functions.

> **Drop-down menus**
>
> The variables `$primary_links` and `$secondary_links` contain only the top-level menu items for their respective menus. If you would like to use a tree-like structure (useful for drop-down or fly-out menus) for your primary or secondary links, you must use the block version of your menu instead of the theme variables. The modules MenuTree and Nice Menus both create drop-down menus from your navigation variables. The project pages for these two modules can be found at `http://drupal.org/project/menutree` and `http://drupal.org/project/nice_menus`, respectively. Compare their features and choose the most appropriate module for your needs.

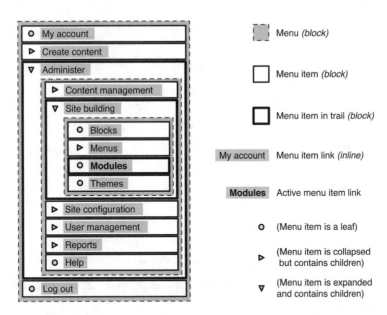

FIGURE 4.5 Menus are built of a menu tree, the menu items, and menu item links.

The primary and secondary links are registered theme variables. You may alter their contents by using the page's preprocess function. The variables themselves consist of an array of links and attributes. To make changes, you must loop through the list of links and alter each one individually. For example, if you decide to add a new class to each menu item that is related to its position in the menu, you could use the code snippet below. This technique would be useful if you wanted to add an icon to each menu item, because it relies on the exact order of the menu items. Once this order is set, you may not alter the order of the menu items without also updating the corresponding CSS styles.

```
function bolg_preprocess_page(&$variables) {
// Make a shortcut for the primary links variables
$primary_links = $variables['primary_links'];

// Loop through the menu, adding a new class for CSS selections
$i = 1;

foreach ($primary_links as $link => $attributes) {
  // Append the new class to existing classes for each menu item
```

```
$class = $attributes['attributes']['class'] . " item-$i";

  // Add revised classes back to the primary links temp variable
  $primary_links[$link]['attributes']['class'] = $class;
  $i++;
}
 // End of the foreach loop


// reset the variable to contain the new markup
$variables['primary_links'] = $primary_links;


} // End of the preprocess function
```

Using the appropriate unique identifier for the primary links, add the new classes to your style sheet:

```
#primary_links .item-1 { /* styles for the first menu item */ }
```

This technique works well if you want to add styles based on the order of options in a menu. Menus are stored in an associative array and have a unique key assigned to each item. To create a unique menu item identifier, replace the variable $i with the variable $link in the snippet given earlier. Your menu items will now be assigned a unique identifier that does not change even when the order of the menu items is altered.

For more information about how menus are constructed and themed, read the API documentation at http://api.drupal.org/api/function/theme_links/6 and http://api.drupal.org/api/group/menu/6 (scroll to the list of theme functions).

Grid Work

In Chapter 1 of this book, you read about Web page design and were introduced to "regions" within a page template. Now you are ready to define the regions within your own page template and to then insert information into these defined spaces. There is no limit on how large or small a region can be within your page template. You may choose to stack many blocks into a region, or you may prefer to have only one block contained in a region. Figure 4.6 shows five of the regions available in the Zen theme

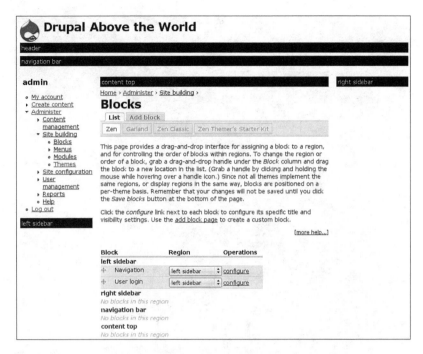

FIGURE 4.6 Five regions in the Zen theme, each with a different position and size.

as black bars. As you can see, the sizes of these regions differ depending on their location in the page.

Regions

Regions are used to place Drupal "blocks" into a Web site. These blocks may include site navigation menus, custom views, module tools, or custom PHP snippets. To see a list of the blocks that are currently available for your site, navigate to Administer, Site building, Blocks. Figure 4.7 shows the blocks that are available for the Hear the North site. This Web site has only a few modules installed, including a newsletter management tool Simplenews.

You can adjust the placement of these blocks by dragging and dropping the crosshair icon to a new region. To enable disabled blocks, drag them to a new region. To disable blocks, drag them back to the "Disabled" section. After updating the placement of blocks, you must click the button "Save blocks" to commit your changes to the

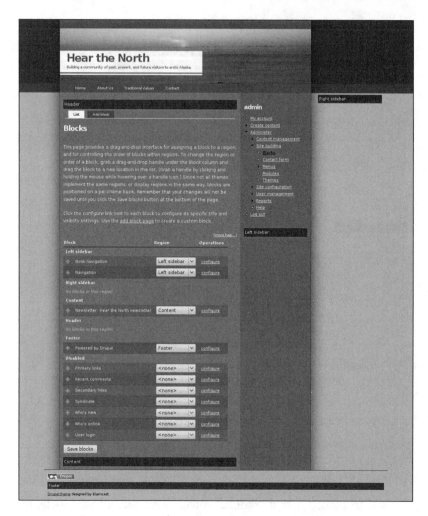

FIGURE 4.7 Blocks available on the Hear the North Web site.

database. You may also change the order of several blocks within a region using the same technique.

Adding a new region to your template is a multistep process:

1. Edit your theme's info file and add the regions as follows:

```
regions[new_region_name] = Human-readable region name
regions[second_region_name] = Another region name
```

2. Edit the file `page.tpl.php` and print your new regions to the structure of your page. Use the variable names you established in your theme's info file.

```
<?php print $new_region_name ?>
```

3. Clear the cache to reset the theme registry and enable the new regions. Navigate to Administer, Site configuration, Performance. Scroll to the bottom of the Web page and click "Clear cached data."

4. You should now be able to place blocks into your new regions by navigating to Administer, Site building, Blocks.

Here is the basic page template repeated from Chapter 3. A few changes have been made including the inclusion of new HTML divisions and one new region (marked in bold) that can be positioned with CSS. Putting these regions after the main content of the site will make the content appear more important to search engines, thereby increasing its rank in search engine results.

```
<!DOCTYPE html PUBLIC "-//W3C//DTD XHTML 1.0 Strict//EN"
    "http://www.w3.org/TR/xhtml1/DTD/xhtml1-strict.dtd">
<html xmlns="http://www.w3.org/1999/xhtml"
    lang="<?php print $language->language ?>"
    xml:lang="<?php print $language->language ?>">
<head>
    <title><?php print $head_title; ?></title>
    <?php print $head; ?>
    <?php print $styles; ?>
    <?php print $scripts; ?>
</head>

<body class="<?php print $body_classes ?>">
<div id="main">
    <div id="page_title"><?php print $title; ?></div>
    <div id="utils-help"><?php print $help; ?></div>
    <div id="utils-messages"><?php print $messages; ?></div>
    <div id="utils-tab"><?php print $tabs; ?></div>
    <div id="main_content"><?php print $content; ?></div>
    <div id="utils-rss"><?php print $feed_icons; ?></div>
```

```
<div id="new-region-name"><?php print $new-region-name; ?></div>
</div>

<div id="sidebar-left"><?php print $left; ?></div>
<div id="sidebar-right"><?php print $right; ?></div>

<div id="footer"><?php print $region_footer; ?></div>
<?php print $closure; ?>
</body>
</html>
```

Blocks

With your regions established, you can now fill them with blocks. Blocks may be generated by Drupal core modules, contributed modules, or custom PHP snippets, including lists of content created by the Views module. For more information on creating a custom view, refer to Chapter 2.

Commonly used blocks include the following:

- Navigation menus (created in Administer, Site building, Menus)
- Lists of content (Views module; see Chapter 2)
- Login forms (Drupal core; turned on by default)
- Site categories (Drupal's Taxonomy module)
- Recent comments (Drupal's Comment module)
- Search (Drupal's search module)
- Author information (Drupal's profile module)
- Five-star ratings (http://drupal.org/project/fivestar)
- Facebook, Digg, and social bookmarking links (http://drupal.org/project/service_links)
- Similar entries (http://drupal.org/project/similar)

You can also create custom blocks with text, images, and even your own snippets of PHP code. Sample PHP snippets are available from the Drupal Web site at http://drupal.org/node/21867. To create a custom block, follow these steps:

1. Navigate to to Administer, Site Building, Modules and enable the PHP Filter module. You may also need to adjust the permissions for this input format by navigating to Administer, Site configuration, Input formats and clicking on the "configure" link next to PHP filter.

2. Navigate to Administer, Site building, Blocks.

3. Select the tab "Add block."

4. Add a "Block description." This description specifies how the block will be identified in the administration area and is a required field.

5. Add a "Block title" if you would like a title to appear at the top of the displayed block. This field is optional.

6. Put your text, images, and PHP snippet into the "Block body." You could also use plain text or HTML markup here if it was appropriate for your block.

7. Update the "Input format" to PHP.

8. Adjust the visibility settings for the "User," "Role," and "Page" roles.

9. Scroll to the bottom of the Web page and click "Save."

> ⚠️ **PHP snippets in blocks**
> Blocks with custom PHP snippets could break the display of your site if they contain errors. Be sure to carefully test your snippets before placing them into a block. Place your PHP snippet into the body of a private page to confirm that it will not break your site before deploying the snippet as a block.

Sites will sometimes have more screen real estate dedicated to blocks than to the main content on each page, especially when the blocks provide additional information for the node that is displayed on the page, such as author profile information or related content. Don't be shy! Enable the most appropriate blocks for each part of your Web site. Blocks are included in Drupal's caching system and will not harm the overall performance of your site. To enable caching for blocks, navigate to Administer, Site configuration, Performance. Under the section "Block cache," choose "Enabled." Scroll to the bottom of the Web page and click "Save configuration."

Customizing the Markup of Blocks

You may change the markup of the blocks displayed in your page template by creating a new template file, `block.tpl.php`. Drupal's default for this template contains only a few wrapper HTML elements:

```
<div id="block-<?php print $block->module .'-'. $block->delta; ?>"
   class="block block-<?php print $block->module ?>">
<?php if ($block->subject) { ?>
   <h2><?php print $block->subject; ?></h2>
<?php } ?>


   <div class="content">
     <?php print $block->content ?>
   </div>
</div>
```

For blocks provided by Drupal core, the variable `$block->delta` represents the order in which this block was created. For example, the first block has a delta value of 1, the second has a delta value of 2, and so on. In rendered HTML, the first line would look like this:

```
<div id="block-user-1" class="block block-user">
```

As you can see, the output is not nearly as complicated as the variables would suggest! Check the output to see what your module is using for its delta value. Some modules provide a text delta instead of a numeric delta.

A full list of block template variables is available from the default block template. This file can be found in your Drupal system files: `modules/system/block.tpl.php`. A full list of the variables is also available online at `http://api.drupal.org/api/file/modules/system/block.tpl.php`.

Search

The default Drupal core engine comes with a module that allows you to search the contents of your site. There are four steps to enabling search on your site: enable the search module; update the permissions for users to search content; index the content on a regular basis through the use of a "cron job"; and display the search form to site visitors.

1. The Search module is not enabled by default. To enable this module, navigate to Administer, Site Building, Modules; enable the module by placing a check mark next to it, scrolling to the bottom of the Web page, and clicking "Save."

2. Next you must enable the permissions for the appropriate roles in your site. Navigate to Administer, User Management, Permissions. To enable searching for all users, make sure "search content" and "advanced search" are enabled for "anonymous user."

3. Drupal's search module does not search the content of the database directly because this operation would be too time-consuming. Instead, it searches an index of your content (similar to an index at the back of a book). To initiate this process of creating or updating the index, navigate to Administer, Reports, Status report. Click on the link "run cron manually." The page will automatically refresh, showing you the cron maintenance task that was last run "less than a few seconds ago." For more information on configuring cron jobs for Drupal, refer to Chapter 2.

4. Two styles of search tools are available for Drupal themes; Figure 4.8 compares these two search forms. On the left side of the screen, the top option is the theme's search box (which has no heading); the second option is the Search form block (which has a heading). If you like, you can customize the Search

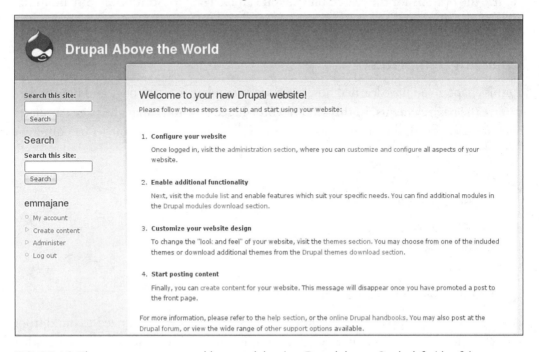

FIGURE 4.8 There are two ways to enable a search box in a Drupal theme. On the left side of the screen, the top option is the theme's search form; the bottom option is the Search form block.

form block to remove the heading. Although these two search forms have a very similar appearance, they are actually applied in quite different ways. The Search form block may be placed only into an existing region; in contrast, the theme's search box may be placed anywhere within the page template.

To enable the theme's search box, add the following PHP snippet to your theme's `page.tpl.php` file at the appropriate location:

```
<?php print $search_box ?>
```

To enable the search block, use these steps:

1. Navigate to Administer, Site Building, Blocks.
2. Scroll down to the "Disabled" section.
3. Select a region for the search form from the select menu.
4. Scroll to the bottom of the Web page and click "Save blocks."

Your search box should now appear as a block within your Web site. To further customize the options for the search block, you can navigate to Administer, Site building, Blocks and click on the "configure" link next to the Search form.

Changing Templates

In this chapter you have learned how to create a template for your page and how to customize the page elements. In this section you will see how to change the page templates that are used for different sections of your Web site. You may want to use different templates for each of the following tasks and types of pages:

- Editing content
- Displaying a content type
- User login
- Front page
- Categories
- Offline or maintenance page

Some of these templates are provided by default; others you will need to build from scratch. The online documentation has a complete list of all default templates provided by Drupal at `http://drupal.org/node/190815`. This section describes several of the page-specific template options.

> **Assigning themes to different parts of your site**
> This section describes how to change the template that is used within a single theme. If you need to assign whole themes to different parts of your Web site, you will need a more powerful toolkit. The contributed module known as sections will allow you to do exactly this. For more information about this project, visit http://drupal.org/project/sections.
>
> If you need to provide even more customization on a per-section basis, you may need The Organic Groups module. This module enables authorized users to create and manage their own "groups." Each group gets its own theme, language, and taxonomy. The techniques described in this book could be applied to each theme for each group on the Web site. For more information about this project, visit http://drupal.org/project/og.

Custom Front Page

What if you need a front page that has more—or fewer—regions than are provided by a certain template? What if the front page needs to have a bigger banner and a smaller content area? What if you need to make so many changes that it feels like the front page needs a theme all of its own? Fortunately, it is very easy to create a custom front page template for your Drupal site—so easy, in fact, that it is difficult to fill up a whole section of this chapter with information about making a new front page template!

To make a custom front page template, follow these steps:

1. Create a new page template file with the name `page-front.tpl.php`. This is a special file name recognized by Drupal as being a unique template to be used on only the front page of the Web site.

2. Clear the theme registry by navigating to Administer, Site configuration, Performance; scroll to the bottom of the Web page and click "clear cached data."

3. Navigate to the front page of your Web site and marvel!

All pages other than the front page will still use the template file `page.tpl.php` (unless additional page-specific templates are used elsewhere in the site).

> **Using a view on the front page**
> If you are using the Views module, you can use the page view to create a custom front page. Once you have created the view and assigned an alias to it, navigate to Administer, Site configuration, Site information. Scroll to the bottom of the Web page and adjust the setting for the "Default front page" so that it uses the new view page alias for the default front page.

Custom Offline Page

Unfortunately, bad things sometimes happen to good Web sites, and the Web sites have to go offline. Drupal provides a default template when a connection cannot be made to the database. In addition, the site can be directed to enter "maintenance" mode so that you can perform some upgrades or other feature enhancements. Figure 4.9 and Figure 4.10 show the default templates for these two offline pages.

The offline message template will appear only to visitors who are not authenticated; administrators will still have access to the Web site as they perform their upgrades when a site is "under maintenance." To customize these pages, complete the following steps:

1. Copy the default maintenance page from the Drupal core directory `modules/system/maintenance-page.tpl.php` to your theme's directory.

2. Make a second copy of the file for the offline template and name it `maintenance-page-offline.tpl.php`.

3. You should now have two new files in your theme's directory:
   - `maintenance-page.tpl.php`: "maintenance" mode
   - `maintenance-page-offline.tpl.php`: "database is offline"

4. Adjust these two new templates to suit your needs.

5. Open your site's configuration file in a text editor. (This file is found in `sites/yourdomainname.com/settings.php`. It is not a theme file, and it is probably write-protected.)

6. Remove the # symbol from the following lines:
   - Line 173: `# $conf = array(`
   - Line 175: `#    'theme_default' => 'your_theme_name'`
   - Line 187: `#    'maintenance_theme' => 'your_theme_name'`
   - Line 214: `# );`

7. Save the changes and make the file read-only again.

The next time you put your Web site into maintenance mode (or if your database server ever goes offline), you will be able to show your customized apology to the world instead of the default Drupal "maintenance" message.

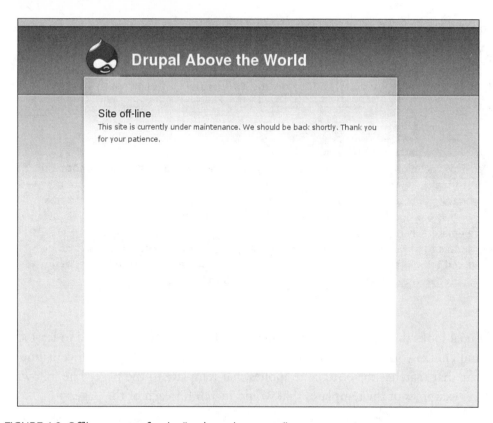

FIGURE 4.9 Offline message for site "under maintenance."

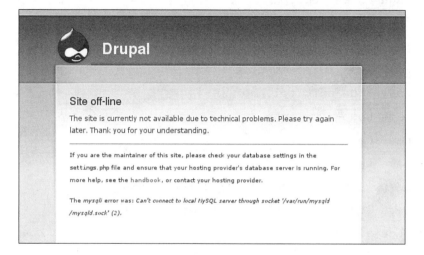

FIGURE 4.10 Offline message when the database connection fails.

In the section "Custom Front Page," you learned how to create a custom front page template. The template was activated when the current page was the front page of the Web site. You may take advantage of this technique to target other types of pages as well. Page templates are activated according to Drupal's internal path for the current page.

> **Internal path and URL alias**
> This technique works only with the internal path for a page. You cannot use URL aliases. You will learn how to work with aliases in the next section. For now, you may only use paths that are related to Drupal core terminology. For example, `node/5` and `node/5/edit` are both internal paths that can be tied to a specific page template, whereas `books/fiction/story-about-ping` is a URL alias. Use the Devel module to obtain a list of suggested template files for each page. If none of the suggested templates matches your needs, consider skipping ahead to the next section to discover alternative ways to create template files.

Drupal looks through a list of suggested templates from most specific to least specific and checks your theme's directory for a matching template file. Once it finds a template that matches the criteria, it applies that template to the page. The following list gives examples of the templates that would match for each of the pages:

- `http://www.example.com/node/5`
    - `page-node-5.tpl.php`
    - `page-node.tpl.php`
    - `page.tpl.php`
- `http://www.example.com/node/5/edit`
    - `page-node-edit.tpl.php`
    - `page-node-5.tpl.php`
    - `page-node.tpl.php`
    - `page.tpl.php`
- `http://www.example.com/admin/build/block`
    - `page-admin-build-block.tpl.php`
    - `page-admin-build.tpl.php`
    - `page-admin.tpl.php`

- `page.tpl.php`
- `http://www.example.com/books/fiction/story-about-ping`
  - `page-node-2665.tpl.php`
  - `page-node.tpl.php`
  - `page.tpl.php`

The last item in the list is using a URL alias. There is not a single template that can be used by default to match any of the words in the URL to assign a template. Instead, you must know the exact node ID for the page to find a node-specific template match. These template suggestions exist automatically, so use them whenever you need to create a new template with the same file name and then theme it according to your needs. You may also need to clear the theme registry to see your new template in action.

Alias: Page

Do you remember the TV show *Alias?* It was full of wigs and disguises and trickery and deception and intrigue! URL aliases are a bit like throwing a wig onto a system path—they change the way the path looks, but keep the content the same. If you want your site to use URLs that are more closely tied to page content than `node/2868`, you will need to use the module Path to create URL aliases. The bad news is that Drupal's theming system cannot recognize the URL aliases that you have created with the wigs and the dark sunglasses. Instead, you must explicitly show Drupal how you want to convert these URLs into a template suggestion. In the next section, you will learn how to further customize this process to create template suggestions for each category.

> **Template overload**
> Do you really need a whole new page template? Think carefully before implementing the ideas presented in this section. For each new page template you create, you will need to maintain the markup for an entirely new page. The more you add, the more you have to maintain. There may be other, less time-intensive ways to simplify a layout—for example, displaying blocks only on certain pages.

The first step in this process is to grab the URL and examine its components before the page template is processed. Using the URL alias, you will compile a new list of suggested page templates. Being careful to match the alias for the page you want to redesign, you then add a new template file to your theme. Now when Drupal looks for the best match for its page template, it will use your new list of suggested file names and find the new page template.

New Templates from Aliased URLs

The work of compiling the new list of suggested templates happens in the page pre-process function in your theme's `template.php` file. If you have already created a `preprocess_page` function in your theme's `template.php` file, you may add this snippet to either the beginning or the end of the function. If you do not already have this function, you will need to include the very first (and very last) lines of this snippet in your theme's `template.php` file.

It takes several steps to compile a new list of suggested templates for the URL alias of your page:

1. Confirm that the module `path` is enabled. Without this module, your site will not have URL aliases and this function will be irrelevant.

2. By default, Drupal allows you to access the system path, but not the URL alias. You need to use a special decoder ring, `drupal_get_path_alias`, to convert the system path back to its URL alias.

3. Break the URL alias into its components using PHP function `explode`. You will use these components to build the new page template file name.

4. Make sure your Web page is not an editing page. If it is, Drupal's templates can be used and this function becomes irrelevant.

5. Create a variable to hold the new template suggestions, and establish the base word for the new template's file names. You could use any word here, but using the base word "page" allows you to keep all page templates together. For example, `page-your-custom-url.tpl.php` would be alphabetically close to `page-front.tpl.php`.

6. Loop through each part of the URL and build new template suggestions. This mimics the way Drupal offers its templates. For example, if your URL alias is `books/fiction/story-about-ping`, you will now be able to create three new page templates: `page-books.tpl.php`, `page-books-fiction.tpl.php`, and `page-books-fiction-story-about-ping.tpl.php`.

7. Add the new template suggestion to a list that will be handed back to Drupal.

8. Finally, return the list of suggested template names back to Drupal.

In your file `template.php`, the PHP snippet for these eight steps is as follows:

```php
function bolg_preprocess_page(&$variables) {
// Step 1:
if (module_exists('path')) {

// Step 2:
$path_alias = drupal_get_path_alias($_GET['q']);

// Step 3:
$alias_parts = explode('/', $path_alias);

// Step 4:
$last = array_reverse($alias_parts);
$last_part = $last[0];
if ($last_part != "edit") {

// Step 5:
  $templates = array();
  $template_name = "page";

// Step 6:
  foreach ($alias_parts as $part) {
    $template_name = $template_name . '-' . $part;

// Step 7:
    $templates[] = $template_name;
  }

// Step 8:
  $variables['template_files'] = $templates;

} // End of the edit check
} // End of the check for the path module
} // End of the preprocess_page function
```

After you place this snippet in your theme's `template.php` file, you may use any part of the URL alias as a page template name. Note, however, that you must refresh the theme registry before Drupal sees your new template suggestions.

Page Templates for Views

The Views module is very clever. When you provide a URL alias for your page view, it automatically performs its version of the function that was described in the previous section. For example, if you have a view with the URL alias `recent/screencasts`, the Views module will automatically generate the following page template suggestions: `page-recent.tpl.php` and `page-recent-screencasts.tpl.php`. The default page template, `page.tpl.php`, will be used there if none of these files exist within the theme's directory.

Adding CSS Classes

The Zen theme allows designers to adapt their layout based on the classes that are applied to the body. You can add this level of customization to your theme as well. To add classes to your page, you will need to alter the contents of the page variable `$body_classes`. This variable contains a list of classes all separated by a space. To add new classes to this variable, you can use the same function that was described previously in this chapter. In the code outlined in the section "New Templates from Aliased URLs," replace step 8 with the following lines (the first line is a comment, not part of the functioning code):

```
// Step 8:
$classes = implode(' page-', $templates);
$variables['body_classes'] = $variables['body_classes'] . ' $classes';
```

This will add your new body classes to the end of the list of default classes.

> **Additional body classes are available**
> If you want to have even more classes available for theming, you may find the Themer module useful. This tiny module creates a suite of CSS classes that can be applied throughout your theme. Additional information is available on the project page at http://drupal.org/project/themer.

Page Templates for Content Types

If necessary, you can change the way a node is displayed within a page with Drupal's node templates. If you knew that one of your content types needed a different page layout, however, you could assign a new page template to that content type. This process is almost the same as that followed in the previous examples.

To make a content type-specific page template, you will need to know which type of content you are looking at. The only time you can know this with certainty is when you are looking at a page that contains only one node. This page would normally use the page template `page-node.tpl.php`.

To create a template suggestion based on content type, you will need to replace steps 6, 7, and 8 of the preprocess function described in the section "New Templates from Aliased URLs" with the following snippet. Notice the use of `arg()` in this example; `arg()` is a special variable that grabs individual parameters from the system path for the displayed page. For example, the value of `arg(0)` for `node/2868` is "node" and the value of `arg(1)` is 2868.

```
if (arg(0) == "node" && is_numeric(arg(1))) {
    $node_type = $variables['node']->type;
    $variables['template_files'] = "$template_name-node-$node_type.tpl.php";
}
```

If you want to make templates for both URL aliases and content types, you can add this snippet *after* step 8 in the code snippet described in "New Templates from Aliased URLs:"

```
if (arg(0) == "node" && is_numeric(arg(1))) {
    $node_type = $variables['node']->type;
    array_push($variables['template_files'], "$template_name-node-$node_type.tpl.
php");
}
```

The examples in this section should give you a solid toolkit for creating unique page templates. You may think of even more ways to customize your templates, too!

Taxonomy Templates

The previous section described how to build new templates based on URL aliases and content type. When you are designing a site to have category-specific enhancements, it is very likely that you want to change the colors or graphical elements of the page template. This section explores ways to create a new page template so as to add color-specific sections and new variables. To accomplish this feat, you will use the same techniques you learned in the previous section.

Unfortunately, categories are easily edited and are not associated with permanent machine names. You may find it helpful to print the taxonomy variable to the page to see how categories are stored and accessed. You can also obtain this information by using the developer module Themer Info tool in the Devel module. Refer to Chapter 2 for more information on using this module.

Here are the contents of one taxonomy variable:

```
[taxonomy] => Array
   (
      [3] => stdClass Object
         (
            [tid] => 3
            [vid] => 1
            [name] => Available for retail and wholesale.
            [description] =>
            [weight] => 0
         )


      [11] => stdClass Object
         (
            [tid] => 11
            [vid] => 2
            [name] => Books Published by The Ginger Press
            [description] =>
            [weight] => 0
         )

   )
```

In this example, the category being used to change the template variable is the first category contained in the array of data in the taxonomy variable. The first four steps of the `preprocess_page` function described in "New Templates from Aliased URLs" section are repeated. At this point, you should adjust the variable `$target_tax` so that it matches the position of the category you want to use to distinguish between sections on your site. This function assumes that you are working within one vocabulary and that each term is a different template. You will need to adjust the scripting if your site differs from this model.

The explanations of steps 1 through 4 can be found in the section "New Templates from Aliased URLs." The new steps perform the following actions:

5. Check whether this page has a system path of `node/nid`. This snippet will work only if you are displaying a single node of any content type.

6. Check whether this page has been assigned a category. Retrieve the whole array of categories if it does.

7. Retrieve the name of the category.

8. Convert the category name to a plain text string of characters suitable for a file name. This operation includes replacing spaces with a dash and converting all characters to lowercase.

9. Add the new template suggestion to the list of page template suggestions; add the category name to the list of existing body classes.

```
function bolg_preprocess_page(&$variables) {
// Step 1:
if (module_exists('path')) {

// Step 2:
$url_alias = drupal_get_path_alias($_GET['q']);

// Step 3:
$alias_parts = explode('/', $url_alias);

// Step 4:
$last = array_reverse($alias_parts);
$last_part = $last[0];
if ($last_part != "edit") {
```

```
// Step 5:
if (arg(0) == "node" && is_numeric(arg(1))) {


// Step 6:
if (isset($variables['node']->taxonomy)) {
    $target_tax = 0;
    $node_tax = $variables['node']->taxonomy;


// Step 7:
    $tid = array_keys($node_tax);
    $name = $node_tax[$tid[$target_tax]]->name;


// Step 8:
    $clean_name = check_plain($name);
    $dash_name = str_replace(" ", "-", $clean_name);
    $lc_name = strtolower($dash_name);


// Step 9:
array_push($variables['template_files'], "page-tax-$lc_name.tpl.php");
$variables['body_classes'] .= $variables['body_classes'] . " tax-$lc_name";


} // End of the taxonomy check
} // End of the node/nid check
} // End of the edit check
} // End of the check for the path module
} // End of the preprocess_page function
```

Graphical Headers

The last function introduced in this chapter allows you to change the template or add a new CSS class to a page based on the category assigned to a page. Wouldn't it be neat if you could change the graphical header for that page as well? With the snippet of code provided here, you will be able to place images into a folder in your theme directory and have them be automatically displayed for unique categories within your Web site.

This snippet can be used as a replacement for step 9 in the preceding section, or it can be used as a further enhancement. It assumes that all of the images reside in a sub-directory of your theme named `tax` and that all image files are named with the lower-case extension `jpg`. You may change these settings, if necessary. The image files should all be named according to the following convention: Using the term name, replace all spaces with a dash and convert all letters to lowercase. A default image should also be available if a matching taxonomy-specific image cannot be found.

```
$image_dir = "tax";

$ext = "jpg";

$default_image_file = "FILENAME.jpg";


$image_dir = drupal_get_path('theme', 'bolg') . "/$image_dir");

$default_image = "$image_dir/$default_image_file";

$image = "$image_dir/$lc_name.$ext";


if (file_exists($image){

    $variables['tax_header'] = theme('image', $image, $clean_name, $clean_name);

} elseif (file_exists($default_image){

    $variables['tax_header'] = theme('image', $default_image, $clean_name, $clean_
name);

} else {

    $variables['tax_header'] = "";

}
```

Remember to put the default header graphic into the appropriate image folder in your theme!

Delivering Plain Content

Sometimes a stripped-down version of your site is more appropriate than one cluttered with bells and whistles. For example, "simpler is better" when you are aiming to provide a print-friendly version of a page or a mobile-friendly version of your Web site.

Print-Friendly Pages

There are two ways to prepare pages for printing. The first is to prepare a unique style sheet for printers. The browser will automatically detect style sheets that have been marked with a media type of "print" and format the page according to the print rules that have been specified. The second method uses a contributed module, Print, to enable links that direct the site visitor to new pages that use a print-friendly template.

CSS Print-Friendly Pages

Cascading Style Sheets (CSS) specify the media type they are targeting. When a page is displayed in a Web browser, you are viewing the styles that have been assigned to the page by the media types "all" and "screen." Eight other media types are available, including "print," "braille," "handheld," and "tv." A full list of media types is available from `http://www.w3.org/TR/CSS2/media.html#media-types`.

The "print" media type specifies how a page should be formatted when it is printed. Figure 4.11 shows a Web page formatted by a "screen" style sheet; Figure 4.12 shows the "print preview" for the same page. Parts of the page that are not relevant to the content being displayed have been eliminated. The elements that have been removed include the header, navigation elements, and quotes in the footer.

Most of the work in creating a print-friendly style sheet focuses on finding regions that can be "hidden" from view. To remove these variables from the print-friendly version of the page, the CSS property and attribute `display: none;` are used. The site name (HICK Tech) is also pulled into the display by using the property and attribute `display: block;`. To add a print-friendly style sheet to your site, you must register the new file in your theme's `.info` file and clear the theme registry by navigating to Administer, Site configuration, Performance; scrolling to the bottom of the Web page; and clicking "clear cached data." A print-specific CSS file is typically named `print.css`; however, there is no absolute requirement to use this file name. Set the print style sheet with the following snippet in your theme's `.info` file:

```
stylesheets[print][] = printstylesheet.css
```

The print style sheet for the HICK Tech Web site contains only the following styles:

```
/* Hide all information that is not unique content for this page */
#header-wrapper, #primary-links, #banner-image, .sidebar-right .sidebar-right,
```

FIGURE 4.11   HICK Tech Web site as it is displayed in a Web browser.

```
.breadcrumb, ul.primary, div.links, #bottomboxes, #footer {
      display: none;
}


/* The site name is set to "display: none"
   in the main style sheet, display it now*/
#print-sitename { display: block; }


/* Use print-friendly fonts */
body {
```

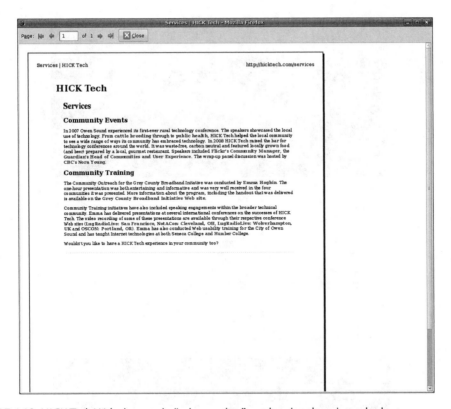

FIGURE 4.12 HICK Tech Web site seen in "print preview" mode using the print style sheet.

```
        font-family: Serif;

        color: #000;

        font-size: 1em;

        text-align: left;

}


/* Make sure the page is white, with no border, and properly aligned */
#wrapper {

        background: #fff;

        border: none;

        margin: 0;

        width: 100%;

}
```

To add your logo to the site name, you could place a background image on the site with the following CSS snippet:

```
#print-sitename {
    display: block;
    background-image: url(/path/to/the/image.gif);
}
```

If you are concerned about exact color matching (saving your visitor's valuable color ink cartridges), consider using a black-and-white logo here instead of your colored logo.

Several Drupal themes provide print-friendly CSS, including the default theme, Garland. Review the following themes for additional examples on how to create a print-friendly style sheet for your theme:

- AD Redoable (`http://drupal.org/project/ad_redoable`)
- NoProb (`http://drupal.org/project/noprob`)
- Pluralism (`http://drupal.org/project/pluralism`)
- Zen (`http://drupal.org/project/zen`)

The A List Apart article titled "Going to Print" by Eric Meyer provides excellent information and strategies for creating print-friendly pages using only CSS. This article can be found at `http://alistapart.com/articles/goingtoprint/`.

Print-Friendly Templates

Sometimes your Web site visitors will simply not believe that a print-friendly page is waiting to greet them in the printer. They may have had too many bad experiences with Web sites that do not provide a print-friendly CSS, and they may not understand the mechanics of Web site construction well enough to know such a thing is even possible. The CrochetMe Web site shown in Figure 4.13 shows a link to a print-friendly page (displayed in Figure 4.14) with all cruft removed. To create custom templates for your content, you must generate new links to the end of each node, create new templates with stripped-down markup, and notify the theme about these new (nonstandard) template files. Sounds like a lot of work, eh?

Print module to the rescue! With this nifty little module, you can easily enable print-friendly, email-this-page, and PDF links to all of your pages. For more information

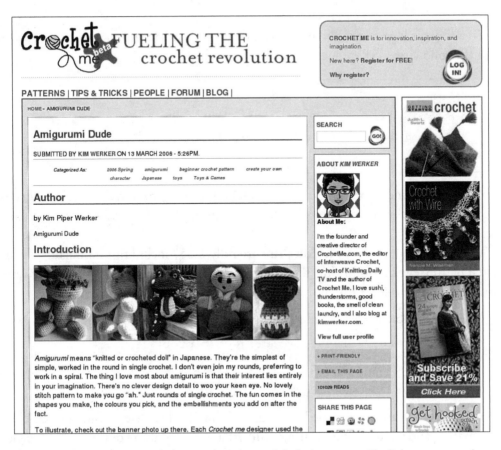

FIGURE 4.13 The CrochetMe Web site uses the Print module for its content. The links appears to the right of the content, below the author information.

about this module, and to download and install it, visit the module's project page at `http://drupal.org/project/print`.

Although this module does have the ability to create PDFs of pages, it requires a helper module. The recommended helper module, which is named `dompdf`, provides full CSS support and allows for excellent reproduction of the Web page. It does not, however, support Unicode character encoding or PDF headers. To install the `dompdf` module, you must install font support on your Web server. If you are not comfortable with system administration, or if you are using a shared hosting service, this functionality will be a little tricky to implement. For more information, visit the `dompdf` Web site at `http://www.digitaljunkies.ca/dompdf`.

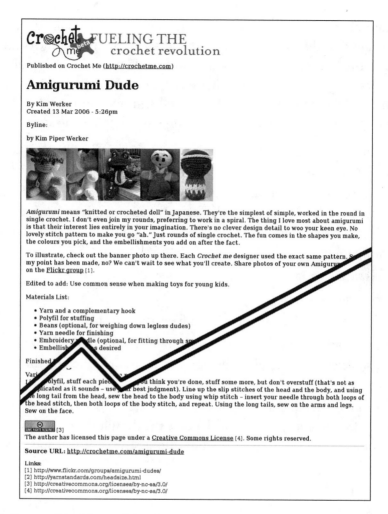

FIGURE 4.14 Output of the Print module—a "print-friendly" page.

Mobile Devices

Handheld devices are becoming more common, to the point that having a site that can be navigated while "on the go" is a must for service-oriented businesses such as restaurants, shops, and social networking sites. If you do not have the resources to develop a mobile application, that does not mean you cannot provide a mobile-friendly version of your Web site. To provide this trimmed-down version of your site template, you may use the Mobile theme. This theme is intended to return only clean HTML with no styling (although images embedded in your content are maintained). The links and sidebars are placed so that mobile or handheld devices can display the content first. For more information about this module, and to download and install it, visit the module's project page at `http://drupal.org/project/mobile`.

Once the Mobile theme is installed, you will still need to provide a URL for the mobile version of your Web site. To do so, complete the following steps:

1. Create a subdomain for the mobile version of your Web site. It is common practice to replace the "www" in your site's domain name with the letter "m."

2. Using the domain name you created in step 1, create a duplicate folder of your current site in Drupal's folder `sites`. For example, if you were adding a mobile version to the site `example.com`, the folder `sites` would include the following folders:

   - `example.com`
   - `m.example.com`

   These two folders contain identical information at this stage.

3. In the new mobile site folder, add the mobile theme to the folder `themes`. You may also delete any graphical themes that are not required by the mobile version of your site.

4. In the mobile site folder, edit the file `settings.php` and look for the section labeled "Variable overrides." Update the default theme to "mobile" and uncomment the relevant lines. Before editing, the code will appear as follows:

```
# $conf = array(
#    'site_name' => 'My Drupal site',
#    'theme_default' => 'minnelli',
#    'anonymous' => 'Visitor',

... approximately 50 lines
# );
```

After editing, it will appear as follows (note the **bold** lines have changed):

```
$conf = array(
  #   'site_name' => 'My Drupal site',
'theme_default' => 'mobile',
  #   'anonymous' => 'Visitor',


... approximately 50 lines
);
```

Your new mobile site is now ready for use! It uses the same database as the main site and, therefore, will always be exactly in sync with the main site. No extra work is required on your part!

Summary

This chapter addressed ways to modify the preprocess function so that you can prepare and alter page template variables, and alert Drupal of new page templates. More specifically, you learned how to perform the follow tasks:

- Dissect a theme into its component template files
- Use sitewide variables in page templates
- Create new sitewide variables with preprocess functions
- Establish a grid for a page template through custom regions
- Configure a sitewide search block
- Change page templates based on taxonomy, page alias, and content type
- Create and implement print-friendly pages using CSS and the Print module
- Create a low-bandwidth site for mobile devices

In the next chapter you will learn how to fill up the "content" region of your page with nodes that are themed exactly as you want them to be.

Chapter 5

Drupal Content

This is the pirate chapter! You have waited patiently to learn how to customize the *content* of your Web site. You have learned about theming tools, preprocess functions, template files, and Web design. In this chapter you will see how to combine all of these techniques to reveal the buried treasure—your content. You will learn how to slice and dice nodes into their component fields. You will learn how to create treasure maps made of beautiful images and how to customize lists of content. Grab your content, matey! It's time to theme it within an inch of its variables. Yarrr!

Node Templates

The node template controls how each unit of content is displayed within the larger page template. By default, this includes everything between the editing "tabs" of the content down to (but not including) the orange RSS feed icon. In Chapter 4, you learned about the various kinds of page templates, including how to create new ones. The node module has, by default, two types of node templates: `node.tpl.php`, for all nodes that do not have a more specific template, and `node-contenttypename. tpl.php`, for each type of content.

To create a custom node template, you must create a new file named `node.tpl.php` in your theme directory. You may print any of the following variables into your node template file:

- `$content`: Node body or teaser depending on the contents of the variable `$teaser`. This variable contains all of the display information for the node stuffed into a single variable. Later in this chapter you will learn how to use the `$node` variable to pick out individual fields for display.
- `$terms`: A list of themed links for each of the relevant Drupal categories for this content.
- `$links`: A list of themed links related to modules other than taxonomy. The links may include "Read more" (which is displayed on the teaser) and "Add new comment" (which is displayed based on the comment settings).
- `$node_url`: The URL of the current node. This link is useful for "permalinks" to the page. It is commonly used to link the date a blog entry was created to the full node.
- `$submitted`: The full themed submission information (for example, "Submitted by Wiarton Willie on 2 February 2009—9:46 am"). This information can be broken into the variable `$date` and the user data (see the last point in this list).
- `$date`: The formatted creation date. This variable uses the Drupal "short" date setting. You can configure formatting of the date by navigating to Administer, Site configuration, Date and time. To display a custom-formatted date, you may use the variable `$created` and the Drupal function `format_date()`.
- User data: `$picture` (the author's profile photo), `$name` (username of node author), and `$uid` (the author's ID).

In this chapter, you will also learn how to replace these variables with smaller units of information. The variable `$title` is available in the node template as well and should be output for lists of nodes; however, you may need to adjust your templates to distinguish between the title displayed in the page template and the title displayed in the node template (especially on pages that display lists of content).

In addition to the variables that you print to the page and are visible to the Web site visitor, many other variables contain information about the node that may help you to format the page appropriately. These variables can be classified into several categories.

Additional Information about the Content. These variables contain information about the node that is being displayed. They include variables that are relevant to a single node display page as well as variables that are relevant to a page containing a list of teasers to several different nodes.

- $type: The content type of the node (for example, story, page, blog, and custom content types).

- $teaser: The variable that announces Drupal is requesting the "teaser" view for the content. When the page is displayed in full, the related variable $page returns true.

- $readmore: If the teaser content of the node does not contain the full content, a "read more" link is displayed.

- $zebra: Displays either "even" or "odd"; to be used for zebra striping in teaser listings.

- $id: Position of the node within a list of nodes (for example, on the front page). This variable is incremented each time a node is output.

- $node: The full array containing all data for the node. This variable may contain "unsafe" data and should be used with caution.

Information about the Site Visitor. These variables are related not to the content, but rather to the visitor who is viewing the content. They can be useful when you are customizing the options for authenticated users and administrators.

- $logged_in: Returns true when the current user is a logged-in member.

- $is_admin: Returns true when the current user is an administrator.

Information about the Comments Related to This Node. These variables are related to the comments for this node, including whether comments are enabled for this node.

- $comment: Indicates whether comments are enabled for this node.

- $comment_count: Number of comments for this node.

Status of This Content. These variables are related to the "Publishing options" for a given node.

- $promote: Identifies whether this node should be displayed on the front page. ($is_front allows you to check whether the page being displayed is the front page.)
- $sticky: Identifies whether this node ought to be displayed at the top of lists of content.
- $status: Identifies whether this page is "published."

A full list of these variables is available from http://api.drupal.org/api/ file/modules/node/node.tpl.php/6. You may also refer to the default node template file within your own Drupal system files. The default template can be found within your Drupal core files at modules/node/node.tpl.php.

The Template File node.tpl.php

Compared to a page template with a full HTML framework for multiple regions and headers, the default node template contains very little markup. The default node template is shown in this section. It includes the default CSS classes that can be used to provide sophisticated and customized context-sensitive designs. Two items of note: If the node being displayed is in "teaser" mode, the node title links to the full page of content. The second item to note is that the page template is also configured to display a title. For example, when the Blog module is enabled, an additional title, "Blogs," appears on example.com/blog. The second title is part of the page template and is set by the module Blog. Note: The editing tabs for a node are actually configured within the page template with the variable $tabs.

```
<div id="node-<?php print $node->nid; ?>" class="node
<?php if ($sticky) { print ' sticky'; } ?>
    <?php if (!$status) { print ' node-unpublished'; } ?> clear-block">
<?php print $picture ?>
<?php if (!$page) { ?>
  <h2><a href="<?php print $node_url ?>" title="
  <?php print $title ?>"><?php print $title ?></a></h2>
```

```
<?php } ?>
  <div class="meta">
  <?php if ($submitted) { ?>
    <span class="submitted"><?php print $submitted ?></span>
  <?php } ?>
  <?php if ($terms) { ?>
    <div class="terms terms-inline"><?php print $terms ?></div>
  <?php } ?>
  </div>
  <div class="content">
    <?php print $content ?>
    <!-- Later in this chapter you will break this into individual fields with the
variable $node -->
  </div>
  <?php print $links; ?>
</div>
```

Gaining More Control Than $content Provides

The variable $content contains both the field labels and the content values for all display information for each content type. The variable $content comes prepackaged, so you cannot use it if you want to insert markup around individual content fields or add explanatory text between fields. To accomplish these kinds of customizations, you must use the variable $node instead. The variable $node is an object containing all node-related data for the node you are viewing. It includes everything from the node ID to the categories for the node. By carefully selecting the right part of the variable $node, you may use any of this information in your template.

Deciphering the Object $node

There are two ways to view the contents of $node. If you have the Devel module installed and enabled, you may use the function dsm() to create an easy-to-read display of the information (see Figure 5.1). More information on the Devel module is available in Chapter 2. In your node template file (node.tpl.php), add the following snippet:

```
<?php dsm($node); ?>
```

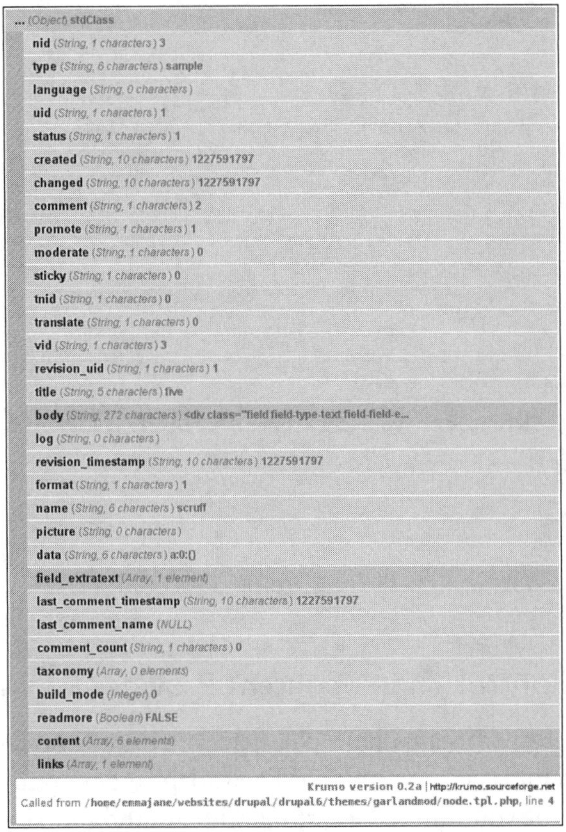

FIGURE 5.1 The node object displayed with the Devel module function dsm.

If you do not have the Devel module enabled, you may use the PHP function print_r instead with the following snippet:

```
<pre>
<?php print_r($node); ?>
</pre>
```

Using the HTML tags <pre> helps you to see each of the indents that represent the structure of the object (Figure 5.2). You may also choose to print the variable without the <pre> tags and view the source of the rendered Web page to see the indents (Figure 5.3).

```
        [log] =>
        [revision_timestamp] => 1227591797
        [format] => 1
        [name] => scruff
        [picture] =>
        [data] => a:0:{}
        [field_extratext] => Array
            (
                [0] => Array
                    (
                        [value] => seven, eight
                        [format] => 2
                        [safe] =>
    seven, eight


                        [view] =>
    seven, eight


                    )

            )

        [last_comment_timestamp] => 1227591797
        [last_comment_name] =>
        [comment_count] => 0
        [taxonomy] => Array
            (
            )
```

FIGURE 5.2 The sample output from the node object displayed with the PHP function `print_r`.

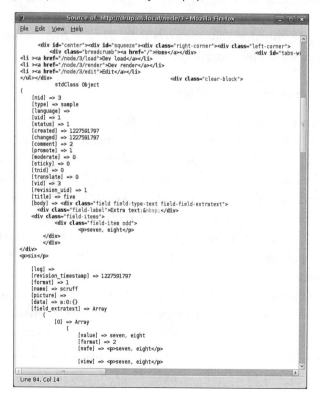

FIGURE 5.3 The source of a printed node object in a rendered Web page.

Each of these items can be accessed by referencing $node->object_property.
For example, if you wanted to print the node ID (nid) content type (type) to the
page, you would include the following snippet in your node template file:

```php
<?php print $node->nid; ?>
<?php print $node->type; ?>
```

This node object contains four subsections:

- body: contains the same data as the variable $content
- field_extratext: a custom field added for this content type
- content: a full listing of the data to be printed to the page as well as formatting instructions
- links: the contents of the variable $links separated into its component parts

Within these subsections, the body contains text and the last three subsections contain
arrays.

This content type contains only one extra field. Thus, if five fields were added to the
content type, there would be a total of eight subsections in the node object.

Accessing Content in the $node Object

Content is contained in multiple places within the node object. For example, the body
field for the node can be accessed from the variable as follows: $node->body and
$node->content['body']['#value']. It makes sense to use the shortest variable
name to access the content you need; however, if you need content that is buried deep
within the node object, it can be a frustrating task to find the right variable name if
you are not comfortable with complex array structures. To show you how to retrieve
information from any point in the node object, the next example retrieves the body
field from the pit of despair ($node->content['body']['#value']). Figure 5.4
shows the expanded array for the content subsection of the node object for the content
type story. This is the default content type story with no additional fields added. The
code is repeated below Figure 5.4 for a clearer view of the contents.

The array contains the following code:

```
content (Array, 5 elements)
    body (Array, 5 elements)
        #weight (Integer) 0
```

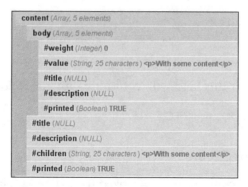

FIGURE 5.4 The dsm printout of the node object expanded to show the content array.

```
    #value (String, 25 characters ) <p>With some content</p>

    #title (NULL)

    #description (NULL)

    #printed (Boolean) TRUE

#title (NULL)

#description (NULL)

#children (String, 25 characters ) <p>With some content</p>

#printed (Boolean) TRUE
```

To access the contents of the body field, you would start with the node object and then walk through each of the nested arrays to build the variable: `$node->content['body']['#value']`.

> **Markup does not always mean sanitized data**
> Although the data was entered without HTML in the example, paragraph tags do appear around the body contents. In this case, these tags indicate that the data has been filtered and is sanitized. In contrast, if the original data contained HTML markup, there would be no way of knowing this was true from merely looking at the contents of the node object.

To access information for custom fields in CCK content types, you can use the content variable (shown above). Much of the same information also appears as a subsection of the node object (see Figure 5.4). The shortcut reveals the content of the field, but not the label. If you need to display the label text as well, you will need to use the contents of the array `$node->content`. For example, to print the contents of the field "Extra text," you could use either of the following variables:

```
$node->field_extratext[0]['safe']
$node->content['field_extratext']['field']['items'][0]['#item']['safe']
```

To access the label for this field, you could use only the following variable:

```
$node->content['field_extratext']['field']['#title']
```

Sanitized Data Is More Secure

The variable $content contains only sanitized data. The variable $node, by contrast, contains a mixture of both sanitized data and raw data. When you use the contents of the node object in your template files, you must ensure that you are using a sanitized version of the data, or else you must clean the data yourself. You can employ the same technique to change the filter that is used for each content field.

Two Drupal functions can be used to sanitize data: check_plain and check_ markup. The first function converts a string of text to plain text. It is appropriate for headings, labels, and fields that are text-only (for example, a person's real name or a phone number). To use this function in your template file, insert the following PHP snippet:

```
<?php print check_plain($text); ?>
```

Of course, you would replace the variable $text with the appropriate variable for your project.

The second Drupal function, check_markup, allows you to apply the appropriate filter to your data field. You may obtain the appropriate filter setting from the array that contains the contents of the field. For example, the following code snippet shows that the field "Extra text" is currently using the filter "2." In this case, the value "2" represents full HTML—your site may have different filters in use.

```
field_extratext (Array, 1 element)
    (Array, 4 elements)
        value (String, 12 characters ) seven, eight
        format (String, 1 characters ) 2
        safe (String, 20 characters ) <p>seven, eight</p>
        view (String, 20 characters ) <p>seven, eight</p>
```

If you wanted to refilter the "Extra text" field with a different filter, you would use the following snippet:

```
check_markup($node->field_extratext[0]['value'], 3, TRUE)
```

The constant TRUE performs an extra test within the function check_markup to ensure that the user viewing the data has sufficient permissions to see the data.

If you were to insert these variables into your template files, matters could get very messy very quickly. In the next section you will learn how to keep your templates neat and tidy!

Node Template Variables

In the last section you learned how to dissect the node object into useful components. You may have noticed that performing this task makes a mess of your node template file. For content types with a lot of fields, it becomes much more difficult to see what is happening in the template when you follow this path. To improve the legibility of the template file, you can create new variables using the node preprocess function in the file template.php.

Creating New Variables

To clean up your node template files, you can create new variables for use in these template files instead of having to dig into the node object as described in the previous section. The techniques you used in that section are applicable here as well, except that this time you will put the contents into a shorter variable name. For this method you will need to adjust the file template.php and the corresponding node template file. If you are working with individual content types, the node template file will have the file name node-contenttype.tpl.php.

In Chapter 4, you learned how to use preprocess functions to tell Drupal to use new page template files based on certain conditions. (These were the "garage blueprints.") In this example, you will use a similar technique, except that this time you will use the function THEMENAME_preprocess_node instead of THEMENAME_preprocess_page. Within the function, two restrictions must be taken into account:

- The content types use specific fields.
- If the field is not set for a content type and you try to work with it, an error message will be displayed to the user.

For this reason, you must check which content type you are working with before you create your new variables. In this example, the theme is named `bolg`; the content type is named `sample`; and the content field uses the machine name `field_extratext`. The function is passed a list of all variables currently set for the node template file. In the snippet below you will add a new variable that contains your node content.

```
function bolg_preprocess_node(&$variables) {
    $node = $variables['node'];
    if ($node->type == "sample") {
        $variables['extratext'] = $node->field_extratext[0]['safe'];
    }
}
```

This example uses a shortcut to make the new variable accessible to the template file. Instead of setting a variable on its own and then pushing it into the array of template variables, this function sets the value of `$variables['extratext']`. The variables in the node template files are built from this array. By setting the variable `$variables['extratext']` in the preprocess function, you ensure that a new variable named `$extratext` will automatically become available in the node template file. If you have several variables to set for each content type, you may add them all through the preprocess function.

This variable will appear only for nodes with the content type "sample." You may create a unique template file `node-sample.tpl.php` to contain only relevant variables. You should always check whether a variable is set before trying to print it within your template file. This snippet could be inserted into either the file `node.tpl.php` or the file `node-sample.tpl.php`:

```
<?php if (! empty($extratext)) { ?>
    <span class="extratext"><?php print $extratext; ?></span>
<?php } ?>
```

This technique is appropriate if you want to control the markup around each of the content fields in the node-related template files.

Changing the Defaults

If you have a lot of different content types, you may not want to maintain individual template files for each content type. In this case you may want to reset the variable $content instead of creating individual variables that contain each data field. To replace the contents of a variable that is defined by Drupal or by contributed modules, you need simply match the variable name. For example, if you wanted to insert the example from the previous section into the variable $content, you would use the following snippet of code:

```
function bolg_preprocess_node(&$variables) {
    $node = $variables['node'];
    if ($node->type == "sample") {
        $variables['content'] = "<span class='extratext'>";
        $variables['content'] .= $node->field_extratext[0]['safe'];
        $variables['content'] .= "</span>";
    }
}
```

This code will completely replace the contents of the variable $content. If you plan to use this technique, you must be careful to include all fields in the new content variable. You may use this revised content variable in the template file node.tpl.php. For pages displaying nodes of the content type "sample," the custom variable $content will be used; for all other pages, the default content variable will be used.

Node Links

Replacing default variables with new content is not limited to the content variable: You may, in fact, replace the contents of any of the node template variables described in the first section of this chapter—including the list of node links. The variable $links contains a formatted list of links relevant to the node of content. This list may include "Add a new comment," "username's blog," and "Read more."

You could replace these links completely by overwriting the variable in the preprocess function. If you prefer to alter only a few items in the list, there are several steps you will need to complete:

1. Set up a preprocess function to alter the node template variable $links.

2. Copy the links array from the node object ($node->links).

3. Make the necessary changes to the array of unformatted links.

4. Pass the new array through the theming function theme('links') to reformat the new list.

5. Reset the node template variable $links with the newly formatted list of links.

6. Use the new list of links in your node template with the variable $links. You may need to clear the theme registry to see your changes.

The array of unformatted links uses the following structure:

```
Array (
    [comment_add] => Array (
        [title] => Add new comment
        [href] => comment/reply/3
        [attributes] => Array (
            [title] => Add a new comment to this page.
        )
            [fragment] => comment-form
    )
)
```

For example, if you wanted to add a new link to the list of links, you could do so by inserting the following PHP snippet in the file template.php. In this example, a link to the front page is added with the visible text of "ET Phone Home" and a title attribute (tool tip) of "ET wants to go home now, please."

```
function bolg_preprocess_node(&$variables) {
    $links = $variables['node']->links;
    $links['home'] = Array(
        "title" => "ET Phone Home",
        "href" => "<front>",
        "attributes" => Array (
                "title" => "ET wants to go home now, please."
        )
```

```
    );
  $variables['links'] = theme('links', $links, array('class' => 'links'));
}
```

To remove a link from the list of links, you need to know the key for the list item. For example, the key in the previous PHP snippet is home. The key for the sample array variable is comment_add. To unset this link item, use the following PHP snippet in the node preprocess function:

```
unset($variables['node']->links['comment_add']);
```

In this case, it makes sense to unset the variable because it is the themed list of links that is printed to the template file, not the variable itself.

Using the techniques described in this chapter, you now have the ability to modify any node template variable and to create new ones as necessary.

Pages and Teasers

So far in this chapter, you have been learning how to theme a full node of content. On summary pages, such as the default front page, Drupal presents a list of content "teasers." These snippets can also be customized in a number of ways. The techniques described in this section are applicable to the summary pages provided by Drupal. Additional information on styling lists of content with the Views module is presented later in this chapter.

Administrative Control of the Default Settings

The front page of your Web site will, by default, display the first 600 characters for the 10 most recent stories. This list contains any items that have been marked "Published to front page" in the "Publishing options" section of the content editing screen. By default, nodes of the content type "story" are promoted to the front page. To adjust the default publishing settings, follow these steps for each content type:

1. Navigate to Administer, Content management, Content types.
2. Select the "edit" link next to the content type you would like to adjust.
3. Scroll down to the "Workflow settings."
4. Select the check box next to "Promoted to front page."
5. Scroll to the bottom of the Web page and select "Save content type."

This change will alter the default setting for new nodes of this content type; it does not affect existing content.

Now that the correct content types appear on the front page of the site, you can adjust the default settings for teasers. From the Drupal administration area, select which items should appear on the summary page and set the length of the teaser (in characters):

1. Navigate to Administer, Content management, Post settings.
2. Adjust the "Number of posts on main page."
3. Adjust the "Length of trimmed posts" to the length (in characters). To use the full text instead of an abbreviated teaser, select "Unlimited" from the drop-down list. You can also adjust this setting on a per-story basis by using the "Split summary at cursor" when creating and editing content.
4. Scroll to the bottom of the Web page and select "Save configuration."

These changes will not affect existing content. If you have adjusted the length of the teaser, you will need to edit and re-save each of the pages appearing on the front page of your Web site to enable the new teaser length.

A Teaser Is Not a Summary

A "summary" is typically a concise synopsis of a whole report, document, or event. In contrast, a "teaser" is a shorter version of the content used to entice you to "read more." Drupal has two ways of preparing these shortened node displays. By default, Drupal creates a "teaser" of each node based on the number of characters in the Post settings. You can override these settings by adding the HTML comment `<!-- break -->` at the point where you want to divide the teaser from the whole content.

The second technique is to create a true summary of your content using the teaser attributes and a custom theme. Figure 5.5 shows the content editing form before "splitting" the node into a "summary" and the full node. Figure 5.6 shows the content editing form after making this split. From a technical point of view, this "Split summary at cursor" operation merely adds the HTML comment break that will override the default settings for the display of content "teasers" as described in the previous paragraph; however, using the button to "Split summary at cursor" reveals a second option: Show summary in full view. This check box allows you to hide or reveal the summary at the top of your node.

When the summary is displayed, it appears as part of the full article and is not visually distinguishable from the main content. Assigning a unique style to the summary

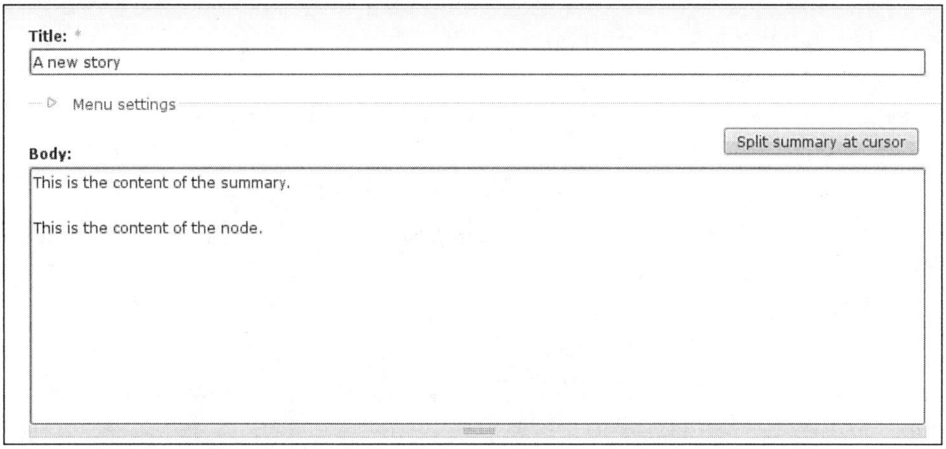

FIGURE 5.5 Before splitting the node editing form into a "summary" and a full node body.

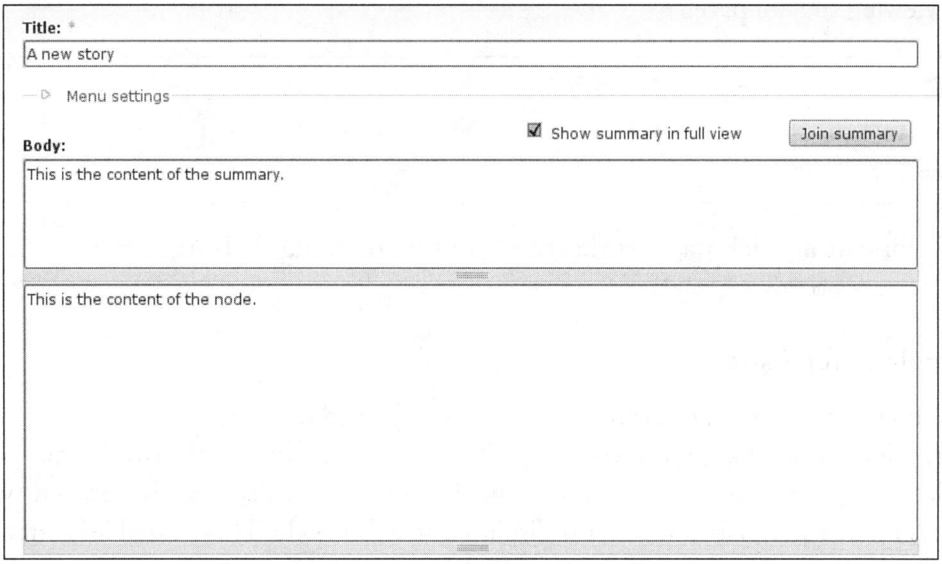

FIGURE 5.6 After splitting the node into the summary (above) and a full node body (below).

on the full node display requires a little bit of Drupal preprocessing acrobatics. Assuming your theme's name is "bolg," add the following code to your preprocess node function in the file `template.php`. You may add this snippet to the beginning or the end of the function if it exists already.

```
function bolg_preprocess_node(&$variables) {
    if ($variables['page'] === TRUE) {
    // Reload the cached node to find the location of <!--break-->
        $node = node_load($variables['nid']);
        if (strpos($node->body, '<!--break-->') == 0) {
            $variables['styled_summary'] = check_markup($node->teaser, $node->format,
FALSE);
        } else {
            $variables['styled_summary'] = FALSE;
        }// End of check for <!-- break -->
    } // End of test for 'is this a page?'
} // End of function bolg_preprocess_node
```

In your node template, you may now use the variable $styled_summary when you are viewing the full page.

```
<?php if ($page) { ?>
    <div class="summary"><?php print $styled_summary; ?></div>
<?php } ?>
```

This formatting trick was first described on the following Web page: http://www.disobey.com/node/1833.

Templates for Teasers

Theming for both full nodes and node teasers is defined in the node template file (and in the file template.php if you are using preprocess functions). Two magic node variables, $page and $teaser, are available to help you distinguish between what shows up in a summary and what is displayed in a full node. These variables contain a Boolean value, rather than content to be displayed. A Boolean variable is a special kind of variable—it may contain only one of two values, either a "positive" or a "negative" value. If the current display ought to be a "teaser," the variable $teaser will return 1 or true and the variable $page will return nothing, 0, or false. Your conditional statement may test against any of these values. as a Boolean value can be all of these values: 1 and true OR nothing, 0, and false. You can also use a simple "existence" test by placing only the name of the variable inside the test statement. The opposite strategy is to use an exclamation mark to test if the variable does *not* exist. Boolean variables are magical that way.

Within your node template file, you must select the elements you want to display or hide for teasers and full nodes. To do so, add conditional statements that hide or display each of the variables and associated HTML markup. For example, the Garland theme provides a linked version of the node title when not displaying a full node. The snippet is as follows:

```php
<?php if (! $page) { ?>
  <h2><a href="<?php print $node_url ?>" title="<?php print $title ?>">
  <?php print $title ?>
  </a></h2>
<?php } ?>
```

This technique works for small customizations within the template file; however, you can also separate the markup completely for the teaser and full views of your content. To enforce this separation, simply split your template file into two parts, using a conditional statement to separate the two sections. For example, in the following template, the display for the "teaser" appears at the top of the template file and the display for the "full node" view is found at the bottom of the template file. Only the relevant part of the file is displayed.

```php
<?php if ($teaser) { ?>
    <!-- HTML and variables for the teaser go here -->
<?php } else { ?>
    <!-- full node template goes here -->
<?php } ?>
```

Images

Several different Drupal modules allow you to integrate images into your Web site. Which module is most appropriate depends on *how* you want to integrate images into your Web site.

If you want to insert an image occasionally and do not want to install image-related modules, you may want to use an offsite hosting service, such as Flickr, to house your images.

Choosing Your Visuals

Each of the techniques for image integration is described later in this chapter. To whet your appetite for using visuals, however, this section begins with a small gallery demonstrating the use of several image modules.

Image Module

Figure 5.7 and Figure 5.8 show how the Image module can be integrated into your Web site—including images embedded into node, a "Random Image" block, and an Image Gallery.

FIGURE 5.7 Images appear in the body of the node (left) and as a Random Image block (right).

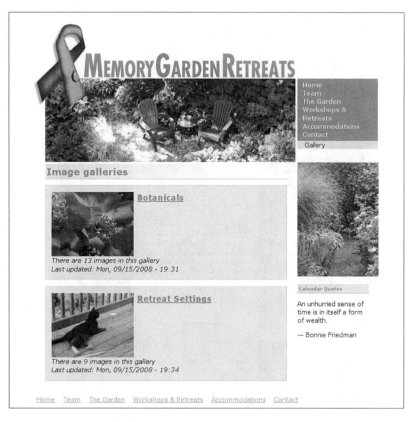

FIGURE 5.8 Images are also available from an image gallery (the Random Image block also appears on the right).

CCK, ImageField, and Image Cache Modules

CCK, ImageField, and Image Cache help you keep your Web site looking consistent. The Toilet Birthdays Web site (Figure 5.9) accepts two images per node—a photo of a toilet and a photo of a person. Different sizes are used for the two images.

Make pictures of words

It can be frustrating to settle for the standard set of installed fonts for headings and titles in Drupal. It is now possible to make image-based headings on the fly. The module Textimage allows you to create images using the GD2 and Freetype libraries. These pictures of words can be used as theme objects, headings, and countless other possibilities. Your new images may have a background, have a background image, or be transparent. There is also limited support for CCK fields. The project page for the Textimage module can be found at `http://drupal.org/project/textimage`.

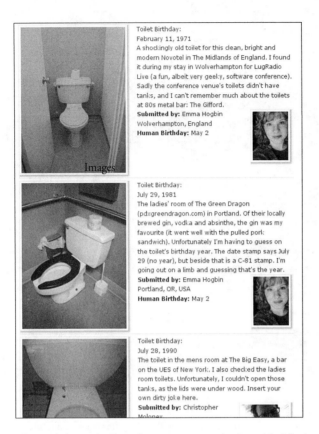

FIGURE 5.9 The Toilet Birthday Web site enforces a common look and feel for images with CCK, Image-Field, and Image Cache.

Images Hosted Offsite

If you want to insert an image occasionally and do not want to install image-related modules, you can use an offsite hosting service, such as Flickr, to house your images. Flickr encourages you to display images from their hosting service in your site. It has two requirements: (1) You must have permission to include the photo in your own work (whether it is your own photo or an image that is available for use under a Creative Commons license); and (2) you must link the photo back to Flickr's Web site.

If you have a rich text editor (such as TinyMCE) installed, you will be able to drag images from Flickr into the text editing window on your own Web site and the image will automatically be linked back to Flickr. Handy and easy, yes?

To provide random images or to include a few of your most recent images, Flickr requires you to create a JavaScript "badge." Log into your Flickr account and navigate to `http://www.flickr.com/badge.gne`. You will then be asked a series of questions to customize your Flickr badge. At the end of this process, you will receive a JavaScript snippet. In your Drupal Web site, perform the following steps:

1. Navigate to Administer, Site building, Blocks.
2. Select "Add block."
3. Add a block description and paste the JavaScript snippet from Flickr into the body of your new block. Change the "Input format" to "Full HTML."
4. Scroll to the bottom of the screen and select "Save block." You will be returned to the Block summary page.
5. Place your new block into the appropriate region. Scroll to the bottom of the screen and select "Save blocks."

If you prefer to host your images offsite, but you want to include a lot of them in your Web site, you should consider using the CCK-related module, Embedded Imagefield. This module allows you to integrate images from third-party services as a CCK field, and it creates links back to the hosting providers as part of the module. The project page for this module is `http://drupal.org/project/emfield`.

Image Module

The Image module is the oldest image-related modules in Drupal. It has been an integral part of many "I can't believe it's Drupal" Web sites, including the online arts community at `http://www.terminus1525.ca`. This module allows users to upload images to Drupal. Images of predefined sizes are automatically created and can be integrated into the site. Specifically, images can be posted individually, included in stories, and grouped into galleries using taxonomy terms. To include a single image per node, users may also use the module Image Attach (which is shipped along with the Image module). A bulk import tool is also provided.

The project page for the Image module is `http://drupal.org/project/image`. Installation instructions are included in Appendix A of this book. Once the module is installed, you will need to enable the appropriate permissions for module-related functions by navigating to Administer, User management, Permissions.

> **Images inside your content**
> The Image module can be integrated with the Image Assist module, thereby allowing users to insert inline images into their posts. Additional information is provided in Chapter 6, which covers theming forms.

When the Image module is enabled, a new content type, "Image," becomes available to users with appropriate permissions. Figure 5.10 shows the form to upload a new image. As with any other content type, you may find this form by navigating to the "Create content" item on the navigation menu (typically displayed as a block).

Default sizes are provided for thumbnails and preview images. You may configure these defaults by navigating to Administer, Site configuration, Images (Figure 5.11). If you change the default image sizes, they will be resized on demand (thereby providing for a distributed server load instead of representing a single hit to the server).

FIGURE 5.10 Uploading a new image with the Image module.

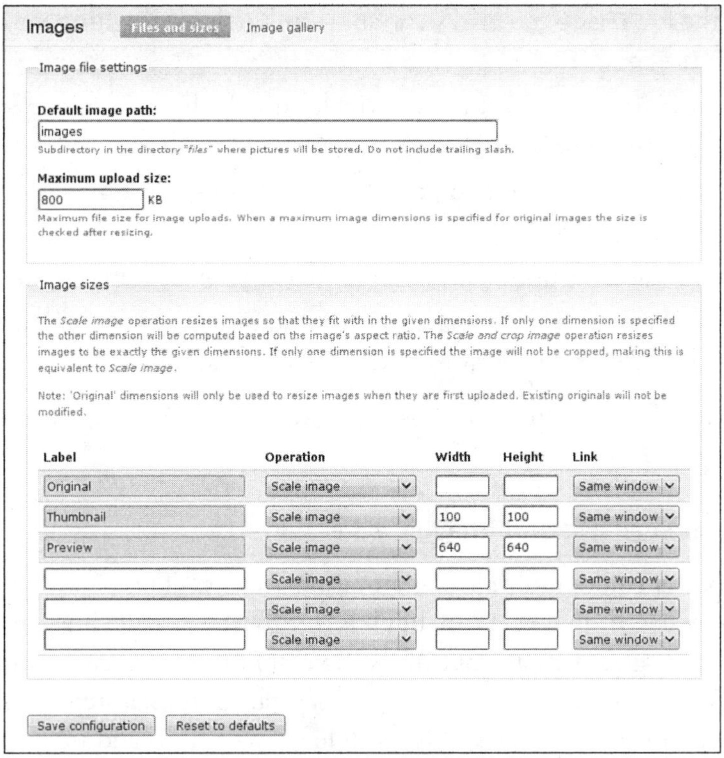

FIGURE 5.11 Configuring the default image sizes for the Image module.

Galleries

You may create both galleries and subgalleries with the image module-related Gallery module. After enabling the Gallery module, navigate to Administer, Content management, Image galleries. Select "Add gallery" and complete the form (including the "Parent" item to distinguish main galleries from subgalleries).

Two theming functions are available for galleries. At the time of this writing, a template file was not available, however. Thus, to theme the gallery, you must copy the relevant function into your theme's `template.php` file and adjust the properties as necessary to suit your needs.

1. In your file system, navigate to your modules directory where the Image module is stored.

2. Navigate to the folder `image/contrib/image_gallery`.

3. Open the file `image_gallery.module` and look for the function `theme_image_gallery`.

4. Copy the contents of this function (including the line `function theme_image_gallery`) to your theme's `template.php` file.

5. Alter the name of the function to `YOURTHEMENAME_image_gallery` (from `theme_image_gallery`).

6. Adjust the contents of this function to match your desired output.

7. Clear the theme registry by navigating to Administer, Site configuration, Performance. Scroll to the bottom of the Web page and click "Clear cached data."

Repeat these steps for the function `theme_image_gallery_img` in the file `image_gallery.module`.

CCK Images: ImageField and Image Cache

"With great power comes multiple configuration screens." This is not quite the advice that Peter Parker gets from Uncle Ben, but it is true for the module ImageField. Whereas the Image module gives you an "out of the box" solution for creating image galleries, ImageField gives you great power but requires several additional steps to configure that functionality. As its name implies, this module allows you to add image upload capabilities to any content type. It requires the modules CCK, FileField, and ImageAPI.

Once the ImageField module has been installed, you must create a new content type for "images." You may also extend an existing content type to include one or more image fields. The content type may use as many fields as are relevant for your Web site. For example, you may want to include fields for the photographer's name and the distribution license. Information on creating custom content types with the CCK module can be found in Chapter 2; information on theming custom content types appeared earlier in this chapter. You will use the Themer Info to identify the correct display image in each instance of your content. Once you have the new content type in hand and have uploaded a few images, you are ready to create galleries using the Views module. This module is covered in the next section.

In addition to the ImageField module, you will need to install the Image Cache module (`http://drupal.org/project/imagecache`). This module allows you to resize images. Although it is similar to the Image module described earlier in this chapter, Image Cache gives you much greater control over the derivative images it creates. For example, you may resize and crop images to create square thumbnails! The online documentation for the Image Cache module is excellent and is kept up-to-date at `http://drupal.org/node/163561`.

Making Lists of Content with Views

Now that you have learned how to customize individual nodes, it is time to customize the entry points into those nodes. You can use the Views module to create lists of nodes that may be displayed as either a block or a page. Chapter 2 introduced the procedure for creating a basic view. If you are not familiar with the module Views, you may want to review the information in Chapter 2 before proceeding with the rest of this chapter.

Views are available as blocks that can be placed into a region, as full pages, and as RSS feeds. In this section, you will learn how to alter the "guts" of these views.

The Views module offers six default lists of content:

- `archive`: Displays a list of months that link to content for that month.
- `comments_recent`: Contains a block and a page to list recent comments. The block will automatically link to the page, which displays the comment body as well as a link to the node.
- `frontpage`: Emulates the default Drupal front page. You may set the default home page path to this view to make it your front page.
- `glossary`: Lists all content, organized in alphabetical order.
- `taxonomy_term`: Emulates the Drupal core's handling of taxonomy/term. It also emulates Views 1's handling by having two possible feeds.
- `tracker`: Shows all new activity on the system.

You may choose to customize these default views, or you may decide to create your own view from scratch. Once your view is created, you may theme it by using a selection of appropriately named template files.

Template Files

Default templates are provided for each view that you have created from scratch or customized from the default views. A sample template file is available within the Views administration area for each view. These "files," which are generated on the fly, contain sample markup as well as the full list of variable names you may use in each template file for each view. To use them, you must copy and paste the sample templates into an actual file in your theme's directory.

To view these files, complete the following steps:

1. Navigate to the administration area for a specific view. For example, follow the path Administer, Site building, Views, edit Archive.

2. Under the Basic Settings, click "Theme: Information." This will reveal a series of template files in three categories: Display output, Style output, and Row style output (Figure 5.12).

The three types of template files for the archive views—Display output, Style output, and Row style output—are common to all views, although some differences in the contents of the sample templates may exist depending on the view. Other views provide additional template file suggestions. Each of the three template categories shown in Figure 5.12 is responsible for theming different parts of the view output:

- Display output: Responsible for the framework of the view, including the header, footer, rows, empty, pager, and feed icon. To alter all views, use the template file `views-view.tpl.php` in your theme.

- Style output: Responsible for the heading and layout of rows. To alter these variables for all views, use the template file `views-view-unformatted.tpl.php` in your theme.

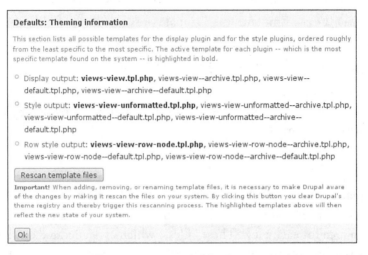

Defaults: Theming information

This section lists all possible templates for the display plugin and for the style plugins, ordered roughly from the least specific to the most specific. The active template for each plugin -- which is the most specific template found on the system -- is highlighted in bold.

○ Display output: **views-view.tpl.php**, views-view--archive.tpl.php, views-view--default.tpl.php, views-view--archive--default.tpl.php

○ Style output: **views-view-unformatted.tpl.php**, views-view-unformatted--archive.tpl.php, views-view-unformatted--default.tpl.php, views-view-unformatted--archive--default.tpl.php

○ Row style output: **views-view-row-node.tpl.php**, views-view-row-node--archive.tpl.php, views-view-row-node--default.tpl.php, views-view-row-node--archive--default.tpl.php

[Rescan template files]

Important! When adding, removing, or renaming template files, it is necessary to make Drupal aware of the changes by making it rescan the files on your system. By clicking this button you clear Drupal's theme registry and thereby trigger this rescanning process. The highlighted templates above will then reflect the new state of your system.

[Ok]

FIGURE 5.12 Suggested template file names are provided for three levels of theming: Display, Style, and Row.

- Row style output: Responsible for the node object. You may use one of the suggested file names, or you may use a node template file to theme the output. For example, you may access the file `node-view-VIEWNAME.tpl.php` in your theme's directory. Check the suggested template file for more information on the most appropriate template file to use for your view.

You will also have a separate template file for each display field. For example, the default view `comments_recent` contains two additional template categories:

- Field Comment: Title (ID: subject)
- Field Comment: Post date (ID: timestamp)

To use template files provided by the Views module, follow these steps:

1. Determine the output you would like to change.
2. Click the name of output to reveal the contents of the default template (Figure 5.13). Copy the contents of the default template that is displayed within the Views administration area.
3. Return to the list of outputs by clicking the link "theming information."
4. Choose the most specific file name that is appropriate for your theming needs.
5. Create a new file in your theme's directory that matches this file name. You may place this file in a subdirectory within your theme's directory.
6. Paste the contents of the sample template provided by the Views Web interface template into your new template file in your theme directory. Customize the PHP and HTML output to suit your needs.

New Variables, with Preprocess Functions

Once you have created the new template file, you may also create new variables with the preprocess function in the file `template.php`. For example, if your theme is named `bolg` and your view is named `All_Goblins`, and you want to create new variables for the template file `views-view.tpl.php`, you could create new variables by placing the following function into your theme's `template.php` file:

```
function bolg_preprocess_views_view__All_Goblins (&$variables) {
    $variables['orcs'] = "<big>goblin</big>";
}
```

```php
<?php
// $Id: views-view.tpl.php,v 1.9 2008/04/16 18:50:49 merlinofchaos Exp $
/**
 * @file views-view.tpl.php
 * Main view template
 *
 * Variables available:
 * - $header: The view header
 * - $footer: The view footer
 * - $rows: The results of the view query, if any
 * - $empty: The empty text to display if the view is empty
 * - $pager: The pager next/prev links to display, if any
 * - $exposed: Exposed widget form/info to display
 * - $feed_icon: Feed icon to display, if any
 * - $more: A link to view more, if any
 * - $admin_links: A rendered list of administrative links
 * - $admin_links_raw: A list of administrative links suitable for theme('links')
 *
 * @ingroup views_templates
 */
?>
<div class="view view-<?php print $css_name; ?> view-id-<?php print $name; ?> view-
  <?php if ($admin_links): ?>
    <div class="views-admin-links views-hide">
      <?php print $admin_links; ?>
    </div>
  <?php endif; ?>
  <?php if ($header): ?>
    <div class="view-header">
      <?php print $header; ?>
    </div>
  <?php endif; ?>

  <?php if ($exposed): ?>
    <div class="view-filters">
      <?php print $exposed; ?>
    </div>
```

FIGURE 5.13 The contents of the default template for Display output.

Note that two underscores appear between `views_view` and the view name, `All_Goblins`.

If you wanted to create a new variable for all views, you would use this simplified function name with the same code snippet as the previous example:

```php
function bolg_preprocess_views_view (&$variables) {
    $variables['orcs'] = "<big>goblin</big>";
}
```

This variable will now be available to you in the relevant template file. In the preceding example, two different preprocess functions were used. The first, `bolg_preprocess_views_view__All_Goblins`, enables the variable in the template file `views-view--All_Goblins.tpl.php`. The second, `bolg_preprocess_views_view`, enables the variable in the template file `views-view.tpl.php`. There is no inheritance from a general template file to a more specific template file name. The variables created in the preprocess function only apply to the function's matching template file. You must clear your theme registry by clearing the cache in Drupal's administration area before the new variables will be available in your template files.

Summary

Thar she blows! It's the end of the pirate chapter, matey! With the skills learned in this chapter, you are now able to theme nodes using template files, preprocess functions, and the Views module. More specifically, this chapter focused on the following tasks:

- Customizing the template files for generic nodes
- Creating new template files for each content type in a Web site
- Displaying individual fields from a content type that has been extended with CCK
- Customizing the summary and full node display
- Choosing between the Image module and the ImageField module for use on a Web site
- Creating galleries with the Image module
- Customizing the output from the Views module
- Using preprocess functions to create new variables for your Views templates

In the next chapter you will learn how to customize the forms that are used to edit content on your Web site.

Chapter 6

Customizing the Content-Editing Forms

Matt Haughey (MetaFilter) once said, "Forms are tedious, confusing, often poorly designed, and most people equate their use with things like paying taxes." In this chapter, you will learn how to alter Drupal's forms so that their purpose is obvious and they are easy to use. Most Drupal themes focus their styles and manipulations on the customization of content, not input forms. As a themer, you may have created a page template and perhaps individual node templates for each of your content types. Forms are often overlooked by themers because the code seems complicated and the forms are "good enough" that the hassle of learning how to code them does not seem to be worth the trouble. This chapter will help transform your forms from "good enough" to "elegant and easy to use."

The chapter begins with a gentle introduction to Web forms. You will learn what happens behind the scenes when Drupal processes a form. From here you will build your own input forms using the Content Creation Kit (CCK) module. Next you will learn how to apply some basic form enhancements using only Cascading Style Sheets (CSS). Several contributed "helper" modules are outlined in this part of the chapter that you may want to download and install. You will learn how to add rich text editing so that your authors may easily **bold** and *italicize* their content (and add links to new pages and images, too).

In the last half of the chapter, you will explore how to take complete control of content editing forms. The techniques you learn in this part of the chapter can also be applied to other Drupal forms (including the contact form and login forms). You will learn how to alter form elements, including how to change text labels and modify the size of input fields, and how to hide form fields from unauthorized users. The chapter will also suggest strategies for dealing with very long forms. Finally, you will learn how to facilitate access to content editing screens by adding helper links to views and blocks.

Web Forms

Throughout this chapter, you will learn how to alter the structure and the visual design of forms. To understand both the limitations of these techniques and the many possibilities that are available to you, it is important to understand how Drupal prepares, displays, and processes its Web forms. When you use a module to build a form, more options become available than would be feasible if you used only the theme layer. From the module point of view, Drupal forms are created as follows:

1. Prepare the form by assembling each of the components from the database that will make up the form.
2. Build the HTML form elements (including any tasks associated with the processing).
3. Display the form.

When the data is submitted (or "posted"), Drupal goes through the first two steps again to assemble the form requirements for comparison against the data that was posted by the content editor. This time, instead of rendering the form for display, Drupal completes the following steps:

1. Validate the submitted data.
2. If the data is valid, save it to the database.
3. If the data is not valid, repeat steps 2 and 3 from the previous list. These actions re-create the form in the Web browser with error messages that allow the content author to revise the form values and resubmit it. These steps are repeated until the data is validated and saved to the database, or the content author abandons the Web form (at which point the content is lost).

Once the form has been successfully submitted, Drupal moves the content author to a page defined in the module. For the submission of content forms, this page is the "view" of the newly saved content. A complete work flow illustration is available at http://drupal.org/node/165104. This illustration is part of a larger Form application programming interface (API) documentation section of the *Developing for Drupal Handbook*. More information about the Form API is available from http://drupal.org/node/204270. Remember, however, that this documentation is written for module developers; as a consequence, many of the steps are not accessible to you as a themer.

In this chapter, you will learn how to create a custom content form with the CCK module. This module allows you to add new fields to your content types, and to change their display order in the rendered form. With your new form in hand, you will then learn how to alter this form using Drupal's Form API.

Form Candy

You may have heard of "eye candy"? It is something that is remarkable for its visual appeal, but not necessarily its demand on your intellect. Analogous to eye candy, form candy consists of Web form enhancements that are remarkable for their visual appeal. These elements may also help users to edit content. This section is dedicated to the modules, CSS tricks, and theme configurations that will take your forms from boring to zippy and fun. Like kittens with a ball of yarn, your editors will enjoy working on their content and will be relieved that they no longer have to fight with forms.

Working with Style Sheets

A lot can be done to improve the visual layout of forms by using both Drupal's default HTML and custom CSS styles. Form-specific files can be added to a separate style sheet in your theme's directory (for example, forms.css). This new style sheet must be added to your theme's .info file using the following line:

```
stylesheets[all][] = forms.css
```

Once you have registered the new style sheet, remember to clear your theme registry's cache. Navigate to Administer, Site configuration, Performance. Scroll to the bottom of the Web page and click "clear cached data."

> **Use Firebug to identify relevant CSS selectors**
> Use the Firefox browser and the Web development extension called Firebug to help you inspect HTML elements in a page and locate specific style classes you can override in a CSS. Download the extension at `http://www.getfirebug.com` and install it into your Firefox browser.

If you would rather work with only your own CSS styles for HTML forms, without having to override the default style sheets provided by Drupal's core, you may replace these files by registering an identical file name in your theme. For example, if you wanted to replace the styles related to basic HTML elements and forms, you would overwrite the file `modules/system/defaults.css`. Check the directory `modules/system` for the full list of CSS files you may want to replace. If you are adding a new style sheet, you must also register it in your theme `.info` file. Be sure to match the file name exactly. For example:

```
stylesheets[all][] = defaults.css
```

You are now able to proceed with the styling of your content editing forms without the hassle of overriding the default Drupal CSS form-related styles. All of the styles described in the rest of this section should be added to the form-specific CSS file or, alternatively, to your main style file if you want to keep all styles together.

Coloring in Required Fields

All Drupal nodes have at least one required field: the title. In some cases, the small asterisk beside the form label is not obvious enough for content authors to notice that this is a required field. Fortunately, Drupal adds a class to the input element that can be used to style the input element. Figure 6.1 shows how even very minor enhancements (coloring the form field, and adding additional instructions) can increase the visibility of a required field. You may also choose to extend the * (asterisk) into a full instruction by using the CSS pseudo-element "after" and the CSS attribute "content." Unfortunately, the CSS "content" attribute is not supported by IE; however, it is a very quick task to add this attribute, and its presence will be appreciated by visitors who use alternative browsers.

Add the following CSS to your file `forms.css`. The background color is a light pink; the border color is red. You may wish to adjust these colors to match your theme. The output of these adjustments can be seen in Figure 6.1.

```
.required {
        background-color: #ffdede;
        border: 1px solid #ff6565;
        border-top: 2px solid red;
        border-left: 2px solid red;
}


/* Some browsers, including IE, will not display this text. */
.form-required:after {
        content: "Required";
}


/* Tone down the "required" text to a light gray */
span.form-required {
        color: #ccc;
}
```

Later in this chapter, you will learn how to adjust individual form elements. With such adjustments, you could add the "Required" text directly to the form element instead of having to rely on browser support of the CSS property `content`.

Focus on Input

Have you ever been busily typing away in a form when you realized that you were actually typing in the wrong place? This kind of problem wastes time and is also mildly annoying. Through the magic of CSS, you can highlight elements that content authors are currently working in. To get this functionality to work, you must use another CSS

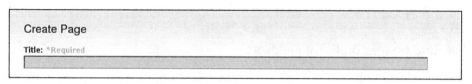

FIGURE 6.1 The required field "Title" is now immediately visible to content authors.

pseudo-element: `:focus`, the long-lost relative of `:hover` (which is typically used in styling links). This enhancement is not supported by all Web browsers.

```
#node-form .form-item input:focus,
  #node-form .form-item textarea:focus {
        background-color: #e0edba;
        border: 2px solid green;
        border-top: 2px solid #eee;
        border-left: 2px solid #eee;
}
```

No fancy JavaScript is required here. Nevertheless, the form element automatically changes color when the content author selects (or "focuses") the field to begin adding their content. The selector that is used in the preceding example will change the color of single input fields, multiline text areas, and input buttons.

In Drupal, form labels are correctly tied to their corresponding input elements. This means you can select a check box by clicking on either the text or the small square beside the label. Unfortunately, this functionality is not immediately obvious to content editors. By setting the CSS property for labels, you can change the cursor that is displayed to a hand that signals to the content author that the label is "clickable." In addition to labels, drop-down menus must be "clicked" for a selection to be made. You can add the cursor enhancement for both selection (drop-down menus) and label elements at the same time by adding the following CSS snippet to your `forms.css` file:

```
select, label {
        cursor: pointer; /* All modern browsers, including IE */
        cursor: hand; /* IE 5.5 and lower */
}
```

Background Images on Form Fieldsets

This enhancement will show you how to add background images to your forms. From a practical point of view, it could be used to add a visual cue to content editors. You might use a background image to mark a fieldset that has all required fields. If your content form collects information about "the person" and "that person's property" you might choose to include a background image with a person for "about you" information and a background image of a house for "about the property" information.

Figure 6.2 shows an example of a form with both an icon and a full-field background image. Both of the images shown in Figure 6.2 were added using only CSS; no additional changes to the theme files were necessary.

Of course, you must be able to identify the fieldset before you can theme it. Firebug comes in very helpful for this task. Right-click on the element you wish to style (or option-click if you are using a Mac). Choose "Inspect Element" from the list of items that appears. Figure 6.3 shows Firebug opened in the footer of the Web browser, with the markup for the element that was selected being highlighted. From here you can see which, if any, classes are set on this form element. If there are no distinguishing characteristics, you can always use the form ID (found in the form tag) to at least distinguish this type of form.

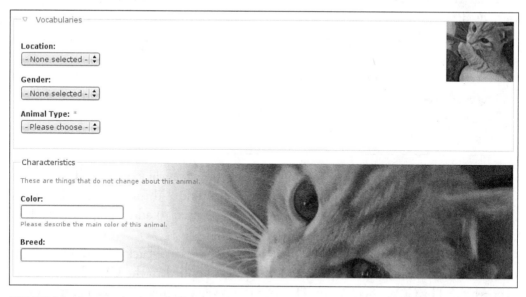

FIGURE 6.2 Kittens as background images. One small image is placed in the corner; another large image fills the whole fieldset.

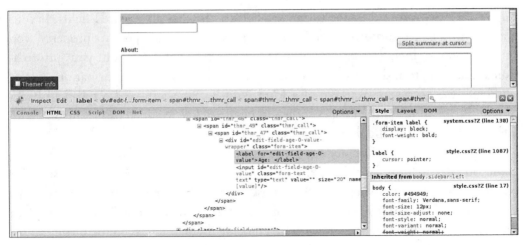

FIGURE 6.3 Using Firebug's "Inspect Element" to find the classes set on a form element.

At the top of Figure 6.3, a small icon (approximately 100 pixels square) was placed as a background image of a fieldset. The following CSS selector and CSS properties were used:

```
form fieldset.collapsible {
    background-image: url(ricky-thumb.jpg);
    background-repeat: no-repeat;
    background-position: top right;
}
```

The CSS selector is very generic and will place the graphical icon into all collapsible fieldsets throughout the site. Figure 6.4 shows an example of the icon repeated in many fieldsets on the same form. This technique could be used to add a graphical wash of color to all fieldsets in your Web site.

In Figure 6.2, a small background image (top) and a large background image (bottom) were used. The larger background image was applied to the CSS class that had been assigned by CCK's fieldgroup. The fieldgroup was assigned the class name group-characteristics. The CSS selector and properties are as follows:

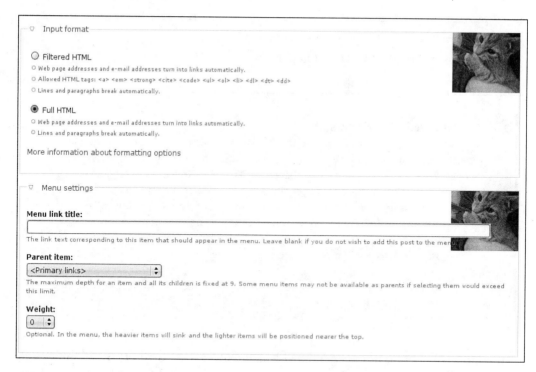

FIGURE 6.4 Using generic CSS selectors, you can repeat the same design elements throughout your Web site.

```
form fieldset.group-characteristics {

     background-image: url(ricky.jpg);

     background-repeat: no-repeat;

     background-position: top right;

}
```

By using a unique class in the CSS selector, you can apply your background image to only one fieldgroup.

Advanced CSS Selectors

In Figure 6.2, the fieldset "Input Format" was assigned a background image. Although it did not have a unique identifier, it was the "adjacent sibling" to the title field, which did have a unique identifier.

```
form#node-form #edit-title-wrapper + fieldset {
    /* Things to display in the "Input Format" fieldset */
}
```

Use advanced CSS selectors
Two very handy CSS selectors are the "adjacent sibling" selector and the "first" pseudo-element. The adjacent sibling selector determines which elements are beside each other at the same level in the document's hierarchy. You can combine as many "siblings" as you need to select the exact form element you wish to style. By combining this selector with the pseudo-element "first," you can count from a very specific position in a document. For example, to select the second paragraph in a `div` with a class of content, you use the following selector: `div.content p:first + p`.

For more information on advanced CSS selectors, visit `http://gallery.theopalgroup.com/selectoracle/`.

For more information on browser support for CSS selectors and CSS properties, visit `http://www.quirksmode.org/`.

If a specific fieldset is not assigned by Drupal, you can use the Forms API and assign a new CSS class to the form element you want to highlight. More information about adding attributes to form elements appears in the section titled "Altering Forms with FAPI" later in this chapter.

Vertical Tabs

The background kittens in the earlier example demonstrated visual enhancements you can add to your form. This section contains information about form usability enhancements implemented with the module Vertical Tabs. This module helps to summarize and compact the bottom third of the form, which most content authors find confusing. Depending on the content author's permissions, the list of possibilities to be used will include Menu options, Revision information, Comment settings, Authoring information, and Publishing options.

Before you install Vertical Tabs, the bottom portion of a node editing form will have the appearance shown in Figure 6.5. After you install Vertical Tabs, content authors will immediately have access to the revised node form layout shown in Figure 6.6.

The project page for this module can be found at `http://drupal.org/project/vertical_tabs`. Instructions for installing modules are found in Appendix A of this book.

FIGURE 6.5 Before the Vertical Tabs module is installed, the contents of the administrative settings for each node are a secret.

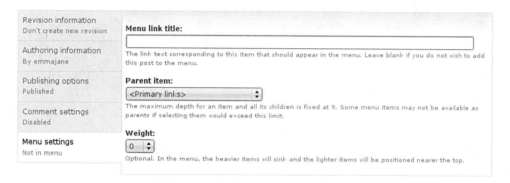

FIGURE 6.6 After the Vertical Tabs module is installed, content authors see a summary of each administrative setting and have a clean and compact interface through which to make changes.

Node Form and Usability Improvements

If you like the module Vertical Tabs, you may also want to try out the development snapshot provided by the Node Form module. This module allows you to change the default layout form for editing nodes when using the Garland theme. Two layout alternatives are currently provided: vertical tabs (Figure 6.7) and accordion style (Figure 6.8). This module is not intended for live Web sites, but rather is a development snapshot that is studying the usability of node editing forms. It is part of the Drupal usability group. You can participate in this group through the site `http://groups.drupal.org/usability`. The module itself can be downloaded from the following address: `http://drupal.org/project/nodeform`.

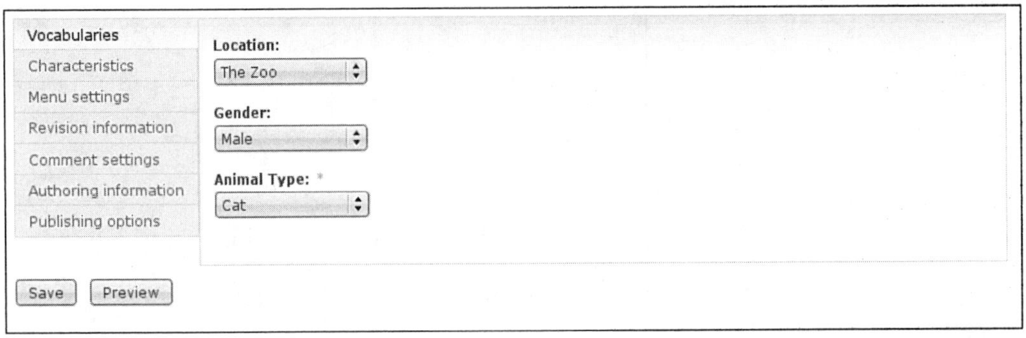

FIGURE 6.7 The Node Form module provides an alternative layout for node forms and does not require any theming per node type. Shown here is the Vertical Tabs layout.

FIGURE 6.8 The Node Form module provides an alternative layout for node forms and does not require any theming per node type. Shown here is the Accordion layout.

Be sure to follow the installation instructions that are provided with the Node Form module carefully. You may be required to copy functions into your theme's `template.php` file. This module is designed to work with only certain forms in the Garland theme. If you are comfortable with PHP and JavaScript, you should be able to replicate some of the module's functionality within your own theme by copying the relevant information into your theme's files and adjusting the function names to match your own theme.

Rich Text Editing

Every Web developer, whether novice or expert, expects to be able to create pretty Web pages with links to other pages and bold text and pictures. To achieve this functionality, you may choose from several Drupal modules that provide rich text editors, also referred to as WYSIWYG ("What you see is what you get") editors. Most of these modules include a third-party JavaScript library that you will need to download and install in addition to the Drupal module. Drupal's full list of filters and editors, which can be found at `http://drupal.org/project/Modules/category/63`, contains rich text editors and filters that will help you to integrate rich media into your Web site. For example, a video filter in this list can help you place YouTube and Google Videos into your content (`http://drupal.org/project/video_filter`); another filter provides for Flickr integration (`http://drupal.org/project/flickr`). If you need more than basic text editing capabilities, look through the full list of available editors and filters—you may find just the right tool for your job. Remember to log into Drupal.org and filter the category based on the version of Drupal that you want to install. It will make sorting through the list much easier!

TinyMCE is a platform-independent, Web-based, JavaScript, HTML, WYSIWYG editor released by Moxiecode Systems AB. It was selected as the example editor for this book because of its integration with the Image Assist module and because of the ease with which it reduces the number of buttons in the editing interface. Another very popular WYSIWYG editor is FCKEditor (`http://drupal.org/project/fckeditor`), which includes a built-in file manager.

Installing TinyMCE

Integrating TinyMCE into a Drupal Web site requires you to complete a multistep installation process. You will need to download both TinyMCE and the corresponding Drupal module. Not all versions of TinyMCE work with every version of the Drupal module, so read the instructions carefully to make sure you download and install compatible versions of the two plugins.

1. Go to the Drupal TinyMCE module page (`http://drupal.org/project/tinymce`) and download the latest version of the module.

2. Unpack the module and look in the `README.txt` file to see if there are restrictions on which version of TinyMCE you must use.

3. If there are no restrictions, download the latest version of TinyMCE from the Web site. If there are restrictions, make sure you obtain the correct version. You can download TinyMCE from `http://tinymce.moxiecode.com/download.php`. Most Web sites will need only the "Main package."

4. Extract the TinyMCE main package and place it in the Drupal `tinymce` module folder in your sites directory. The path for the TinyMCE package will be `sites/all/modules/tinymce/tinymce`.

You are now ready to enable the TinyMCE module from within Drupal.

1. Navigate to Administer, Site building, Modules.

2. Find the TinyMCE module and put a check mark beside its name.

3. Scroll to the bottom of the Web page and click "Save configuration."

4. Navigate to Administer, User management, Permissions.

5. Enable the correct TinyMCE permissions for the appropriate roles. You may choose who has rights to use TinyMCE and who may administer it.

6. Scroll to the bottom of the Web page and click "Save permissions."

Configuring TinyMCE

With TinyMCE installed, you are ready to configure this module for each of the roles that will have access to use TinyMCE. You may create a different profile for each Drupal role. Repeat these steps for each different profile that you want to create. If you are exposing a number of buttons, you should switch the default input filter for your content types from Filtered HTML to Full HTML.

Follow these steps to add a TinyMCE profile:

1. Navigate to Administer, Site configuration, TinyMCE.

2. Click the link at the top of the page to "create a new profile."

Six sections must be configured to create a new profile. Figure 6.9 shows the default layout of the settings page for the creation of a new TinyMCE profile.

Basic Setup

In the "Basic setup" section you will find many configurable options. The most important of these are highlighted here:

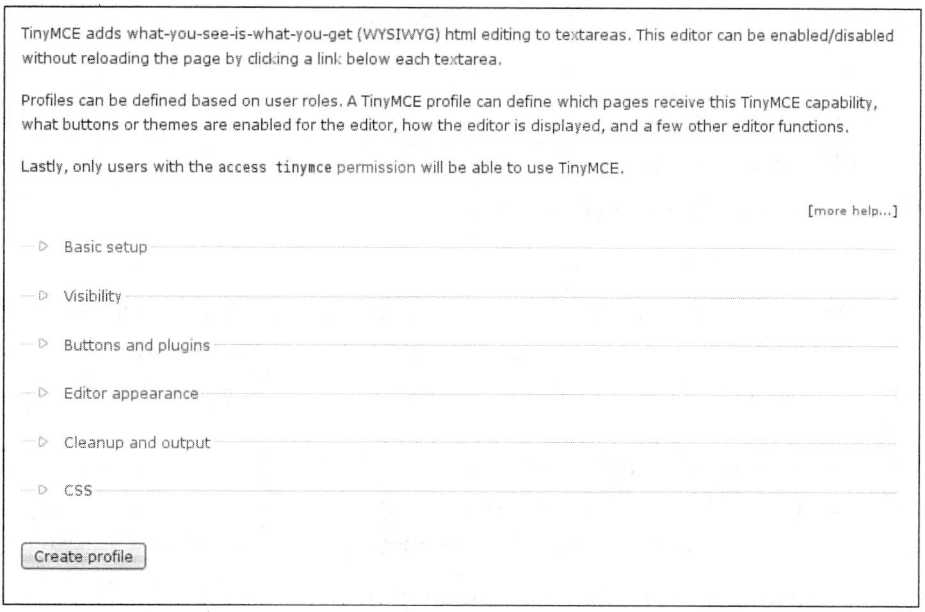

TinyMCE adds what-you-see-is-what-you-get (WYSIWYG) html editing to textareas. This editor can be enabled/disabled without reloading the page by clicking a link below each textarea.

Profiles can be defined based on user roles. A TinyMCE profile can define which pages receive this TinyMCE capability, what buttons or themes are enabled for the editor, how the editor is displayed, and a few other editor functions.

Lastly, only users with the access tinymce permission will be able to use TinyMCE.

[more help...]

▷   Basic setup

▷   Visibility

▷   Buttons and plugins

▷   Editor appearance

▷   Cleanup and output

▷   CSS

[Create profile]

FIGURE 6.9 The editor profiles in TinyMCE have six sections.

- Profile name (for example, "author" or "advanced editor")
- Roles allowed to use this profile (you must select at least one role)
- Default state (choose "enabled")
- Allow users to choose default (choose whatever is most appropriate)

Visibility

In the "Visibility" section, you will choose the pages on which TinyMCE will appear. By default, all of the node, user, and comment creation and editing pages will have TinyMCE turned on. For most Web sites, it is appropriate to remove rich text editing capabilities everywhere except on the node editing pages (this includes all content types). If you want to be more specific and allow only some content types, you will need to use a PHP snippet instead of simply listing the pages.

Buttons and Plugins

Use the "Buttons and plugins" option to choose which buttons will be available for your rich text editor. The following types of buttons are appropriate for nearly all Web sites:

- bold
- italic
- bullist (bullet list)
- numlist (numbered list)
- link (creates a link to a new page)
- unlink (removes a hypertext link)

Start with only the most basic of editing options. As an example, Figure 6.10 shows TinyMCE with only these buttons in the toolbar. If your pages absolutely require more options, you may add them at any time. (Image integration is discussed later in this chapter.)

At this time, all visible buttons will pass easily through the most restricted content filter. If you have added more buttons, you may need to allow more HTML elements to pass through your content filters. To add elements to a filter, follow these steps:

1. Navigate to Administer, Site configuration, Input formats.
2. Click the link "configure" next to the input format "Filtered HTML."
3. Click the "Configure" tab at the top of the page.
4. Adjust the list of "allowed tags" to include the tags for which you have enabled buttons in TinyMCE.
5. Scroll to the bottom of the Web page and click "Save configuration."

To enable users to drag and drop images from Flickr, you must add the tags <span> and <img> to the list of allowed tags.

FIGURE 6.10 TinyMCE with only the following buttons enabled: bold, italic, bullet list, numbered list, create a link, and remove a link.

Editor Appearance

The "Editor appearance" option controls the outside shell of the TinyMCE editing window. By default, the toolbar of buttons is located along the bottom; however, content authors will expect to find these buttons at the top of their editing window. Change the setting "Toolbar location" to "top."

Cleanup and Output

The default options are almost always acceptable for the "Cleanup and output" option. Nevertheless, it is a good idea to read through the options in case your site has unique requirements.

CSS

The CSS settings control the inside text display of the editing window. The "TinyMCE default" is typically the most appropriate option. You may also wish to use your theme's style sheet or to define a custom style sheet that is relevant only to the editing interface.

With each of these settings configured, scroll to the bottom of the profile configuration page and click "Create profile." You will be returned to the summary page, where your new profile should be listed.

Image Integration

Offering the ability to perform rich text editing without the ability to place images is a bit like having a candy store with no candy! TinyMCE integrates well with the Image Assist module. The combination of the two enables content authors to click a button on TinyMCE's toolbar to upload an image and integrate it immediately into the page they are editing. This module can be used without rich text editing; in such a case, however, content authors will see only the HTML for the image, not the image itself.

The advantage of using this combination of modules is that content authors can place their images into exactly the right spot on the page using only a few mouse clicks. The Image Assist module creates a new node for each image uploaded. These images can be placed into galleries automatically on upload, which saves you from the burden of having to maintain images in two separate locations.

> ⚠ **Version issues for TinyMCE**
> As of this writing, the Drupal Image Assist plugin did not integrate correctly with the TinyMCE version 3 plugin architecture. It was necessary to download version 2 of TinyMCE if integration with Image Assist was desired.
> The link to the version 2 plugin is not available from the main page of the TinyMCE site. Instead, go to the full list of all TinyMCE packages, found at `http://sourceforge.net/project/showfiles.php?group_id=103281&package_id=111430`. From this list, select the Zip file for the latest version 2 release of TinyMCE (for example, 2.1.2).

Image Assist can also be integrated with Drupal's Image module. To do so, you must download both modules, but be aware that version-specific requirements must be satisfied if the two modules are to work together. Start by downloading the Image module (`http://drupal.org/project/image`), noting which version you have downloaded. Then go to the project page for the Image Assist module. Read the instructions carefully and choose the appropriate version of Image Assist. Both the Image and Image Assist modules need to be placed into your site's modules directory and installed according to the instructions in Appendix A. Be sure to check the new permissions for each module and confirm that they are correct. Navigate to Administer, User management, Permissions and confirm that the appropriate roles are able to create new images and use the Image Assist module.

Configuring Image Assist and TinyMCE

Once the Image and Image Assist modules have been installed, they must be configured for use with TinyMCE:

1. In the Image Assist module directory (`img_assist`), locate the subfolder `drupalimage` and move it to `tinymce/tinymce/jscripts/tiny_mce/plugins/`.

2. In the main TinyMCE directory, edit the file `plugin_reg.php`.

3. To the file `plugin_reg.php`, add the following lines anywhere above the `return` statement at the end of the file (this code can by copied from the Image Assist file `INSTALL.txt`; you do not need to retype it!):

```
$plugins['drupalimage'] = array();
$plugins['drupalimage']['theme_advanced_buttons1'] = array('drupalimage');
$plugins['drupalimage']['extended_valid_elements'] = array('img[class|src|border
=0|alt|title|width|height|align|name]');
```

4. Navigate to Administer, Site configuration, TinyMCE and enable the `drupal-image` plugin in your TinyMCE profile. It will appear at the very bottom of the Buttons and Plugins list.

Figure 6.11 shows the new camera icon available in the TinyMCE editor toolbar. Clicking this button will open a pop-up window where you may perform either of the following actions:

- Choose a previously uploaded image
- Upload a new image

Extending TinyMCE

The TinyMCE can be integrated with the IMCE module to enable the following features, among others: File/Image Manager, Quota, Auto Resize, folder per user, file upload, file delete. Additional information is available in the TinyMCE module directory that you created, in a file named `README.txt`.

Altering Forms with FAPI

As you learned earlier in this chapter, much can be done to improve Web forms with just CSS. Sometimes, however, the content of the forms Drupal creates is inappropriate. Unfortunately, CSS cannot alter the content that is available on a page; it can only be used to style the content that is provided. In this section you will learn how to alter the structure of your forms with Drupal's Form API (FAPI). Although you will not be able to create new database fields, you will learn how to alter the text associated with form elements and how to change those elements' order and display settings. You will

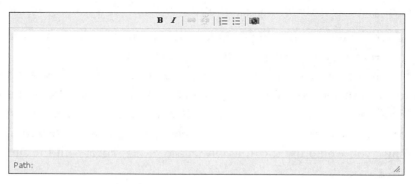

FIGURE 6.11 The TinyMCE toolbar has been updated and now incorporates the Image Assist button, allowing users to upload a new image file or choose a previously uploaded image.

also learn how to add new class attributes to form elements to make the selection of form elements easier for CSS customizations.

Changing Forms Throughout Your Site

Theming a form allows you to change what Drupal has prepared into just the right form to be displayed. Coding best practices offer some guidance when doing so—namely, all changes to the logic or data of the content Drupal has prepared must be made from your theme's file `template.php` and not from the `tpl.php` files.

> **Keeping template.php free of clutter**
> To keep the file `template.php` free of clutter, you can put your form alterations into a separate PHP file, such as `template-forms.php`. To activate this file, simply include it from the main `template.php` file using the following PHP snippet:
> ```
> include_once('template-forms.php');
> ```

Although you may use several different functions to theme your forms, there are only three key points you will need to know to alter forms using FAPI:

1. Form elements (including the whole form) can be themed by using themeable, form-related functions. A full list is available from `http://api.drupal.org/api/group/themeable/6`. Be aware that this list also includes non-form-related functions.

2. Drupal uses an array to store the form-related variables it needs to build a form. These variables, including their contents and order in the array, can be manipulated from the form's themeable functions (see point 1).

3. You may add new themeable form functions for each form on your Web site.

Using these three form theming techniques, you can alter all of the forms in your Drupal site. To apply your changes across all forms, you can use the theme functions described in the list of themeable functions in point 1. To apply these functions just within your own theme, you must alter the name of the function from `theme_HOOK` to `yourthemename_HOOK`. For example, to alter the text that appears on the "Save" buttons for all content-related forms in your entire Drupal Web site within a theme named "bolg," you would use the function `theme_node_form` with the altered name `bolg-node-form`.

When you take this approach to editing the site, you will still need to know which item in the form array needs to be changed. To make this determination, use the Devel module to find the item in the form array that you want to change. For example, in Figure 6.12 the "Save" button has been selected for detailed examination. The parent function theme_node_form has been selected from the list of related functions that can be themed. From here, it is possible to examine the form array to isolate the variable that needs to be changed.

The following PHP function should be added to your theme's template.php file. It will allow you to change the value of the submit button for all node forms across your Web site. Of course, you will need to replace "bolg" in the following snippet with your theme's name.

```
function bolg_node_form ($form) {
        $form['buttons']['submit']['#value'] = "Save these changes";
        return (drupal_render($form));
}
```

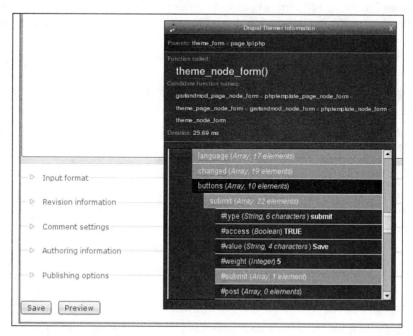

FIGURE 6.12 Use Themer Info to isolate the functions and form array items you need to change.

This function affects all "node" (or "content") forms sitewide, including both core content types (such as Page and Story) and any new content types that you have created or will create in the future. The guts of the function illustrate the first two rules in theming forms: (1) The content of forms can be altered by using themeable functions and (2) Drupal stores form information in a complex data array. The preceding function highlights three key concepts:

1. The form array was updated and now contains a new value for the submit button.
2. The new value was converted from an array back into a form element with the function drupal_render.
3. The rendered form element was returned to Drupal.

If any of these steps are omitted, the submit button will not be altered.

Use the right theme
Make sure you have set the administrative theme to be the same as the template files you are modifying. It may not be sufficient to set the administrative theme to "Default Theme." To confirm you are using the right theme, navigate to Administer, Site configuration, Administration theme. Set the theme to match the template files you are working with.

If you use the preceding function exactly as written, you would notice that the buttons no longer appear at the bottom of your form. To sink the buttons to the bottom, you must change another form array item and increase the "weight" of the buttons in the form. Note that the weight is adjusted for both the preview and submit buttons in the form. The final function is as follows:

```
function bolg_node_form ($form) {
        $form['buttons']['submit']['#value'] = "Save my changes";
        $form['buttons']['#weight'] = 40;
        return (drupal_render($form));
}
```

Now that you know how to make sitewide changes to your content editing forms, it is time to get a little more specific about form-related changes.

Changing Specific Forms

To change a specific form, you will first need to identify the ID of the form you want to alter. You can find this information using the Themer Info provided by the Devel module. Once the Themer Info window has been opened and you have highlighted the form, scroll down to the array key, `form_id`; the information you need can be found beside the key name, `#value`.

> **Finding form IDs without Themer Info**
> The form ID is stored as a hidden field located toward the end of the form. Look for the hidden input field that contains the name attribute of `form_id`. In HTML, forms match name-value pairs. In this case, the name attribute for `form_id` corresponds to the value attribute. For example, in this form the value attributed that is paired up with `name="form_id"` is `value="portfolio_node_form"`:
> ```
> <input id="edit-portfolio-node-form"
> type="hidden"
> value="portfolio_node_form"
> name="form_id"/>
> ```
> The HTML attribute `id` can be used for CSS styling; however, this attribute is not used by Drupal to identify themeable forms.

Armed with the value of the `form_id`, you can begin the customization process. You will need to edit the file `template.php` to add the customizations for your theme's forms. First, you must alert the theme to the form you would like to alter. This step is necessary only if there is not a themeable function registered in the Themer Info list of "parent" functions specific enough to meet your needs. For example, `theme_node_form` will alter all content forms in the Web site. If you want to make changes for one of your custom content types, however, you will need to register a new function name. This can be accomplished with the following function. Of course, you will need to replace "bolg" with your theme's name and "portfolio" with the `form_id` you want to change.

```
// Alert the theme you will be altering its form contents
function bolg_theme() {
  return array(
    'portfolio_node_form' => array(
      'arguments' => array('form' => NULL),
    ),
  );
}
```

Now that you have registered the new function name, you can use the same technique that was used previously to rename the text on the submit button. This time, however, the changes will apply to only one form. In the following snippet, only the text in **bold** has changed from the previous version of this function.

```
function bolg_portfolio_node_form ($form) {

        $form['buttons']['submit']['#value'] = "Save my changes";

        $form['buttons']['#weight'] = 40;

        return (drupal_render($form));

}
```

Using the Themer Info toolkit, you can find every element that is displayed on a form. In conjunction with the weight attribute, you can use this information to alter the layout of your forms.

Changing Display Text in Forms

Any form element that is displayed can be changed at the theme level. In the last section we used the weight to sink the submit button to the bottom of a custom form. In addition to changing the order of the form elements, you can change the displayed label text for any of the form elements. These changes are made from the template. php file and fit into the relevant theme functions for your form.

Following are examples of three kinds of form elements whose text you can alter. In each example, the new text has been sanitized by using either t() (appropriate when you want to translate the text later) or check_plain() (when you want to sanitize the text entered, with no intention of translating it later).

Label for the core content field "Title" available in all content-related forms:

```
$form['title']['#title'] = t("New label text");
```

CCK field label for a custom content type field named field_age:

```
$form['field_age'][0]['value']['#title'] = t("New label");
```

"Save" button at the bottom of the form:

```
$form['buttons']['submit']['#value'] = check_plain t("Yarrr! Save me timbers!");
```

To change the default size of a text input, you could use the following code:

```
$form['field_age'][0]['value']['#size'] = 2;
```

To change the default height of a text area, you could use the following code:

```
$form['body_field']['body']['#rows'] = 20;
```

The column width is set by the system style sheet. If you want to change the width of a text area, you must also remove the default width setting.

Removing Fields from the Form

Sometimes you may want to limit which users can fill out specific form fields. By using the module Content Permissions, you can control which roles can view and edit every field for each content type. These changes are made across all forms for the entire Web site. The Content Permissions module is part of the CCK set of core modules and is not enabled by default. To enable it, you must navigate to Administer, Site building, Modules and select the Content Permissions module. You may then adjust the permissions for each form field and each role on the Permissions pages. To access this page, navigate to Administer, User management, Permissions. Scroll down to the content_permissions module and adjust the settings for each of the content fields in your site.

If you want to make these changes on a per-form basis (rather than sitewide), you can follow one of two approaches: (1) You can create new fields for each different scenario, or (2) you can use the theme layer to remove fields from the individual forms before they are rendered and displayed. In the theme layer, you can remove fields from the form in the preprocess function for content type. You will likely want to limit access based on the user's role (including whether the user is logged in), although you could use other tests as well. Each of these snippets should be added to your form's theme (for example, bolg_portfolio_node_form). You should also check whether the field you are trying to restrict is a required field—use the Theme Info tool to find the appropriate form variable to test for each field type.

Drupal has provided a special variable, $logged_in, to test whether users are logged in. You can use it as follows:

```
if ($logged_in){
        // Do something for authenticated users

}
```

If you want to test that a user is not logged in, you can use the following snippet. Note the use of an exclamation mark to negate the statement. In English, this statement would be read as follows: "If the NOT logged-in user."

```
if (! $logged_in){
        // Do something for anonymous users

}
```

Drupal also provides a special variable, $is_admin, to test whether users have been granted permission to access the administration pages. You may use $is_admin in the same way as the variable $logged_in. For example:

```
if ($is_admin){
        // Do something for users with administrative privileges

}
```

If you want to test for a specific role, use the following test:

```
if (in_array('content editor'), array_values($user->roles)){
        // Do something for content editors
        // This user role must match one that exists at admin/user/roles

}
```

Inside these tests, you should "unset" the form elements you want to hide. To obtain the name of the field you want to hide, navigate to Administer, Content management, Content types and select "managed fields" next to the content type you are working with. The fields are listed under the "Name" column. You can also use the Theme Info module to find the same information. For example, if you wanted to unset the Project Web site (field_url) for everyone except those users with the role of "content editors," you would use the following code snippet:

```
if (! in_array('content editors'), array_values($user->roles)){
       unset($form['field_url']);
endif}
```

You will still need to use the function `drupal_render($form)` at the end of your function; however, Drupal will now omit the Project Web site field from the form.

You will learn more about how to control the display of "private" content in Chapter 8.

Changing Form Widgets

For some fields, such as the image field, it makes more sense to have the "help" text appear directly below the form label. Depending on which form element you want to alter, there are two ways to approach this problem. Most form elements are controlled by the Drupal function `theme_form_element`. If you want to change a CCK multiple-form value (for example, `imagefield`), you need to theme the function `theme_content_multiple_values`.

To alter the default theme provided by Drupal or one of its modules, the easiest strategy is to copy the full function from the module file and paste it into your theme's `template.php` file. Drupal stores its theme information for forms in the file `includes/form.inc`. From this file you will need to copy all of the function as follows:

```
function theme_form_element($element, $value) {

       ....

       // Lots of stuff goes here

       ....

       return $output;

}
```

You can also find this function in Drupal's online API Web site at `http://api.drupal.org/api/function/theme_form_element/6`.

In addition to using Drupal's themes for individual form elements, you can use CCK, which provides its own formatting information. CCK stores its theme information in the file `cck/content.module`. This folder is found in your site's module directory (for example, `sites/all/modules`). This time you need to copy the following function:

```
function theme_content_multiple_values($element) {

    ....
    // Lots of stuff here

    ....
    return $output;

}
```

You can find this function in CCK's online API Web site at `http://api.freestyle-systems.co.uk/api/function/theme_content_multiple_values/6`.

After you have copied the function into your theme's `template.php` file, you must change the name to match your own theme. To do so, replace the first word in the function with your theme name. For example, if your theme is named `bolg`, you would rename `theme_form_element` to `bolg_form_element`, and rename `theme_content_multiple_values` to `bolg_content_multiple_values`.

Look carefully at the contents of these two functions. You will quickly realize that to alter the `form_element` function, you must swap the `$value` and "description" output lines so that the description is appended to `$output` ahead of `$value`. To change the placement of the help text within the `content_multiple_values` function, move `$description` from the bottom(ish) of the function to the top. Add the `$description` to the `$header` via the data array key. Here's a code snippet that accomplishes this task:

```
'data' => t('!title: !required',
        array('!title' => $element['#title'],
        '!required' => $required)) . $description,
```

Note the trailing comma after `$description`: This change is part of a larger array.

Multiple-Page Forms

Sometimes forms get long—very long. You may decide to create a wizard-style form that asks different questions based on the data entered, or perhaps you want to set up a multistep registration form you know will take several attempts to complete. Or maybe you have a completely different reason for having a multistep form. Unfortunately, this type of development is not something that is easily accomplished at the theme level. Instead, such a task is better suited to custom module development.

Some modules, such as the Drupal core Profile module, automatically separate groups of content into separate input forms. If you are trying to accomplish a specific task, you should check the list of Drupal content modules for one that suits your needs. This list is available at `http://drupal.org/project/Modules/category/57`. Module developers may also find the Drupal Handbook page "Multipage forms with CCK" useful; find it at `http://drupal.org/node/162373`.

Webform

The Webform module helps you build forms that can be filled out and submitted by Web site visitors. The module collects response data, which can then be output into various formats. For example, a `.csv` file to be imported into a spreadsheet application such as Microsoft's Excel or OpenOffice.org's Spreadsheet. Typical uses for Webform are to create questionnaires; contact, request, and register forms; surveys; and polls. This module has also been used as an issue-tracking system.

The Webform module also includes features that allow you to notify a specific person whenever a Webform has been submitted. It collects all submissions as a single node. The resulting data are not intended to be viewed in the same way as "regular" node-based content.

The project page for the Webform module can be found at `http://drupal.org/project/webform`.

Altering Flow

After creating or editing content, Drupal redirects the content author to the content's full node display. In some circumstances, however, it may be more appropriate to take the content author somewhere else. Using the Form API and its redirect property, you can change the final destination for content authors after the successful submission of a form. Forms, however, are well constructed and are rebuilt by Drupal after content authors have submitted their data, which means changes that you make to the redirect property at the theme layer are lost when the form is rebuilt after submission. Although you can check the contents of the `$_SERVER` variable in your theme's preprocess function for the page and redirect the user to a new page based on the previously viewed page stored in the variable `$_SERVER`, it is more appropriate to alter the flow of your forms through a custom module. For more information on module development, refer to the online guide at `http://drupal.org/node/231276`.

You may also want to review the module Pageroute. This flexible module provides a user-friendly wizard for creating and editing several nodes. Although stable Drupal 6 module has not yet been released, a beta version is available. Additional information about the Pageroute project is available at `http://drupal.org/project/pageroute`.

Improving Access to Edit Screens

The more you customize Drupal's interface, the more likely it becomes that the content's "edit" button will disappear. There are a number of ways you can make it easier for content authors to edit Web site content. One option is to add this functionality to your theme; a second option is to install one of the contributed modules that will add these links for you. If you are working with Zen as the base of your theme, you may already have some of this functionality available as part of your theme! In contrast, if you are working with an existing site and want to add this functionality without altering your theme, these modules are a great way to quickly improve access to editing screens.

Admin Links

There are many different ways to get from where you are to where you can edit content in Drupal. Unfortunately, this navigation route can be cumbersome. Figure 6.13 shows a typical front page story. Content authors often ask, "But how do I edit the front page?" The answer: "Well, you click on the title and then click 'edit.'" This process is awkward and not at all intuitive. An alternative is to navigate to Content

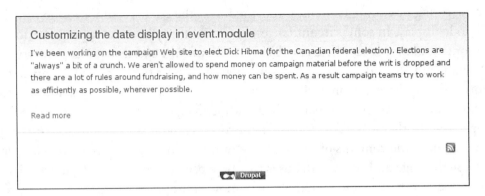

FIGURE 6.13   By default, there is no obvious way to edit content that appears on the front page or in a view.

management, Content page and filter the content to find the page you want to edit—but this approach is also time-consuming.

There are two ways to improve access for content authors: customize the "teasers" to include a link directly to the content editing form for each content type, or install the Admin Links module. This module adds "edit" and "delete" tabs for authenticated users to all "teasers." It is easy to install and does not require additional theming.

The project page for the Admin Links module can be found at `http://drupal.org/project/admin_links`. The installation instructions in Appendix A provide more information on the process of downloading and installing this module.

Once the Admin Links module is installed, no additional configuration is required. All permissions are gathered from the existing permissions defined in the Content management, Permissions table. If you are an authorized content editor, you will immediately see "Edit" and "Delete" links at the bottom of all content teasers (as shown in Figure 6.14).

Editing Blocks

If you are using the Zen theme, you already have the ability to configure blocks from a link in the block itself. Figure 6.15 shows the "configure" and "edit menu" links that appear when you hover on a block. If you are not using the Zen theme, you can copy this functionality to your own theme. If your theme is not already a subtheme of something else, consider adding Zen as the base theme to enable this functionality, and more.

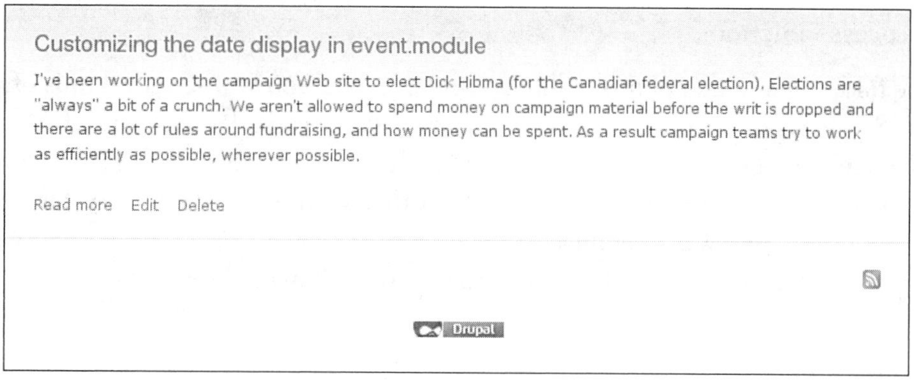

Customizing the date display in event.module

I've been working on the campaign Web site to elect Dick Hibma (for the Canadian federal election). Elections are "always" a bit of a crunch. We aren't allowed to spend money on campaign material before the writ is dropped and there are a lot of rules around fundraising, and how money can be spent. As a result campaign teams try to work as efficiently as possible, wherever possible.

Read more   Edit   Delete

FIGURE 6.14 The Admin Links module adds "Edit" and "Delete" links for authorized content editors to all teasers.

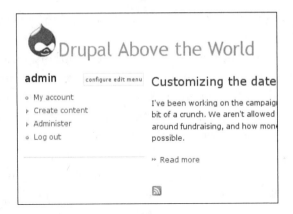

FIGURE 6.15 The Zen theme includes a set of configuration links that allow authenticated users to edit the block from a link that appears in the block.

Three files must be modified in this case: `template.php` sets up the variables; `block.tpl.php` places the links in the structure of the block; and your style sheet customizes the appearance of the configuration links.

To enable this functionality, you must download the Zen theme from `http://drupal.org/project/zen`, extract it into your theme folder, and enable the theme. You should enable the theme as a "personal theme" (described in Chapter 3) if you are working on a live Web site so that you do not affect the public view of the Web site. Once the theme is enabled, two new links will appear when you hover on the block (neat, eh?).

Preprocess Functions

In the folder `zen/zen`, open the file `block.tpl.php`. You will see two kinds of variables. Some begin with `$block->SOMETHING`; these variables are part of Drupal's core variables and are available to all themes. The other variables (`$edit_links` and `$block_classes`) were prepared by the Zen theme's file `template.php` before the file `block.tpl.php` was assembled.

Open the file `template.php` and search for the following line:

```
function zen_preprocess_block(&$vars) {
```

This function is responsible for preparing the additional variables `$edit_links` and `$body_classes`. The function name, `zen_preprocess_block`, is derived from three different words. "Zen" and "block" you should recognize; they indicate you will be building variables that are relevant only to the Zen theme and only to blocks. When you copy this function to your own theme, you must change the word "zen" to your theme's name. This leaves one word in the middle of the function name—"preprocess." This keyword tells Drupal that the guts of the function are a recipe for new variables that will be used by "zen" in the "block" template.

Structure of the preprocess_block Function

The function `preprocess_block` receives a copy of all of variables prepared by Drupal for blocks (`$vars`). This list includes everything (its ID, the module that created the block, the region where the block should appear, and the title of the block). In addition to blocks, special preprocess functions are available for pages, blocks, and nodes. To obtain a full list of all variables created by this block, issue the following PHP command inside the preprocess function to print the variables to the page:

```
print_r($vars);
```

If you have the Devel module installed, you can generate a formatted version of the same information with the function `dsm`:

```
dsm($vars);
```

New variables that are placed back into the array `$vars` are automatically passed along to the associated template file. In most cases, this location is indicated by the rightmost word in the preprocess function name; for example, the template file for `preprocess_block` is `block.tpl.php`.

Inside Zen's preprocess block function, several sections can be seen:

- Definition of CSS classes used to hide and show editing links
- Test for permission to administer blocks
- Test for views-related blocks (type of this block and permission to administer views)
- Test for menu-related blocks (type of this block and permission to administer menus)
- Assembly of links

Adding Block-Editing Capabilities to a Theme

If you have chosen a different parent theme as your subtheme, you will not have access to the Zen Edit block function. Moving the functionality from the Zen theme to your own theme is not difficult, however, and requires only careful copying and pasting. Follow these steps to merge the necessary Zen functions into your own theme:

1. Open the Zen theme file `template.php` and copy the contents of the function `zen_preprocess_block`.

2. Open your own theme's file `template.php` and look for the function YOUR-THEMENAME_preprocess_block. If this function does not exist, you must create it now by adding the following PHP snippet:

```
function YOURTHEMENAME_preprocess_block (&$vars) {
// The edit block links snippet goes here
}
```

3. To your theme's `preprocess_block` function, add the contents of the Zen theme's `preprocess_block` function, which you copied in step 1.

4. Remove the Zen-specific settings. For example, the Zen theme includes a test to check whether block editing is enabled for the Zen theme.

```
// Zen's template (remove the next line from your theme):
 if (theme_get_setting('zen_block_editing') && user_access('administer blocks')) {
// Your template (add this line to your template):
 if (user_access('administer blocks')) {
```

5. Place the new variables into your theme's `block.tpl.php` file. To print them at the bottom of every block, add the following PHP snippet to the end of the file, but before the `</div>` tag in your theme's file `block.tpl.php`:

```
<?php print $edit_links; ?>
```

6. Clear the cache for your site by going to Administer, Site configuration, Performance. Scroll to the bottom of the screen and click "Clear cached data." Block

administration links should now be visible at the bottom of all of your blocks. You may style these as appropriate for your site with CSS.

If you would like to use the appear/disappear trick, you must also copy the Zen style sheet for block editing (`block-editing.css`) to your own theme's directory. Instructions for adding a new style sheet to your theme can be found in Chapter 3.

Administrative Interfaces

This book devotes an entire chapter to the creation and customization of the Drupal administrative interface. For more information on how to improve the administration of Drupal, read Chapter 8.

Summary

This chapter focused on ways to style and alter Drupal forms. Several techniques were covered—from simple CSS modifications to complex functions that alter the way a form is displayed on the page. Specifically, the following abilities are key ways of working with forms:

- Improving the usability of content editing forms with simple CSS enhancements
- Installing and configuring a rich text editor to make it easier for content authors to add simple styles to content on their Web pages
- Using modules developed by the Drupal usability group to alter the layout of content editing screens
- Using preprocess functions to create new variables for use in block template files
- Hiding form fields
- Combining form fields into relevant groups to enhance the usability of content editing forms

## Chapter 7

Users and Community Participation

With its excellent core modules and thousands of contributed modules, Drupal is capable of providing a rich interaction platform for online communities. In this chapter, you will learn how to theme different kinds of contents that will be added to your Web site. You will also learn how to enable, theme, and control comments—and discover the potential spam that may arise from having anonymous comments enabled on your Web site.

Users

If you are running a community Web site, you will need to distinguish between anonymous Web site visitors and active Web site contributors. Asking users to create accounts on your site will create persistent, but editable, identities for individuals wishing to collaborate in content creation and communication on your Web site. Drupal now offers two ways for users to create an account on your Web site: (1) You may force users to create identities that are unique to your Web site, or (2) you may enable the core OpenID module and allow users to use a previously created digital identity to log into your Web site. For more information on OpenID, visit `http://openid.net/`.

User Profiles

A number of Drupal modules will extend the basic user profile by adding new tabs and new information summaries. Each of these modules has its own theme functions that can be modified to suit your needs. In this section we will look at ways to modify the display at the theme layer. In Drupal 6, you can easily modify the default profile to include new fields.

To start the customization process, you must enable the Profile module:

1. Navigate to Administer, Site building, Modules.
2. Find and enable the Profile module.
3. Scroll to the bottom of the Web page and click "Save configuration."

You may now add new fields to the user profiles:

1. Navigate to Administer, User management, Profiles.
2. Select a new type of field to add. You may choose from any of the following options:

   - Single-line text field
   - Multiline text field
   - Check box
   - List selection
   - Free-form list
   - URL
   - Date

3. Fill out the corresponding form for the field type that you added. Figure 7.1 shows an example of the form for a multiline text field.
4. "Category," "Title," and "Form name" are all required fields. The "Category" is the group this field will appear within. If you begin typing, Drupal will attempt to complete the name by offering a list of categories that begin with the same letters. The "Title" is the label for the form field and will display on the page by default. The "Form name" is the database field name and is also used as a CSS class.
5. Scroll to the bottom of the Web page and click "Save field."

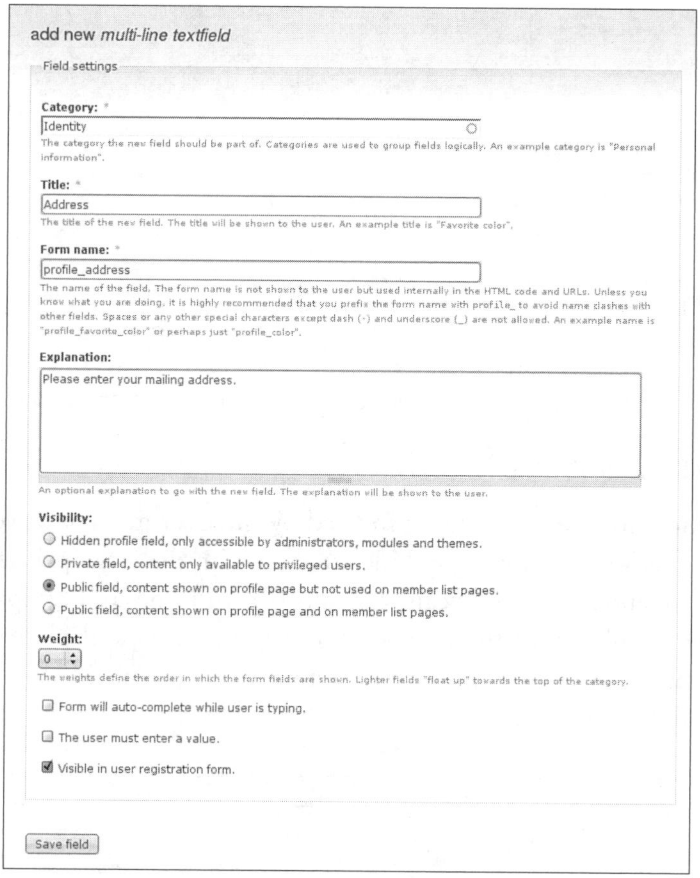

FIGURE 7.1 Profile fields can be added and easily customized. These fields may also be a requirement to create an account on a Web site.

As you add fields, you may want to change their display order. To do so, click on the crosshair icon and drag the field to its new position. Fields may be moved from one category to another as well. Figure 7.2 shows an example of a field that has been moved. You must click the "Save configuration" button to commit the changes back to the database.

When the user edits his or her profile, the categories will appear as separate tabs across the top of the page (Figure 7.3). Be sure to add enough visual cues so that your Web site account holders will be certain to see these tabs. You may also want to give text instructions as part of a help file on your Web site.

Title	Name	Type	Operations	
Family				
⊹ Family	profile_family	textfield	edit	delete
Identity				
⊹ Real Name	profile_real_name	textfield	edit	delete
⊹ Address*	profile_address	textarea	edit	delete

* Changes made in this table will not be saved until the form is submitted.

Save configuration

FIGURE 7.2 Fields can be moved to any position in the form through a drag-and-drop interface.

Theming the Default Profile

Drupal 6 includes four template files provided by the User module. If you would like to modify the user profile, it is a good idea to start with these template files. They are well documented and are automatically downloaded with the core Drupal installation. You may copy the files from the directory `modules/user/` and place them in your theme directory. To take advantage of these template files, you will also need to enable the Profile module.

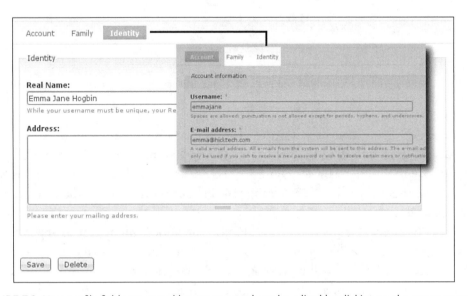

FIGURE 7.3 User profile fields are sorted by category and can be edited by clicking on the category name after enabling the edit functionality.

These template files are responsible for the display of user images and the main profile page.

user-picture.tpl.php

This file provides the HTML wrapper for the image that is displayed on a person's profile. To use it, you must first enable picture support in the User settings:

1. Navigate to Administer, User management, User settings.
2. Scroll (almost) to the bottom of the page and find the Pictures section.
3. By default, Pictures are disabled. Change this selection to enabled.
4. A new series of options will appear. For most Web sites, the default settings for user pictures are acceptable (see Figure 7.4).

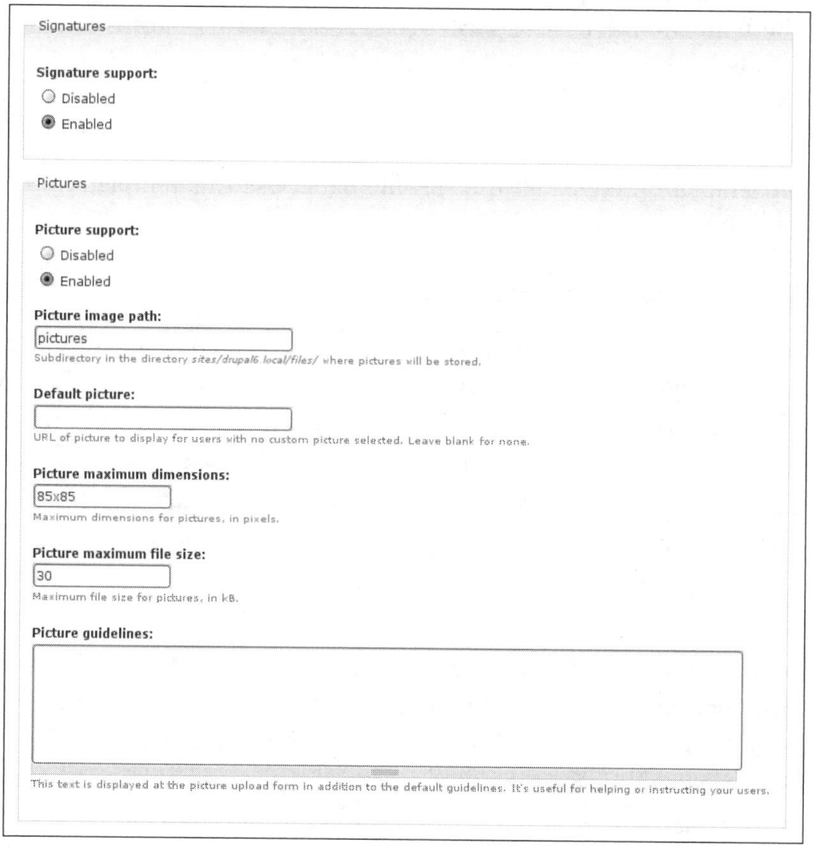

FIGURE 7.4 The default configuration options for user pictures are good choices for most Web sites.

5. You must also enable this option for your theme. Navigate to Administer, Site building, Themes.

6. Click the link "configure" beside your default theme.

7. In the Toggle Display area, enable "User pictures in comments." You may also want to enable "User pictures in posts" if your Web site has multiple authors.

8. Scroll to the bottom of the Web page and click "Save configuration."

user-profile-category.tpl.php

This template file is created for each of the different groups of information for a user profile. For example, if you created a new category called "Real Identity," its display would be controlled by the template file `user-profile-category.tpl.php`. By default, each category is displayed as a definition list. You may alter this HTML by changing the template file called `user-profile-category.tpl.php`. One default category is provided by the user module, called "History."

user-profile.tpl.php

This default template presents all user profile data. Use this template to change the overall layout of user profiles.

user-profile-item.tpl.php

This template is used to loop through and render each field configured for the user's account. It can also render the data from modules. The output is grouped by categories. If you like, you can change only the wrapper for this page. If you want to exert finer-grained control over the information that is printed to the page, however, you will need to work with the individual fields. They can be accessed through the `$profile` array. To print all possible information, use the following PHP snippet:

```
<?php print '<pre>'. check_plain(print_r($profile, 1)) .'</pre>'; ?>
```

This command is also stored in the default template provided in the `modules/user` directory. You may wish to copy and paste it to avoid typographical errors in copying.

In a default Drupal installation, this command will print remarkably little information. You may access this information using two different variables. The first variable, `$profile`, contains an array of all currently stored profile variables; the second variable, `$user_profile`, contains a formatted user profile, ready for printing. To modify the display of your profile, use the individual components stored in the variable `$pro-file`. To add material to the default profile display, use `$user_profile`. Figure 7.5 shows an example illustrating the output of these two variables.

Adding More Content

Modules typically provide you with all of the variations you will need to display for the information they collect. There may be cases, however, when you want to display data that is not available from the module's default variables. For example, the data collected by the Profile module is very limited. In addition to using the content contained in the variables `$profile` and `$user_profile`, you may want to pull in other content that is relevant to the user account for display on the account page. To assemble a richer set of variables for display on the user's profile, you must use Drupal's preprocess functions.

The following snippets show how to create a new variable with information retrieved from the database. The information that is retrieved in this snippet could be more appropriately retrieved using the module Views; however, it is given here as an example of what can be done at the theme layer to supplement the data provided by existing module variables.

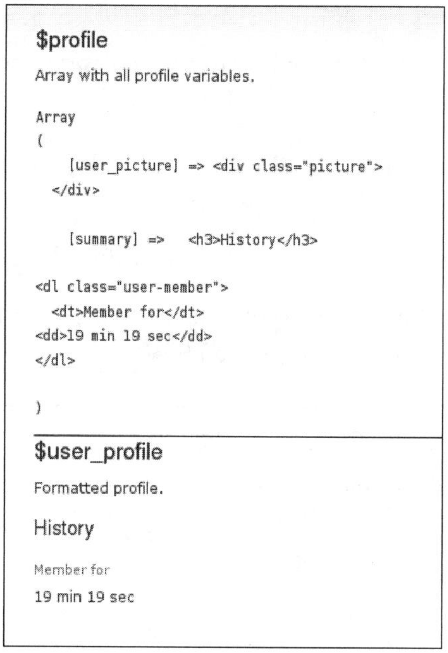

```
$profile
Array with all profile variables.

Array
(
    [user_picture] => <div class="picture">
    </div>

    [summary] =>    <h3>History</h3>

<dl class="user-member">
  <dt>Member for</dt>
<dd>19 min 19 sec</dd>
</dl>

)
```

```
$user_profile
Formatted profile.
```

History

Member for
19 min 19 sec

FIGURE 7.5 `$profile` and `$user_profile` are two variables that allow you to retrieve profile information for different types of display.

In the theme file `template.php`, information is retrieved from database and the contents are placed into a new variable.

```php
function bolg_preprocess_user_profile(&$variables) {
  global $user;
  $result = db_query_range("SELECT nid, title, created FROM {node} WHERE
type='page' AND uid = $user->uid order by created DESC", 0, 8);
  $nodes = array();
  while ($row = db_fetch_object($result)) {
    $nodes[] = l(check_plain($row->title), "node/" . $row->nid);
  }


  if ($user->uid > 0 && count($nodes) > 0){
    $nodes = theme('item_list', $nodes);
  }


  return $variables['recent_nodes'] = $nodes;
}
```

In the previous snippet three special Drupal theming functions were used:

- `l()` creates a Drupal link.
- `check_plain()` encodes special characters in a plain text string for display as HTML. This allows you to "see" HTML markup printed to the page.
- `theme('item_list', $nodes)` is a list builder helper function.

Once the new variable has been prepared, it can be inserted into the template file `user-profile.tpl.php` for display in a Web page:

```php
<div class="user-contrib-content">
<h2><?php print t("Recent Content"); ?></h2>
  <?php if ($recent_nodes){ ?>
    <?php print $recent_nodes; ?>
  <?php } else {
    print t("No content, yet!"); ?>
  <?php } ?>
</div>
```

In the template file, one special Drupal theming function is used: `t()`. This function checks for translations of the text passed to the function. All human-readable text should be passed through this function, which in turn allows content editors to translate the text. This approach is the secure way of passing text from Drupal to the Web browser. For more information, read the document found at `http://drupal.org/node/28984`.

Additional information on ways to extend the display of user profiles with custom PHP snippets can be found on the Drupal Web site at `http://drupal.org/node/35728`. If you want to allow users to syndicate their off-site blogs into their user profiles, you should consider using the SimpleFeed module.

At the time when this book was written, a number of sophisticated Drupal 5 modules were available that customized the user account page (or user "home" page). Several module teams were preparing to work together to create one really great user profile module for Drupal 6. The Advanced Profile Kit combines several modules to give a comprehensive profile useful for social networking Web sites. More information on this tool can be found at `http://drupal.org/project/advanced_profile`. The MySite module allows users to create their own home pages with blocks that are of greatest use to them. These "home pages" could also be made public. For more information about this project, visit the project page at `http://drupal.org/project/mysite`.

Granting and Restricting Access

In a Drupal Web site, you control the things that users do. This section is placed front and center as a reminder that you must set permissions for each new task that you enable on your Drupal site. If you are logged into the system as `user/1`, you will be able to do everything without setting permissions. This is not true for any other user in the system. You may want to perform your administrative duties from another user account to remind yourself to set the permissions explicitly for functionality that you add to your Web site.

Defining Roles

Drupal allows you to grant access to "roles" within your Web site. By default, there are two roles: "authenticated" and "anonymous" users. You may add as many new roles as you would like. There are no limits on how many, or how few, users can be added to each role. If there is a specific task you would like only one user to perform, you could create a role and assign only one user to that role. You may use any naming convention for your roles. You may wish to use names that are related to site capabilities—for example, content author, moderator, administrator. Alternatively, you may decide to use names that are related to job titles—for example, student, professor, associate dean.

Creating a role is very easy (Figure 7.6). Once your new role has been added, you can use the link to "edit permissions" to change what users with this role may do within the site. Use the following steps to add a new role to your Web site:

1. Navigate to Administer, User management, Roles.

2. Enter the name of the new role at the bottom of the current list of roles.

3. Click "Add role."

To change the name of the role, or to delete one of your custom roles, click the "edit" link beside the name of the role. There are no other configuration options available in the "edit" option.

Granting and Revoking Permissions

To change the permissions available to each user, you may click on the link "edit permissions" next to the name of the role. To see the full matrix of all permissions for all roles, navigate to Administer, User management, Permissions. The role summary page also contains a text link to this page.

The programming team for every module has made some decisions about the default permissions for its module. In most cases, all permissions are not enabled when a new module is installed. In Figure 7.7, you can see the permissions for a few modules that have been installed. Some modules listed are core modules (block and comment modules); others are contributed modules (advanced_help module).

Name	Operations	
anonymous user	locked	edit permissions
authenticated user	locked	edit permissions
administrator	Add role	

FIGURE 7.6 A new role, administrator, is created. Permissions will now need to be configured for the new role.

Permissions

Permissions let you control what users can do on your site. Each user role (defined on the user roles page) has its own set of permissions. For example, you could give users classified as "Administrators" permission to "administer nodes" but deny this power to ordinary, "authenticated" users. You can use permissions to reveal new features to privileged users (those with subscriptions, for example). Permissions also allow trusted users to share the administrative burden of running a busy site.

Permission	anonymous user	authenticated user	administrator
advanced_help module			
view advanced help index	☐	☐	☐
view advanced help popup	☐	☐	☐
view advanced help topic	☐	☐	☐
block module			
administer blocks	☐	☐	☐
use PHP for block visibility	☐	☐	☐
comment module			
access comments	☐	☑	☐
administer comments	☐	☐	☐
post comments	☐	☑	☐
post comments without approval	☐	☑	☐
controlpanel module			

FIGURE 7.7 Most permissions are disabled for each role by default when a module is installed.

If you wish your roles to override the permissions for these two states, unselect the permission from the default settings and apply the permissions as you would like to your custom roles. For example, if you want only authenticated users with the role of "content manager" to add new pages, you would unselect the permission to "add page" from "authenticated" users and add the permission to the role of "content managers."

Checking Access at the Theme Level

In addition to assigning privileges via the permissions matrix, you may control access at the theme level. For example, you might want to allow only users with a specific role to view content through a specific template. You may also use this technique to limit access to specific fields of content. For example, you might want to enable members of a grant application committee to view all financial data submitted by a group, but permit "peer" reviewers to see only the text-based proposal (and not the financial data).

> **More control than permissions alone**
> To limit the display of fields at the theme level, you will need to edit your template files for the relevant content type. PHP snippets found throughout this chapter can be added to the appropriate places in your *.tpl.php files.

There are three types of permission-based functions you should be aware of at the theme level:

- user_is_logged_in()
- user_access('permission')
- in_array('name_of_role', array_values($user->roles))

Each of these options would be used as a test. For example:

```
if (user_is_logged_in()) {
    // Do something for logged-in users
}
if (user_access('access administration pages')) {
    // Allow this user to do administrative tasks
}
if (in_array('administrator'), array_values($user->roles)) {
    // Allow this user to do something administrators should be allowed to do,
    // but there is no permission defined by the module itself.
    // Useful for displaying specific content fields to selected roles.
}
```

If you are testing for the "administrator" role, you may also want to test for the main site administrator. This can be done by extending the third test to look to see which user is logged in.

```
if (in_array('administrator'), array_values($user->roles)
   || $user->uid == 1) {
    // Allow all administrators and the root user to do very special things
}
```

If you are looking at specific permissions that are created by a module, you should also confirm that the module is enabled. To do so, use the function `module_exists('name_of_module')`. For example, in Chapter 6 you learned how to add a search form to the error screen when the user requests a page that is a "404 Page Not Found." In this example, we checked whether the module was enabled (`module_exists('search')`) and the Web site visitor had permission to use the form (`user_access('search content')`). The module name to use with `module_exists()` is the word prepended to "module" on the permissions page. The specific permission to use with `user_access()` is the exact text (with spaces, if there are any) that appears next to your check boxes on the same permissions page.

Extending the Administrative Role to More Users

Drupal allows "all" permissions for only the first account on the site. If you need to have more than one account with this level of access, you should consider installing the module known as "Admin role." This module is a little helper for maintaining an administrator role that has full permissions. By default, only one user has full administrator rights in Drupal; this module changes that situation.

For more information, and to download the Admin role module, go to the project page at `http://drupal.org/project/adminrole`.

Community Comments

Drupal excels at being a platform on which people can interact. If you are producing Drupal Web sites, you probably considered its audience participation features to be among Drupal's key advantages. Over the next few sections we will examine how these interactions can be styled to fit with the rest of your Web site design.

Customizing Comment Display

As with the user profile, the comment module comes with three template files that you can modify. These files can be copied from the directory `modules/comment`.

comment.tpl.php

The main comment file, `comment.tpl.php` controls the whole output for a comment. The default template includes options to print out at least the commenter's picture (if this individual has an account on the Web site); whether the comment is new; the title of the comment (if it is enabled); the date when the comment was submitted; and the actual comment. For information on how to add additional CSS classes to comments, review the template file `comment.tpl.php` in the Zen theme and the template file `template.php`. In this file, Zen shows you how to add classes based on the following considerations:

- "Comments by me"
- Status-related information (published or unpublished)
- Comments written by the same author who wrote the original content

These variables are all added to the comment template as part of the preprocess function. Within the zen folder, look for the following line in the template file `comment.tpl.php`:

```
function zen_preprocess_comment(&$vars, $hook) {
```

This function contains the logic to create new variables that can be used in the template file.

comment-folded.tpl.php

This file defines how the comments will look if they are hidden or "folded" away. In this case, users have to click a link to view the comment. By default, the subject of the comment and the author appear (as well as a "new" flag if relevant).

comment-wrapper.tpl.php

This file includes the HTML `<div>` for all comments that have been created. It is the container in which all comments are placed for display. You may wish to add some kind of title to this file, explaining that content displayed here consists of user-contributed comments. In the Zen theme the following heading is added:

```
<h2 id="comments-title"><?php print t('Comments'); ?></h2>
```

Note the use of the function `t()`. It is the correct and secure way of handling text in templates. This function will also escape any characters that are not plain text by running the text through the function `check_plain()`. It is especially important to be secure when you are allowing content from untrusted Web site visitors.

The comment settings can also be configured based on the type of content. Figure 7.8 shows the range of options that can be set for your comments, which include the following possibilities:

- Default display mode (flat list versus threaded list)
- Display order (newest first or oldest first)
- Number of comments to show per page
- Location of the comment controls
- Anonymous commenting
- Whether a subject field should be provided
- Whether people leaving comments must "preview" their comments before submitting them
- Location of the comment submission form

FIGURE 7.8 Many configuration options for comments exists. Comments can be configured in a unique fashion for each different content type on your Web site.

Adding User Identity to Comments

In addition to the configurations that are available to each of the content types, you may choose to include the profile image of authenticated Web site commenters. Of course, this possibility arises only when the commenters have an account on the Web site with a user profile image. These settings are adjusted in the theme configuration area. To include user pictures in comments, for example, you must complete the following steps:

1. Navigate to Administer, Site building, Themes.
2. Find the theme you are currently using and click the "configure" link.
3. Scroll down to the "Toggle display" area and add a check mark beside "User picture in comments." You may choose to enable "User pictures in posts" as well, although this option is less relevant on a Web site where there is only one content manager.

If you want to adjust the position of the profile image, you must use the file `comment.tpl.php`. The template file can be copied directly into your theme directory.

Disqus

Disqus (pronounced "discuss") is a service and tool for facilitating web comments and discussions. The Disqus comment system can be plugged into any Web site, blog, or application. It makes commenting easier and more interactive, while connecting Web sites and commenters to create a thriving discussion community. Disqus makes it easier for people to comment and track their contributions on a single profile, which they can display as a comment blog. After all, there really is no difference between a great comment and a great published article. In addition to allowing authors to track their own comments across multiple Web sites, Disqus allows Web site visitors to reply to comments through email or mobile technologies, and to edit their own comments after submission.

Integrating Disqus into your Drupal Web site is a two-part procedure. First, you must download and install the Disqus module from Drupal and create an account on the Disqus Web site. From your Disqus account, you can manage the comment systems for multiple Web sites. Second, after you have installed the Drupal Disqus module and created your account on Disqus, you need to configure your Drupal Web site.

1. Navigate to Administer, Site configuration, Disqus.
2. Enter your configuration settings from the Disqus Web site.

3. Set the node type for which you would like to enable comments.

4. Scroll to the bottom of the Web page and save your configuration.

5. Disable Drupal's comment module. Navigate to Administer, Site building, Modules.

6. Unselect the comment module. Scroll to the bottom of the Web page and save your settings.

7. Set the permissions so as to allow users to use Disqus. Navigate to Administer, User management, Permissions.

8. Select the appropriate roles who may "view disqus comments." Scroll to the bottom of the Web page and save your settings.

9. Enable the Disqus block. Navigate to Administer, Site building, Blocks.

10. Select the region where you would like the Disqus block to appear. Save your settings.

User-Generated Content

Blogs, forums, wikis, content, and more content! There are many different ways that community members may potentially contribute to a Web site. This section provides a brief overview of some of the modules you may want to install to support different kinds of user-generated content (UGC) as well as the template files you should be aware of for each content type.

Blogs (and Comments)

Although comments were covered in the previous section (and spam will be covered in a later section in this chapter), a brief note on blogs is appropriate here. Drupal includes a Blog module as part of its core. Although this module does not offer a lot of extra functionality, it makes "blogging" easy for content editors who are new to Web site participation and know they are supposed to be creating blogs as part of their jobs. You can easily filter blog entries using the Views module to take advantage of exactly the right combination of authors. You may also want to provide a summary page of all blog entries that have a specific tag (or category or taxonomy term).

To enable the blog navigate to Administer, Site building, Modules. Look for the Blog module in the list of Core-optional modules. Enable it by selecting the check box beside its name, scrolling to the bottom of the Web page, and clicking "Save configuration."

With the Blog module installed, you should confirm the default settings for this content type using the following steps:

1. Navigate to Administer, Content management, Content types.

   a. Click the "edit" link for the Blog content type.

   b. Adjust the description so that content authors know their blog entries will be filtered to the correct page automatically.

   c. Confirm the following settings: Submission form settings; Workflow settings; Comment settings.

   d. Scroll to the bottom of the Web page and click "Save content type."

2. Navigate to Administer, Site building, Themes.

   a. Click the "configure" link at the top of the page.

   b. Confirm the display of post information for blog entries. Although the list of blog entries will be controlled by the view, you will still have the default veiw provided by the module itself. You may also choose to alter this display with a template file.

   c. Scroll to the bottom of the Web page and click "Save configuration."

Although there are no default templates for the Blog module, you can easily configure the display of a blog entry through the `node.tpl.php` template. If you would like to have a more specific template for only blog entries, within your theme directory create a copy of the template file `node.tpl.php` and name it `node-blog.tpl.php`. Make your changes to this new file for blog-only theming.

Forums

Drupal also provides a Forum module as part of its core. This discussion system relies on a combination of other core modules including taxonomy, nodes, and comments. Because several modules are involved in the creation and display of Drupal's discussion system, you must look in several places to find the default templates. Fortunately, the entire forum system and its related modules have been converted to template files. You will not need to go on a hunt through the module files for theme functions; instead, you can simply copy the related template files into your theme directory and begin the process of theming the forums to match your site.

To style the display of a forum post, use the template file `node-forum.tpl.php`. You may start with the default node template file `node.tpl.php` for a very basic node (if your theme already has a node template file, you may wish to use it as a base for your forum templates). The Zen theme also provides a sample template for forum content. The responses to a forum topic are technically comments.

Once you have the content themed, you may want to review the larger theming picture—that is, how forum topics and listings are themed. The Forum module provides you with six template files through which to alter the forum-specific data:

- `forum-icon.tpl.php`: Displays an appropriate icon for a forum post.
- `forum-list.tpl.php`: Lists forums and containers. This list shows the broadest overview of all forum categories.
- `forums.tpl.php`: Default theme implementation to display a forum that may contain both forum containers and forum topics.
- `forum-submitted.tpl.php`: Gives information about the author of the post and the date on which it was submitted.
- `forum-topic-list.tpl.php`: Lists forum topics. This list is displayed on screen after the Web site visitor has selected a topic from the `forum-list.tpl.php` page.
- `forum-topic-navigation.tpl.php`: The topic navigation string that appears at the bottom of all forum topics.

To alter the individual forum pages, you will need to add theme information for nodes of the content type forum as well as comments related to these nodes. The comment template files can be obtained directly from the comment module. The Zen theme provides a template for the first message in each topic in the template file `node-forum.tpl.php`. Zen's forum template is essentially the same as a plain node. The only thing that differs is the addition of Zen's shortcut for assigning new classes based on the status of the content being displayed. If you have already created a `node.tpl.php` file, consider using it as the base template file for new forum messages as well.

Wikis

It is always best to use the most appropriate tool for the job. Even though there are a lot of very sophisticated wiki platforms, Drupal should not be overlooked when considering a platform for community-editable documentation. As with its forums support, Drupal's wiki system is created by combining several modules. To create a wiki site, you will need to install the following modules:

- `book` (core): Use this module for automatically generated navigation.
- `wikitools` (contributed): Provides Wiki features such as node creation, deletion, and move protection.
- `flexifilter` (contributed): Use Wiki-style text formatting (available at `http://drupal.org/project/flexifilter`).
- `freelinking` (contributed): Create links between nodes with the CamelCase-Title for the destination page (available at `http://drupal.org/project/freelinking`).

To create a wiki, you must install each of the modules listed above. Refer to Appendix A for more information on how to install a contributed module. Each of these modules must also be configured as follows:

1. Rename the book content type to "Wiki page." Navigate to Administer, Content management, Content types. Click the "edit" link next to "Book." Update the "Name" and "Description" to suit your Web site.
2. Update the revision control defaults for your wiki pages. These setting are found under the "Workflow settings" tab. Force a new revision for each edit of the page by enabling "Revision Control."
3. Configure the "Wikitools" to match your site's needs.
4. Enable and configure the flexifilter module. Enable the default Mediawiki filter. Consider importing more filters from `http://drupal.org/node/212417`.
5. Enable and configure the freelinking module. Update your settings in the "Wikitools configuration" screen to enable "Hijack freelinking module."
6. Configure the input format to use the new filters.
7. Update the default input format for wiki pages (formerly book nodes).
8. Update the permissions for your new content type. All Web site visitors should be able to view content and view revisions. Depending on the "openness" of your wiki, you may set the appropriate permissions to revert changes, create new pages, and edit existing pages.

Extending your Drupal wiki

Charlie Gordon (http://www.cwgordon.com) also recommends the following additions:

- Use the talk module to add a "talk" tab to each applicable node page.
- Use the table of contents module to insert a table of contents on pages of your choice.
- Use the diff module to show the differences between various revisions. This feature is useful for finding and reversing spammy posts.

Recipes and Specialized Content

In many cases, it is completely acceptable to build your own content type using the Content Creation Kit (CCK). In contrast, if your needs are specialized enough that you might consider making a custom content type, you should consider wandering through the hundreds of submitted modules in the Content category at http://drupal.org/project/Modules/category/57. This list of modules includes some highly specialized, but highly useful modules. For example, the Recipe module includes a calculator that changes the ingredient quantities in a recipe based on the number of servings you want (Figure 7.9). For more information about the Recipe module, visit its project page at http://drupal.org/project/recipe.

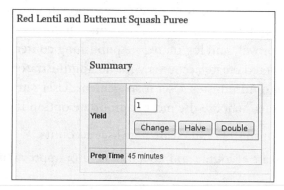

FIGURE 7.9 The Recipe module provides a form on which Web site visitors can alter the quantity for the ingredients in a recipe based on the number of servings required.

Spam

Any Web site that allows visitors to add content, or create a membership so as to create content, faces the risk of having unwanted content added to the site. This undesirable content is referred to as "spam"—a term that comes from the British comedy troop Monty Python's 1970 "SPAM" sketch. In the sketch, Mr. and Mrs. Bun try to order breakfast from a menu that contains mostly canned, spiced ham (brand name, "SPAM"); however, a group of raucous Vikings keep drowning out their order by singing a tune almost entirely composed of the word "spam." During the short skit, the word "spam" is used more than 80 times. In the 1980s, the term was adopted when individuals began to maliciously disrupt conversations with senseless, unwanted content. Early "spam attacks" consisted of a simple flood of the word "Spam" into bulletin board systems and chat rooms. The term now has a much wider definition and is used to describe any unsolicited and unwanted receipt of digital content (email, blog comments, discussion board postings, and so on).

In the Drupal context, "spam" refers to any content created by a computer program that has been designed to seek out Web forms and publish unwanted content. Although individual Web site visitors may create spam, such attacks are more typically generated by an automated process that is disconnected from individual people. The computer programs that create the spam content are referred to as "bots" or "spambots." (Although "bot" is short for "robot," bots are worthy of the same disdain awarded to the parasitic botfly.)

Several approaches can be taken to prevent spambots from publishing content on your Web site. The fastest way to lock down your site is to force each visitor to create an account (that you approve), and log in, before publishing content. By default, Drupal allows Web site visitors to create accounts with no administrator approval. To change this setting, navigate to Administer, User management, User settings. Under the heading "Public registrations," choose the most appropriate option for your Web site:

- Only site administrators can create new user accounts.
- Visitors can create accounts and no administrator approval is required (selected by default).
- Visitors can create accounts but administrator approval is required.

Be sure to update the authenticated role's access permissions accordingly. Navigate to Administer, User management, Permissions. Confirm the settings for the "authenticated" role. You may need to add or remove permissions as appropriate. You may also need to add a new "administrative" role if your settings initially focused only on the default roles of "authenticated" and "anonymous" users.

CAPTCHA

Forcing individuals to create an account before leaving a comment on your Web site is a barrier to participation that many visitors will not take the time to surpass. If visitor participation is limited to comments on a blog, you may wish to consider adding a "challenge" to your comment form instead of forcing users to create an account if they want to leave a comment on your Web site. These challenge questions added to Web site forms are known as "Completely Automated Public Turing tests to tell Computers and Humans Apart" (CAPTCHA). The Turing test was first described by Alan Turing in 1950 and was described as a test to distinguish humans from computers. It asked, "Can machines do what we (as thinking entities) can do?" Web CAPTCHA tests have since been implemented in several different ways:

- As a graphic test (read a scrambled word and type it into the response box)
- As a logic test (perform a simple math calculation or select a word from a list, and type the result into the response box)
- As an audio test (listen to a word and then type it into the box)

The graphic test is one of the most commonly used tests, but it is also relatively inaccessible to Web site visitors who have low vision or who are blind. The graphics-based CAPTCHA test is often paired with an audio test to provide low-vision and blind users with an alternative way to prove their humanity.

Several CAPTCHA modules are available for Drupal. The basic module, CAPTCHA, can also be extended by other modules to include different types of tests (and logic questions that you have created!).

- CAPTCHA: A basic module appropriate for most uses (`http://drupal.org/project/captcha`)
- reCAPTCHA: Implements the reCAPTCHA service (`http://drupal.org/project/recaptcha`)
- CAPTCHA Pack: Many different lightweight, text-based CAPTCHA tests; requires the basic Drupal CAPTCHA module (`http://drupal.org/project/captcha_pack`)

- Captcha Riddler: Allows you to create your own test questions; requires the basic Drupal CAPTCHA module (`http://drupal.org/project/riddler`)

Comment Closer

Many Web sites that allow comments on their content are blogs and, therefore, do not need to leave comments open indefinitely. If this is true for your Web site, you should consider installing the Comment closer module. This simple module does exactly what its name implies: After a fixed amount of time, it disallows visitors from commenting on specific types of content.

To install the Comment closer module, follow the instructions in Appendix A that explain how to install a Drupal module. The project page for this module can be found at `http://drupal.org/project/commentcloser`.

Once installed, the module can be easily configured by navigating to Administer, Site configuration, Comment closer. A simple menu allows you to choose which content types should have their comments automatically turned off, and at what point this termination should happen (see Figure 7.10).

You must configure three options with the Comment closer module:

1. Node type: the type of content you want to control with comment closer.

2. Older than: the age of the content that should be closed.

3. Execute: how often the creation date of the content should be checked.

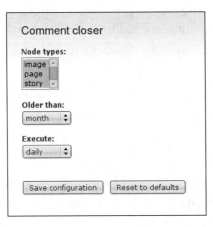

FIGURE 7.10 Comments can be easily closed on a timed basis using the Comment closer module.

The Comment closer module should be "executed" more frequently than the age check. For example, you would check for content "older than" a week every day.

This module requires the simultaneous use of cron, Drupal's automated scheduling tool. To confirm that cron is running automatically, navigate to Administer, Reports, Status report. Look for the section on "Cron maintenance tasks." If cron has not run recently, you will need to configure your Web server to trigger Drupal's scheduling tool. Chapter 2 of this book describes how to set up a cron job.

Spam Filtering Services

The techniques described in this section are geared toward evaluating Web site visitors *before* they submit their content to your Web site. More sophisticated services are also available that will help you to evaluate content *after* it has been submitted to your Web site. These services include Akismet and Mollom.

Akismet was one of the earliest community-powered spam assessment tools. It harnessed the brain power of everyone who subscribed to its service to identify patterns of spam (unwanted content) and ham (desired content). Mollom goes beyond this simple filtering service and attempts to block fake user accents. In recognition of its additional features, Mollom is currently receiving more active development and support in the Drupal community. If you have used Akismet in the past, you should consider switching to Mollom!

Installing Mollom is a two-step process. First, you will need to download and install the Mollom module; second, you must create a Mollom account on the Mollom Web site.

To perform the first step, follow the instructions in Appendix A on how to install a Drupal module. The project page for this module can be found at `http://drupal.org/project/mollom.`

Once the module is installed, you will need to attach your Web site to the Mollom service. To do so, you must create a user account on the Mollom Web site. Within your user account, you will need to tell Mollom which Web sites will be using its service. This notification is made via the "Manage sites" tab, where you then ask Mollom to "add subscription."

At the end of the configuration process, you will be able to "view keys" for each of your Web sites. Two keys are provided: public and private. These keys should be placed in the configuration page of your Drupal Web site. A sophisticated spam filtering toolset will be presented to you once the keys have been entered.

For more detailed information on how to configure Mollom, visit its Web site at http://www.mollom.com.

Private Web Site Areas

There are many ways to create a private area within your Web site. One option is to use CCK and create a new type of content that is "private" and available only to users with a specific role. This technique is quite limited, however, and does not allow you to reuse content for both the public and private areas of your Web site. Alternatively, you might like to display some fields' content to some users, but not to all users.

Member-Only Sites

A quick way to separate different kinds of content is to use the Taxonomy module. Within Drupal, the concepts of "tags" and "categories" are collectively referred to as taxonomy (in fact, "taxonomy" is sometimes referred to as "categories" within the Drupal administrative area). It is easy to add categories to different pieces of content. One way to categorize content could be to make a simple distinction between "public" and "private" content. Unfortunately, Drupal cannot act on these categories without some extra help from a contributed module.

Although you could build your own private content area with views and custom templates, it is much easier to download and install the Taxonomy Access Control Lite module. This module restricts access so that some users may view content that is hidden from other users. A simple scheme based on taxonomy, roles, and users controls which content is hidden. The Taxonomy Access Control Lite module uses the same concepts that you could implement by hand as a themer, but gives Web site administrators a graphical interface through which to accomplish these tasks.

To install the Taxonomy Access Control Lite module, follow the instructions in Appendix A on how to install a Drupal module. The project page for this module is located at http://drupal.org/project/tac_lite. Once you have downloaded and installed the module, you may need to rebuild the content access permissions tables.

With the permissions tables rebuilt, you can configure Taxonomy Access Control Lite. If you have not already created the categories you would like to use to distinguish between private and public content, you should do so now.

1. Navigate to Administer, Content management, Taxonomy.
2. Add a new vocabulary that will distinguish between public and private content. Click on the "add vocabulary" tab at the top of the page.

> ⚠ **Rebuilding database tables**
> A warning message will appear after you have installed the Taxonomy Access Control Lite module and clicked "Save." Follow the on-screen instructions to perform the necessary database updates. If you are having problems accessing content, you may need to rebuild the permissions cache. This can be done by navigating to Administer, Content management, Post settings. Click the "rebuild permissions" button to clear the cache related to permissions.

3. Enter as much information as you can at this stage. Make sure you enable this vocabulary for at least one content type. Scroll to the bottom of the Web page and click "Save." You can also choose at this time whether you would like to have this category as a requirement for submitted content.

4. Add terms that will act as flags for content authors to set their content as either "public" or "private." Click the "add terms" link and fill out the form using the appropriate category names for your Web site.

You are now ready to set up TAC Lite.

1. Navigate to Administer, User management, Access control by taxonomy.

2. Select the vocabulary you would like to use to distinguish public and private content. Click "Save configuration."

3. Click the link at the top of the page for "Scheme 1." This is the configuration screen for your vocabulary.

4. Fill out the configuration screen using defaults that are appropriate for your Web site. For example, for private pages, you would use the following settings (Figure 7.11):

   • Scheme name: private, read-only access

   • Permissions: view

   • Access for anonymous user: none (this is a default role, provided by Drupal)

   • Access for authenticated user: private (this is a default role, provided by Drupal)

   • Access for administrator: private (this is a role created by navigating to Administer, User, Roles))

5. Scroll to the bottom of the form and click "Save configuration."

6. Repeat steps 1–5 to create additional permissions (for example, any authenticated user can edit content with the category "private").

You may also want to consider using the Nodeaccess module. Nodeaccess is a Drupal access control module that provides view, edit, and delete access to nodes. Users with the "grant node permissions" permission will have a grant tab on node pages that allows them to grant access to that node by user or role. Administrators can set default access controls per content type, and they can also define which roles are available to grant permissions to on the node grants tab. The Nodeaccess module allows you to set limits such as "node 123 can be viewed by authenticated users and edited by admin users and joeplumber." As an added bonus, update and delete permissions are kept separate, so you can make sure users with edit permissions cannot accidentally delete pages.

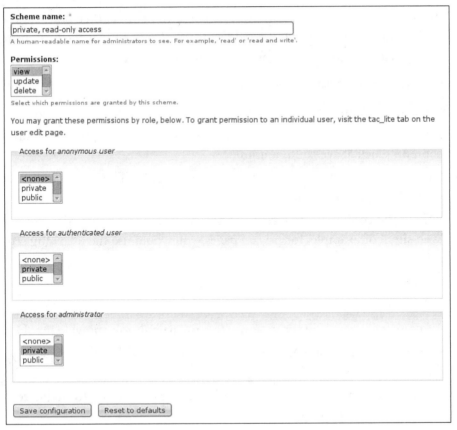

FIGURE 7.11 Setting the permissions is controlled by the schemes configuration screen.

When this book was being written, a major rewrite of the Nodeaccess module was in the planning stages. Many user interface changes were being planned. You can review the status of this module, and download it, from its project page at `http://drupal.org/project/nodeaccess`.

You may also wish to enhance the navigation of your Web site for the public and private areas by using the Views module to create custom lists of content. For more information about creating administrative views of content, refer to Chapter 8. For more ideas on how to implement a private Web site, refer to Drupal's online documentation page, "Private forums and member-only sites," at `http://drupal.org/node/111576`.

Private Content Fields

You may wish to have some content fields that have restricted visibility. Within the template file for each of your content types, you can perform tests on each of the content fields to limit its visibility. Common tests include the following:

- Test whether the user is viewing content he or she has authored:

```
if ($GLOBALS['user']->uid == $node->uid) {
```

- Test whether a user is viewing his or her own user profile:

```
if ($GLOBALS['user']->uid == $user->uid) {
```

- Test whether the logged-in user has a specific role:

```
if (in_array('administrator'), array_values($user->roles)){
```

- Test whether the logged-in user has a specific permission:

```
if (user_access('access administration pages')){
```

Each of these if statements must be ended with }. For example, to provide a link to the Administration area only for users with sufficient permission, you could use the following PHP snippet:

```
if (user_access('access administration pages')){
    print l("Administration Drupal", "admin");
}
```

This example uses the l() function to format an internal Drupal link. It correctly handles aliased paths, and it allows themes to highlight links to the current page correctly.

If you are working within the user profile and want to limit the display of certain fields, you have four more options at your disposal:

- Hidden profile field: Accessible only to administrators, modules, and themes
- Private field: Content available only to privileged users
- Public field: Content shown on profile page but not used on member list pages
- Public field: Content shown on profile page and on member list pages

Within your template file, make sure you are using the variable $profile to display each of your profile fields to protect information according to the settings listed above. Private profile fields can be viewed only by the account holder (in other words, a user can view his or her own information) as well as users with the "administer users" permission. Hidden fields, by contrast, can never be manipulated by the user. They may contain information about the user. The hidden profile field was originally implemented to keep track of community contributions. The higher the number of contributions (tallied based on the number of nodes added to the Web site), the higher the user's assigned role. Although it is very useful for module developers, it is unlikely you will use the hidden profile field on a regular basis in your work as a themer.

By limiting the visibility of certain areas on the profile page, you can change the profile page from a boring account history to a private home page for users who are viewing their own accounts. If you wanted to create a "friends-only" view of a profile, you could install either the Buddylist2 module (http://drupal.org/project/buddylist2) or the User Relationship module (http://drupal.org/project/user_relationships) to establish relationships between account holders.

Summary

This chapter described ways to create and style a Web site that has a lot of user-contributed content. More specifically, it covered the following topics:

- Styling user profile pages
- Customizing the access profiles for different types of roles in your Web site
- Enabling different kinds of user-generated content
- Creating custom pages of user-generated content
- Controlling spam
- Creating private areas in your Web site

Using suggestions from your community and the basic techniques covered in this chapter, you will now be able to theme your Web site according to the needs of your community of users.

Chapter 8

Administrative Interfaces

It is easy to be lulled into thinking the only area of the Web site that can be controlled by a theme is the very front-end design—the part that Web site visitors see. In fact, with a little bit of thinking about the common tasks your Web site administrators are performing, you can create a completely customized Drupal administration area. This will help to speed up work flow and will reveal new ways of thinking about how common tasks could be made even easier. When using any administrative system, take notes about functionality that you do, and do not, like. Think about how you could apply these lessons to your own Web sites. Does it make more sense for you, and your Web site administrators, to use iconic cues, or would a series of text-based links work better than a bunch of cryptic images?

In this chapter, you will learn how to enhance or replace elements in Drupal's administrative interface. Specifically, this chapter includes sections on using the core Drupal tools to customize your administrative interface and on using contributed modules to create control panels and administrative dashboards. A large part of this chapter focuses on the Views module, including use of this module to create unique lists of content that can be used by content administrators to filter out pages that need moderation or that have been omitted from the main site (perhaps unintentionally). The chapter ends with a brief discussion of the customization of error messages and error pages.

Creating a Custom Administrative Interface

Drupal's default administrative interface is based on functionality created by developers. It is not easily administered by novice Web site managers. Fortunately, Drupal is highly flexible, even in the administration area, and you can easily update the interface to reflect the tasks that your content managers will need to accomplish.

Applying a Separate Administrative Theme

Content managers and Web site administrators may be accustomed to having a visually distinct management area within the Web site that looks very different to the public Web site. By default, Drupal uses the same theme for both the administrative and public versions of a Web site. This behavior is unlike that of other Web publishing platforms. For example, WordPress uses an administrative dashboard with a distinct "view site" link near the top of the page. In Joomla!, the administrative area is known as the "control panel," and it comes equipped with a "preview" button to view the live site.

Both approaches offer both their own advantages and disadvantages. In Drupal, the administrative interface provides a seamless experience for Web site administrators. Administrators can delve into the administration of the site without having to learn a different style of pages, which might otherwise cause a jarring switch between the administrative and public views for the site. This distinction may also be a drawback, however, as visitors can sometimes overlook the powerful administrative options because they feel those options are part of the public side to the Web site; thus visitors may not realize they have the full set of administrative tools available to them.

To set an administration theme, you select the theme from a list, as shown in Figure 8.1. If you want to do additional configuration of your administration theme, use the steps in Chapter 3 to configure a sitewide theme; alternatively, you must navigate to Administer, Themes and choose the "configure" option beside the administrative theme that you would like to alter.

> **Use a flexible administration theme**
> If you are using a fixed-width theme for your main Web site, you may want to use a fluid design for your administration theme. Many of the administration tables are quite wide and may not be displayed properly in a fixed-width theme.

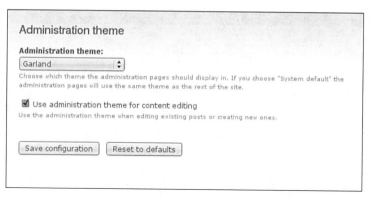

FIGURE 8.1 Use the Theme settings administration area to select the theme you want applied to your Web site.

The administrative theme is set in the "Site Building" part of the administration screen.

1. Choose the "Administer" link from the navigation options on the left side of the screen (or choose "administration section" from the front page).
2. Choose "Administration Theme" from the list of options on the main administration screen.
3. Select the Administration Theme you would like to use.
4. At the bottom of the configuration screen, click "Save configuration."

A separate administration theme should now be applied to your Web site.

RootCandy

RootCandy is a theme designed explicitly for the administration of Drupal; it is not meant to be used as a public interface theme. This contributed theme must be downloaded and installed before it can be applied to a Web site. RootCandy features icons across the top of each page in the administration area highlighting each of the main administrative functions (Figure 8.2). Wherever possible, screens expand to the full width of the page. In sections with subnavigation possibilities, the options are tucked neatly to the left of the main screen (Figure 8.3). This theme can also be recolored to complement the main part of your Web site using the Color module, which is also used by the default theme, Garland.

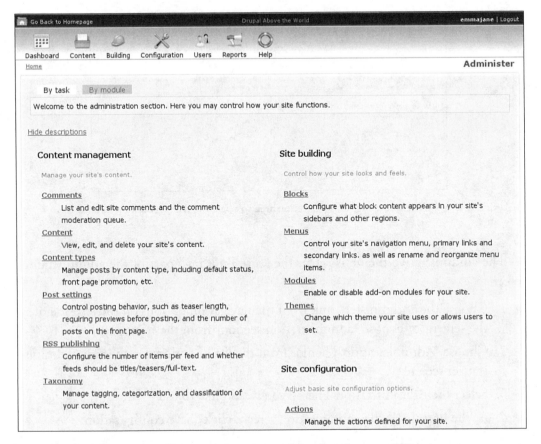

FIGURE 8.2 RootCandy is an alternative administrative theme focusing on usability.

You should download and install the RootCandy theme to see how the administration area of Drupal might potentially be themed. You may not choose to use it as your final administration theme, but RootCandy will likely serve as a source of inspiration, suggesting the many possibilities that are available to you. To install the RootCandy theme, follow these steps:

1. Download the project files from `http://drupal.org/project/rootcandy`.

2. Unpackage the files and put them into the site-specific directory `sites/yoursitename.com/themes` or a general directory for all sites using this Drupal code base: `sites/all/themes`.

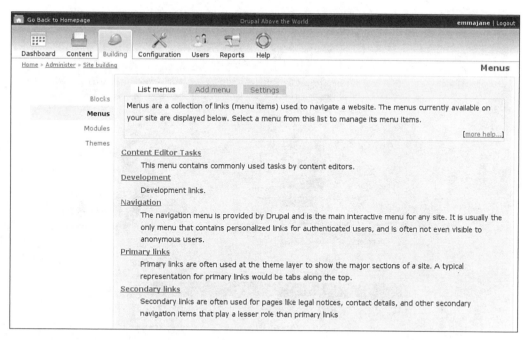

FIGURE 8.3 The RootCandy theme emphasizes the best possible use of space on each screen.

3. Enable RootCandy as the administration theme. Navigate to Administer, Site configuration, Administrative Theme. Choose RootCandy as the administrative theme. Scroll to the bottom of the Web page and click "Save configuration."

Other configuration options are also available for this theme, including changing the base colors (Figure 8.4).

1. Navigate to Administer, Site building, Themes.

2. Click the "configure" link next to the RootCandy theme.

3. Customize the display options for this theme, including the color.

4. Scroll to the bottom of the Web page and click "Save configuration."

Now that you have seen how Drupal's administrative area can be altered, it is time to start thinking about how you, too, can improve the experience for your administrators. If you are working with a small Web site that requires few custom tasks, Root-Candy might be enough for your needs. If you have a lot of custom tasks, however, you should consider creating a customized experience for your content administrators.

FIGURE 8.4 RootCandy allows you to customize the colors to match the main theme of your Web site.

Task-Based Navigation

Regardless of the type of Web site you have created, there will be some tasks that you need to perform on a regular basis. These tasks may range from creating a simple blog entry to undertaking a more complex series of tasks, such as editing, reviewing, and publishing content submitted by multiple Web site authors. Drupal provides a navigation block for users who are logged into the Web site that contains links to "Create Content," "Administer" the site, and "Logout" from the site. This block features the user's name as the title of the block and typically appears on the left side of the page in a default Drupal installation as shown in Figure 8.5.

While the Administer menu does contain a number of useful links, it is long and somewhat overwhelming for new Web site administrators. Using the "Site building" and "Site configuration" features requires the administrator to memorize each of the

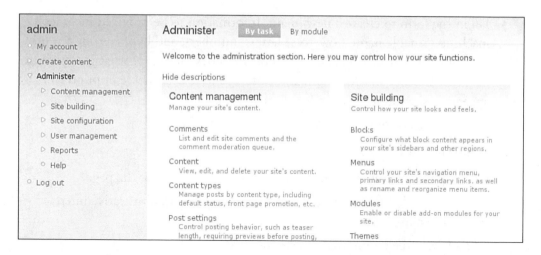

FIGURE 8.5 The default navigation block lists the Administer menu option; however, only those people who are very familiar with each of the sections will be able to effectively use this menu.

options contained within them. In many cases it is easier to go to the main "Administer" page and choose from the detailed list of all options found there.

To overcome the problems of having a too-long administrative menu, you may create your own custom menus for frequently performed administrative tasks within your site. For example, Web site administrators, content managers, and basic users have different sets of tasks that they need to accomplish. Customized menus for each of these groups can be placed into a specific region on your page by enabling the block for that menu. You will also be able to limit the access to each of these blocks according to the user's role.

When developing these menus, first list the common tasks that are needed by each different type of user. Consider the order in which these tasks should appear on the menu. In most cases it will be appropriate to put the most frequently performed tasks at the top of the list. You will be able to change the order of the menu items at any time. You may also use links to external Web sites for your menus—an ability that can prove especially useful if you use an external service, such as mailman, to administer the mailing lists for your Web site.

Creating Custom Menus

To create a custom menu, follow these steps:

1. Navigate to Administer, Site building, Menus.
2. Click "Add menu" from the configuration options across the top of the page.

3. Fill in the form to create a new menu. Information to be provided includes a machine-readable name (lowercase letters, numbers, and hyphens but not underscores), a human-readable title, and a brief description of what is contained in the menu. Use meaningful names, and be aware that the description will appear on the summary page for all menus.

4. Scroll to the bottom of the Web page and click "Save."

Your menu is now ready to have items added.

1. Click on the "Add item" configuration option at the top of the page.

2. You will be able to create new menu items using the administrative interface shown in Figure 8.6:

   • "Path" may be an internal or external link.

   • "Menu title" contains the words that will appear in the menu. Be as clear as possible with this text.

   • "Description" will appear as a tool tip when the user hovers the mouse over the menu item. Try to use a concise description that does not repeat the "Menu title" text. (In other words, in the dictionary, under the word "redundant," the definition should not say, "See redundant.")

   • Your menu item can have several subsections. When you specify the "Expanded" option, menu items nested under the current option will appear.

   • If you wish to move your menu item to another menu (or to move it within the hierarchy of the existing menu), change the "Parent item."

   • You can also change the order of the items within the menu. Use the "Weight" to move items up and down. This positioning of items can be easily edited in future screens.

3. When the menu item has been added and configured to your liking, scroll to the bottom of the Web page and click "Save."

4. Add additional items to the menu by repeating steps 2–7.

Once you have added your menu items, you can easily change their order, as shown in Figure 8.7, by dragging and dropping items to the correct location.

1. Navigate to Administer, Menus.

2. Choose the menu you want to alter by clicking on its title.

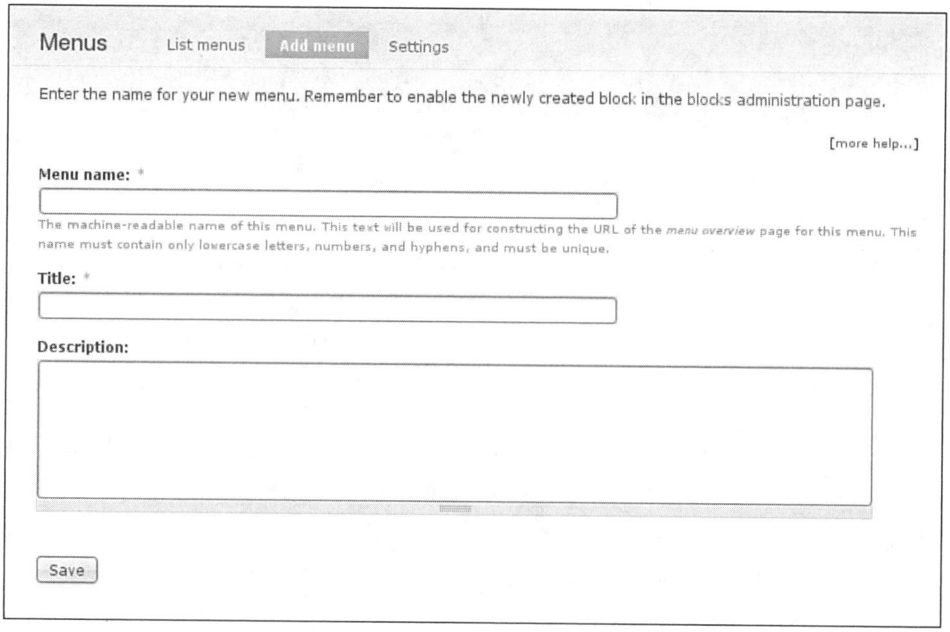

FIGURE 8.6 Items can be easily added to any menu in Drupal.

3. Use the crosshair icon at the left side of each menu item to drag and drop the menu item to a new location.

4. Scroll to the bottom of the Web page and click "Save configuration" to retain these changes.

If you do not have JavaScript enabled, you can move menu items by changing the weight in the drop down-box for each menu item.

Deploying Custom Menus

Once you have created the custom menu, you will need to enable it on your site. To do so, you must place a "block" for the menu into a "region" on your template. To enable the menu, follow these steps:

1. Navigate to Administer, Site building, Blocks.

2. Note the yellow bars, which will appear throughout the site to show you regions where blocks can be placed (the color may vary depending on the administrative theme you are using).

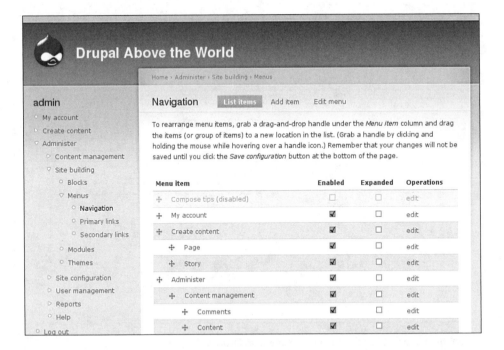

FIGURE 8.7 To change the order of a menu item, use the crosshair icon on the left side to drag and drop the item to a new location. If JavaScript is not enabled, use the "Weight" drop-down menu to change the position of each menu item.

3. Scroll down to the list of "Disabled" menu items and find your new menu. Drag the block up to the region you would like it to appear under and in the order you would like it to appear within the given region.

4. Scroll to the bottom of the page and click "Save blocks."

With the blocks saved, you can now configure their visibility:

1. Scroll to the block that contains your custom menu. Click "configure" next to the block.

2. On the configuration screen, you can override the name of the menu and set three different visibility options:

   • User-specific settings

   • Roles that may view the block

   • Pages on which the block can appear

Administrative Menus

Several contributed Drupal modules are available that will allow you to keep the full navigation options open for the Administration area without cluttering up the overall Web site layout. These modules are not part of the Drupal core, but rather must be downloaded and installed separately. Information about each of the project's pages is included here, along with a description of the module.

Remember to enable the permissions

If you are logged in as the primary site administrator, you will have these administrator menus available when the module is installed. If you have other Web site administrators who also want to access these menus, you will need to set the permissions on a per-role basis by navigating to Administer, User management, Permissions.

Admin Menu

The Admin Menu module creates a new menu containing all administrative menu items along the very top of your Web site. This module is not part of the Drupal core and must be downloaded and installed separately. The Admin Menu module is especially helpful for new Drupal administrators, because it gives them a quick overview of the available options without having to click through to each of the screens. It is also useful for experienced Drupal administrators, because it provides a shortcut to administrative tasks. An example of the Admin menu in action can be seen in Figure 8.8.

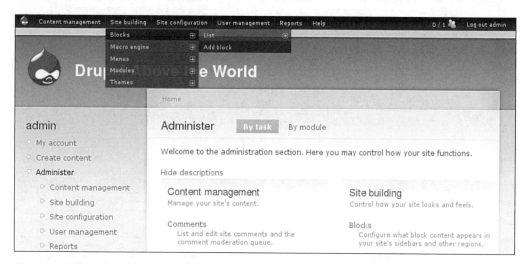

FIGURE 8.8 The Admin Menu module contains a shortcut to all links in the Administer menu.

To install the Admin Menu module, follow the instructions in Appendix A on how to install a Drupal module. The project page for this module is located at `http://drupal.org/project/admin_menu`.

Once the module has been installed and enabled, you will immediately see a black menu bar at the top of your Web site. Figure 8.9 shows the Admin Menu with no options selected. You will be able to use the Admin Menu as a shortcut to all administration pages as well as some commonly run administrative tasks.

The Drupal icon on the far left end of the Admin menu also contains a menu. This menu includes links to the following task:

- Visiting the Administer home page
- Running cron (see Chapter 2 for more information)
- Running updates
- Disabling the Devel module
- Accessing a shortcut to the Drupal.org issue queue

If the Devel module (see Chapter 2) is installed, you will also see links to three other tasks:

- Generating items ("dummy" content, users, and taxonomy items)
- Emptying the cache
- Using the Variable editor

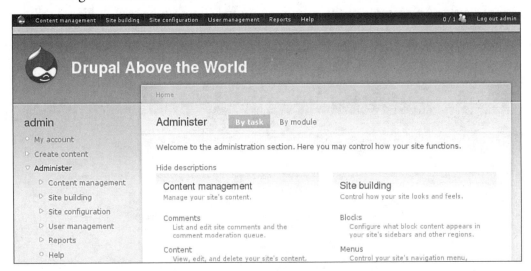

FIGURE 8.9 The Admin menu sits neatly at the top of your page and contains shortcuts to all administrative pages.

The Admin menu alters the modules page

By default, the Admin menu collapses fieldsets on the module pages. If you would rather that each section remain open on this page, you will need to change the default settings for the Admin menu. Navigate to Administer, Site configuration, Admin menu. Remove the check box next to "Collapse fieldsets on modules page." Scroll to the bottom of the Web page and click "Save configuration."

The Admin menu is designed for use by administrative users. If you need a drop-down menu as a replacement for a complete menu (for example, the default Navigation menu or a custom menu that you have created), you will need to use the SimpleMenu module instead of the Admin Menu module. It can be downloaded from `http://drupal.org/project/simplemenu`.

Teleport

Another useful shortcut tool for site administrators and expert users is the Teleport module. This module is an on-demand search widget. It appears as in Figure 8.10 when the user presses a series of keys. The teleporter locates titles and paths that match the text as you begin typing. You can then select from a list of possible options in the drop-down menu. Use of this module requires JavaScript.

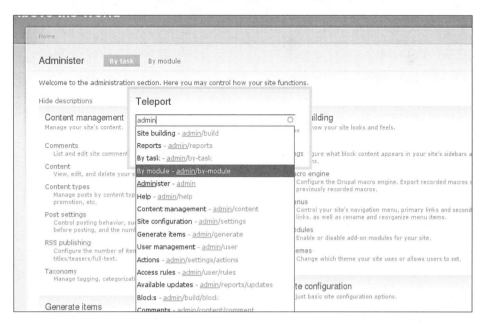

FIGURE 8.10 The Teleport widget allows you to quickly jump to another page in your Web site.

The Teleport module can be downloaded from the project page at `http://drupal.org/project/teleport`. Instructions for its installation can be found in Appendix A.

Once the Teleport module is installed, you may configure several options, including the shortcut keys used to access the teleporter (Figure 8.11).

1. Navigate to Administer, Site configuration, Teleport.

2. Configure the following options for the module:

   - Default shortcut key

   - The types of things to include in the search (Only titles and paths are indexed, not the content of the pages.)

   - The content types to search

3. Scroll to the bottom of the Web page and click "Save configuration."

Navigate

Navigate is an administrative menu that truly separates site administration from the theme. From this administrative menu, you can readily navigate through pages;

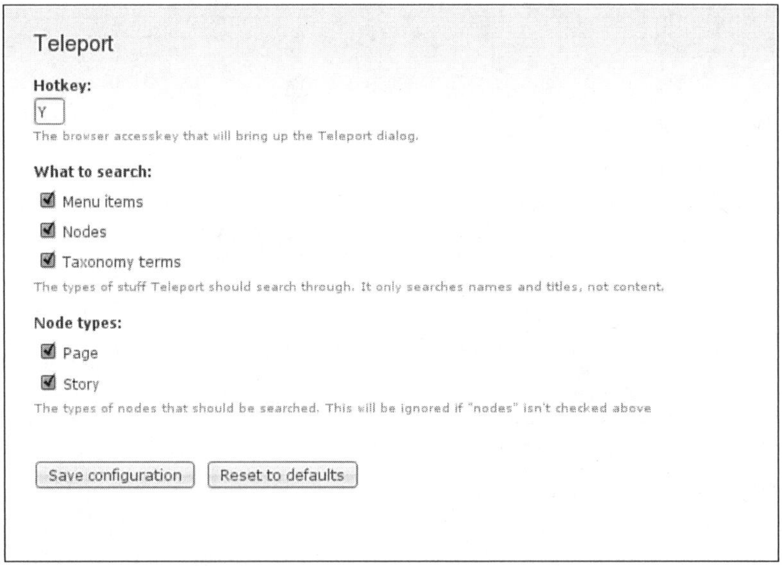

FIGURE 8.11 The shortcut keys for the teleporter can be easily configured.

you can also search through your navigation and pages (Figure 8.12). Pages can be bookmarked and saved in the Navigate menu for future use. Although there are no additional module dependencies, Navigate is heavily dependent on AJAX and will not work as advertised if you do not have JavaScript enabled.

The Navigate module can be downloaded from the project page at `http://www.drupal.org/project/navigate`. Instructions for its installation can be found in Appendix A.

Once the Navigate module is installed, you may configure several options.

1. Navigate to Administer, Site configuration, Navigate settings.

2. Configure the following options for the module:

   • Help text

   • Default home page

   • Number of history items to save

   • The header image for the administration frame (This can also be removed, as shown in Figure 8.12.)

3. Scroll to the bottom of the Web page and click "Save configuration." If the Devel module is installed, each of the shortcuts from the devel block are also

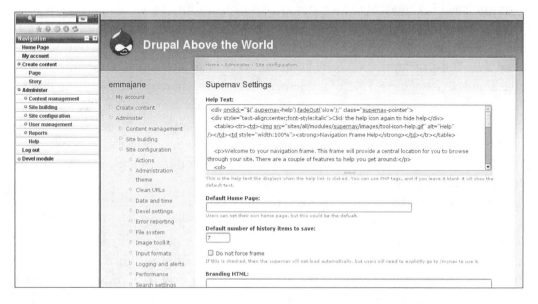

FIGURE 8.12 Navigate is an administrative menu that separates site administration from the theme.

available from this page. This includes a set of handy links to the following tasks:

- Emptying the cache
- Listing the output from `phpinfo()`
- Accessing documentation for recently used Drupal functions
- Listing currently set variables
- Resetting menus and reinstalling modules

Administrative Dashboards and Control Panels

The distinction between an administrative menu, a control panel, and an administrative dashboard might be viewed as a bit pedantic. These controls offer either graphical or text-based, administrative navigation that is visually prominent within the site's design. Both RootCandy's set of icons across the top of the administrative pages and the Control Panel module allow you to easily build your own graphical administrative dashboard to administer Drupal.

Control Panel

Control Panel is a module that creates a series of icons for the administration of your Drupal installation. It matches the administrative URL from a menu onto a graphical icon. A control panel can be built from any Drupal menu. With the Control Panel module, a full-page option is created and can serve as an alternative to the administrative home page (Figure 8.13). To implement this approach, replace the existing link to the Admin page with a link to the control panel. You may also choose to create a block from any menu and place it in any region of your Web site.

The Control Panel module can be downloaded from the project page at `http://drupal.org/project/controlpanel`. Instructions for installing modules can be found in Appendix A.

The sample block shown in Figure 8.14 uses the default menu for Administer and contains links to Content management, Site building, Site configuration, User management, Reports, and Help. Although the display is not perfect, altering the titles of the longest menu options tightens up the display significantly as shown in Figure 8.15. Instead of changing the names of the menu items, you may wish to build your own custom menus containing each of the options your users will need.

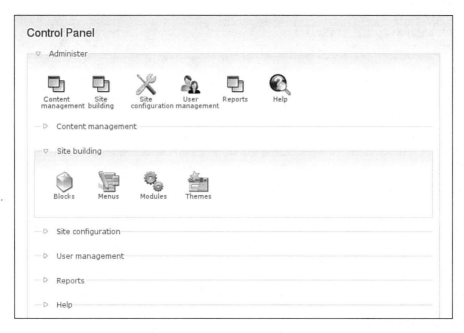

FIGURE 8.13 A control panel can be used as a full-page display to replace the main administration home page.

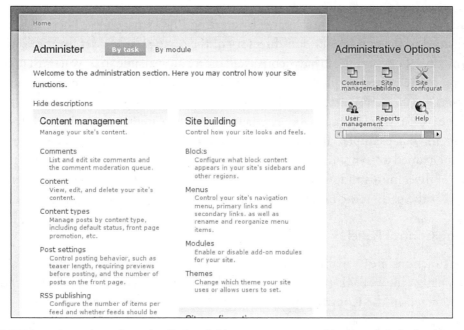

FIGURE 8.14 Control panels can be displayed either as a page or as a block. By default, the titles are a bit long for display in most sidebars.

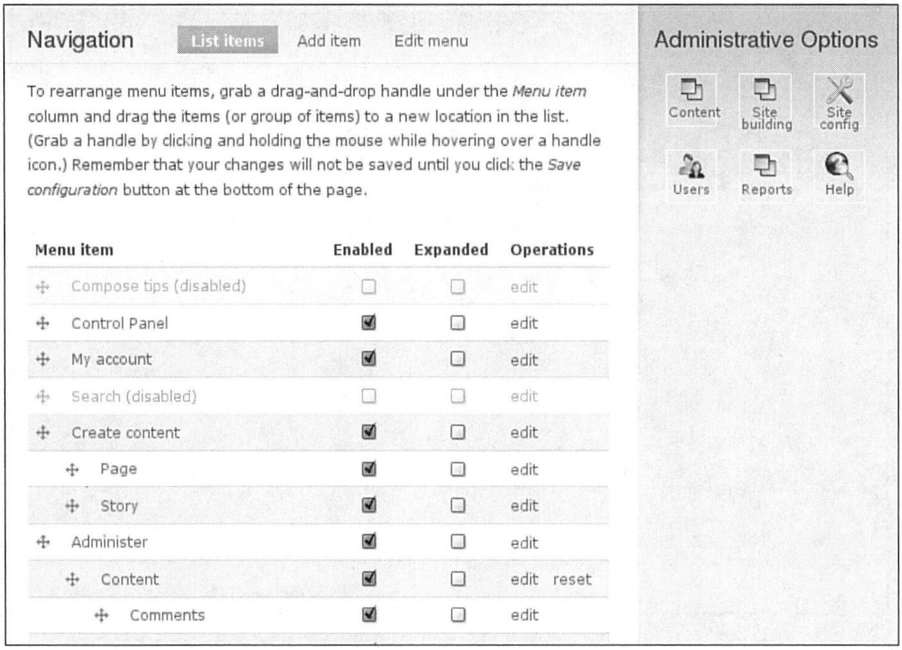

FIGURE 8.15 By altering the name of the menu items, the text of the control page is now legible.

You can add icons to a control panel by creating PNG image files. These files must be uploaded to the appropriate sub-directory of the `images` subfolder for the Control Panel module. For example, to have icons available for all available sizes, you must upload the appropriately sized graphics to each of the following directories: `controlpanel/images/16x16`, `controlpanel/images/24x24`, `controlpanel/images/36x36`, and `controlpanel/images/48x48`. Image file names should match the path for the menu item. For example, an image representing the path `admin/build/modules` should be named `admin_build_modules.png`. You may also provide icons for paths outside of the administration area by using the same naming convention. For example, an icon for the path `node/add/blog` would be named `node_add_blog.png`.

Theming Control Panel

Theme functions are available for the Control Panel module. These functions allow you to change the HTML that surrounds each item in the control panel. Two views can be themed in the Control Panel module: main panel view and child panel view.

The first function alters the output for the first row of the control panel icons displayed in Figure 8.13. The second function alters the output for subsections displayed in subsequent rows (for example, for "Site building" in Figure 8.13).

To change the output of these two views, you must create a replacement function in your theme. Instead of printing what the module programmer has put into the module, Drupal will then use your HTML when printing the output for the control panel. The steps outlined here can be used to theme the output from any module with a theme function.

1. Open the module file in a text editor. This file will be found in the `controlpanel` subdirectory of the modules directory—for example, `sites/all/modules/controlpanel/controlpanel.module`.

2. Look for the function that can be themed. It begins with:

```
function theme_controlpanel_panel_view ($menu, $block = NULL) {
```

3. Copy the contents of this function. You will need everything from the word `function` to the final `}`. This data will be approximately 20 lines long.

4. Open the file named `template.php` for your theme. If this file does not exist, create it now.

5. Paste the function into the file `template.php`. Although this function can be placed anywhere in the file, you may prefer to list your functions alphabetically to keep the file neat and tidy.

6. Change the name of the function so that the word "theme" matches the name of your theme. For example, if your theme was named `bolg`, the function would be renamed from `theme_controlpanel_panel_view` to `bolg_controlpanel_panel_view`.

7. Using the provided output as an example, you may now reconfigure the inside of the theme to produce whatever HTML you would like to print to the browser page. Make sure the end of your function "returns" content back to Drupal.

8. Repeat these steps for the second function that can be themed in the Control Panel module. It is named `theme_controlpanel_child_panel_view` in the file `controlpanel.module`.

You may repeat this entire process for the second function that can be themed.

Custom Administrative Screens

Even with the rich offering of themes and modules from the Drupal community, it is very possible that your site may need a little bit more customization than what is offered by these solutions. If this is the case for your site, consider building a new content administration area that exists independently of the main administrative area. By redirecting site administrators to your version of how the administration ought to work, you can create a whole new experience for the administration of Drupal.

The first thing you will need to do to create a custom administration experience is to think about the tasks that each of your administrators will need to perform. You may have placed some of these tasks into menus and then blocks earlier in this chapter. In some cases, however, it is difficult to confine the tasks to a single block. For example, you may want to create a list of all pages that are waiting for approval before being published, or you may want to list all images that are not currently assigned to a gallery. Thinking about the tasks you perform on a regular basis may help you to realize that life would be a lot easier if only you could have a summary of a specific kind of content.

Using the Views module, you can easily create a customized list of any content you may need. This tool is essentially a point-and-click database query tool. The results of a query can be returned as a page, as a block, or as a feed (or a combination of these). The list of content that is returned can be themed so that it fits with the rest of your Web site.

You may decide to filter the list based on the content's characteristics or based on the URLs that a visitor uses. For example, you could have a single view that shows "unpublished content" for each of your Web site categories based on the URL that is called. In this case, two conditions would be put onto the list of content that is returned: The first condition (only unpublished content) is called a "filter" within views; the second (variable categories) is referred to as an "argument." A filter is fixed within the view, but an argument can change depending on which URL is visited.

The origins of an argument
The word "argument" is a programming term. It refers to pieces of information that are passed from the outside world into a specific section of a script. You may also be familiar with the term "parameters." Parameters are the variables that are passed to a specific section of a script. Arguments, by contrast, are the actual values that are assigned to the parameter variables when a script is executed. In Web-based applications, arguments are typically thought of as extra bits of information collected from the URL of a Web page.

New Content View

Using the Views module, you can create lists of content that are relevant for your Web site administration. For example, you could create a view containing the 20 most recent items published on your Web site. You must have the contributed Views module enabled for this section. Additional information about the Views module can be found in Chapter 2. This view is comparable to the front page of a blog as well as to the content management administrative interface found by navigating to Administer, Content management, Content. You may wish to use this view as a block, a page, or a feed. For this view we will start by cloning the default "frontpage" view. You must first enable it using the following steps:

1. Navigate to Administer, Site building, Views.
2. Click on the link to "clone" the "frontpage" view. This will reveal the first configuration screen, "Clone view frontpage." See Figure 8.16.

FIGURE 8.16 The first configuration screen in the View interface allows you to configure information about your new view.

3. Change the "View name" to `all_recent_content`. The "View name" should be a machine-readable name that contains only letters, numbers, and underscores.

4. Update the "View description" to match the new functionality for this view. Provide a helpful description—for example, "Creates a list of the most recent content published to the Web site."

5. Add relevant tags for this view to the "View tag"—for example, "new content."

6. You cannot change the "View type" when you are cloning a view. Note that type for this view is "node." If you want to use a different type of content, you must either create a new view or clone a different view.

7. Scroll to the bottom of the Web page and click "Next."

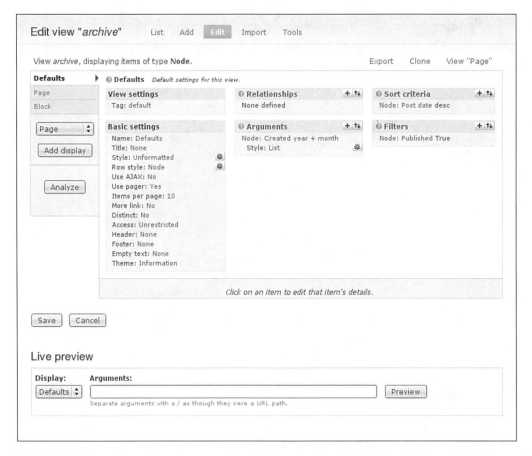

FIGURE 8.17 The main configuration screen for the Views module allows you to configure your view.

The main configuration screen for your view will now appear. See Figure 8.17.

For the altered "All recent content" view, several items need to be changed from the default "frontpage" view. For each configuration option, click the text and then change the appropriate options in the configuration screen that appears at the bottom of the page. Click "Update" to save your settings.

Basic Settings

Under the "Basic settings" section of the Views administration screen, you must configure the following options:

- **Items per page: 10.** Update this number to display more than 10 items.
- **Name: Defaults.** Update the view name to match the new content that will be displayed.
- **Title: None.** This is an administrative view; it will be useful to add a page title.

Filters

Under the "Filters" section of the Views administration screen, you must configure the following option:

- **Node: Promoted to front page.** This filter is no longer required. Click the "Remove" the option in the configuration screen.

Sort Criteria

Under the "Sort criteria" section of the Views administration screen, you must configure the following option:

- **Node: Sticky.** This filter is no longer relevant, as we want only the newest content. Click the "Remove" option in the configuration screen.

Page Display

You must also create a new URL for this view. Click the "Page" tab to the left of the main configuration screen. Under "Page settings," click the text next to "Path." Update the path to the new URL for this page. For example, you would change "frontpage" to "all_recent_content."

After adjusting each setting and clicking "Update," scroll to the bottom of the page to see a preview of what will appear for this view. Once the view is correctly configured, click "Save" to finalize all changes made. To use the new view, integrate a link to the new page into your custom menus created previously in this chapter, or enable a block to give a summary of all content for this view.

Orphan Images View

Another useful list of content that you can create with the Views module is a list of orphaned images that are not included in an image gallery. This view requires you to have taxonomy enabled and configured with the Image and Image Gallery modules. It will be most useful as a full page (as opposed to a block or a feed). To create this view, you will start from scratch instead of cloning an existing view.

1. Navigate to Administer, Site building, Views.
2. Click on the link to "Add" a new view. This will reveal the first configuration screen. Set the following information for this view:
   - View name: orphan_images.
   - View description: A list of all images not integrated into a gallery.
   - View tag: orphan image. (You may also have orphan book pages or other types of content.)
   - View type: node.
3. Scroll to the bottom of the Web page and click "Next." The main configuration screen for your view will now appear.

Update the settings for this view. You will need to set the node type as well as the categories. You should set the fields before you set the filters; otherwise, you will get an error message.

Page Display

You must also create a new URL for this view. Click the "Page" tab to the left of the main configuration screen. Under "Page settings," click the text next to "Path." Add a new URL for this page—for example, `orphan_images`.

Fields

Under the "Fields" section of the Views administration screen, you must configure the following options:

- Click the + sign next to the "Fields" heading to add a display field.

- In the configuration screen, change the "Groups" to "node" and wait for the new list of fields to appear.
- Choose Node: Title, Node: Edit, Node: Delete, and Node: View from the list of fields. Click "add" to enable these four fields.

Filters

Under the "Filters" section of the Views administration screen, you must configure the following options:

- Node type: images

  1. Click the + sign next to the "Filter" heading to create a new filter.
  2. In the configuration screen, change the "Groups" to "node" and wait for the new list of filters to appear.
  3. Scroll down to the filter "Node: type" and enable it by selecting the check box.
  4. Set the operator to "Is one of" and the node type to "Image."
  5. Click "Update" to save these settings.

- Not in a gallery

  1. Click the + sign next to the "Filter" heading to create a second filter.
  2. In the configuration screen, change the "Groups" to "taxonomy" and wait for the new list of filters to appear.
  3. Scroll down to the filter "Taxonomy: Term ID" and enable it by selecting the check box and clicking "Add."
  4. Set the vocabulary to "Image Galleries" and the selection type to "Dropdown." Click "update."
  5. Change the operator to "Is none of" and select all image galleries from the list on the right.
  6. Click "Update" to save these settings.
  7. Repeat these steps to add additional filters.

Basic Settings

Under the "Basic settings" section of the Views administration screen, you must configure the following options:

1. Choose the basic style for this view—for example, Grid, List, Table, Unformatted. Configure the display settings for the style you choose.

2. Restrict this view to only authenticated users. The assumption here is that because the image is not in a gallery, it should not be a public image. Click on "Access: unrestricted." Change "By role" to "authenticated users." You must set this access correctly or the page will not display any images even if there are some!

After adjusting each setting and clicking "Update," scroll to the bottom of the page to see a preview of what will appear for this view. Once the view is correctly configured, click "Save" to finalize all changes made. To use this view, integrate a link to the new page into your custom menus created previously in this chapter, or enable a block to give a summary of all content for this view.

Theming the View

At this time, the image module does not provide hooks to display images as part of the view. Instead, a custom theme template is required to do so. A default template is included as part of the Views module.

1. Under the "Basic settings," click "Theme: Information." This choice will reveal a series of template files.

2. Beside the "Row style output" link, you will see a series of file names. Choose the most specific file name for the fields for this view—for example, `views-view-fields--orphan-images.tpl.php`. Create a file in your theme directory that matches this file name.

3. In the new template file, add the following code snippet:

```php
<?php $node = node_load($row->nid); ?>


<h2 class="image"><?php print check_plain($node->title);?></h2>
[ <?php print l("view", "node/$node->nid"); ?> ]
[ <?php print l("edit", "node/$node->nid/edit"); ?> ]
[ <?php print l("delete", "node/$node->nid/delete"); ?> ]
<div class="image">
<?php print theme_image($node->images["thumbnail"], $node->title, $node->body,
NULL, TRUE); ?>
</div>
```

FIGURE 8.18 Using a simple template file, images can be added to the output of the view for orphan images.

This code will display the list using the thumbnail images and provide a set of view, edit, and delete links for each image. (See Figure 8.18 for an example of this output.) The images that are displayed from this list differ from the main image gallery layout shown in Figure 8.19.

This view can now be added into a custom administrative "Gallery" menu that allows you to perform a variety of tasks. Following is a list of suggested tasks, with the administrative path appearing in parentheses:

- Upload Image (node/add/image)
- Edit Gallery Categories (admin/content/image)
- Orphan Images (orphan_images)
- View Galleries (image)

FIGURE 8.19 The main image gallery contains only one image, which has been assigned the category of "Hay-on-Wye."

Unpublished Content by Category

A third example of a custom administrative view would be one created by selecting unpublished content on a per-category basis. This view is easily created from the default view of `taxonomy_term`.

1. Navigate to Administer, Site building, Views.
2. Enable the `taxonomy_term` view.
3. Click the "clone" link to create a copy of the view.
4. Update the "View name," "View description," and "View" tags. For the "View name," you may wish to use `unpublished_by_term`.
5. Scroll to the bottom of the Web page and click "next."

On the next administration screen you will be presented with a new set of configuration options.

1. Alter the filter "Node: Published or admin" by clicking on the filter name.
2. Click "Remove" for this filter.
3. Add a new filter by clicking on the + next to the "Filters" heading.
4. Choose the "Node: published" filter. Scroll to the bottom of the Web page and click "Add."
5. Without selecting "Published" click "Update." This option will filter the view so that only unpublished content is listed.

6. Under the "Basic settings" for the "Page" type, update the "Path" to `taxonomy/term/%/unpublished`. Click "Update" to commit the changes.

7. The "Core feed" and "Views 1 feed" displays can be removed. Click "Save" to commit the changes.

This view can now be accessed by adding "unpublished" onto the end of any taxonomy page—for example, `taxonomy/term/1/unpublished`.

Error!

Sometimes bad things happen. Drupal allows you to easily create custom error pages to deal with those (infrequent, one hopes) mishaps. Several solutions are presented in this section to help you decide how to best deliver useful error messages to your Web site visitors. Always remember to test your error pages and error messages. The last thing you want to have is an error-filled error!

Error Messages

Drupal has two main ways of delivering system-related messages to the user: help and messages. Both are rendered in the `page.tpl.php` template file, where they are available as `$help` and `$messages`, respectively. With some very simple styling, you can easily ensure that these messages match your existing theme.

Three types of Drupal messages can be displayed to the Web site user: status, warning, and error. These messages are always displayed in a `div` with the additional class of `messages`. For example, an error message has the following markup:

```
<div class="messages error">Bad things happened!</div>
```

Within your theme's CSS file, the following classes can be used to override Drupal's default theming for these messages:

```
/* Define the box shape for all messages */
.messages {
    padding: 7px;
    border: 1px solid black;
    margin: 10px;
}
```

```
/* Define the colors for error messages */
.error {
    border-color: red;
    background-color: #FFDDDD
    color: #AA0000;
}


/* Define the colors for warning messages */
.warning {
    border-color: yellow;
    background-color: #FFFFDD
    color: #CCAA00;
}


/* Define the colors for status messages */
.status {
    border-color: green;
    background-color: #EEFFAA
    color: #668833;
}
```

404, Page Not Found

By default, Drupal allows you to create two types of error pages: one for "404, Page not found" errors and a second for "403, Access forbidden" errors. These error pages are actual pages stored within the database. You may use any content type for these pages. Once the pages have been created, navigate to Administer, Site Configuration, Error reporting. Enter the path for the two error pages you created as shown in Figure 8.20.

Technically, that was very easy. Creating the text of the error page, however, requires a bit more thought. Here are a few tips to creating good error pages:

1. Use a friendly and human tone on your error message page.
2. If you have a site map, offer a link it. You may also want to include the site map as part of your error page.
3. Offer a link to the site search, or include the search form in the error page. This can be done with a PHP snippet within the actual page.

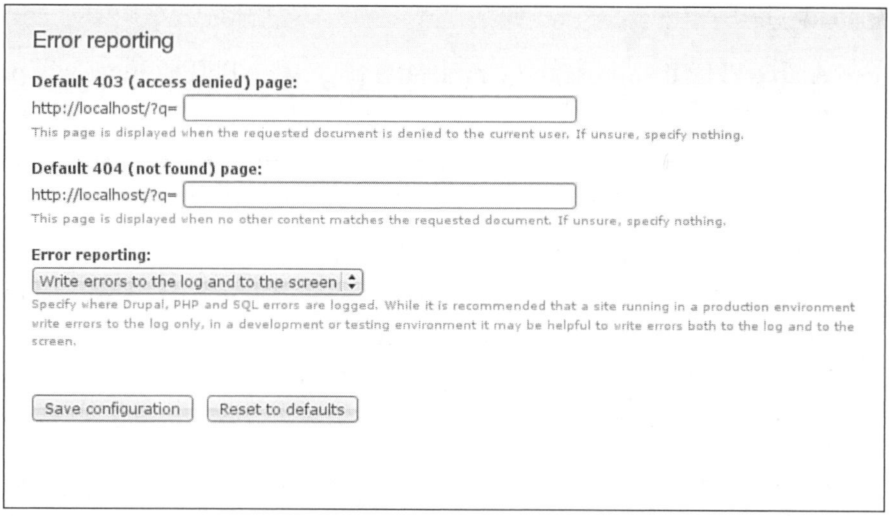

Error reporting

Default 403 (access denied) page:

http://localhost/?q= [   ]

This page is displayed when the requested document is denied to the current user. If unsure, specify nothing.

Default 404 (not found) page:

http://localhost/?q= [   ]

This page is displayed when no other content matches the requested document. If unsure, specify nothing.

Error reporting:

[Write errors to the log and to the screen ‡]

Specify where Drupal, PHP and SQL errors are logged. While it is recommended that a site running in a production environment write errors to the log only, in a development or testing environment it may be helpful to write errors both to the log and to the screen.

[Save configuration] [Reset to defaults]

FIGURE 8.20 On the error reporting page, enter the path for the error page that you have created.

4. Offer a link to a guided tour (if you have one) or the "About the site" page.

5. Include a contact form for visitors to fill out if they were looking for specific information.

6. Read "The Perfect 404" (`http://www.alistapart.com/articles/perfect404`) for additional tips on dealing with missing pages.

Custom Error

One of the disadvantages of using the built-in Drupal error-handling techniques is that the error pages are actual nodes in the database. As a consequence, they may show up in search results pages. An alternative to this approach to error handling is to use the Custom Error module. This module can be downloaded from the project page at `http://drupal.org/project/customerror`. Instructions explaining how to install modules can be found in Appendix A.

Once the Custom Error module is installed, you will need to configure the error messages and enable the custom error screens. To do so, you first enter the text for the error message page. You may use HTML tags and/or PHP snippets. To update the error text, follow these steps:

1. Navigate to Administer, Site configuration, Custom error.

2. Enter the title and text you would like to use for the error pages ("404, not found" and "403, access denied").

Sample 404 Page

Be sure to enable PHP if you use the sample 404 page. The PHP snippet will provide a search form on the error page.

```
<p>We couldn't find your page. We're sorry. But look what we did find: It's a
search form! Cool, eh?!</p>

<?php

// Confirm the search module is enabled, and the visitor is allowed to use it

if (module_exists('search') && user_access('search content')) {

// Copy a sanitized version of the requested URL into the search box

$search_terms = strtolower(preg_replace('/[^a-zA-Z0-9-]+/', ' ', $_
REQUEST['destination']));

print drupal_get_form('search_form', NULL, $search_terms, 'node', 'Look it up');

}

?>
```

Sample 403 Page

Be sure to enable PHP if you use the sample 403 page. The PHP snippet will provide a login form to Web site visitors who are not logged into the Web site.

```
<p>Sadly, you are not important enough to view this page.</p>
<?php
// Check whether the visitor is logged in...
if (user_is_logged_in()) {
  print "SuXor, eh?";
} else {
  print "Would it help if you were logged into the site?";
  print drupal_get_form('user_login');
}
?>
```

Once you have created the text, you must enable the custom error pages:

1. Navigate to Administer, Site configuration, Error reporting.
2. Set the "Default 403 (access denied) page:" to "customerror/403."

3. Set the "Default 404 (not found) page:" to "customerror/404."

4. Scroll to the bottom of the Web page and click "Save."

Additional information on custom page templates for offline messages can be found in Chapter 4.

Summary

Customizing the Drupal administrative experience can be as easy as creating a few blocks with highly useful links or as complex as implementing an entirely new theme with pages that replace the main administrative navigation. This chapter covered the following topics:

- Installing administrative themes
- Creating administrative shortcuts for frequent tasks
- Installing and configuring administrative control panels and dashboards
- Using views to create custom lists of content
- Customizing error pages

Regardless of whether you create an entirely new Drupal administrative interface or simply add a few time-saving taskbars, you should consider checking in with the Drupal Usability Group. They may have uncovered some tools that will help you customize your site more effectively. Visit this group at `http://groups.drupal.org/usability`.

Chapter 9

Learning JavaScript

With the rise of the technology called AJAX (for **A**synchronous **J**avaScript **and X**ML) in 2005, JavaScript lost its image as a poor amateur language, which it had since its first appearance in 1995. This image was mostly due to the language being used to achieve things that were regarded as useless gimmicks. If you were a Web developer in the late 1990s or early 2000s, you may be familiar with popular JavaScript effects from that time, such as status bar tickers, text flying after the mouse cursor, automatic resizing of windows, or annoying pop-ups.

In recent years, the art of writing good JavaScript has shifted its focus as Web developers began applying common programming techniques. They also started to use function libraries and began to harness the full power of the language. Actually, JavaScript itself has not really changed a lot since its introduction; rather, the way it is used has undergone dramatic changes.

In Drupal, JavaScript is mainly used to enhance functionality that is already there. Usually the JavaScript facilitates the process of doing something—for example, the file upload JavaScript allows the user to upload a file without having to reload the entire page. That way, the user can upload a file in the background while still writing the content or changing other details about the node. It is not good practice to build things with JavaScript that aren't accessible when JavaScript is unavailable. Instead, you should provide a basic version that is usable without JavaScript and then gradually enhance the functionality by incorporating JavaScript features.

Drupal uses the powerful jQuery library for most of its included JavaScript functionality. Settling on one JavaScript library included in the core allows third-party module developers to rely on this library and not worry about including their own. Although writing JavaScript using jQuery certainly differs from writing plain JavaScript, it is nonetheless essential to know the fundamental features of JavaScript. Just knowing how to write jQuery code does not allow you to create truly flexible and portable JavaScript "widgets." For this reason, this chapter focuses on the core language first. If you know some basic PHP (like that used in templates), you should understand the general syntax of JavaScript as presented here.

Chapters 10 and 11 explain jQuery in greater detail and demonstrate how you can integrate your JavaScript code with Drupal.

JavaScript versus DOM

JavaScript in the browser consists of two main components: the core JavaScript language and the DOM (Document Object Model). The DOM is responsible for providing access to elements of the Web page currently loaded, such as `divs`, forms, and virtually any other aspect of the document. The DOM provides the `document` and `window` objects and all their methods. Unfortunately, it can be quite difficult to use the DOM even for simple tasks, because this model usually requires the use of long function names like `document.getElementsByTagName()` and because it lacks convenient navigation methods. Additionally, the implementation of the DOM is not fully standards-compliant across browsers and a lot of weird edge cases crop up, especially with Internet Explorer.

Luckily, jQuery steps into the breach to provide a unified interface on top of the DOM (see Figure 9.1). It takes a lot of the pain out of writing cross-browser-compatible code. Because we are able to use jQuery when working with Drupal, the DOM won't be covered in greater detail here. Instead, we will focus on using jQuery to achieve the same things in a much faster and clearer way. But first, we look at JavaScript itself to learn some quite useful things and explore its mechanics.

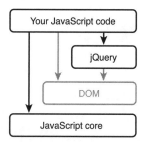

FIGURE 9.1 The JavaScript and jQuery development stack.

The JavaScript Language

Like PHP, JavaScript is a scripting language. That means you don't have to compile it to be able to run it; instead, you feed the JavaScript into an "interpreter" that goes through the source code and executes the commands as it goes. Even though JavaScript has syntax similar to PHP, there are some differences between the two: For example, functions don't have to have names, JavaScript is less strict about semicolons, and the syntax for defining arrays is more concise than in PHP. This section explores the basics of writing and executing JavaScript and provides a quick glance at the most important concepts of the language.

First Steps: Executing Code

For now, the easiest way to execute snippets of JavaScript code is the Firefox extension called Firebug. If you have not already installed it, now is a good time to do so. You can download Firebug from `http://getfirebug.com`. If you don't want to use Firefox, you can use another browser that has a JavaScript console, such as Safari 3+ or Opera; however, Firebug's console is probably the easiest to use. You don't have to open a real Web page—a blank page is sufficient for our first JavaScript experiments.

To run JavaScript code, just open the console by clicking on the icon on the right side of the status bar, as shown in Figure 9.2.

Next, type `alert("Drupal rocks!");` after the prompt at the bottom of the Web page. Congratulations, you just ran JavaScript code—not bad for the start! `alert()` is a function that displays an alert box. Keep in mind that JavaScript is a case-sensitive programming language (unlike PHP), which means that it considers `alert`, `Alert`, and `aLeRT` to be completely different things. It also means that running `Alert("Drupal rocks!");` won't work.

FIGURE 9.2 Firebug's JavaScript console.

Declaring Variables

If you want to write more complex scripts, you will most likely want to store data or other items using variables. In JavaScript, a simple assignment closely resembles its counterpart in PHP: `myVariable = "Drupal";`. After making this assignment, you can use the variable by simply specifying its name: `alert(myVariable);`. This statement will produce an alert box with the contents of the variable `myVariable` as a message. Note that variable names (and all other "identifiers") are case sensitive as well and must start with a letter, an underscore, or a dollar sign.

> **The dollar sign**
> In JavaScript, you could prefix variable names with the dollar sign just like you do in PHP; however, it is not common practice in the JavaScript world to do so. The JavaScript code in this book does not use variable names prefixed with the dollar sign. In your own code, you can prefix all variable names with $, but that step is not required.

The Variable Scope

There is one subtle but very important difference between JavaScript and PHP: If you use a variable without prefixing it with `var` the first time you're using it in JavaScript, the variable is automatically considered to be "global" and, therefore, is automatically defined in any section throughout your entire script.

You might be familiar with the concept of "scope" from PHP. If you have not previously encountered this idea, here is a short explanation: When a variable is defined first, you can specify its scope, where *scope* refers to the area for which the variable is defined. If you define a variable in a function, it is available only in that particular function, but not in other functions. As a rule of thumb, a variable "ceases" to exist

```
var detail = 1;

function hello() {
    var orange = 'internal';
    red = 'global';
    alert(detail);
}

hello();
alert(orange); // Error!
alert(red);
```

FIGURE 9.3 The scope of a variable.

when the current function is closed (in JavaScript and PHP, when the final } character appears after a function).

By default, variables are defined as global in JavaScript when you create them manually. In reality, you rarely want to use global variables. To keep a variable from being available outside of the scope in which it was defined, you must prefix it with var like this: var myVariable = "Drupal";.

Figure 9.3 illustrates this concept. In the figure, the global variable detail is available inside the function, so the function alerts 1. The local variable orange is defined inside the function but is not available to access initiated from outside the function. Trying to access it will result in an error. The variable red is defined without the var modifier and, therefore, is considered global. Accessing this variable from outside the function is possible, but only after the function has been executed and defined the variable. If you try to access this variable before the function has been run, you will get an error. After the function is run, red contains the string "global".

> **Camel case names**
> You might have noticed that the variable name we used (myVariable) is not typical for Drupal. This naming scheme, which is called "camel case," is used nearly everywhere throughout JavaScript. Instead of separating words with a space or an underscore, the first letter of a word is written in uppercase and appended immediately to the preceding word without whitespace between them. The first letter of the entire phrase usually appears in lowercase. You can adopt this scheme or use the variable naming scheme known from PHP—either way will work.

Data Types

So far, we have used strings (enclosed with the " character). In fact, several other data types are also available in JavaScript:

- **Strings** contain sequences of characters (e.g., words or sentences, though their content can also be the source of an entire HTML document). They are enclosed by either double quotes (") or single quotes ('). If you want to use the enclosing delimiters themselves, you must "escape" them by prefixing them with a backslash. The backslash in a string is represented by a double backslash (\\; an "escaped" backslash).

- **Numbers** represent numerical data such as integers or floating-point numbers. JavaScript doesn't distinguish between `int` and `float`—it treats all numbers in the same way. For example, if you type `3.5 * 4` into Firebug's JavaScript prompt, it does not return `14.0` but rather `14`.

- **Booleans** can have two values: `false` or `true` (just like in PHP). Always write these two keywords in lowercase (JavaScript is case sensitive, remember?). Internally, `true` corresponds to `1` and `false` corresponds to `0`. Type `1 == true`, `2 == true`, `true + 2`, and `0 == false` into the prompt to verify that.

- **Functions** are data types in JavaScript. No, you didn't misread the previous sentence: You can assign functions to a variable, pass functions as arguments, return them from another function, and so on. Functions are full-blown, first-class objects in JavaScript—more on that in the section "Using Functions" later in this chapter.

- **Objects** are omnipresent in JavaScript. Everything in JavaScript is an object, and even the other data types can be used as objects because they are automatically converted to a "wrapper object" around the actual data type. The section "Object Orientation in JavaScript" explains objects in greater detail.

Even though **Arrays** are actually objects, they are often considered a separate data type because they have their own syntax and behavior. Arrays in JavaScript don't behave exactly like their counterparts in PHP: You can only number items sequentially starting from 0 instead of using your own keys. You can use objects as counterparts to the associative arrays in PHP, however. Arrays can be defined as a list of comma-separated values within square brackets:

```
var myArray = [ 'green', 'red', 'blue', 'purple' ];
console.log(myArray[2]); // Prints 'blue' to the console.
```

> **Displaying debugging information**
> You can write data to Firebug's console by using the function `console.log()`.
> Many different formatting options are available, as documented on `http://getfirebug.com/console.html`.

Operators

In JavaScript, just as in PHP, you can use several operators to perform calculations or other operations. On numbers, you can use the +, -, *, /, and % operators just as in PHP. For concatenating strings in JavaScript, however, you must use the + operator instead of . (dot).

The **Boolean operators** || and && also behave slightly differently in JavaScript. While PHP returns `true` or `false` when you concatenate multiple expressions with these operators, JavaScript returns the actual value of the expression that stopped the evaluation of the entire expression. Here's a short example from `misc/drupal.js`:

```
var Drupal = Drupal || {};
```

This short snippet makes sure that the `Drupal` variable is defined without overwriting previous contents. It is evaluated in the following way: When the first part (before the ||) evaluates to `true`, it is returned (and subsequently assigned to `Drupal`, so nothing really happens). When it does not (e.g., it is not defined, 0, or `false`), the second part of the expression is checked. If it's `true`, it is returned; if not, the next part is checked, and so on. In this case, the second part is the last expression, so it is always returned, even if it evaluates to `false`.

The same mechanism can be used to check multiple variables in sequential fashion, with the first variable that meets the criteria being used. An example of this behavior can be found in `misc/progress.js` in the `Drupal.progressBar` function:

```
Drupal.progressBar = function (id, updateCallback, method, errorCallback) {
  // ...
  this.method = method || "GET";
  // ...
};
```

When the function is called without specifying the method parameter (or by passing a value that is null or false), it automatically uses GET as an HTTP method; otherwise, the specified method is used. This behavior saves you from writing code like this:

```
if (method) {
  this.method = method;
}
else {
  this.method = "GET";
}
```

Controlling the Flow

JavaScript also features control structures such as if, while, for, and switch. These types of statements can be used in much the same way as their counterparts in PHP. Although JavaScript lacks a keyword called foreach, it is nonetheless possible to iterate over an array or an object. To do so, you would use a special syntax for the for loop, which is illustrated in the misc/autocomplete.js file in the function Drupal. jsAC.prototype.found:

```
for (var key in matches) {
  var li = document.createElement('li');
  $(li)
    .html('<div>'+ matches[key] +'</div>')
    .mousedown(function () { ac.select(this); })
    .mouseover(function () { ac.highlight(this); })
    .mouseout(function () { ac.unhighlight(this); });
  li.autocompleteValue = key;
  $(ul).append(li);
}
```

The code in this loop is executed for each item that can be found in the array matches. At this point, you need not worry about the code surrounded by the { and } characters. The key variable contains the index (in the case of an array, it is 0, 1, 2, . . .) and allows you to retrieve the actual value of the array element or object property. Keep in mind that PHP's foreach loop returns the value (and optionally the key); JavaScript always returns the key, but never the value. Also keep in mind that you should always define the variable used for storing they key using the `var` keyword—otherwise, it becomes global!

JavaScript also has a **ternary "operator"** that acts like an abbreviation of an `if` statement. The following example stems from the `Drupal.tableDrag.prototype.dragRow` function found in `misc/tabledrag.js`:

```
self.rowObject.direction = y > self.oldY ? 'down' : 'up';
```

If the expression (the part between the equal sign and the question mark) evaluates to `true`, the first expression after the question mark (separated by a colon) is executed. If that is not the case, the second expression is executed. In this case, the direction the user is dragging a row is calculated. `y` is the current coordinate and `self.oldY` is the origin of the row. When the new `y` coordinate is bigger than the original coordinate, the user is dragging in a downward direction; otherwise, the user is dragging upward.

Although these statements can make your code more concise, you should not overuse them: Your code can quickly become an unreadable tangle!

Object Orientation in JavaScript

Unlike most programming languages, JavaScript is a "prototype-based," object-oriented programming language. In other words, you won't find a `class` keyword in this language, because JavaScript doesn't have regular classes. Instead, everything is an object in JavaScript. In traditional object-oriented languages, classes define an entity; you then create instances of these entities. By contrast, in JavaScript, you create new objects that are derived from another object. The new objects inherit all prototypes of the original object, even if they were defined after the derivation. However, it's still possible to mimic the "regular" classes known from most programming languages with object orientation. We will explore the exact details of how objects and prototypes work in JavaScript later in this chapter.

The "Everything Is an Object" Approach

Unlike a couple of other object-oriented programming languages, JavaScript does not draw a real distinction between primitive data types (such as integers and Booleans) and objects. Everything in JavaScript is an object. Integers and other numbers are objects, strings are objects, arrays are objects, functions are objects, regular expressions are objects, and so on.

As mentioned earlier, JavaScript also doesn't distinguish between integers and floating-point numbers. Numbers in JavaScript are basically "copies" of the `Number` object: `(42).constructor;` returns `Number`. However, numbers have some special traits that other objects lack and are restricted in some other ways. Nonetheless, we can do some interesting experiments with numbers. In some edge cases and in some versions of Firebug, executing the preceding script in the console will not work. Instead, you must create a plain HTML file with a `script` tag in the header, as shown in the following code example. This approach is also useful when you want to test slightly different versions or more complex code because it can be a bit of a hassle to write longer code in the JavaScript console.

```html
<!DOCTYPE html PUBLIC "-//W3C//DTD HTML 4.01//EN">
<html>
<head>
  <title>JavaScript testing</title>
  <meta http-equiv="Content-Type" content="text/html; charset=UTF-8">
  <script type="text/javascript">

  // Insert code here.

  </script>
</head>
<body>
  <p>No page content</p>
</body>
</html>
```

Comments in JavaScript work the same way as in PHP: You can start a single-line comment with a double slash (`//`) and enclose a multiple-line comment with `/*` and `*/`.

You can now replace the comment with your testing code and load the file into a browser.

```javascript
Number.prototype.squared = function() {
  return this * this;
```

```
};
```

```
console.log((42).squared());
```

This code extends the `Number` objects and adds a function to all numbers named `squared`. In the last line, we create a new number object just by writing out the number and calling the number's `squared()` method! Using such functions makes the code much easier to read because the resulting code looks and sounds more natural. For example, suppose you have a lot of hexadecimal codes that you want to convert to their RGB equivalents. You can simple extend the `String` object with a function that takes the string and converts it to the respective RGB values: `"66CCFF".hexToRGB();`.

Adding functions to an object (and all instances of that object) is achieved via the `prototype` property. Later in this chapter, the "Prototypes" section explains this process in greater detail and shows an implementation of the `hexToRGB()` function. For now, just be aware that basically everything is an object in JavaScript.

Yes, functions are also objects. As a consequence, you can do anything with functions that you could do with other objects. You can store functions in variables, use them as parameters to other function calls, add properties to them, and so on. And because properties of an object are regular variables, these properties can also contain functions! That means you can add "subfunctions" to functions:

```
function foo() {
  console.log("foo");
}


foo.value = "Drupal";


foo.bar = function() {
  console.log("My value is: " + this.value);
};


foo();
console.log(foo.value);
foo.bar();
```

> **⚠ Semicolons in JavaScript**
> In JavaScript, you should end an assignment with a semicolon, just like any other command. JavaScript is not as strict about semicolons as other programming languages, but to improve readability and compatibility, you should always add semicolons to separate commands. If you omit the semicolons, line ends are considered the end of the command if the current context allows it.
>
> Not adding semicolons is considered bad programming style and can sometimes even break the script—for example, when it is compressed by removing whitespace. Line breaks are also considered whitespace and, therefore, will be removed. If you do not add semicolons, the commands will be glued together and the JavaScript engine will no longer be able to parse the script.

The preceding code prints "foo", "Drupal", and "My value is: Drupal", in that order, to the console. Using this technique, you can create full-blown objects that are not instances of any class. This approach is very similar to the programming pattern commonly known as a "singleton". (More on design patterns in JavaScript can be found in Chapter 11 of this book and in the highly recommended book *Pro JavaScript Design Patterns* by Ross Harmes and Dustin Diaz.)

Defining and Working with Objects

You can define new objects in JavaScript in two ways:

- `var myObj = new Object();` uses the `new` keyword to create a new "instance" of an object. While this approach works adequately, it's considered obsolete by many programmers because the syntax is quite verbose.

- `var myObj = {};` creates a new, empty object that you can now fill.

Due to its brevity, we'll use the latter syntax throughout the book. This syntax is used by JSON (as described in Chapter 10, in the section "Calling the Server with Xml-HttpRequest") and most other people as well. You can add properties to a class in two ways: (1) add the properties directly when defining the object or (2) add the properties after the object is defined.

```
var configuration = {
  "id": 1634,
  "firstName": "John",
  "lastName": "Doe",
```

```
  "birthday": "1982-03-17",
  "permissions": {
    'create': true,
    'update': true,
    'delete': false
  }
};
```

The preceding code block contains an example object, where the object consists of key–value pairs. The string (or integer) found to the left of the colon is the key; the item found to the right of the colon is the value that corresponds to the key. Key–value pairs are separated from one another by commas. As everywhere else in JavaScript, the whitespace doesn't matter here—we could just as well have written everything on one line. It is also possible to arbitrarily nest objects: The value corresponding to a key can also be an object, for example. Finally, because everything is an object in JavaScript, values can be anything.

> **Commas in arrays and objects**
> Unlike in PHP, you shouldn't add a comma after the last element of the object in JavaScript. Mozilla browsers won't complain, but many other browsers will just stop the execution of the script!

You can add new keys to an object by using the following syntax:

```
function IDtoKey(id) {
  //...
  if (id == 236) {
    return "lastName";
  }
}


var configuration = {};
configuration.id = 1634;
configuration["firstName"] = "John";
configuration[IDtoKey(236)] = "Doe";
configuration["birth" + "Day"] = "1982-03-17";
```

```
configuration.permissions = {};
configuration.permissions.create = true;
configuration["permissions"].update = true;
configuration["permissions"]["delete"] = false;
```

> **Inspecting the contents of an object**
> With Firebug, you can print any object to the console. Just enter `console.`
> `log(configuration);` and you'll see a new line showing some values of the
> object. By clicking on that line, you can inspect the object fully and even dig
> deeper into it.

The dot syntax used in the preceding example corresponds to PHP's arrow syntax for objects. Alternatively, you can use an array-like syntax when accessing properties of the object. You can also use variable names or other arbitrary commands to specify the key in the square brackets; it's even possible to call a function that returns the key. These ways of accessing an object's properties work on deeper levels and can be freely mixed, as shown in the preceding example. To add new properties to an object, you do not need to declare those properties beforehand—just assign them. If the property didn't exist before, it will be created from scratch by this step; if it did exist before, it will be overwritten.

Prototypes

Most other object-oriented programming languages support the concept of classes. Classes are basically blueprints for objects (the objects created from a class are commonly known as *instances*), as shown in the left part of Figure 9.4. In contrast, JavaScript does not have classes. Instead, it allows objects to have a special property that acts as template for "instances" created from that object—namely, the `prototype` property.

This special property contains the blueprints for other objects created from that object, as illustrated in the right part of Figure 9.4. Everything in that area of the figure is available in the instance. However, an object must meet one requirement before it can act as base object: It must be a function (Functions *are* objects, remember?) that serves as constructor. This point might seem subtle, but there really is a difference: The prototype is an object as well, which means that it can be extended at any time—not just when it is defined for the first time.

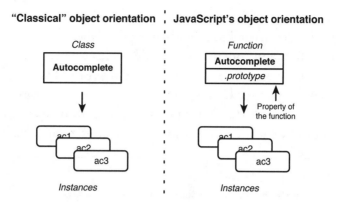

FIGURE 9.4 Classical object orientation versus JavaScript's object orientation.

Creating Your Own Objects with Prototypes

We will now illustrate these ideas with some code examples.

```
// Creates the constructor function for the autocomplete object.
function autocomplete(url) {
  // Saves the correct url for this object.
  if (url) {
    this.url = url;
  }
}


// Adds a function to "autocomplete's" prototype.
autocomplete.prototype.doStuff = function() {
  console.log("This object autocompletes from " + this.url);
};


// Adds some default properties to the prototype.
autocomplete.prototype.url = 'http://example.org/js/node/title';
autocomplete.prototype.maxItems = 8;
```

This source code shows the basic definition of a "prototype-enabled" object. We start off with a regular function, which will become the "constructor" of the object. A constructor is a function that is executed when a new instance of the object is created—in this case, when a new text field is enabled for autocompletion. We then add a function and some other variables needed to that object's prototype.

The constructor function contains some code, which we next examine a bit further: If the parameter url is not false, it is saved to this.url. The if statement checks whether a URL has been passed to the function; when that is the case, it saves the URL into the object. We'll discuss that behavior later. For now, here's some code to create instances of the object we just created (add this code to the object definition):

```
var ac1 = new autocomplete();
var ac2 = new autocomplete("http://example.org/js/taxonomy/title");


ac1.doStuff();
ac2.doStuff();


ac1.maxItems = 12;
console.log(ac2.maxItems);
```

The first two lines of this code create new instances of the autocomplete object. The first instance doesn't pass a URL to the constructor, so nothing is saved to this. url. The second instance does pass a URL to the constructor. When the two functions ac1.doStuff() and ac2.doStuff() are called, they will log their URL to the console. The first line appearing in the console is "This object autocompletes from http://example.org/js/node/title." This URL is the "default" URL for that object as defined in the prototype! As long as the properties of the instance aren't overwritten or changed in some way, they contain the values of the prototype. The second line in the console contains the custom URL that was passed to the constructor for ac2.

You can also change the value of an instance directly. For example, we can just change maxItems to another number. Printing out the value of maxItems from the *other* instance shows that the assignment only altered one object. To easily see what values a certain object contains, we can just print the object to Firebug's console with console.log(ac1);. Clicking on the object in the console allows for further inspection of it, as shown in Figure 9.5.

Extending Existing Objects

One of the best things about JavaScript is that it's extremely flexible. JavaScript allows you to modify anything at any given point. In the case of object orientation with

FIGURE 9.5 Displaying an object in Firebug's console.

prototypes, that statement means that you can alter the prototype of the base object at any time. If you do, all instances of that object will also get the newly added properties. Thus you can add and override functions even after you create instances of them, and these new instances will automatically be "updated."

Let's look at an example (add this code after the object definition from the previous two code examples):

```
// Function for creating the drop-down menu.
autocomplete.prototype.createDropdown = function() {
  // Dummy code for creating a drop-down menu.
  console.log("Creating the dropdown with " + this.maxItems + " items");
};


// Increase the number of items displayed by default.
autocomplete.prototype.maxItems = 10;


ac1.createDropdown();
ac2.createDropdown();
```

First, we add a new function to the prototype of the `autocomplete` object. This function will be available to all new instances created from the `autocomplete` object as well as to all existing instances. Next, we increase the default item limit for `autocomplete` objects to 10. When we call the new function `createDropdown()`, it prints the number of items to be displayed for that particular instance of the `autocomplete` object. In this case, it displays 12 for `ac1` and 10 for `ac2`. In this way, the new value propagates to existing instances, although it will not overwrite values we already have overridden. In the preceding code example, we set `ac1.maxItems` to 12, thereby overriding the value provided from the prototype.

We can also extend predefined objects, such as the `String` object from the Java-Script core. That ability allows us to execute code such as `"66CCFF".hexToRGB();` and to understand how this implementation can be done. Because all strings are instances of the `String` object, we simply add a new function to `String.prototype` and all strings will gain that functionality automatically! Here's the code:

```javascript
String.prototype.hexToRGB = function() {
  return {
    'r': parseInt(this[0] + this[1], 16),
    'g': parseInt(this[2] + this[3], 16),
    'b': parseInt(this[4] + this[5], 16)
  };
};
```

You can paste this code into the bare-bones HTML document and test it in Firebug's console. The function `parseInt` converts numbers from different bases (hexadecimal numbers are base 16) to regular base 10 numbers.

> **Operator overloading**
>
> A small problem in JavaScript is that the + operator is overloaded. In other words, this operator can operate with a multitude of data types, including both strings and numbers: It concatenates strings, but adds numbers. Consider `4 + 5 + "6"` as an example: It first adds 4 and 5 and then concatenates 6, resulting in `"96"`.
>
> If you get odd results when doing calculations, check whether all operands are of correct data types. You can convert strings that contain numbers to actual numbers with `parseInt()`. Thus `4 + 5 + parseInt("6")` returns the correct result.
>
> This problem doesn't exist in PHP because the concatenation operator in PHP is the dot operator (`.`), whereas adding numbers is done with the + operator.

This function obviously lacks some capabilities, such as checking that the string is, in fact, a hexadecimal value. The conversion could also be performed in one step and the color channel parts can be extracted using the modulo function. Our function should also allow the hash sign to appear as the first character, and so on.

Using Functions

As mentioned earlier, functions are first-class objects in JavaScript. That fact allows us to do many things in JavaScript that are not possible in other programming languages.

Anonymous Functions

Anonymous functions describe functions that are not associated with a name; they are just *there*. You can define anonymous functions virtually everywhere. It's even possible to define a function directly in the argument list to a function call!

```
function(param1, param2, ...) { /* Function body */ }
```

This example shows what an anonymous function looks like. The difference between a regular function and an anonymous function is that you omit the function name after the keyword `function`. You might find this format familiar, and you are correct: We used the same notation to assign the function to a variable name or an object property, thereby removing its anonymity.

```
function functionCaller(func) {
  console.log("Calling function...");
  func();
  console.log("Function has been called!");
}


functionCaller(function() {
  alert("Anonymous function");
});
```

The preceding code example shows that you can simply define functions in another function's argument list. First, we create a function called `functionCaller` with one parameter. We print some debugging information and call the anonymous function that is passed to this function. `func` contains the function passed to that function; `func` can just be treated like a regular function. The second part of the code calls the function with an anonymous function as the parameter.

This technique is commonly used in jQuery and various other programming patterns because it allows you to easily customize an action by passing in custom code that is called in another function. In fact, it is quite similar to what Drupal does in some places in its PHP code. For example, when you are defining a new menu item, you must specify a `page callback`, `access callback`, and various other callback functions that are called when the menu item is invoked or displayed. The only difference here is that PHP (unlike JavaScript) doesn't allow you to define these functions directly in place (at the time of this writing), but rather forces you to use a string that contains the function's name.

You can define anonymous functions in many other places. For example, you might want to return a function from a function (Yes, functions are everywhere in JavaScript!):

```
// A function that returns a function.
function logCall(func) {
  return function() {
    console.log("Calling function %o.", func);
    var ret = func();
    console.log("Function %o returned %o.", func, ret);
  };
}


function doStuff() {
  alert("Executing function");
}


// Create a version of the doStuff() function that is being logged.
var doStuffLogged = logCall(doStuff);
doStuffLogged();
```

The first function, logCall, returns another (anonymous) function with no parameters. This code is *not* executed when the function logCall is invoked; rather, the inner function is created. In that inner function, we log the function that is being called, execute the function (named func), and print the return value for that function. The next section in this book examines the nitty-gritty details of how the function scope works and explains why the inner function can access the variable func.

The second function, doStuff, is just a dummy function that will be used later. We call the function logCall with that function as a parameter. logCall returns a new function that executes doStuff when it is executed (phew!); that anonymous returned function is saved to a variable. In the next line, we execute this function, which is now stored in the variable doStuffLogged.

When you execute this code snippet in a browser, you'll see "Calling function doStuff()." in the console window, then the alert will appear. After you click "OK," the text "Function doStuff() returned undefined." will appear. That message indicates we just "extended" a function by adding logging capabilities, so that the function now informs us every time it is called. How neat is that!?

The Function Scope

We've talked about the *function scope* before, but what does that term actually mean? In general terms, the scope is the environment or context in which a piece of code (read: a function) is executed. The scope comprises all things that can be accessed or reached from a certain point in the code.

In a function, the scope includes the defined local variables in that function (using the var keyword), the parameters to that function, and all global variables (e.g., objects that JavaScript provides itself, such as the Math object, and objects that the Document Object Model provides, such as window and document). Additionally, in JavaScript, the scope of a function includes all variables of the function it is defined in (the "parent function"). As we saw in the previous code example, the inner anonymous function can also access the parameters of the outer function in which it is defined.

This kind of scope is called "lexical scope" (or static scope). Although it is somewhat uncommon, it is not that complicated and is certainly very convenient: The things you can access are the items that are defined or available above the function in the *source code*. The scope doesn't depend on the context in which the function is executed, but rather on the context in which the function is defined. Let's look at an example:

```javascript
function scopeTest(param) {
  var funcs = [];

  for (var i = 0; i < 10; i++) {
    funcs[i] = function(j) {
      console.log("i: %o; param: %o; j: %o", i, param, j);
    };
  }
  funcs[3](42);
  return funcs;
}


var functions = scopeTest('successful');
functions[3](21);
```

This example defines a function with one parameter. The for loop creates 10 functions and stores them to the funcs array so that they can be executed later on. The functions created print various variables to the console so that we can see which values they contain. We then pick a random function, execute it with the additional parameter 42, and return the entire array with the created functions.

When we look at the output of this JavaScript snippet, we see that i is always 10, param is always "successful", and j is 42 in the first case and 21 in the second case (executing other functions than the one with index 3 gives the same result). The sources of the values of param and j are clear: "successful" is from the call of scopeTest, and 42 and 21 are the arguments passed to the created functions.

The value of i is 10 because the for loop counted until 10 until it stopped. But . . . i had a different value when the function was created in the loop, you say? That doesn't matter, because we used only the variable i. Although the value of that variable may change, the inner function always uses the current value of the variable.

The last line of the example shows that the scope of the function scopeTest survives even until after the function has returned. It exists as long as it is necessary—as long as you still can execute functions defined within scopeTest, the scope is guaranteed to exist.

One kind of function does not have only one static scope. In fact, each invocation of such a function creates a new "copy" of the scope, leaving the other scopes intact. That behavior is called **closures.** Using the same scopeTest function from the preceding example, we now create a second set of functions with a different parameter:

```
var otherFunctions = scopeTest('failed');

functions[3](21);

otherFunctions[3](21);
```

The variable otherFunctions now contains another set of functions. When we call one of the original functions, param remains "successful" because the function was defined in a scope(!) where param was set to that value. Calling the newly created copy prints "failed" for param—because the scope that function was declared in contains a *different* variable with the name param.

As shown in Figure 9.6, executing the preceding code means that you end up with two copies of the scope when the function is called twice. These scopes are completely unrelated and can have entirely different values and states. Code that is operating inside that scope can change variables in the scope (the state of the scope), even after the

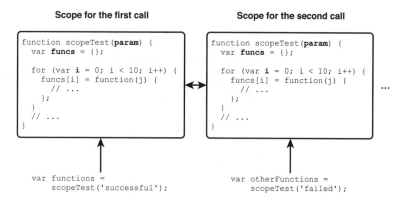

FIGURE 9.6 Different scopes of one function.

original function returns. The scope is discarded only when it becomes impossible to execute any code found in that scope.

This notion of functions and scope is not an easy concept to understand, but there are many different ways to leverage that particular feature of JavaScript. You can use this capability to encapsulate JavaScript widgets so that they form one single component instead of being distributed in the entire namespace. You can tightly integrate components with one another without *actually* making them depend on each other (more on that in Chapter 11).

Aliasing and Calling Functions

So far, we have called functions simply by adding () after the function name (or after the variable name in which the function is stored), optionally with some parameters. This is not the only way to call functions in JavaScript, however. Because functions are objects, they also have methods. Specifically, the two methods named `call` and `apply` both basically do one thing: execute the function.

In contrast to the practice of appending parentheses, which simply executes the function, the `call` and `apply` methods can also modify the `this` variable available in the function as well as pass parameters in another way. The `call` method executes the function to which it belongs, where `this` is the first parameter of `call()` and the rest of the parameters is shifted by one to the left (see Figure 9.7). The `apply` method also uses the first parameter as `this` and takes the second parameter (which must be an array) as the parameter list. As a result, you can execute a function with a variable parameter list very easily.

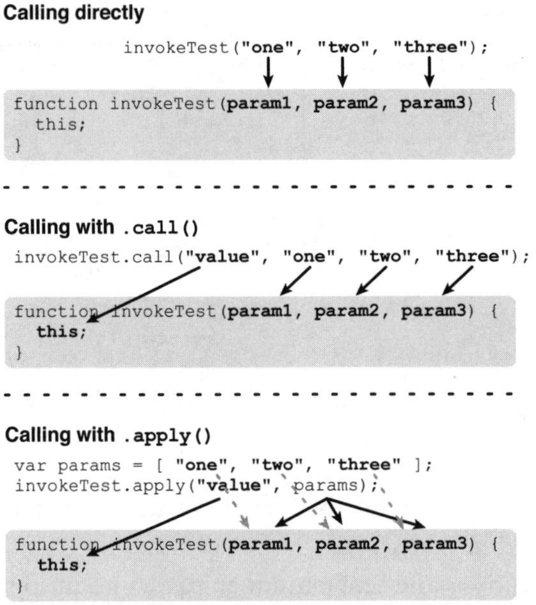

Calling directly

```
        invokeTest("one", "two", "three");


function invokeTest(param1, param2, param3) {
   this;
}
```

- -

Calling with `.call()`

```
invokeTest.call("value", "one", "two", "three");


function invokeTest(param1, param2, param3) {
   this;
}
```

- -

Calling with `.apply()`

```
var params = [ "one", "two", "three" ];
invokeTest.apply("value", params);


function invokeTest(param1, param2, param3) {
   this;
}
```

FIGURE 9.7 Various ways of calling a function.

With those two functions, you can manipulate the `this` variable. But what is `this`? As a general rule of thumb, `this` is *the object for which the function is executed*. When you add click events to an element, `this` refers to the element the event handler was attached to (the element that was clicked). When you execute the method of an object, `this` is the object itself, and so on. When the function is not called for a specific object, `this` is a generic pointer to `window`, the root element of the browser environment. Let's look at an example:

```
var myObj = {};

myObj.name = "Banana";


// Create a function that tells us something about this object.

myObj.tellMeAboutYou = function() {

  console.log("My name is " + this.name);

};


// Now execute that function.

myObj.tellMeAboutYou();
```

When you execute this snippet, you'll see that `this.name` does, indeed, refer to `myObj.name`. In this example, `this` is the same as `myObj` because the function `tellMeAboutYou` is executed as a member of `myObj`; thus it is executed *for* `myObj`. Remember that `this` is not tightly bound to the place where it was defined, so in our example, `this` does not necessarily always refer to `myObj`. We already have seen that its value can be altered. In fact, if you reference a function from another object and call the function as method of that other object, `this` points to that other object:

```
var myOtherObj = {};

myOtherObj.name = "Kiwi";

myOtherObj.tellMeAboutYou = myObj.tellMeAboutYou;


// Execute the referenced/copied function.

myOtherObj.tellMeAboutYou();
```

This code snippet prints out "Kiwi": Because of the way in which this function was called, `this` refers to `myOtherObj`. This behavior can both be a good thing and a bad thing. It often proves useful because you can easily reuse functions—after all, `this` is not bound to a specific object.

Summary

This chapter took a broad view of JavaScript. A variety of language constructs are specific to JavaScript, and some of JavaScript's features differ somewhat from those of PHP. In this chapter, we played with JavaScript's data types and examined how they behave. Probably the most important part of this chapter dealt with JavaScript's object orientation. Don't worry too much if you didn't understand every detail; in Chapters 10 and 11, you will become more comfortable with the sometimes unusual aspects of JavaScript.

Functions are first-class objects in JavaScript, and much of the language's emphasis focuses on them. Two concepts—scope and context—are also very important in JavaScript.

In the next chapter, we take a step back from the innards of the JavaScript programming language and have some fun with jQuery.

Chapter 10

An Introduction to jQuery

Chapter 9 introduced the Document Object Model (DOM); the DOM has also been mentioned earlier in this book. The DOM is the means used to access, create, manipulate, and delete parts of the Web page on which JavaScript is operating. It also allows the Web page to react to events that happen on the page, such as the user clicking on a certain element, moving the mouse, or typing letters. Furthermore, it provides an interface to some of the browser's user interface (UI) elements (the chrome) and other status information, such as the screen resolution or the scroll bars.

The DOM is not specific to JavaScript, nor is it specific to certain browsers. Put simply, the DOM defines a certain way to do things with a hierarchically structured document tree—and that's what a Web page is! All (X)HTML documents are structured in a tree-like fashion: As shown in Figure 10.1, they contain a root element (html), which has two children (head and body), which in turn can have their own child elements, and so on.

The DOM is actually a *model* to interact with such a tree-like structure. It can also be used in a back-end application (such as Drupal) to create, read, and manipulate HTML or XML documents.

```
▼<html xmlns="http://www.w3.org/1999/xhtml" xml:lang="en">
  ►<head>
  ▼<body>
    ▼<div id="wrapper">
      ▼<div id="header">
        ►<h1>
          <h4>A Company that Makes Everything.</h4>
        ►<ul id="navigation">
        ►<form id="language" action="/" method="get" title="Select a language to view the site in">
        ►<form id="search" action="/" method="get">
        </div>
      ▼<div id="body">
        ▼<div class="teaser">
          ▼<a href="#" class="lead-image">
            <img src="files/teaser.jpg" alt="Bank on a beach">
          </a>
          ►<p>
        </div>
        ▼<div class="columns">
          ►<div class="column" id="column-products">
          ►<div class="column" id="column-news">
          ►<div class="column" id="column-misc">
          </div>
        </div>
      ▼<div id="footer">
        ►<ul id="footer-nav">
        ►<p class="message">
        </div>
      </div>
    </body>
</html>
```

FIGURE 10.1 An HTML document tree.

Unfortunately, the JavaScript methods and functions to interact with the DOM are not easy and straightforward to use. Even simple tasks, such as adding a class name to all paragraphs, require some verbose code and are vulnerable to errors because of some not-so-obvious pitfalls. Also, the DOM is not consistently implemented across browsers. As a consequence, if we tried to use the DOM directly, we would have to take all kinds of weird edge cases into account.

This is where jQuery comes into play: It provides a clean and easy-to-use interface to the Web site. Internally, it uses DOM functions; externally, it provides a coherent interface that remains consistent across all browsers. jQuery deals with all of the browser-related differences at the internal level—that is, invisibly to the user—so the user (in this case, the jQuery programmer) doesn't have to worry about them.

This chapter explains most aspects of jQuery. As you follow along with the examples here, you'll learn to find your way around an HTML document; create, manipulate, and delete elements; attach and remove events from them; and explore many more of jQuery's features. You will also see how to make calls to the server (commonly known as AJAX, although it's technically not AJAX for the most part) and how the returned data can be processed efficiently. First, however, we take a look at the basic usage of jQuery.

A First Look at jQuery

In this section, we will briefly look at how jQuery can be used and encounter the most commonly used features in jQuery. Even though jQuery is designed to be easy to use, you should be aware of a few exceptional cases.

Setting Up jQuery

The most current version of jQuery can be found at `http://jquery.com/`. Drupal 6 ships with jQuery 1.2. For testing purposes, the uncompressed version is the best one because it allows you to easily examine the code. For production Web sites, the other version is a better choice because of its smaller file size.

Making jQuery available on a Web site requires you to write only a single line of code, which includes the `jquery.js` file:

```
<script type="text/javascript" src="jquery.js"></script>
```

That's it. (You must replace the path to `jquery.js` with the location where your version of jQuery resides, of course.) Drupal automatically adds jQuery to a generated page when it is needed—that is, when there's another JavaScript file or code on that page.

You can use one of two approaches to make Drupal aware of JavaScript files in a theme:

- Use the `drupal_add_js()` function in your theme.
- Add the JavaScript file name to the theme's `.info` file.

For experimenting with jQuery, the second solution is the easiest option. (You'll learn how to use the more powerful `drupal_add_js()` in Chapter 11.) In your theme's `.info` file, add the following line:

```
scripts[] = mytheme.js
```

This line tells Drupal's template engine that this JavaScript file is required for this theme, so it automatically includes it. You can test that it works correctly by adding `alert("file loaded!");` to the `mytheme.js` file. Make sure you empty the cache before you begin the test. You can add as many JavaScript files as you want by just repeating the line. Because a JavaScript file is added to the page, Drupal will automatically add `misc/drupal.js` and `misc/jquery.js` as well. You don't have to download jQuery—your Drupal installation already has it!

jQuery itself doesn't do anything by default; it simply sits on the page and waits to be used. When your Web page contains multiple JavaScript files, you should include jQuery first because other scripts might rely on jQuery. Browsers execute JavaScript code in the exactly same order it is included in the HTML document, so simply placing the `script` tag that includes jQuery above all other `script` tags ensures that this feature is available to all remaining JavaScript code. Drupal ensures that jQuery is always the first file, so you don't have to worry about the order in which files are made available.

Some people prefer to experiment with JavaScript and jQuery in a clean and controlled environment. If you're one of them, you will find a sample HTML page in the files accompanying this book; they can be downloaded from `http://frontenddrupal.com`. The sample file includes the jQuery library and contains some markup and CSS code that you can use for experimenting with Drupal. (The template may not work properly in Internet Explorer 7 or earlier versions, but it's just a test template anyway.)

Executing Code on Page Load

The most common way of executing JavaScript code is immediately after the page loads. That strategy takes care of housekeeping issues early on, by ensuring that all kinds of setup and initialization tasks are performed, event handlers are attached to elements, and so on. Executing JavaScript when the page loads might not seem like a big deal; after all, you could just write code into a JavaScript file and include it in the HTML page. In fact, you have already seen that you can execute JavaScript code in this way because you were `alerted` that the "file loaded."

Now let's move on to our first jQuery command: `$('h2').hide();`. Write that line into the JavaScript file you just created and open a Drupal page in a browser. (Make sure there *are* h2 tags in the source code; if there aren't, you can use any other tag name.) Depending on your browser and many other circumstances, you might even see an effect; in most browsers, however, you will not notice any visible change. If you already know some jQuery, you will recognize that this command is correct and makes all h2 elements in the page disappear (we'll get to the nitty-gritty of the syntax soon).

JavaScript code is always evaluated *as soon as possible*—that is, as soon as all preceding JavaScript code is loaded and executed. Oftentimes, JavaScript code is evaluated before the entire page is loaded (before the closing `</html>` has even reached the browser). When you put code directly in the `head` of a document or a file loaded in that place, there is no guarantee that you will be able to access the DOM at that point, because it might not be loaded completely. For example, our earlier jQuery code tried to find all h2 elements in the page, but it found none because the document was not yet loaded completely when the code was executed. To prove this fact, try replacing this code with `console.log($('h2').size());` to confirm that it didn't find any h2 elements.

When we talk about loading the DOM, we are referring to only the HTML source code—not to other elements such as style sheets or images the page needs. Thus the ideal point to execute JavaScript code that should run when the page loads is precisely when the HTML page itself is loaded.

Luckily, jQuery has a ready solution to handle this issue. We can tell jQuery to execute a function as soon as the *DOM is ready* by using the `onready` event:

```
var init = function() {
  $('h2').hide();
};


$(document).ready(init);
```

When you insert this code into your JavaScript file, the function `init` is called when the document is ready. All h2 headings should disappear when you load the Drupal page containing that file.

> **The onload event**
> The onready event is provided by jQuery and is not part of the regular DOM event collection provided by the browser. Although some people use the native onload event to execute JavaScript code on page load, that's not a good idea because the onload event isn't triggered until *everything* has been loaded, including any style sheets and media files such as images.
>
> Usually, the user sees the page before all elements are loaded (with placeholders indicating the positions of unloaded images). The user can interact with the page at that point, even though the JavaScript code that changes parts of the page has not yet executed. To avoid this kind of problem, you should always use jQuery's onready event when you want to execute code immediately when the page loads. Use the onload event if you really want to execute code only when *all* elements of the page have been *fully* loaded.

Now, let's dissect the code we've just written step by step:

```
$('h2').hide();
```

The dollar sign at the beginning of this line is the name of a function (functions and variables can start with a dollar sign in JavaScript—in fact, you can create a function named $). That function lies at the heart of jQuery and acts as a dispatcher for all of its functionality. In other words, every piece of jQuery functionality is encapsulated within the dollar object. Actually, the dollar function is just an alias to a function called jQuery, which is used to make statements shorter. You'll discover the implications of this behavior in the section "Using Other JavaScript Libraries" later in this chapter.

The dollar function is called with a single parameter, 'h2'. jQuery allows you to find elements in a page using CSS syntax; therefore this selector finds all h2 tags inside the page. The dollar function call returns a jQuery object that has several methods, one of which is named hide; that's the method we are calling.

Alternatively, we could have written the first statement in this way:

```
var headlines = $('h2');
headlines.hide();
```

The first syntax is more commonly used, however, because it's cleaner and more concise. As you can see, jQuery has a very expressive syntax that requires you to type in only a few characters. By comparison, the equivalent statement in regular JavaScript, utilizing the DOM directly, would be written as follows:

```
var headlines = document.getElementsByTagName('h2');

for (var i = 0; i < headlines.length; i++) {
  headlines[i].style.display = 'none';
}
```

You can probably understand what that code means, but it's significantly longer.

The second line in our initial code, $(document).ready(init);, is similarly structured. This time, we don't pass a string to the dollar function, but rather a variable named document. This variable is predefined by the browser environment and contains all kinds of settings and methods related to the currently loaded document. (Similarly, the window object contains properties and methods for obtaining information about the window or changing aspects of the browser window in which the page is loaded.)

The $(document) part of the second line creates a "jQueryified" version of that object; in other words, the object returned by that function call contains all jQuery functions and acts on the document object. It does not change the original object, but instead wraps it in a jQuery object to provide more functionality. The ready() method of the returned jQuery object attaches a function to the list of events to execute when the element has finished loading. When functions are used in this way, they are usually termed "callbacks" or "callback functions."

There are, of course, even shorter ways to achieve the same goal:

```
$(document).ready(function() {
  $('h2').hide();
});
```

The preceding code takes advantage of the fact that we can declare anonymous functions (see Chapter 9 for more information on anonymous functions) that can be defined in the argument list of a function.

```
$(function() {
  $('h2').hide();
});
```

This code is a jQuery shortcut for attaching a function to the document's `onready` event. jQuery can detect when the first parameter is a function and attaches that function to the event list (more on events later in this chapter).

Navigating the DOM Tree

We've already seen that the dollar function has some unique features. There are five ways to call that function, three of which we've already encountered:

- `$("selector")` finds all HTML nodes matching the CSS selector passed.
- `$(document)` wraps the passed (HTML node) object as a jQuery object.
- `$(func)` attaches the passed function to the document's `onready` event list.

The dollar function also allows us to restrict the search for HTML nodes matching a selector to a certain area in the DOM tree by passing the root of the area (also called a *context*) as second parameter:

```
var headline = $('h2');
var image = $('img', headline);
```

The variable `image` now contains all `img` elements that are *inside* the items in `headline`.

The selector syntax allows you to use many different kinds of CSS selectors. You can query elements based on their ID, search by class name, select only elements with a certain property or a certain state (e.g., disabled), and so on. In addition, as in CSS, you can use multiple selectors in one statement by concatenating them with commas. The best part is that all of these selectors also work in Internet Explorer (even though Internet Explorer doesn't support some of these selectors for CSS).

You can try out all of these selectors in the sample document, either by wrapping them in a function called `onready` or by typing them into Firebug's console. To see the resulting elements in Firebug, append `.get()` to all of these functions to get a plain list of the elements found. When you hover over this list in Firebug, each element will be highlighted in the body window; when you click on that element, you can inspect its position in the document tree.

Without further ado, here are some examples of jQuery's extensive selector support:

- **$(".links")** finds all elements that belong to the class `links`. This selector is not exclusive, so it also finds elements that have other classes besides the one searched for. For example, this query might find `<div class="links">`, but also `<ul class="links inline">`.

- **$("li:contains('comment')")** matches all list items that contain the word "comment" somewhere. (It also matches partial words, so it also finds "comments".)

- **$("#header h1 a[href^='http']")** finds all hyperlinks whose `href` attribute begins with "http" and that are inside a `h1` tag, which in turn is inside an element with an ID of `header`.

- **$("input:submit")** finds all `input` elements that have `type="submit"`; thus it finds all submit buttons.

Some of these selectors might not produce any results on a Drupal page because there are just no matching elements available. To test that the searching strategy actually works, modify your theme (or the content of a node, for example) so that you get results.

The jQuery documentation found at `http://docs.jquery.com/Selectors` has a complete and up-to-date listing of all supported selectors, along with examples of their use and detailed documentation for the selectors. You should look at all selectors at least once—you will almost certainly find a selector you didn't know exists, but proves to be very useful.

Be aware that the "jQuery version" of an element and the native JavaScript object of the element itself (which is provided by the DOM) are not identical. The jQuery object allows you to perform all actions that can be done with jQuery (hiding, moving, applying CSS, animating, . . .). By comparison, the native object directly represents the object and doesn't contain any jQuery actions.

The left side in Figure 10.2 depicts various plain HTML nodes floating around. When you use `$('.content')` to select elements, jQuery will collect only the matching elements and wrap them in a jQuery object, thereby providing abstraction and more features to all enclosed nodes.

To access the actual native objects, you can use array syntax. With this syntax, `$(".columns")[0]` is the first element found, `$(".columns")[1]` is the second element found, and so on. In addition, the function called `.get(N)` returns the Nth object found. Calling `.get()` without a parameter will retrieve an array of all DOM objects in the jQuery object.

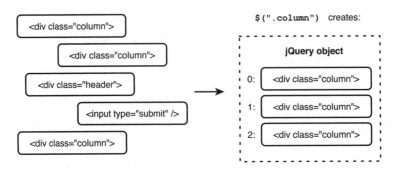

FIGURE 10.2 A jQuery object is a wrapper for one or more DOM objects.

Using jQuery

As discussed earlier, jQuery always acts on lists of elements. When you execute an action, it is (usually) applied to all elements that are part of the jQuery object. On many occasions, there will be just one element wrapped into a jQuery object. Nevertheless, keep in mind that jQuery isn't restricted to manipulating only one DOM object at a time.

To do something with a jQuery object, you call one of its methods. There are lots of possibilities in terms of actions you can perform. The jQuery documentation at http://docs.jquery.com/ divides these actions into the following categories:

- **Attributes** methods allow you to retrieve attributes from the matched DOM elements and change them. There are special methods for changing classes as well. It's also possible to retrieve and manipulate the value attribute of form elements.

- **Events** can be attached and removed from elements with various methods. You can also artificially trigger events.

- **CSS** methods retrieve and set CSS properties of the elements matched. jQuery also provides methods for calculating the absolute position of the element in the viewport as well as measuring and setting the dimensions of the element.

- **Traversing** methods allow you to change the matched elements inside the jQuery object. It's possible to find other elements based on the currently selected element (e.g., by selecting parents, children, or siblings). It's also possible to filter out elements from the current selection.

- **Manipulation** methods change the position of the element in the DOM tree. It's possible to move around DOM nodes, wrap them in other markup language, clone them, or delete them. It's also possible to change the contents of the elements matched (i.e., the material between `<tag>` and `</tag>`).

- **Effects** methods allow you to add visual cues to your Web page by animating movements, fading elements, and showing or hiding them. It's also possible to queue multiple animations so that they execute sequentially.

The other sections don't refer to actions that can be performed with DOM elements. Some of the described methods also fit into multiple categories. Here, we look at the most important methods. We start by considering how events are managed in JavaScript and jQuery because that is what we will do most of the time: do something in response to the user's actions.

Events

Events are *things that happen*. A *thing that happens* can be the user clicking on something, moving the mouse, scrolling down, double-clicking, submitting a form, pressing a key, or resizing the browser window, among other actions. The browser allows you to act upon those events—that is, to execute code when an event occurs.

To do so, the DOM maintains a set of `on...` properties for almost all properties. For example, you can set the `onclick` property of any DOM element (which is *not* the jQuery object—a jQuery object wraps DOM elements) to a function, and the browser will then call that function when the user clicks on that element. This approach has one drawback, however: When you set the property, the previous value is overwritten.

Oftentimes, you want to add multiple functions to a single event of a single element. Different scripts might add different functions, but when you just set the DOM element's `on...` property, the script that runs later will overwrite the first script's event callback function. Luckily, jQuery offers an interface through which you can add events to an element—and it does so without overwriting existing functions. Internally, jQuery has only one function, but that function calls in turn all of the other functions you attached using jQuery.

Let's add our first event-handling function:

```
$('#body .teaser p').mouseover(function() {
  alert('Mouse is here');
});
```

In the preceding code, you should replace the selector `#body .teaser p` with a selector that matches an element on your Drupal page. You can, of course, use a selector that matches multiple elements. In that case, every instance will react to the mouseover event. You can either run that code snippet directly in Firebug (or a JavaScript console in another browser) or write it into the JavaScript file you created. If you follow the latter path, don't forget to execute the code when the DOM has finished loading by wrapping it in `$(document).ready(function() { ... });`.

The code in the previous example "attaches" a function to the `onmouseover` event of the paragraph selected. Event functions in jQuery are named without the leading `on`, so calling the `.mouseover()` method adds a new method to the `onmouseover` event. The parameter to that function is an anonymous function. (If you don't know what an anonymous function is, revisit the section "Anonymous Functions" in Chapter 9.) The function does only one thing: Send an alert message when called.

Now, let's add another `mouseover` event to the same set of elements:

```
$('#body .teaser p').mouseover(function() {
  $(this).animate({ opacity: 0.5 });
});
```

Make sure to change the selector in the preceding code to whatever you used in the first `mouseover` event. When adding this event in addition to the previous one, you'll notice that *both* functions are executed when you hover over a selected element. The second function fades the hovered element to 50% of its original opacity, so it will appear semi-transparent.

> **What's the dot before the function name?**
> In this book, we use dot notation to refer to jQuery methods instead of "regular" functions. A dot before the function name indicates that the function cannot be called by that name, but rather has to be called as a method of a jQuery object—for example, `$('div').mouseover(...)`.

When you load the page, you should see a message box as soon as you *enter* the paragraph selected with your mouse cursor. Note that the `mouseover` event is fired only when the user *enters* the paragraph, not when the user moves the cursor around on the paragraph.

Let's look at another event function:

```
$('#header h1 a').click(function() {
  alert("This link leads to the home page.");
  return false;
});
```

When you click on the selected element, the specified anonymous function is called. It first sends an alert message and then returns `false`. Try to remove the `return false;` line and see what happens. With that statement, nothing should happen after the alert; without the statement, you should follow the link. It is the return value of an event callback function that matters. When the function returns `false`, the handling of the event stops (the event no longer "bubbles" up, in DOM lingo); otherwise, execution of the code continues with the remaining event handlers, which include the "default" action that would happen if no other JavaScript handlers were added to the element.

jQuery also allows you to remove event-handling functions you have added previously. You have two options for doing so. First, you can add an event-handling function that is automatically removed after the event occurs once:

```
$('#header h1 a').one('click', function() {
  alert("This link leads to the home page.");
  return false;
});
```

Run this code on the example page and then click on the logo. The first time, you should see the alert message; the second time, the link should actually take you to the linked page. This callback function is added with the `.one()` method. Its first parameter is the event name (without "on"), and its second parameter is the function.

Alternatively, you can call the method `.unbind()`, which works via the same mechanism: The first parameter is the event from which you want to remove a callback function; the second parameter is the event function you want to remove. If you use this approach, you must save a reference to the callback function, because otherwise you won't be able to remove it. Here's an example:

```
$(function() {
  var searchText = "Enter your search terms";

  var focusSearch = function() {
```

```
    if ($(this).val() == searchText) {
      $(this).val("");
    }
  };


  var blurSearch = function() {
    if (!$(this).val()) {
      $(this).val(searchText);
    }
    else {
      $(this)
        .unbind('focus', focusSearch)
        .unbind('blur', blurSearch);
    }
  };


  $('#edit-keys')
    .val(searchText)
    .focus(focusSearch)
    .blur(blurSearch);
});
```

This example actually does something useful: It adds text into the search text field. When the user gives the focus to that text field, the text is removed. When the user leaves the field again, the text is inserted again, if the user didn't enter any text of his or her own. Once some actual text is entered, the event handlers are removed completely so that the script no longer messes with the user's input. Figure 10.3 shows the possible states of the input field.

Let's dissect the preceding script line by line. The first and the last lines are the "wrapper" that ensures that the code in between them is executed only until after the DOM finishes loading. (The note entitled "The onload Event" provides further information on that topic.) The second line defines a variable that holds the text, thereby ensuring that we don't have to write the same text over and over each time we need it. Note that var is used to make the variable local to the surrounding function. As a consequence, this variable cannot be accessed from outside and doesn't "pollute" the global namespace.

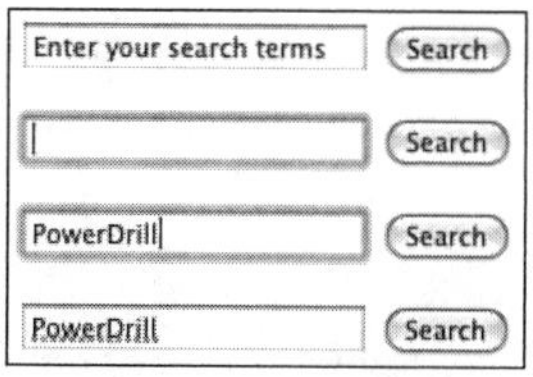

FIGURE 10.3 The possible states of a text field with a default value.

Next, the function `focusSearch` is defined. It sets the value to an empty string when the value of the text field is the default text. To refer to the text field, we use `this`. The function is used as an event-handling function, such that when the event is triggered, `this` refers to the element associated with the event. Because we have attached the function to the "focus" event of the text box, `this` in that function refers to that text box. This relationship is a good thing: It allows us to use the same event callback function for lots of different events because `this` always refers to the element that is the target of the current interaction.

You might have noticed that `this` was wrapped into `$()`. In event callback functions, `this` is a native DOM element, so we must wrap it as a jQuery object first to be able to use jQuery functionality.

The `blurSearch` function works in a similar fashion: It checks whether the value of the text box evaluates to `false` (using the `!` operator). When the text box is empty, the original value is restored. When the user has entered text, the `else` branch is executed and the events are removed from the text box with the `.unbind()` function.

You might find the syntax used in the preceding script a bit awkward: No semicolon appears after the first line, which wraps `this` as a jQuery object. Instead, the next line calls the `.unbind()` function for the first time. But this line doesn't end with a semicolon, either: The command continues on the next line with another call to `.unbind()` with other parameters. This example demonstrates one of jQuery's greatest features: You can "chain" several commands together without specifying the jQuery object over and over again. Without chaining, these lines would have to be written in this way:

```
$(this).unbind('focus', focusSearch);
$(this).unbind('blur', blurSearch);
```

In this example, `$(this)` is relatively short, but you could also use longer selectors. Repeating them multiple times would certainly be tiresome. Also, there is some overhead associated with creating a jQuery version of an object and searching through the document for elements matching that selector. When you chain together several methods to be applied to one jQuery object, you eliminate that overhead.

> **How chaining works internally**
> The chaining technique is actually quite simple: Each jQuery method returns itself (using `this`). JavaScript allows you to call a function from the object returned from another function call, which in turn allows you to chain together an infinitely long series of method calls. However, some functions don't return `this`, so you can use those functions only as the last item in a chain. These functions usually return something related to the elements, such as their contents or the value of an HTML attribute.

Back in our text field script, the last three lines actually do something right away: The first line fills the search field with the text, and the next two lines attach the event handlers for the `focus` and the `blur` event. The `focus` event is triggered when the user moves the cursor into the element (either by clicking on it or by moving the cursor with the keyboard). The `blur` event is triggered when the user moves the cursor away.

Of course, you could do many other things with this kind of script. For example, you might try to develop a script that automatically submits the form when the user picks another language. Drop-down menus based on the `select` syntax have a `change` event that is triggered when the user selects something. Forms can be submitted by calling `.submit()` for the form. Once the form is submitted automatically, you can hide the submit button as well. If you're stuck or your solution isn't working, look into the package downloadable from `http://frontenddrupal.com`, which contains an example solution. (Hint: The script requires fewer than five lines of code.)

Setting and Retrieving Attributes

Now let's continue to work on our sample HTML page. It contains several objects that we can modify.

```
$('#column-products a').attr('target', '_blank');
```

This line looks for all links within the element with the ID "column-products" and changes the `target` attribute to `_blank`. Try clicking on a link in the "Products" column before you execute the code and again after you execute the code. The attribute opens the link in a new window or tab (assuming you didn't disable that functionality in the browser). In Firebug's HTML inspector, you can also see that the links received the target attribute.

The .attr() method can be called in many different ways. This flexibility—one function accepts parameters in different ways—is typical of jQuery.

- .attr('attribute', 'value') sets the attribute of the elements in the jQuery object to the second parameter (which is a string or an integer).

- .attr('attribute') returns the value of the attribute from the *first* matched element. This is an exception to the rule that a jQuery method always works with all matched elements. Methods that return information about an element usually return information only for the first element.

- .attr({ 'attribute': 'value, ... }) takes an object consisting of attribute–value pairs as its only parameter. As a result, you can set multiple attributes at once without calling .attr() repeatedly.

- .attr('attribute', func) calls the function func for each element and sets the element's attribute attribute to the return value. This capability makes it possible to dynamically calculate the value for each element. The function's this value is the element, and the first and only parameter for that function is the index (all elements in a jQuery object are numbered from 0 to *N*).

The .attr() function offers a good example of jQuery's flexibility, as it features a lot of patterns used throughout jQuery. It is often possible to specify an object using key–value pairs instead of just one key and the corresponding value. jQuery also allows you to pass functions that are called subsequently for every element to do something (e.g., to determine a value).

A very commonly used feature in jQuery is the ability to add, remove, and toggle classes from elements. Theoretically, you could perform those operations with the .attr() function, by calling .attr('class', 'myClassName'). However, elements can have multiple classes and .attr() always replaces the entire value. Given these possibilities, jQuery offers a more convenient and less destructive way to deal with classes. The names of the three methods used for this purpose—.addClass ('myClassName'), .removeClass('myClassName'), and .toggleClass('my ClassName')—explain their usage. .toggleClass "toggles" the class, removing the class if it is present and adding the class if it is not. Trying to remove a class that is not

present or to add a class that is already present does not have any effect. The method
`.hasClass('myClassName')` checks whether at least one of the matched elements
has the class name.

Consider the following example:

```
$('ul.menu a:first').toggleClass('active');
```

This line looks for the first link in a menu and toggles the `active` class. This class is
not set by default, so running this code for the first time adds it (if the class has not
been added previously). Running the code for the second time removes it again.

Similar to what happens when you add and remove classes, you can modify CSS
directly (You could just change the `style` attribute, but the `.css()` method provides
a much nicer, easier, and more consistent interface). The function `.css()` can be
called in much the same way that the function `.attr()` can be called. Let's look at
some examples to see how this works (the selectors work on the sample HTML page
provided, but you can change them to something else and test the examples on your
Drupal page):

- `$('.teaser p strong').css('font-size', '16px');` changes the font
  size of the introduction sentence to 16 pixels.

- `$('#column-products li a').css({ 'color': 'blue', 'text-dec-
  oration': 'underline' });` makes the links in the products column blue
  and underlined.

- `$('#column-misc li:first img').css({ 'paddingTop': '30px' });`
  increases the top padding of the first image in the rightmost column.

As the last example demonstrates, the names for the CSS rules are slightly different
from actual CSS. Usually, property names are replaced with camel-case variants (i.e.,
the dashes are removed and the next letter is capitalized). Although there are some
differences among browsers, jQuery smoothes out those variations so we don't have to
take care of them.

While it's fast and easy to change CSS directly in jQuery, adding and removing
classes is usually a better strategy for two reasons. First, you don't have to mix presentational CSS rules into the behavior layer. Second, you can control the look of your
JavaScript widget by altering the code in just one place. It is recommended that you
use `.css()` only when the CSS rules aren't strictly serving presentational purposes and
your JavaScript component requires them to be present. For example, you could set the

position to absolute or relative, but you shouldn't change the font size if it can be moved into a regular style sheet and applied using classes.

You can also change the content of elements, where the content refers to what appears between the opening and closing tags of the matched element. To do so, you can use `.html('<div>New markup</div>')` and `.text('New text')`. The first method replaces the content of the elements with the specified markup, and the second method accepts only text. When you call these functions without parameters, they return the current content. Consider the following example:

```
$('#column-products h3').text('Products & Services');
```

Running this code changes the heading in the "Products" column to "Products & Services". Note that you don't have to use HTML entities when you call `.text()`. However, running that code removes the a tag in the heading. To preserve that tag, you could use the selector `#column-products h3 a` or execute

```
$('#column-products h3').html('<a href="#">Products &amp; Services</a>');
```

to change the entire HTML content of the heading. Actually, this is not the ideal approach: You could have reused the a tag and just changed its contents and possibly the `href` attribute to achieve your goal. When events are attached to elements on a Web page and execute actions when the user clicks on the target link, they will *not* be moved over when you use `.html()` to replace the content. Conversely, they *are* preserved when you change the anchor's content. If you want to add a callback to an element, you should not replace the element itself but only its content; that strategy retains the callback.

Finding Elements

You already know how to find elements on a Web page with CSS selectors (if you're unsure about how to do that, check the section "Navigating the DOM Tree" in this chapter). However, you can find your way around the Web page in other ways.

When you have a set of DOM elements in a jQuery object, you can filter them by using `.filter()` with a CSS selector. jQuery will then weed out all elements that don't match the selector. For example, `$('li')` finds all list elements and `$('li').filter(':first-child')` filters out all of those list items that are not the first element within their container (which is usually a ul or ol tag in this case). The jQuery object with which you use this method acts as a "base" set; jQuery then removes the items that don't match the selector from the current set.

Calling `.filter()` alone is sometimes useful. jQuery also provides an `.end()` function, which restores the state of the jQuery object before the last "destructive" action—that is, it restores the object to its state before elements were added or removed. This capability, when combined with method chaining, allows you to create extremely powerful statements that require you to write very little code.

Another command, `.find()`, also takes a CSS selector as parameter. It searches for elements matching this selector. It doesn't search through the entire document, however, but only searches the children and descendants of the currently selected elements. The results then replace the current selection so that you can apply other methods to the result set. As with `.filter()`, you can reverse a `.find()` operation by calling `.end()`.

jQuery includes many more methods for performing specific operations, such as finding the next sibling of all elements, filtering all siblings of the current DOM elements with a CSS selector, climbing up the DOM tree by selecting parents, adding other elements to the current selection, and selectively removing elements. A detailed list of all available methods can be found at `http://docs.jquery.com/Traversing`.

Inserting, Moving, and Removing Elements

Sometimes, in addition to changing the existing elements that are already in a page, you want to add new elements to the mix. jQuery facilitates that operation to a high degree. Consider the following example:

```
var col = $('<div class="column">...</div>');
```

This line creates a new DOM element, wraps it in a jQuery object, and stores it in the variable `col`. You can use arbitrary valid markup as part of this operation—even nested elements are possible. Of course, this code just creates the elements; it doesn't insert them in the document anywhere. That means the elements are *there* (i.e., they exist) but are not *somewhere* (i.e., in a specific location) in the document.

Elements are inserted into the page relative to other elements. In other words, you can insert elements before, into, and after other elements. When inserting an element as a child of another element, you can choose between inserting it as the first child or as the last child. Figure 10.4 shows the possible ways for insertion relative to the highlighted element.

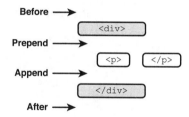

FIGURE 10.4 Inserting elements.

The insert methods take the element to be inserted as first parameter. Thus calling `$('body').append('<p>Lorem Ipsum</p>');` inserts a new paragraph as last element inside `body`. The parameter can be either an HTML string (as in this example), a jQuery object, or a native DOM object. The `.prepend()` method works similarly, but it inserts the element as first inner element. The methods `.before()` and `.after()` insert the element before and after the element, respectively (on the outside).

Let's look at an example. Here we are rearranging the "Products" list:

```
var construction = $('li.construction');
$('li.pharmaceuticals').after(construction);
```

In the first line, we select the element we want to move so that we can easily reference it in the next line. The second line inserts the elements of the jQuery object `construction` *after* the list item with the class `pharmaceuticals`. When changing the positions of items that are already in the document, these items are *moved* away from their original positions and inserted into their new positions; they aren't duplicated but rather are moved by default.

Of course, you could also write the preceding statement in one line by replacing `construction` with its value:

```
$('li.pharmaceuticals').after($('li.construction'));
```

We can easily insert a new list item at any place in similar fashion:

```
$('li.electronics').before('<li class="furniture"><a href="/furniture">Furniture</
a></li>');
```

Note that we pass just a plain HTML string to the `.before()` method as opposed to an actual jQuery object or DOM element. jQuery is smart enough to figure out whether you pass an element or an HTML string to it and accordingly takes the

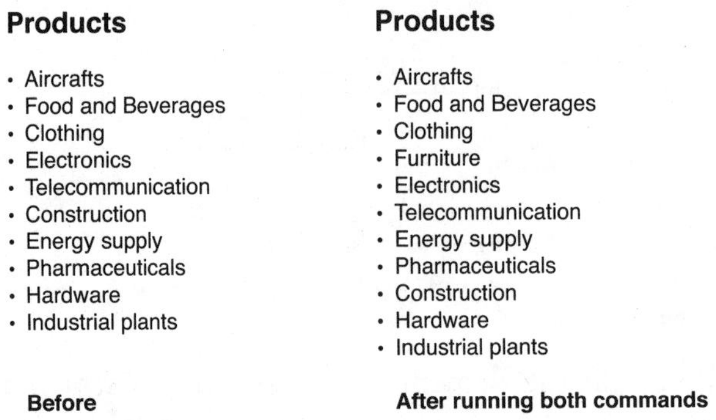

Products

- Aircrafts
- Food and Beverages
- Clothing
- Electronics
- Telecommunication
- Construction
- Energy supply
- Pharmaceuticals
- Hardware
- Industrial plants

Before

Products

- Aircrafts
- Food and Beverages
- Clothing
- Furniture
- Electronics
- Telecommunication
- Energy supply
- Pharmaceuticals
- Construction
- Hardware
- Industrial plants

After running both commands

FIGURE 10.5 A list before and after executing the commands.

appropriate action. Figure 10.5 shows the changes to the "Products" column of the sample page.

The methods we have examined so far insert another element relative to a certain element (the elements in the jQuery object). It's also possible to work in the reverse direction by using `.prependTo()`, `.appendTo()`, `.insertBefore()`, and `.insertAfter()`. These four methods insert a jQuery object relative to another element, jQuery object, or selector.

This discussion is a bit theoretical, so let's look at a practical example. We will compare these two methods:

- `$('li.pharmaceuticals').after($('li.construction'));`
- `$('li.construction').insertAfter('li.pharmaceuticals');`

Both lines do the same thing—they move the "Construction" item after the "Pharmaceuticals" item—but their "point of view" is different. In the first line, the destination item is the focus; in the second line, the original item is the focus. It doesn't really matter which method you use, as both are useful in some situations. For example, if you are changing other attributes of a jQuery object, it's easier to chain a `.insertAfter()` to that operation than to make a `.after()` call in another line.

Note that `.insertAfter()` and its brethren can also take a string as parameter. This string will be interpreted as a CSS selector instead of HTML code. You can, of course, use jQuery objects and DOM elements as well, just as you would with all other methods.

The `.remove()` method allows you to delete the currently selected items from the document. These items are retained in the jQuery object, however. Thus you can remove

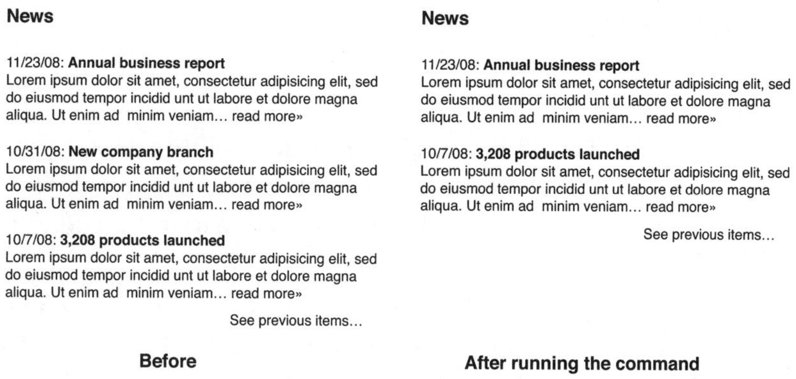

News

11/23/08: **Annual business report**
Lorem ipsum dolor sit amet, consectetur adipisicing elit, sed
do eiusmod tempor incidid unt ut labore et dolore magna
aliqua. Ut enim ad minim veniam… read more»

10/31/08: **New company branch**
Lorem ipsum dolor sit amet, consectetur adipisicing elit, sed
do eiusmod tempor incidid unt ut labore et dolore magna
aliqua. Ut enim ad minim veniam… read more»

10/7/08: **3,208 products launched**
Lorem ipsum dolor sit amet, consectetur adipisicing elit, sed
do eiusmod tempor incidid unt ut labore et dolore magna
aliqua. Ut enim ad minim veniam… read more»

See previous items…

Before

News

11/23/08: **Annual business report**
Lorem ipsum dolor sit amet, consectetur adipisicing elit, sed
do eiusmod tempor incidid unt ut labore et dolore magna
aliqua. Ut enim ad minim veniam… read more»

10/7/08: **3,208 products launched**
Lorem ipsum dolor sit amet, consectetur adipisicing elit, sed
do eiusmod tempor incidid unt ut labore et dolore magna
aliqua. Ut enim ad minim veniam… read more»

See previous items…

After running the command

FIGURE 10.6 The "News" column before and after removing an item.

items temporarily and store them in variables so that they can be inserted somewhere else at a later date. If you do not store the removed element (or the jQuery wrapper), it is destroyed when the variable goes out of scope. For example, $('#column-news li:eq(1)').remove(); removes the second news item from the page as shown in Figure 10.6 (enumeration starts with 0, so 1 is the second item).

Several other methods that modify item positions, such as .wrap() and .replace(), are documented on the jQuery Web site at http://docs.jquery.com/Manipulation.

Leveraging jQuery's Full Potential

So far, we've used only basic code snippets to demonstrate jQuery functionality. In reality, jQuery offers many more capabilities: You can animate items in various different ways, call the server, write plugins for jQuery, and so on. Additionally, jQuery features some useful functions that make everyday programming much easier. After considering these aspects of jQuery, we'll take a quick look at jQuery UI, a library built on jQuery that implements commonly used functionality that is not covered by jQuery, such as drag-and-drop, date pickers, tabs, and so on.

Animations

jQuery provides an easy-to-use interface for animating elements of the Web page. Using this system, you can quickly move elements, change their sizes, and fade their opacity. Plugins may offer even more animation capabilities, such as fading the color and implementing different styles of animation.

Let's look at an example:

```
$('.menu').slideUp();
```

Paste this code into your theme's JavaScript file (make sure that it's executed `onready` and not right away). When you load the page, notice how the menus slide up (given that your menus do have the class `menu`). The other animation functions can be used in a similar fashion.

All animation functions take a parameter indicating the duration of an animation. You can either specify the time in milliseconds or use one of the default lengths by specifying `"slow"` (600 milliseconds), `"normal"` (400 milliseconds), or `"fast"` (200 milliseconds).

Animation functions also take the parameter "callback," which can consist of a callback function. This function is executed when the animation is finished. You could, for example, add a function that removes the element after the animation is finished, when you `.fadeOut()` an element, or when you `.slideUp()` an element. Some animation functions take different or more parameters; you can find out more about them on `http://docs.jquery.com/Effects`.

Like most other jQuery methods, animations can be chained. Animations are executed sequentially, not in parallel (executing several animations in parallel is discussed later in this chapter). In other words, the next animation doesn't start until the first animation finishes. This statement applies only to animations, however. When you change other aspects of the Web page—for example, the font color with `.css()`—the change is executed right away, even when it seemingly occurs after the animation. For this reason, you should put commands that need to run *after* the animation finishes in the callback function of that animation.

It's possible to stop animations as well. This ability comes in handy when the user performs an action while the element that should do something different is in the middle of its animation. At this point, the new action can simply `.stop()` the animation and do something else with it. For example, suppose a slide widget moves in new slides from the right when the user clicks the "Next" button. If the user immediately clicks the "Previous" button after clicking the "Next" button, the slide continues to move in, even though it should actually move in the other direction. In this case, clicking the "Previous" button can stop the animation and start a new animation in the other direction.

The animation functions we have encountered so far are shortcuts for the `.animate()` function. This function is the central hub for animating things in jQuery. Its first parameter contains all information related to how the elements should be animated. Other options, such as the duration of the animation and the callback function, can be specified as well. (Refer to the `http://docs.jquery.com/Effects` page for more details.)

Let's investigate the first parameter of the `.animate()` function. It allows you to specify almost any CSS property that takes numbers as its parameters, from the dimensions to the opacity, to the position, to the font size, to paddings and margins, and more. (The exception to this rule is that you cannot animate background URL changes.) Let's look at an example:

```
$('.teaser p').animate({
  fontSize: "12px",
  left: -100,
  opacity: 0.5
});
```

This animation changes the font size to 12 pixels, changes the left position of the animation to −100 pixels (the element is positioned relatively, so the animation will move away from its original position), and fades the text to 50% opacity. Depending on your browser, this font size might make the animation look either smooth or clumsy. Firefox 3 animates it perfectly with non-integer font sizes, but most other browsers will render only integer font sizes. The default text is set at 14 pixels, so animating it at a size of 12 pixels requires only one intermediary step in most browsers. Given that the animation usually occurs relatively quickly, that's rarely a problem.

During animations, the values are always changed from their current state. If the animation would end in the same value as is already set, no animation occurs (because the final state is already in place); thus it's safe to execute the same animation twice. jQuery takes care of all cross-browser compatibility issues. Using jQuery's `opacity` property also works in Internet Explorer, even though it doesn't support the `opacity` CSS property.

The `options` parameter allows you to specify callback functions that should be executed either after each animation step is finished (an animation consists of many intermediary steps) or after the entire animation is completed. You can also modify the queuing behavior, the duration of the animation, and the easing. *Easing* means the behavior of the animation over time. The default (and the only value available in the jQuery core) is "linear," which means that each of the animation steps changes by the same amount.

Other easing methods might first animate slowly, then more quickly, and before the completion of the animation move more slowly to provide a more natural feeling.

Using jQuery Helper Functions

jQuery also provides some functionality that is not related to manipulating the DOM. A full list of these functions can be found at http://docs.jquery.com/Utilities. In this section, we'll look at the jQuery.extend() and jQuery.each() methods more closely.

The jQuery.extend() function allows you to merge objects together. That means all values and their associated keys are copied from one object to another, overwriting the former values. The jQuery.extend() function copies all objects starting from the second parameter into the object passed as first parameter (the "target") and returns this object. This capability is useful when you want to merge in parameters, add default values, and so on. Here's an example:

```
var slideshow = function(params) {
  jQuery.extend(this, {
    start: 0,
    duration: 7000
  }, params);
};
```

The preceding code extends this first with the default options specified in the object and then with the options specified in params. This order ensures that passed parameters (as part of the params object) overwrite default values. This technique is commonly used in JavaScript to allow passing function parameters by name. Oftentimes, you will have a considerable number of parameters for a function (or an object constructor, as in this case), but you want to pass only certain parameters to the function. The jQuery.extend() function allows you to name which parameters you want to change, thereby ensuring that the actual parameters are merged into the default parameters.

The jQuery.each() function takes two parameters: (1) an object with keys and their associated values and (2) a function. It executes the passed function for each of the items of the object, passing it the index, the key, and the value. This technique represents an alternative to looping over the object, albeit with a slight, but important difference: Because a function is called for each element, a new scope is created for each element. As a consequence, you can do with the passed values whatever you want without worrying that their contents might change during the loop. In a loop, exactly *one* variable holds the value, and the loop mechanism changes the contents in each step. In `jQuery.each()`, a *new variable* in each step continues to hold its value, though there can be several distinct variables with the same names living in different scopes.

Calling the Server with XmlHttpRequest

You almost certainly have heard of AJAX, a term coined in 2005 for the process of loading data within the lifetime of a Web site. AJAX makes it possible to develop Web sites that change their content dynamically without needing to preload all possible content or resorting to reloading the page. AJAX, which stands for "Asynchronous JavaScript and XML," is based on the XmlHttpRequest technology introduced by Microsoft in Internet Explorer.

XmlHttpRequest was originally created to facilitate the process of requesting data in XML format (thus the "XML" in the AJAX acronym). In reality, it doesn't matter *which* content you transmit—it doesn't have to be XML. In fact, most of what is today described as AJAX doesn't use XML at all, but rather either HTML code, which is then inserted into the page directly, or JSON.

JSON ("JavaScript Object Notation") basically describes JavaScript's object literal syntax (the one with the curly braces). It has become increasingly popular as an alternative to XML because it's easier to parse and has less overhead. Here's a short JSON example:

```
{
  'status': true,
  'id': 49836,
  'title': 'Lorem Ipsum',
  'body': 'An important way to im...',
  'tags': {
    'technology': 'Technology',
    'business': 'Business'
  },
  'link': 'http://example.com/story/lorem-ipsum',
  'related': [ 28983, 34985, 38475 ]
}
```

Using JSON, you can arbitrarily nest JavaScript objects. In addition, you can use arrays (with the bracket notation) and most other data types available in JavaScript.

Drupal provides a (PHP) function named `drupal_to_js()` that converts a PHP array to JSON. The function `drupal_json()` automatically adds the right content type to the HTTP header and outputs the passed array as JSON. Use this function when you want to create a response from within Drupal.

The "Asynchronous" part of the AJAX acronym means that the browser doesn't wait idly until it receives a response from the server, but rather continues to execute other JavaScript in the meantime. If that were not the case, the browser would be completely locked up and the user could not do anything while an XmlHttpRequest was performed (it's also possible to carry out synchronous calls). At some point, the request finishes and the return value must be processed. For this purpose, it's possible to specify a callback function that is executed when the request finishes.

Figure 10.7 shows the difference between a synchronous call and an asynchronous call. Performing asynchronous calls is a bit more complicated because you must take into account that the user can do something else while the request is processed. Nevertheless, it's generally worth the effort to use asynchronous calls because synchronous calls completely block the browser while the request is performed.

The .load() Function

The easiest way to load data from the server is to use jQuery's `.load()` function. This function loads an HTML fragment and replaces the jQuery object's elements with the new content. The first parameter is the URL from which data should be loaded; the other parameters are optional and allow you to add parameters to the request and specify a callback function to be executed when the data has been loaded.

It is a bit trickier to demonstrate the usage of this function than it is to show pure jQuery functions because you also need a server that produces the appropriate responses. For this reason, a `fed_ajax.module` is available on this book's Web site at `http://frontenddrupal.com/`. Install this module to your Drupal site (see Appendix A for a guide on installing modules), and you can then use the module's responses to follow along with the examples in this section.

Another barrier to demonstrating the use of the `.load()` function is that, for security reasons, all browsers forbid loading data from domains other than the one on which the page performing the load is located. For this reason, the `fed_ajax.module` also provides a copy of our sample HTML page that you can work on at `/fed_ajax`.

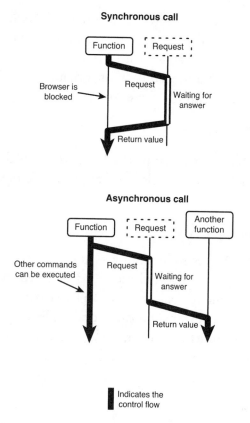

Figure 10.7 Synchronous call versus asynchronous call.

First, we will load another teaser into the page. On the sample HTML page loaded from your Drupal installation, execute `$('.teaser').load('/fed_ajax/teaser');` in the browser's JavaScript prompt. The browser will load the URL in the background and then replace the teaser with the newly returned content. If your Drupal installation is not located at the root level of your Web server, you must prefix the URL `/fed_ajax/teaser` with your base path. For example, if your installation is located at `http://localhost/drupal/`, the URL should be `/drupal/fed_ajax/teaser`.

The `.load()` function has another nice feature: It allows you to automatically select a specific part of the returned HTML and insert only that portion instead of the entire return value. This ability is useful when you don't want to write specific functions that return just the data you need; with this feature, you can load the entire

HTML page and replace only the relevant part using a CSS selector. This CSS selector is not a separate parameter to the .load() function, but rather must be inserted after the URL (in the same string), separated with a space.

We can use this mechanism to load back the original teaser by simply loading the exact same page and selecting just the teaser part:

```
$('.teaser').load(document.location.href + ' .teaser');
```

document.location.href contains the URL from which the current page was loaded. We now add a space and the selector that plucks the right part from the newly loaded page.

Loading Data with jQuery.getJSON()

While loading plain HTML is sometimes very useful and simplifies matters greatly on the client side, having the data available in a structured format is equally useful. The jQuery.getJSON() method allows you to retrieve data in the JSON format and then operate on that data. This function cannot be applied to a set of elements in the same way as the .load() function; rather, it is a stand-alone function in the jQuery namespace (which is accessed by the $ shortcut by default).

```
var callback = function(data) {
  console.log("Request finished; returned data:");
  console.log(data);
};


$.getJSON('/fed_ajax/json', { id: 1 }, callback);
console.log("Request started...");
```

In this example, we first define the callback function to be executed when the request is finished. The first parameter contains the returned data, already parsed into a Java-Script object. We then print the data to the console. In a real-world situation, you would most likely perform actions with the data, such as looping over all returned elements and inserting them somewhere into the page or adding them to a data store.

The $.getJSON call first specifies the URL (again, prefix this identifier with your actual path to Drupal). The second parameter can contain data for the request. It should be either a ready-made query string (such as "id=1&action=fetch") or a

JavaScript object with key–value pairs that is transformed into a query string and appended to the URL by jQuery. The third parameter is the callback function that will be executed when the data has been retrieved. Note that any code you execute immediately after the call to $.getJSON is executed right away: $.getJSON does not wait until the request finishes, but rather returns immediately after starting the request (as outlined in Figure 10.7).

The $.getJSON function should *only* be used for obtaining data from the server. Requests to the specified URL should not change anything on the server (by creating new data or deleting items, for example). This restriction applies because $.getJSON uses a GET request. HTTP has different request modes, of which the most frequently used are GET and POST. The HTTP definition specifies that GET requests should be nondestructive (of course, you *can* modify the database for logging the request). The POST type is used for requests that have side effects, such as the creation of content, deletion of items, or modification of elements. In short: GET is for retrieving content, POST is for creating content.

The All-Arounder: $.ajax()

All of jQuery's AJAX functions use the $.ajax() function internally. The .load() and $.getJSON functions are just wrappers for that function, intended to simplify commonly performed tasks. If you need more flexibility, you can use $.ajax directly and configure whatever functionality you need. Many configuration options are possible—so many that we can't possibly show all of them here. This function is extensively documented at http://docs.jquery.com/Ajax/jQuery.ajax.

The $.ajax() function makes use of the named parameter mechanism, which was outlined in the section "Using jQuery Helper Functions." This function takes one parameter, which contains key–value pairs for all other parameters. A large number of parameters available, including the following options:

- type can either be GET (default) or POST; it determines the HTTP type.
- url is the URL for the request.
- data can either be a string or an object with key–value pairs.
- dataType specifies how the returned data should be interpreted. It can be "json", "html", "xml", or "text". (Other values are also available; see the documentation.)
- success is a callback function that is executed when the request was completed successfully and the data could be parsed.

- `complete` is a callback function that is executed when the request finishes (on both success and failure).
- `error` is a callback function that is executed when the request fails.

`$.ajax` works in the same way as `$.getJSON`: It returns immediately after the request has been *started* and the code after the call to that function is executed. (This isn't true when you select the synchronous transfer mode by setting the `async` parameter to `false`.)

Plugins for jQuery

jQuery allows you to create custom operations that will then become available for jQuery objects. You can use that feature to create new shortcuts for existing functions or to implement completely new functionality. You add functions to a jQuery object by adding them to the `jQuery.fn` namespace (this is, in fact, just a reference to `jQuery.prototype`). Here's a small example:

```
jQuery.fn.log = function() {
  return this.each(function() {
    if (console.log) {
      console.log(this);
    }
    else {
      alert(this);
    }
  });
};
```

This plugin adds the `.log()` function. Because jQuery objects may contain several DOM elements, you must use the `this.each()` function to execute the action for each of the contained elements. The inner function logs the DOM element to the console when that functionality is available; otherwise, it sends an alert message to the user.

Of course, this is just a very small example; there's much more to say about jQuery plugin development. The `http://docs.jquery.com/Plugins/Authoring` page has a bit more information available. In addition, several more advanced books ably cover this topic—for example, *jQuery Reference Guide: A Comprehensive Exploration of the Popular JavaScript Library* by Jonathan Chaffer (Packt Publishing). A vast repository of ready-made jQuery plugins can also be found at `http://plugins.jquery.com/`. Add them to your page, and you will immediately be able to take advantage of the new functionality.

jQuery UI

jQuery UI (located at `http://ui.jquery.com/`) is a collection of jQuery plugins and APIs that implement commonly used functionality that is not part of the jQuery core. It features drag-and-drop support; APIs for making elements resizable, sortable, and selectable; and frequently used controls such as a date picker, a dialog window, a progress bar, and tabs. If you are considering implementing drag-and-drop functionality, you should definitely think about using jQuery UI's APIs for that purpose. These plugins will eliminate a lot of the pain associated with implementing drag-and-drop functionality across browsers.

Using Other JavaScript Libraries

Although Drupal exclusively uses jQuery, your project might not. If you're porting an existing application that was built using another library, such as Prototype/Scriptaculous, you might want to continue using these libraries in your existing scripts. That way, you will not have to convert all code to jQuery, possibly introducing new bugs.

Unfortunately, both jQuery and Prototype use the $ variable, but only one library can have that name. In most cases, the library that is loaded later overwrites the library that is loaded first. Fortunately, jQuery is aware of the fact that the $ variable is coveted, and it is designed to run even if it's not stored in the $ variable. To remove jQuery from this variable, you would execute the command `jQuery.noConflict();` immediately after jQuery loads; jQuery will then not modify or overwrite that variable.

Making jQuery not use the $ variable is relatively easy, but many scripts (including the scripts that ship with Drupal) rely on jQuery being available in $. There is an easy fix for this problem: Create a new scope (through a function) and overwrite $ with jQuery in just that scope. The code looks like this:

```
(function($) {
  // Put your code using $ as jQuery here.
})(jQuery);


// $ is not jQuery here.
```

The solution is to create a new function and execute it right away, passing jQuery as parameter that then maps to $ *just inside that function*. Inside the function, $ is jQuery; in the outside world, it's not. Note that a lot of JavaScript code from contributed modules relies on jQuery being available in $, so you should take this step with great care. If a module doesn't work when jQuery is not available in $, go to the module's project page on `http://www.drupal.org` and create an issue telling the author to make the module compliant.

Summary

This chapter introduced jQuery, a JavaScript library that allows you to perform common tasks using a very concise and easy syntax. Even though jQuery focuses mostly on manipulating the DOM tree, it also has some useful helper functions. Most importantly, jQuery provides an interface for making AJAX-style server requests. jQuery plugins and jQuery UI are other key components of the jQuery environment, as is getting jQuery to live in harmony with other libraries.

Chapter 11

JavaScript in Drupal

This chapter explains how to apply the JavaScript skills you acquired or polished while working through Chapters 9 and 10. You will learn how to add JavaScript to Drupal and to themes in particular, and you will get to know the various ways of providing additional information in the form of variables for the JavaScript that runs on a page. You will also see how JavaScript can interact with the server and discover how you can return results from a server query.

The majority of this chapter, however, explores ways to create self-contained and portable JavaScript "components"—pieces of functionality that can greatly enhance your Web site. You will learn how to create a horizontal scroller, step by step. Finally, you'll learn about more ways to add interaction to your Web site by leveraging the vast pool of ready-to-use jQuery widgets and the jQuery UI.

Server-Side Drupal Integration

Now that you know quite a bit about both JavaScript and jQuery, it's time to go back to Drupal and see how to integrate JavaScript with Drupal. Drupal provides some functionality for dealing with JavaScript, but you should always keep in mind that JavaScript is run in the browser, after Drupal has completely finished creating the HTML page. As a result, you cannot call PHP functions from your JavaScript code. If you need to obtain additional data from the server, you must specifically advise Drupal to react to certain requests by creating a menu callback, as discussed later in this section.

Adding JavaScript to a Page

Drupal provides a function named `drupal_add_js()` that allows you to add all kinds of JavaScript to a page. Using this function, you can add files, variables, and custom code, depending on which parameters you use. The `drupal_add_js()` function is extensively documented at `http://api.drupal.org/api/function/drupal_add_js/6`. Its behavior heavily depends on the *second* parameter, which defaults to `'module'`.

Adding Files

The most common use of `drupal_add_js()` is for adding files. This behavior is triggered when the second parameter for `drupal_add_js` is neither `'inline'` nor `'setting'`. You can add JavaScript files to a page everywhere except for `page.tpl.php` (this exception occurs because the list of files added is a variable in `page.tpl.php` and so cannot be changed after it has been generated). In the download package that accompanies this book, you will find a `demo.module` that you can place in `sites/all/modules`. In a module, a call to that function would look like this:

```
drupal_add_js(drupal_get_path('module', 'mymodule') . '/mymodule.js');
```

The first and only parameter is constructed of two parts: The path to the module's folder is concatenated with the name of the JavaScript file in that folder. When the JavaScript file is located in a theme directory, the usage is similar: Just replace `'module'` with `'theme'` and insert the theme's name as the second parameter in the `drupal_get_path()` call.

When adding JavaScript files for a theme, you should set the second parameter for `drupal_add_js()` to `'theme'`. This will guarantee that this JavaScript file is included *after* any module or Drupal core JavaScript files.

By setting the `$scope` parameter to `'footer'`, you can include the script at the bottom of the page instead of within the `<head>` section. This step is sometimes necessary to include scripts that can be run only when the document has already been loaded, but that don't use jQuery's `document.ready()` method. To add a JavaScript file to the footer, use the following code:

```
drupal_add_js(drupal_get_path('module', 'mymodule') . '/mymodule.js', 'footer');
```

Other, rarely used parameters for `drupal_add_js()` are documented on the API Web site.

Adding JavaScript to a Theme in the .info File

There is another, easier way to add JavaScript to your theme: Add a line in the theme's `.info` file. In much the same way that you would add style sheets there, you add a line in the following format:

```
scripts[] = file.js
```

Drupal's theme layer then automatically adds this file to every page with that theme. This behavior is ideal for JavaScript files that should always be available on a page—for example, for functionality that is shared among all or most pages. You can add as many lines as you want, as long as each starts with `scripts[]` = and is followed by the path to the script relative to the theme. It is not possible to add scripts to other scopes or use any other parameters with this approach, nor is it possible to add JavaScript files only to certain pages. After adding a script to the `.info` file, flush the theme registry by going to the theme administration page or using `devel.module`'s link.

The Settings Storage

Oftentimes, you will want to pass certain parameters to your JavaScript code. The settings storage in `Drupal.settings` is the perfect place to carry out that task. `drupal_add_js()` lets you add arbitrary values to that storage; those values will then be made available on the Web site to your JavaScript code.

To add settings, the second parameter must be `'setting'` and the first parameter must be an array that contains the actual settings. The other parameters aren't used in this way for calling `drupal_add_js()`. Here's an example setting:

```
$data = array(
  'items' => 3,
  'data' => array(
    342 => 'http://example.com/files/slideshow01.jpg',
    386 => 'http://example.com/files/slideshow02.jpg',
    440 => 'http://example.com/files/slideshow03.jpg',
```

```
  ),
);
```

```
drupal_add_js(array('slideshow' => $data), 'setting');
```

This code adds an array with just one key named `slideshow`; `slideshow` contains the actual data. This approach prevents our data from appearing directly in `Drupal.settings` on the client side. Instead of `Drupal.settings`, that array is stored in `Drupal.settings.slideshow`. By putting everything in `Drupal.settings.slideshow`, we can ensure that no other module interferes with our data and everything is nicely grouped in one place. It's a good idea to use your module or theme name to create a namespace.

To access data added with `drupal_add_js()`, you can use the `Drupal.settings` object. To access this object, type `Drupal.settings` in Firebug. You can then click on the object and inspect it further, as shown in Figure 11.1.

Be careful to not add your data twice or PHP's array merge function might produce unexpected results. If you add the same key twice, PHP will convert that value into

FIGURE 11.1 Exploring the `Drupal.settings` object with Firebug.

an array that contains both the original value and the new value. The following code example illustrates what might happen:

```
drupal_add_js(array('mymodule' => 4), 'setting');
drupal_add_js(array('mymodule' => 8), 'setting');

// This will result in:
//   array(
//     'mymodule' => array(4, 8)
//   );
```

To prevent this result, you may not add exactly the same key twice. A solution to this dilemma is to store your variables somewhere else and add them only when you add variables for the last time.

Inline JavaScript

The `drupal_add_js()` function also allows you to add custom JavaScript code to a page. To do so, the second parameter must be `'inline'` and the first parameter consists of a string with the actual JavaScript code (don't include `<script>` tags here):

```
drupal_add_js('alert("Hello World");', 'inline');
```

When you insert this line in any module or template file (except for `page.tpl.php`), it will add this JavaScript code that sends an alert message of "Hello World" when the page loads. You should use this feature only rarely, however, and only when it's absolutely necessary. If you want to add larger quantities of code, move that code to a separate JavaScript file; when you want to add just configuration options, use the settings functionality described in the previous section.

Creating Menu Callback Handlers

Although this book doesn't cover module development, you still need to know how to integrate your JavaScript code with Drupal. In the previous section, JavaScript was added to a page from within Drupal. Once the JavaScript is executed on the client side, you might want to call back to the server to request additional data—a technique commonly known as AJAX (see Chapter 10 for a discussion as to why this name is misleading).

The Drupal menu system is used for more than simply creating and maintaining the visible menus and the menu items in it. In fact, Drupal's menus are primarily a system to "dispatch" requests to different page functions. Thus Drupal allows you to create menu items that are not visible in the menu system ("menu callbacks") and map them to a function that generates the content.

In the menu hook of a module, you can define the menu items for your page. Read more about hooks at `http://api.drupal.org/api/group/hooks/6` and more about the menu system at `http://drupal.org/node/102338`.

Let's see how to define a menu item:

```
function demo_menu() {
  $items = array();

  $items['demo'] = array(
    'title' => 'Demo module',
    'description' => 'A demo page for testing code.',
    'access callback' => 'user_access',
    'access arguments' => array('access content'),
    'page callback' => 'demo_page',
  );

  return $items;
}
```

You can find this menu item code in `demo.module` (which is included in the download package from `http://frontenddrupal.com`). You just have to return an array with menu item structures (which are also arrays). Many different settings are possible, as shown on the documentation page. Usually, you need only a few of them, as illustrated in this code example.

The preceding code defines a new menu item with the path `'demo'` (in the square brackets after `$items`). You can also define access restrictions; currently, this menu item is available for everyone who has `access content` permissions, which is everyone by default. The last line is probably the most interesting line. Here you define the "page callback function"—that is, the function called when the user accesses this menu item. In that function, you should generate the content and return the resulting *HTML* code. This menu item is a visible item; you should see it in the navigation block, as shown in Figure 11.2.

Creating JSON

When we call the server to obtain data, we don't always want to use HTML code. Instead, JSON is often used for this purpose (see Chapter 10 for more about JSON). Luckily, Drupal provides a `drupal_json()` function that generates a JSON object from a regular PHP array. It also sends the correct HTTP headers so that browsers recognize this input as JavaScript code. The `drupal_json()` function is documented at `http://api.drupal.org/api/function/drupal_json/6`. When using this function, you don't have to return anything from your page callback function.

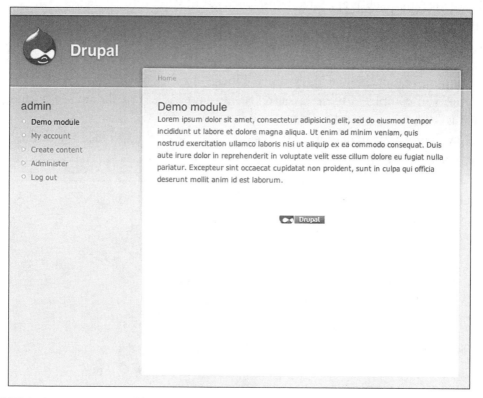

FIGURE 11.2 A page generated by a custom module.

Let's look at an example JSON callback menu item:

```
$items['demo/json'] = array(
  'access callback' => 'user_access',
  'access arguments' => array('access content'),
  'page callback' => 'demo_json',
  'type' => MENU_CALLBACK,
);
```

The last line specifies that this menu item is a callback item (the menu system defaults to visible items) and ensures that it does not appear in the menu tree. Insert this menu item into the demo_menu function and go to /demo/json as specified. You'll probably see the same page as appeared with /demo—but why? Drupal caches menu items, so just inserting new code into the menu hook won't do the trick. Instead, you must explicitly tell Drupal to flush the menu cache. To do so, go to /admin/build/modules. You can also install the devel module available from http://drupal.org/project/devel, enable the "Developer" block, and click on "Empty cache."

Once you completed these tasks, reload /demo/json. You should see nothing—which is what you expected.

Now that our menu definition works, we must create the specified menu function demo_json():

```
function demo_json() {
  $data = array(
    'items' => 3,
    'data' => array(
      342 => 'http://example.com/files/slideshow01.jpg',
      386 => 'http://example.com/files/slideshow02.jpg',
      440 => 'http://example.com/files/slideshow03.jpg',
    ),
  );

  drupal_json($data);
}
```

When you reload `/demo/json` again, you should see the data in JSON format:

```
{ "items": 3, "data": { "342": "http://example.com/files/slideshow01.jpg", "386":
➥ "http://example.com/files/slideshow02.jpg", "440": "http://example.com/files/
➥ slideshow03.jpg" } }
```

And that's all it takes to make your data JavaScript-compatible. Of course, the data does not take the form of a static array, but is usually generated dynamically, based on the parameters of the request. The parameters are available in `$_GET` or `$_POST` depending on the request type. Be careful when you use these values, because they are not checked for malicious input. The menu system also provides some facilities for retrieving parameters. Check the menu documentation for more information.

Architecting a Component

Oftentimes, you don't just want to make a few minor enhancements to a website, such as automatically submitting the form after a drop-down box changes, but rather want to develop larger components with which the user can interact. In this section, we'll first look at some of the key principles you need to know when creating a new JavaScript component:

- **Compatibility.** In the early days of developing JavaScript components, developers acted as if they were alone. Specifically, they used global variables everywhere. Eventually, this led to conflicts between different components when both used the same variable name. On today's Web sites, your script is not likely to be the only one present; therefore, you should try to keep all of your components together in one space. Drupal uses the `Drupal` object to group all Drupal-related things, such as the settings storage, behaviors, and translations. Ideally, your script should reside in one unambiguously named variable.

  Additionally, you should make sure that you use the `var` keyword when declaring local variables; otherwise, they become global variables, which can lead to random behavior when other scripts also forget to use the `var` keyword. To see whether you might have missed one, execute a couple of JavaScript actions and then check the `window` object in Firebug. It lists all global variables. `Drupal`, `jQuery`, and `$` should be the only user-provided variables, as shown in Figure 11.3. The other variables are provided by Firefox add-ons or the browser itself.

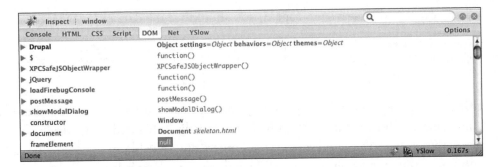

FIGURE 11.3 The global JavaScript objects in Firefox.

- **Reusability.** It is recommended that you write as many of your functions as possible in such a way that those functions are not fixed for exactly one use case. For example, instead of making the function use an implicit variable from `this`, you can make the function operate on a parameter. That way, other scripts can also make use of your widget.

  Another aspect of reusability is to create your components in such a way that it's easy for other components to reuse the entire functionality of the component. As an example, consider a "modal overlay" widget that displays a page overlay. An ideal modal overlay widget would expose all required functionality so that other components can simply create a new modal widget with custom content in one or two lines of code.

- **Flexibility.** Oftentimes, you will need to create complex HTML markup for displaying your widget. Different elements will inevitably have different functionality when interacting with such widgets. To avoid coupling your JavaScript component too closely with a specific markup tree, you should assign class or IDs to all elements that will get an event handler assigned to them. In your JavaScript, you can just "search" for this class name within a given HTML structure to select the element. This approach should always be preferred over relying on a specific HTML structure and navigation with `.prev()`, `.next()`, or `.children()` because it allows you to almost arbitrarily change your HTML markup while retaining all functionality.

- **Encapsulation.** On many occasions, you will want to use not just a single instance of the component on one page, but several of them. For example, having just one slideshow on a given page is not always a good idea; instead, you may decide to create several of them. This is also a time where it's vital that your components be encapsulated (see the "Compatibility" bullet point) and not interfere with one another. However, sometimes it makes sense to have shared parts of a component—for example, when you create a function that performs a calculation but doesn't have any side effects. It would be a waste of resources to create a copy of this function for every component instance.

- **Speed.** When developing a Web site, you will often test the site with one or two instances of a component. Of course, some components are used even more often on one page. This consideration is critical, especially if the Web site users will somehow be able to create new instances of something. You should never underestimate a user's ability to do something to an excessive amount. Test at least once whether the component you've developed still performs acceptably when the Web page contains several hundred instances of it. If it doesn't, you should reconsider your use of poorly performing CSS selectors or spread out calculations over time as opposed to calculating everything at one single point.

Example: Horizontal Scroller

In this section, we will actually implement a JavaScript component while obeying the preceding rules. The point of this example is to help you create more modular, reliable, and stable components. Here we will develop a horizontal scroller widget that allows you to horizontally scroll images by clicking on left/right buttons. In Figure 11.4, you can see the finished product.

The features of this widget include the following items:

- The left/right buttons are hidden when they have no functionality.
- The scroller scrolls to the first item that is not completely visible.
- The scroller degrades gracefully when JavaScript is not available.
- The items in the scroller can be of variable width.

FIGURE 11.4 The final horizontal scroller, featuring images and left/right buttons.

- The "page transitions" are animated.
- Resizing the window does not cause the scroller to break, just because fewer or more items fit into the view at once.
- The scroller works in Internet Explorer 6.

It's always helpful to first write a list of the features you want; later, you can check whether your component really does everything you need. In addition, the results of this exercise make for a good checklist when you are testing the component in various browsers.

The Component Skeleton

When developing a component, it's often easier to *not* start directly within Drupal, but instead to first develop the JavaScript code in a controlled environment. In other words, you take a plain HTML page, add jQuery and the required JavaScript files to it, develop the base widget there, and then move the component to Drupal. This approach has several advantages:

- The page reloads more quickly, and you don't have to wait for Drupal to render that page.
- You don't have to clean Drupal caches repeatedly to see the change you've made.
- This strategy reduces distractions caused by other elements on the page.
- You can actually read the jQuery code when stepping through a function with the debugger because you can use a non-minified version of jQuery.

Of course, starting in another environment also has a few drawbacks:

- The result is not 100% Drupal, and you might encounter some minor problems when finally moving your component to Drupal.
- You can't really test interaction with the server via AJAX without refraining from using Drupal for supplying data.
- Not all components can make use of the proposed component skeleton.

The download package for this book includes a folder named `component-skeleton` that contains a component development environment. Just rename every file named "skeleton," and replace "skeleton" in all files with the name of your component. This skeleton contains the `drupal.js` from Drupal 6 as well as jQuery 1.2 in an uncompressed version. The included `drupal.js` file provides some commonly used functionality as well as the basic infrastructure for some of the JavaScript-related concepts that are specific to Drupal. `skeleton.js` contains a wireframe for starting off with a new component. You can reuse the code found in this file or replace it with your own.

We'll name our example component "horizscroll." For your own component, choose a name that is not in use and that is unambiguous, yet concise. Of course, you can change the name at any point—but to do so, you must rename everything, which can become quite a hassle.

Creating the Markup

The `skeleton.html` file is just a bare-bones HTML file that contains some content and a section where the widget will reside. Depending on your widget, you may have to change the markup to suit your needs. The HTML file also includes a place where you can add further settings variables that normally would be added during Drupal's page generation process.

We can—and should—create most of the component's look with plain HTML and CSS. Always do as much as possible with HTML/CSS, reserving JavaScript and jQuery for creating behavioral functionality. Even though it might be tempting to use jQuery's `.css()` function to fix a small bug, don't go down this road: Finding potential errors introduced during this process becomes a lot more complicated (e.g., you can't use Firebug to see the source of the formatting).

Drupal's JavaScript Behaviors

The component code will reside in `skeleton.js`. The renamed "behaviors" function looks like this:

```
/**
 * Initializes the horizscroll component.
 */
Drupal.behaviors.horizscroll = function(context) {
  $('.horizscroll:not(.horizscroll-processed)', context).each(function() {
```

```
    // <<< Insert the code to process each horizscroll here >>>

  }).addClass('horizscroll-processed');

};
```

Behaviors are specific to Drupal, but the underlying concept is easy to understand: Oftentimes you have code that does something when the page is loaded, such as initializing a component. However, when you modify the page afterward by requesting additional data via AJAX or AHAH (AHAH is Drupal's way of making dynamic forms without writing JavaScript code), the component HTML code that is part of the newly inserted code does not receive the same treatment by default—because your code looked for such elements only at the very beginning of the process.

This is where Drupal's *behaviors* jump into the breach: Whenever new code is inserted, the `Drupal.attachBehaviors()` function is called, with the first parameter being the root of the newly inserted elements. The `Drupal.attachBehaviors()` function calls all functions that appear inside the `Drupal.behaviors` namespace with that parameter. Your behavior function is then responsible for initializing any components of its type inside that new page part.

Usually, this process occurs in the manner illustrated in the sample code: You call an anonymous function for each `.horizscroll` element you can find inside that context, except when it already has the class `horizscroll-processed`. The anonymous function then performs initialization tasks before the `addClass()` function adds the class `horizscroll-processed`, which prevents the same component instance from being initialized twice.

When you insert HTML code into the page, you should call the function `Drupal.attachBehaviors()` yourself to allow other JavaScript files to initialize components that might be contained in that code. For more information on this feature, see the source code documentation in `drupal.js`. The document at `http://drupal.org/node/120360` describes how this functionality came to be part of Drupal.

The slider will work as illustrated in Figure 11.5. As shown in the figure, the items reside inside a content section with infinite width. The content section itself is included in a container, which cuts off the container at a certain width using `overflow:hidden;`. Because the content box has infinite width, the items inside it won't float into several lines but rather will stay together in one line. Additionally, left and right buttons allow the user to change the currently displayed items. A click on the slider will move the content box to the left so that another part becomes visible inside the viewport provided through the container.

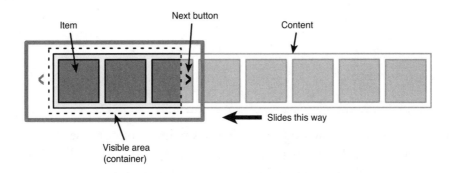

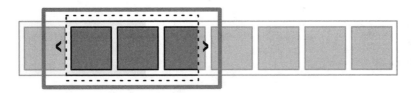

FIGURE 11.5 How the slider works internally.

We can identify five kinds of elements for the slider:

- Each slider can contain an arbitrary amount of **items.**
- A **content box** is repositioned when the slider moves.
- The **container** provides the viewport for the item.
- The **left and right buttons** allow the user to change the currently displayed items.
- An overall **container** encapsulates everything (this element is somewhat optional but makes life a lot easier).

This list of elements leads us quickly to the following markup:

```
<div class="horizscroll">
  <a class="horizscroll-left" href="#"><</a>
  <a class="horizscroll-right" href="#">></a>
  <div class="horizscroll-container">
    <ul class="horizscroll-content">
      <li>Item #1</li>
      <li>Item #2</li>
```

```
    <li>Item #3</li>
    <!-- ... -->
  </ul>
</div>
</div>
```

The left and right quotation marks serve as pointers in our case, but you can also replace them with text, an image, or a background image. After all, this code is just HTML and CSS. We can now style that HTML, but we must use some specific rules to ensure that we get the functionality we want:

```
.horizscroll-container {
  position:relative;
  overflow: hidden;
}


.horizscroll-content {
  width: 32767px;
  position: relative;
  top: 0;
  left: 0;
}


.horizscroll-content li {
  float: left;
}
```

These are the absolute minimum styles for the script to function correctly. Of course, you might want to add additional CSS rules—for example, rules to remove the bullets from each list item. The width of the content box is set to a very large value. When you have a large number of items, you might have to increase that number, but generally you won't run into problems with this value.

The container has a `relative` position, which means it becomes the new offset origin for all containing children. As a consequence, the rules `top: 0` and `left: 0` refer to the origin of the container, not to the origin of the browser window. For the final CSS rules, check the `horizscroll.css` file in the `horizscroll` folder in the book download package.

Unfortunately, you must deal with some of the oddities of Internet Explorer 6 when creating a widget in this way, because the code presented here is actually just pure HTML and CSS. Still, writing the JavaScript code is much less of a hassle, thanks to jQuery's cross-browser abstractions.

Filling the Component with Functionality

In Chapter 9, you learned about JavaScript's object orientation—and this is the right place to use it. In the skeleton's JavaScript file, you will find a definition for an instantiable object. Here is the constructor, renamed appropriately for our `horizscroll` project:

```
Drupal.horizscroll = function(options) {
  // Store a reference to this so that anonymous functions
  // can reference it.
  var that = this;

  // Merge in the options object.
  $.extend(this, options);

  // <<< Insert more constructor code here >>>
};
```

This code already does several useful things (which you can ditch in your own project if you don't want them): It aliases `this` to `that`; as a result, we can create anonymous functions that can also access the outer `this`. A quick reminder: `this` contains the newly created instance of the object for which this constructor is being executed. For an explanation for why this is necessary, see the sections entitled "The Variable Scope" and "The Function Scope" in Chapter 9. The second line implements the "named parameters" pattern commonly used in jQuery. To learn more about the `$.extend()` function, see "Using jQuery Helper Functions" in Chapter 10.

The rest of the skeleton JavaScript file contains placeholder functions for the new object's prototype:

```
Drupal.horizscroll.prototype = {
  /**
   * Method documentation.
   */
  'method': function() {
    // <<< Insert code here >>>
  },

  /**
   * AnotherMethod documentation.
   */
  'anotherMethod': function() {
    // <<< Insert code here >>>
  }
};
```

Breaking Down the Functionality

If you like, you can simply rename these methods and use them as is. Before we begin to add more code, let's take a step back and try to split up the features into functions:

```
Drupal.horizScroll = function(options) {
  // Store a reference to this so that anonymous functions
  // can reference it.
  var that = this;

  // Merge in the options object.
  $.extend(this, options);

  // Store references to the container, the content, and so on.

  // Set the first element as the "target item."

  // Add callback functions to the left and right buttons.
```

```
    // Initialize the button status.
};


Drupal.horizScroll.prototype = {
    // Function that updates the button status based on the
    // position of the content.
    'updateButtons': function() { },

    // Function that moves the content box to a particular item.
    'scrollToItem': function() { },

    // Function that calculates the next target item.
    'findTarget': function() { }
};
```

When you think about it, that's all that's necessary to create the described component. While writing your code, it's often useful to create "stub functions" that don't actually do anything, but simply serve as placeholders for features that are yet to be implemented. When you have a clear idea of how the functionality is split among the various functions, it becomes much easier to implement each feature in the appropriate place. Every time you need a specific task done, call that function. You can worry about that function's implementation later. Coming up with a good breakdown of functionality is not always easy, but here are some tips to help you think about the issues:

- Go through your widget step by step and write down all the things you need to do (in plain text, not code).

- When you have to do a certain thing more than once, that task is a good candidate to be split out in its own function.

- Try to generalize functionality. In our example, we have "calculate the next target item," but it's also called to calculate the previous item when the user clicks the left button.

Of course, you will often have to change the way you originally broke down the functionality during the development process for a component. For example, you might find that you want to reuse a certain code snippet, so you move it to its own function. Conversely, you might discover that some other functionality is better performed inside another function, because splitting it out to a function would introduce too much overhead. Despite the likelihood that changes will be necessary, getting a good overview of the desired functionality before you start to code the component usually results in better-structured and -architected code.

Bootstrapping the Component

In the constructor, we start to write our own code by storing the elements that make up the component, the container, the content, and so on. This step ensures that we can later reference those items easily without having to search the whole document tree each time:

```
this.left = $('.horizscroll-left:first', this.root);

this.right = $('.horizscroll-right:first', this.root);

this.container = $('.horizscroll-container:first', this.root);

this.content = $('.horizscroll-content:first', this.root);
```

This code finds the first occurrence of that class within the component's HTML root. Unfortunately, there seems to be a lot of duplicate code; all lines look exactly the same, except for the name.

In our second attempt, we use a loop:

```
var items = ['left', 'right', 'container', 'content'];

for (var i in items) {

  this[items[i]] = $('.horizscroll-' + items[i] + ':first', this.root);

}
```

That's much better. When we want to change the way these items are selected, we have to change just one line instead of four.

There's also a third way to accomplish this goal, by using jQuery's `.each()` function:

```
$.each(['left', 'right', 'container', 'content'], function() {

  that[this] = $('.horizscroll-' + this + ':first', that.root);

});
```

(that is this from the constructor function; this in the anonymous function refers to the currently processed item, so it's one of 'left', 'right', ...).

For this task, it doesn't really matter which version you use; all of them have the same effect. However, if you're performing more complicated tasks, having an own function scope for each "loop" iteration is beneficial.

When scrolling through the items, we keep a "target" item, which is a reference to the item that is currently being displayed as the leftmost item. This approach is useful because it allows us to quickly calculate position differences between items. However, when initializing the component, the targeted item is the first item. Let's fetch this item using our previously created references:

```
this.target = this.content.find('> :eq(0)');
```

The CSS selector finds the first direct child of the elements in this.content. Because this child is the <ul class="horizscroll-content">, this.target will end up being the first <li> of that list. Note that we are not using completely fixed selectors, so the content box doesn't have to be a <ul>; it might also be wrapped in more markup.

To verify that the commands work correctly, you can use Firebug's console and the method console.log(). You should always confirm that you do, in fact, get what you're trying to select. If you skip this testing, you may end up with hard-to-spot errors because jQuery doesn't produce any warnings or error messages when the result set is empty (in fact, jQuery lets you perform arbitrary actions on empty sets).

The scrollToItem() Function

We can add the rest of the constructor code later; let's move to the real functionality of the scroller now. We'll tackle the scrollToItem function first. To test this functionality, add the following code to the end of the constructor:

```
this.scrollToItem(this.content.find('> :eq(3)'));
```

You should also modify the content of the scroller to contain more items (at least four in this case; numbering starts at 0). To do so, either come up with your own content (images are perfect) or use the HTML code from the finished implementation and copy the images folder to your development folder. To perform the scrolling, we must determine the offset to move the content to. Look at Figure 11.6 to get an idea of the distances and offsets.

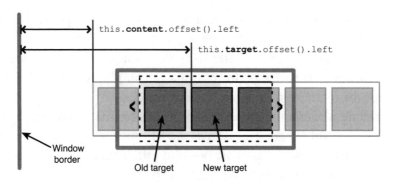

FIGURE 11.6 Distances for the content and the new target item.

We don't need the current target's position, so we can just replace `this.target` with the new target. The new target is supplied as a parameter:

```
'scrollToItem': function(item) {
  // Set the item as target.
  this.target = item;
},
```

Luckily, jQuery 1.2 provides a function named `.offset()` that calculates the current left and top positions of an element, relative to the document origins. This function returns an object with two keys, `left` and `top`. As you can see in Figure 11.6, the distance between the left offset of the new target item and the content box is exactly the number of pixels by which the content box should be positioned left of the container box. The content box and the container have `'relative'` positions, so we can just specify `left: -200px;` for the content box to move it 200 pixels left of the container. The parts that are left of the container will be invisible. To calculate the value for `left`, we use this code:

```
var pos = this.content.offset().left - this.target.offset().left;
```

The resulting value is negative, because all elements are always right of the content box. Thus `this.target.offset().left` is greater than `this.content.offset().left`. Of course, we have to use negative offsets anyway. Using the command

```
this.content.animate({ 'left': pos });
```

we can move `this.content` to the new position. Using the animation function ensures that the transition goes smoothly and that the content slides to the left.

So far, we've only talked about moving items to the left. What about moving items in the opposite direction? Actually, the code we've written already takes that possibility into account: The positions from .offset() are always the absolute position on the page; when we select a new target item that is farther on the left than the current target item, the difference becomes smaller. In such a case, the value for left becomes larger (i.e., less negative). jQuery's .animate() method will automatically figure out how to move the content box depending on its current position and the new value.

For the moment, then, our scrollToItem() function looks like this:

```
'scrollToItem': function(item) {
  // Set the item as target.
  this.target = item;

  // Animate the content frame to the new target position.
  var pos = this.content.offset().left - this.target.offset().left;
  this.content.animate({ 'left': pos });
},
```

Finding the Next Target Item

The .findTarget() method is a little more complex. We have two options here: We could split this method up into two distinct functions that determine the next target item depending on the direction, or we could try to keep everything in one function. We will take the latter approach. First, we consider which information we need to determine the next target. Figure 11.7 provides an overview of all the distances and positions.

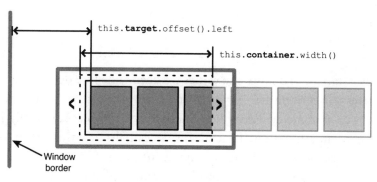

FIGURE 11.7 Data needed when calculating the next target item.

The basic algorithm includes four steps:

1. Set the new target item to the next item.
2. Look at the next item.
3. If the distance between the current target item and the next item is smaller than the container width, set the new target item to the current item and continue at step 2.
4. Otherwise, stop.

This algorithm ensures that we move by at least one item, which makes sense (e.g., when the container is narrower than an item). It also allows the user (or the developer) to resize the slider at any point. The algorithm for finding the next item will automatically use the current width. Even though the width and number of items in the scroller may change, this algorithm always determines the correct position. Now, how does that look in code?

```
'findTarget': function(direction) {
  var width = this.container.width(),
      origin = this.target.offset().left,
      current = this.target[direction](),
      next = current[direction]();

  while (next.size() && Math.abs(next.offset().left - origin) <= width) {
    current = next;
    next = current[direction]();
  }

  return current;
},
```

The first var statement defines the values we need. The line defining current is of particular interest: It runs either .prev() or .next() on this.target, depending on the direction parameter. Recall how methods of an object are really just regular variables that contain a function. That means we can also use this syntax to reference such a member variable and call the contained function. (The section entitled "The Function Scope" in Chapter 9 offers another example of this syntax.) next contains the next but one item, whose position we will then check to see whether it is still within the container's width.

The loop condition first checks whether a next item exists. If that's not the case, it aborts the loop immediately. If there is a next item, the distance between the current target item (`offset`) and this item is calculated and compared to the container width. If the distance is smaller, the loop continues; otherwise, it aborts, leaving the `current` item alone. When the loop body is executed, it moves the next item to `current` because it's still within the limits as confirmed by the loop condition. Finally, we calculate the next item and store it to `next` for the loop condition to check.

Just returning `current` after the loop has finished does the trick, but there's room for improvement. Issue a `console.log(current);` command and inspect the results in Firebug. As shown in Figure 11.8, a series of nested `prevObject` keys contain the preceding objects (so that you could use `.end()` at a later point).

We don't need these keys and they just take up space. Fortunately, there's an easy solution to get rid of them—just wrap `current` in `$()` so that the return line looks like this:

```
return $(current);
```

To thoroughly test this function, you would issue various `findTarget()` calls in the constructor. To programmatically move the slider to another position, you can give the command `this.content.css('left', -300);` in the constructor function and then call `findTarget('prev')`. Make sure to use debug outputs with `console.log()`

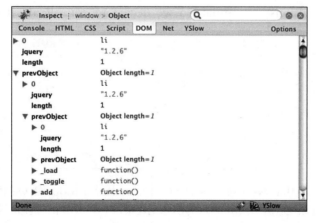

FIGURE 11.8 Nested `prevObject` properties.

so that you can check with Firebug whether the found object is actually the correct item.

Enabling the Buttons

Now that we have implemented two of the three functions, let's try to make the buttons functional. This operation is done only once, so we'll add it to the constructor function:

```
this.left.click(function() {
    that.scrollToItem(that.findTarget('prev'));
    return false;
});


this.right.click(function() {
    that.scrollToItem(that.findTarget('next'));
    return false;
});
```

In these functions, we reference the newly created `horizscroll` object using `that`—because `this` is something else when the function is called as a click event-handler callback. In the callback functions, we first find the next (or previous) target and then pass the returned item to `scrollToItem()`. Finally, `false` is returned so that the default action for that link is not executed.

These two functions are similar, so we decide to consolidate them into a more generic version:

```
$.each({'left': 'prev', 'right': 'next' }, function(key, direction) {
    that[key].click(function() {
        that.scrollToItem(that.findTarget(direction));
    });
});
```

This time, it's vital that we use `$.each()` instead of a loop. If we did not take this step, `key` and `direction` would change on the second loop iteration, but the function created in the first iteration would reference the same variables—effectively doing the wrong thing.

Now try clicking the "next" button. You should see the slider move to the right. If not, something went wrong. Make absolutely sure that you followed the steps outlined previously. You can also peek at the final code (which is available in the downloadable package for this book at `http://frontenddrupal.com`) and compare it with your own code to see whether you missed something.

Still no luck? Try the following steps:

- Make sure your JavaScript code is loaded correctly and that JavaScript is not turned off in the browser.

- Using the JavaScript console, try to find where the code fails.

- Check whether all variables are assigned correctly and whether you made typos.

- Use JavaScript Lint (`http://jslint.com`) to verify that your code parses correctly.

- Use a debugger such as the one found on Firebug's "Script" tab to step through the code. Hover over variable names to see their values.

- Use `console.log()` in Firebug to print out each step in the process, verifying that nothing went wrong.

If your code doesn't run on the first try, don't worry. Most of the time, you won't get it right the first time. (If you do, congratulations!) Thankfully, debugging support for JavaScript has greatly improved in recent years. With Firebug, you have an amazing tool that can assist you during development.

Debugging in Internet Explorer

Microsoft provides a tool for debugging scripts in Internet Explorer that comes bundled with Visual Studio. A free alternative is also available from Microsoft: Microsoft Visual Web Developer 2008 Express Edition, which is available at `http://www.microsoft.com/express/vwd/`. This tool was originally built for ASP.NET development, but there's an easy trick to get it to debug the JavaScript code in your Drupal application: Load an empty project and click the Preview button. Visual Web Developer starts Internet Explorer and loads the empty page. Now you can just enter your own URL or file name, but debugging still works. If your script produces an error, the backtrace is displayed in Visual Web Developer, and you can use the debugger to step through your code.

The current version of our code still contains one bug, though: If you click the right button repeatedly, you'll eventually end up at the rightmost item. Clicking again will result in a JavaScript error, indicating that jQuery is using `.offset()` on an empty result. To avoid that problem, you can wrap all of the code in `.scrollToItem()` into an `if` branch that checks whether a target item exists:

```
'scrollToItem': function(item) {

  if (item.size()) {

    this.target = item;

    var pos = this.content.offset().left - this.target.offset().left;

    this.content.animate({ 'left': pos });

  }

},
```

Updating the Buttons in updateButtons()

At this point, most of our code is complete. Indeed, users can scroll the content flawlessly. Only one thing is missing: When the item is at the rightmost or leftmost position, the buttons to scroll to the left or right are still functional; doing nothing in the ideal case. To implement this behavior, instead of using jQuery's `.show()` and `.hide()` functions, we will use classes again. This choice enables us to do other things besides hiding elements as well. For example, we could reduce the component's opacity, change the background image, or even alter the position of the scroller.

Here is the code for updating the left button:

```
var leftmost = this.target.is(':first-child');
this.left[leftmost ? 'removeClass' : 'addClass']('enabled');
```

This code is actually quite straightforward: When the target is the first element, we *remove* the class `enabled`; otherwise, the class is added. Insert this code in the `update-Buttons()` function and add a call to `this.updateButtons()` in the constructor to test it. Here we use `enabled` instead of `disabled` for a simple reason: When JavaScript is disabled, the button will stay in the `disabled` state instead of having an "enabled" appearance. You should always make sure that your UI elements have a meaningful appearance and behave as expected when JavaScript is not available (e.g., when the user is browsing on a mobile phone or when the user has manually disabled JavaScript). Look at the CSS file in the downloadable package's `horizscroll` folder to see which styles we use in the final script.

> ### Graceful degradation for style sheets with html.js
>
> Sometimes you may want to change the default look of your page, based on whether JavaScript is enabled or disabled. Drupal provides a good solution for that situation: When JavaScript is enabled, it adds the class `js` to the `<html>` tag. Then, in your style sheets, you can precede your selectors with `html.js` to overwrite CSS rules when JavaScript is enabled:
>
> ```
> .horizscroll-container {
>     overflow:auto;
>     position:relative;
> }
>
> html.js .horizscroll-container {
>     overflow:hidden;
> }
> ```
>
> These CSS rules ensure that the container receives a horizontal scrollbar by default (try disabling JavaScript and reload the page). When JavaScript is enabled, however, the scrollbar is removed because the slider buttons are functional. This technique allows your users to access all scroller items, albeit in a slightly different way.

Updating the right button is a bit harder, but the idea is the same as the one we used in the loop condition for `findTarget()`: If the distance between the last item and the current target item is smaller than the container width, the last item is already fully visible and we no longer need the right button. Here's the code:

```
var last = this.content.find('> :last-child');

var rightmost = (last.offset().left + last.width() -
              this.target.offset().left) <= this.container.width();

this.right[rightmost ? 'removeClass' : 'addClass']('enabled');
```

First, we grab the last item in the list and use it to calculate whether the rightmost item is visible. We use `last.offset().left + last.width()` to perform this operation because we have to check whether the item is fully visible inside the container; thus we need the offset of the right border. We then add or remove the `enabled` class based on the value of this variable. Adding the same class multiple times is not a problem, because jQuery will detect that condition and discard the request for addition when the class is already present.

This technique works well in Firefox, but Safari may not show the button after initializing the widget. At the time of this writing, Safari returns 0 for the offset and width of the last item if the item is positioned too far outside the browser window or if it is not associated with a fixed width. For this reason, we check whether the item actually has a width; if it doesn't, we show the right button just in case. We can issue the command `var hidden = (last.width() === 0);`, to see whether the item has a width.

The final function looks like this:

```
'updateButtons': function() {
  var leftmost = this.target.is(':first-child');
  this.left[leftmost ? 'removeClass' : 'addClass']('enabled');


  var last = this.content.find('> :last-child');
  var hidden = (last.width() === 0);
  var rightmost = (last.offset().left + last.width() -
                  this.target.offset().left) <= this.container.width();
  this.right[(!hidden && rightmost) ? 'removeClass' :
                                'addClass']('enabled');

},
```

Now that all of our functions work, we should confirm that the button is updated appropriately. We need to add a call to `this.updateButtons();` in two places: at the end of the constructor and at the end of `scrollToItem()`. That's it—our horizontal slider is now fully functional!

Making the Component Data-Source Agnostic

We won't stop here, of course; we still can improve many things. Currently, the horizontal slider component can only take the HTML code that is already there and add interactivity to it. It would be useful to let the horizontal slider *ask* for new items each time more items should be displayed. This approach offers a key advantage—namely, not all items need to be available as HTML code at page load time. (Most browsers will load these images, even though they might not yet be displayed because they're outside the viewport.)

The idea is to create a `datasource` function that takes care of obtaining new items when the slider requests such an item. This function can be supplied when the widget is created and will be "merged" into the new `horizScroll` object. The command `$.extend(this, options);` takes care of this task. In case the developer doesn't supply a `datasource` function, we must make sure a fallback data source is available:

```
if (!this.datasource) {

  this.datasource = Drupal.horizScroll.settingsDatasource;

}
```

We add this code after the `.extend()` call. We then define the function referenced there (note that we just use the function name—we don't *call* the function):

```
Drupal.horizScroll.defaultDatasource = function(index) {

  var el = $('> :eq('+ index +')', this.content);

  if (el.size()) {

    return el.html();

  }

};
```

This function is just a placeholder that returns the HTML code of the element that is already present. If the specified index doesn't exist, the function doesn't return anything, so the return value is `undefined`.

We can write a number of different data source functions that take data from the `Drupal.settings` object, create the data on the fly, or load it via AJAX. A data source function that loads data from the settings object might, for example, look like this:

```
Drupal.horizScroll.settingsDatasource = function(index) {

  return Drupal.settings[this.datasourceKey][index];

};
```

Note that this is the scroller object when this function is called, so it can access any values it needs. This function requires another key to be present, the datasourceKey, which must also be supplied when we create the scroller object.

Let's take a quick look at how we would create a horizontal scroller with a nonstandard data source works:

```
new Drupal.horizScroll({
  'root': $('#posts'),
  'datasource': Drupal.horizScroll.settingsDatasource,
  'datasourceKey': 'postsScroller'
});
```

This code uses the settingsDatasource function we defined earlier. That function then takes as input the data from Drupal.settings.postsScroller as specified with the datasourceKey.

To test this function, add some item data to the HTML file's settings section, as shown here:

```
<script type="text/javascript"><!--//--><![CDATA[//><!--
  jQuery.extend(Drupal.settings, {
    "basePath": "/",
    'postsScroller': [
      '<img src="images/con01.jpg" />',
      '<img src="images/con02.jpg" />',
      '<img src="images/con03.jpg" />',
      // ...
      '<img src="images/con26.jpg" />'
    ],
  });
//--><!]]></script>
```

At this point, you should either change how horizscroll components are created or change the class name and add a custom initialization function. When you watch Firebug's "Net" panel, you'll notice that—in contrast to the previous version—not all files are loaded immediately. (You can also confirm this behavior by inspecting the HTML code; new items should be added as you progress farther to the right.)

Integration with Drupal

The actual task of integrating our new component with Drupal is not that complicated: You've learned earlier in this chapter how you can use the PHP function `drupal_add_js()` to include a JavaScript file on a page. In the same way, you can add the settings required for the `settingsDatasource` version of the scroller. Usually, a custom-built module gathers the required data, adds it to the page, and exposes it to the theme layer. It might seem tempting to gather the data directly in your template, but this is not a good idea: You're moving the functionality into the theme layer, which makes it more complicated to switch your theme later or upgrade to a new version of Drupal.

Using Plugins and jQuery UI

An alternative to creating JavaScript components yourself is to integrate one of the many freely available jQuery plugins you can find on the Web. The jQuery Web site provides a platform for sharing such plugins at `http://plugins.jquery.com/`. However, not all jQuery plugins are listed there.

Sparklines

In this section we explore the "sparklines" plugin, which is available at `http://plugins.jquery.com/project/sparklines`. Sparklines are small information graphics that can be placed inside text, as shown in Figure 11.9. Usually, they display some sort of numerical data, perhaps plotted over time or depicted as a pie chart. The inventor, Edward Tufte, describes sparklines as "data-intense, design-simple, word-sized graphics." They usually don't contain axis descriptions but are intended solely for making a point or giving the user a very quick overview of the latest developments.

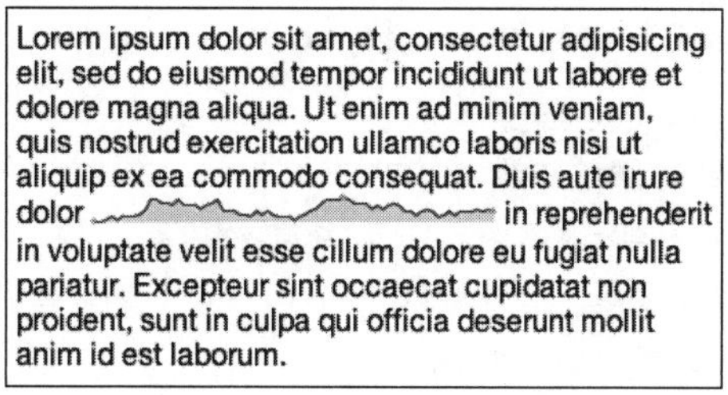

FIGURE 11.9 A sparkline information graphic.

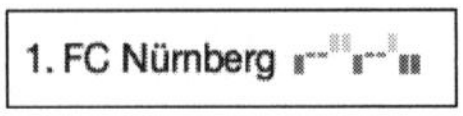

FIGURE 11.10 Lost and won games of 1. FC Nürnberg from the July 2008 Bundesliga season.

Suppose we have a CCK node titled `team`; this module contains a field with multiple values that allows you to track the wins and losses of the team. Wouldn't it be cool to show a small graphic that indicates whether the team has lost, won, or achieved a draw in its last few matches? Figure 11.10 shows what this graphic could look like. This type of graphic is called "tristate" because it has three possible states: "plus," "neutral," and "minus." It is a perfect choice for showing the results of recent games.

Using jQuery plugins is generally a rather simple process: You download the jQuery plugin file and create a new Drupal behavior (see the previous section for an explanation of behaviors) that initializes the jQuery plugin in your preferred way. The sparklines plugin is documented in the source code and on its author's Web site at `http://omnipotent.net/jquery.sparkline/`. There are two ways of inputting data into a sparkline: The sparkline can take the data that is embedded in the HTML code or you can provide an array of data when initializing the plugin. To simplify matters, we use the HTML initialization technique.

In a module or a template file, you must aggregate the required data (aggregate the data in a template file that is already available in the node object—for example, you can syndicate data from different CCK fields, but you shouldn't perform database queries to collect the data). Then print the data, separated by commas, into an element, like this:

```
<span class="winslosses">-1,0,0,1,1,-1,0,0,1,-1,-1</span>
```

Here −1 indicates a loss, 0 indicates a draw, and 1 indicates a win.

Next, call `.sparkline()` on this element. Make sure to add the `jquery.spark lines.js` file to your page before trying this code:

```
Drupal.behaviors.winslosses = function(context) {
  $('.winlost:not(.winslosses-processed)', context)
    .sparkline('html', { type: 'tristate' })
    .addClass('winslosses-processed');
};
```

This is the general behaviors pattern: Look for nonprocessed elements, process them, and then add the class indicating that the element has been processed.

There are many other jQuery plugins besides the sparklines program available on the jQuery Web site. Of course, not all plugins are of outstanding quality. Most, though, are worth giving a try.

jQuery Drupal Modules

As an alternative to adding jQuery files yourself to the theme or with a module, you can download a Drupal module that adds it to your Web site. The Drupal Web site has many JavaScript/jQuery modules available for download. Check the "JavaScript Utilities" section at `http://drupal.org/project/Modules`. Most of the time, adding these files is a simple matter of installing the module. Some of the JavaScript modules don't do anything by themselves, however. Instead, they exist to provide a central instance of, say, jQuery UI. That way, other modules that use jQuery UI can just add a dependency on the jQuery UI module and don't have to ship with their own version of jQuery UI.

Another useful module is the jQuery Update module. This module replaces the jQuery version that shipped with your Drupal version with the most current one. It also makes sure that all of the JavaScript files that came with Drupal are compatible with the new jQuery version. This module can be found at `http://drupal.org/project/jquery_update`.

jQuery UI

jQuery UI (downloadable at `http://ui.jquery.com/`) is a collection of plugins and frameworks that implement frequently used features. You can use some of the components of jQuery UI directly, such as the Accordion and Tabs plugins. Other parts of jQuery UI provide APIs on which you can build your own components. For example, the Draggable and Droppable interfaces allow you to easily add drag-and-drop capabilities to your widget. jQuery UI also provides a variety of easing options as well as more effects. It is developed independently of jQuery, however, so it may not be as stable and well tested as jQuery is. Nevertheless, jQuery UI is certainly ready for production use.

The usage of jQuery UI APIs is generally not complicated: You simply tell jQuery how you want your components to interact. Enabling drag-and-drop functionality between two lists might work like this:

```
$('ul.source li', context).draggable({ 'helper': 'clone' });
$('ul.target', context).droppable({
  accept: '.source li',
  drop: function(e, ui) {
    $(this).append(ui.draggable);
  }
});
```

This code allows list items from a list with the class source to be dragged to lists with the class target. It first makes the list items draggable with the "Draggable" API, and then makes the target list accept items with a certain selector by using the "Droppable" API. Next, the drop callback function moves the item from the old list to the new one by appending the dragged object (which is stored in ui.draggable) to the target list (which is this). Many more options are also available for the Draggable and Droppable interfaces.

Summary

This chapter described how you can add JavaScript files to your Drupal template and to modules. As explained in this chapter, you can feed data and configuration options into JavaScript code either directly in the page header or via an AJAX request. When creating a JavaScript component, it is important to adhere to the key principles outlined in this chapter.

To demonstrate the creation of a component, we implemented a horizontal slider in JavaScript, first making a rough skeleton and then filling in the features, making sure that everything works in each step. To make this widget even more useful, we converted the horizontal slider to use a dynamic data source function that adds new items to the slider as they are about to be displayed. An alternative to writing JavaScript components yourself is to use one of the many readily available jQuery plugins and Drupal JavaScript modules.

Of course, the JavaScript chapters in this book do not cover all aspects of the JavaScript world. Entire books have been dedicated to jQuery and jQuery UI as well as to JavaScript and JavaScript programming techniques. Check out these resources if you want to learn even more about JavaScript development.

Appendix A

Installing Drupal

Even though Drupal is a powerful content management system, its requirements are modest: a Web server (preferably Apache, but IIS or other server software will work as well) with at least PHP 4.3 and a database back end (MySQL or PostgreSQL) are needed. In this appendix, the setup of an Apache Web server and MySQL is briefly outlined, as this is by far the most common approach to using Drupal.

Setting Up a Development Server

When developing a theme or tweaking a Drupal Web site, a local Web server is very handy to speed up the process of developing and testing. Several software distributions that come preconfigured with Apache, PHP, and MySQL are available; their use largely simplifies the setup of a Web server. These packages usually have a straightforward installation routine: download the package, extract the files, and click the "Start server" button.

Of course, there are many ways to install a server; only a few of them are presented here. If you already have a development Web server set up, you can most likely reuse it for running Drupal.

Windows

A popular free server package is XAMPP, which comes in two flavors: the regular version and a light version. Both can be downloaded from `http://www.apachefriends.org/en/xampp.html`. The light version contains all software that is required for running Drupal. If you want to conveniently upgrade your servers later, however, you will have to stick with the full version.

> **What the heck is XAMPP?**
> The name XAMPP is compiled from the components this package contains. The X stands for any operating system, A is for Apache, M for MySQL, the first P for PHP, and the second P for Perl. You might also see the acronym LAMP, which similarly stands for "Linux, Apache, MySQL, PHP"—a common Web host configuration.

On the XAMPP Web site, choose your operating system and follow the steps detailed on the subsequent page. The Windows version of XAMPP ships with a convenient installer that guides you through the installation process. During setup, you can opt to install Apache and MySQL as a "service." That means that these server programs are started automatically when you boot your computer. If you don't want to do that right now, you can always install or uninstall the service in XAMPP's control panel. Your new Web server can be reached at `http://localhost`.

If you are stuck in the installation process or experience other difficulties, you can find extensive support documentation on the XAMPP Web site.

Linux

If you are using Linux, keep in mind that a lot of distributions already have Apache, PHP, and sometimes even MySQL preinstalled. If not, you might want to take a look at your package manager—it might provide for easier installation. The default location of your document root depends on your distribution, and you might want to edit it to suit your needs. In case you don't want to stick with your distribution's packages, XAMPP also comes in a Linux version.

Mac OS X

Mac OS X also ships with Apache and PHP. To enable the Apache server, go to the "Sharing" section in the "System Preferences" and check "Personal Web Sharing." By default, every user has a Web root, which is the "Sites" folder in your folder; it is accessible at `http://localhost/~username/` (where `username` is your login name). The files located at `/Library/WebServer/Documents` are available at `http://localhost`.

Even though Mac OS ships with Apache preinstalled, you still need MySQL (or PostgreSQL). There are installation packages available for Mac OS X on the vendors' Web sites: `http://dev.mysql.com/downloads/mysql/` for MySQL and `http://www.postgresql.org/download/` for PostgreSQL.

Unfortunately, the Apache and PHP versions in Mac OS X 10.4 and earlier are quite old (Apache 1.3.x and PHP 4.x), so you might want to consider installing Apache 2 with PHP 5. Mac OS X 10.5 Leopard ships with server and PHP versions that are sufficient for Drupal. However, you have to remove the hash sign before the `LoadModule php5_module libexec/apache2/libphp5.so` line in the `httpd.conf` (see below for more information on where you can find that file).

In most cases, it's a lot easier to use a preconfigured package called MAMP (Mac OS X, Apache, MySQL, PHP), which is available at `http://www.mamp.info`. It contains all required components for running Drupal. The regular version will suffice. MAMP's default document root is `/Applications/MAMP/htdocs`.

Configuring Document Root and Virtual Hosts

If you're unhappy with the default document root (the place where your Web server files are located), you can change it by modifying Apache's configuration file. To do so, you typically have to locate `httpd.conf`, as it is the main configuration file. Use Table A.1 to find the file location for your setup.

TABLE A.1 Locating httpd.conf

Setup Method	Configuration File Path
Windows (XAMPP)	`C:\xampp\apache\conf\httpd.conf`
Linux	Type `locate httpd.conf` in a shell
Mac OS X Tiger	`/private/etc/httpd/httpd.conf`
Mac OS X Leopard	`/private/etc/apache2/httpd.conf`
Mac OS X (MAMP)	Use the MAMP control panel (Preferences/Apache) or `/Applications/MAMP/conf/apache/httpd.conf`

In the configuration file, look for a line beginning with `DocumentRoot`. The path that follows this directive (in double quotes) is the document root. It must not end with a slash (or a backslash). Write down the old directory and enter the new directory here. Then search for the old document root directory until you find a line that looks like `<Directory "C:/xampp/htdocs">` (the path is your old document root). Enter the same new path here as well and save the file. This part of the configuration file could look like the following code example:

```
#
# DocumentRoot: The directory out of which you will serve your
# documents. By default, all requests are taken from this directory, but
# symbolic links and aliases may be used to point to other locations.
#
DocumentRoot "/Users/kkaefer/Sites"


[...]


#
# This should be changed to whatever you set DocumentRoot to.
#
<Directory "/Users/kkaefer/Sites">
    [...]
</Directory>
```

For the changes to take effect, you have to restart the Apache Web server. To do so, follow the instructions found in Table A.2.

TABLE A.2 Starting and stopping Apache

Setup Method	Restarting the Method
Windows (XAMPP)	Use the XAMPP control panel
Linux	Type `apachectl restart` or `/etc/init.d/apache restart`
Mac OS X	System Preferences/Sharing, uncheck/check "(Personal) web sharing"
Mac OS X (MAMP)	Use the MAMP control panel application (Preferences/Apache)

Installing Drupal—and Common Hurdles to Its Installation

Once your Web server is working, installing Drupal is usually a fairly easy task. You may encounter some small hurdles when setting up the CMS, but these can be overcome quickly. As we walk through the installation process, you will get to know some of them.

1. **Download Drupal.** Go to `http://drupal.org` and select "Drupal 6" in the download section. Unpack it and copy the contents of the Zip file to your document root (or wherever you want Drupal to be located).

> **Hurdle 1**
> When copying the package, make absolutely sure that you also copy the .htaccess file located in the Drupal root folder. It is required by Drupal, especially for clean URLs. Most operating systems tend to hide this file by default because it begins with a dot. To make sure you copy the file, you can either turn on the display of files of that type, move the entire folder that contains the Drupal root, or move the files from the command line.

2. **Create a database.** Drupal needs a database in which to store its data. Databases can be created via the command line, but it is easier to use graphical user interfaces such as phpMyAdmin for that purpose. XAMPP and MAMP already ship with phpMyAdmin preinstalled, and almost every shared hosting provider has it installed as well.

   If you're prompted with a "collation," select something with UTF-8, as this is Drupal's default character set (it contains almost all known characters on earth). If you can't select a charset, Drupal will take care of that task later. You should note the username, password, and database name for Drupal's installation process.

3. **Install Drupal.** Once you have downloaded and extracted the Drupal files and created a database, you are ready to run Drupal's installer. This piece of software automatically creates all required database tables and sets some default settings. To launch the installer, navigate to the URL where your Drupal installation is reachable over your Web server (e.g., `http://localhost`, `http://localhost/drupal`, or whatever you have chosen).

   You'll be automatically redirected to the installer, which guides you through the whole installation process. If you prefer, you can install Drupal in another language, but that requires additional effort, as there are no translations supplied with the Drupal core package.

Hurdle 2

On most systems, you will see a warning message saying that you don't have enough permissions to write to a configuration file. The automatic installer requires you to copy the `settings.default.php` file in the `/sites/default/` folder and to give PHP write permissions to that folder. The installer needs this permission because it writes the database configuration data to that file.

If you're on Windows, you will likely not see this warning. Windows uses a different rights management system.

On Mac OS X, navigate in the Finder to that folder, duplicate the file, and rename it to `settings.php`. Then select the "Get Info" item in the file's context menu (right-click or Ctrl-click). In the "Permissions" section of the info window, set all access permissions to "Read & Write." If the access permissions drop-down options are disabled, click on the lock icon to authenticate first.

On a Linux shell, navigate to your Drupal installation's root folder and type in the shell command `chmod 777 sites/default/settings.php` (this technique also works on Mac OS X).

When you're done installing Drupal, make absolutely sure to set the access rights to "read-only" to prevent attackers from being able to compromise your system. In Mac OS X, just set the drop-down option back to "read only"; on Linux systems, execute the same command, but with `644` instead of `777`.

4. **Perform site setup.** After the Drupal installer managed to write the settings file to the disk and successfully set up the database, you will be presented with a page containing settings for the most important configuration options for your site, such as the site's name and the email address. You are also required to set up an administrator's account here. This account will always have all access rights. It is vital to keep the account data safe.

5. **Perform the initial configuration.** Once you're done setting up Drupal, you'll be automatically logged in to Drupal. When you are on the "Administer" main page (see Figure A.1), you will most likely see a little warning message at the top telling you that there are problems requiring your attention.

On the "Status report" page as shown in Figure A.2, you will see an overview of most of Drupal's dependencies and an indication as to whether they're met.

If you receive a "Configuration file" error message, you must change the access permissions. See the "Hurdle 2," which explains how to change these permissions.

The next thing that will most likely appear as problematic is the "Cron maintenance tasks" page. Cron is a piece of software that is well known from

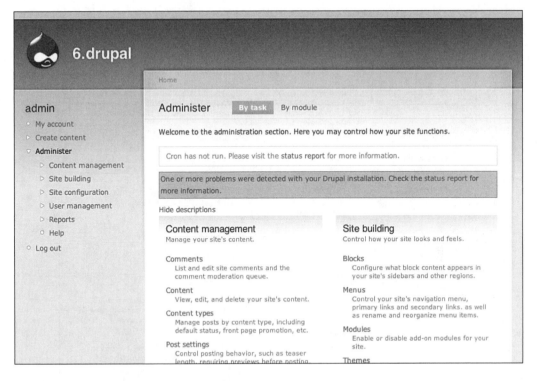

FIGURE A.1 Administration home screen showing warning messages.

UNIX-based systems (Linux, Mac OS X); it allows scheduling of repeating tasks. (In Windows, the corresponding feature is the "Task Planner," which works differently). Drupal requires a task setup that calls the page `http://example.com/cron.php` (where `example.com` is the URL to your Drupal installation) regularly. This setup is needed for maintenance tasks, such as creating the search index or temp folder cleanups. When you're just running a development site on your local machine, you can skip this step (keep in mind that the search will not work correctly in this case!). Some hosting companies have an interface for creating cron tasks. If your hosting company does not, you can try dropping its help staff a nice email and asking for it.

The last item that is likely to bear a warning sign after installation is "File system." Drupal stores all files uploaded by users in a central files directory. To create this directory, create a folder named `files` in your Drupal installation's folder and set access permissions to read and write (see "Hurdle 2" for further instructions). Alternatively, you can create a folder with an arbitrary name, set

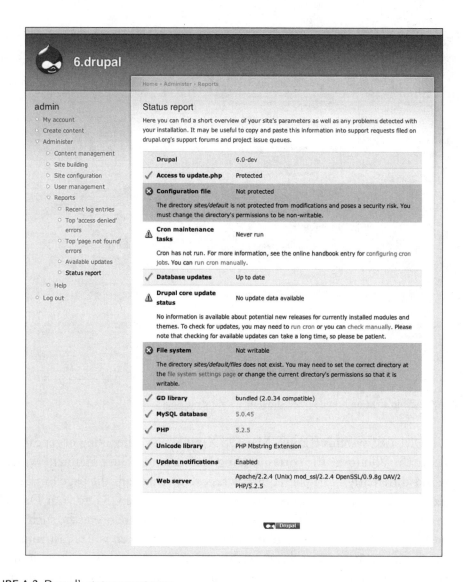

FIGURE A.2 Drupal's status report page.

its permissions, and change where Drupal stores its files by going to Administer, Site configuration, File system.

A Quick Glance at the Admin Area

Drupal's administration area is, by default, split into four sections: Content management, Site building, Site configuration, and User management. In addition, Reports and Help areas are available. Modules can extend these main categories arbitrarily. The Organic Groups module, for example, adds a new root-level administration item called Organic groups.

- The **Content Management** section contains all administrative settings related to the creation and management of content. You can use this area to create new content types, alter the publishing work flow, moderate comments, and manage posts on your Web site.

- The **Site building** area controls the actual functionality of your site. You can manage which modules and themes are enabled, which blocks are visible, how your menu is structured, and so forth.

- **Site configuration** contains all settings related to the general Web site. If a settings page cannot be associated with either content (i.e., nodes or comments) or users, it's likely that the page can be found here, as this section acts as a kind of "catch-all."

- **User management** contains all actions and settings concerning users of your site. In this area, you can get an overview listing page, manage permissions, block users. and so forth.

- The **Reports** item comprises various messages that have been accumulated while running your site, such as error and status messages. It is also the place to look for the updating notifier, which informs you about new versions of Drupal or installed third-party modules. A great place for finding out what's wrong with your site is the "Status report" page, which lists all sorts of information about your system and points out misconfigurations.

- The **Help** section holds various help texts for many Drupal components, but acts more like an introduction to the general capabilities of Drupal and its modules rather than providing actual help when something is broken. Nevertheless, it is worth checking out to get a basic idea of what a certain module does, as this information is not specifically covered in this book.

Installing Modules

Some of the features that made Drupal what it is today are not included in the core distribution you just installed. Drupal features a very flexible and well-documented plugin architecture that allows plugin developers to do almost anything they want without modify the core of Drupal. These plugins are called *modules* in the Drupal world. Most Drupal Web sites use at least the CCK module and the Views modules, among others.

Installing modules is usually relatively easy and takes just a few steps:

1. Download the latest version of the module from the project's page. Make sure that it matches the Drupal version you are running. Modules are not compatible across major Drupal releases. For example, you can't use Drupal 7 modules with Drupal 6, and vice versa.

2. You may choose to unpack the files before uploading them if your Web server does not have the appropriate tools to unpack the files or if your Web server runs on your local machine.

3. Place the module folder in the `sites/all/modules` folder on your Web server.

4. Navigate to Administer, Site building, Modules.

5. Enable the module by selecting the check box next to the module name, scroll to the bottom of the screen, and click "Save configuration."

Usually it's a good idea to read a module's `README.txt` or `INSTALL.txt` file before installing the module. This file contains information explaining which additional steps may be required to install the module, help text on how to use or set up the module configuration, and warnings.

APPENDIX B

Supplemental Code

On http://frontenddrupal.com, you can download the example code used throughout the book. Additionally, this appendix provides a short overview of the code as well as the most important example code, grouped by folders.

template

In Chapter 10, a sample template is used for practicing jQuery code in a clean environment. The template folder contains all required files for running code. Insert new code into the index.html file.

index.html

The index.html file serves as a playground for experimenting with JavaScript code. Just insert the JavaScript code you want to try in the marked section in the header.

```
<?xml version="1.0" encoding="UTF-8"?>
<!DOCTYPE html PUBLIC "-//W3C//DTD XHTML 1.1//EN"
   "http://www.w3.org/TR/xhtml11/DTD/xhtml11.dtd">


<html xmlns="http://www.w3.org/1999/xhtml" xml:lang="en">
<head>
   <title>ACME Inc.</title>
   <link rel="stylesheet" href="files/styles.css" type="text/css" />
   <script type="text/javascript" src="files/jquery-1.2.6.js"></script>
   <script type="text/javascript">


$(function() {
   // Place your JavaScript code here.
});


   </script>
</head>


<body>


<div id="wrapper">
   <div id="header">
      <h1><a href="http://frontenddrupal.com">ACME Inc.</a></h1>
      <h4>A Company that Makes Everything.</h4>


      <ul id="navigation">
         <li class="active"><a href="#"><strong>Home</strong></a></li>
         <li><a href="#">Products</a></li>
         <li><a href="#">Brands</a></li>
         <li><a href="#">Company</a></li>
         <li><a href="#">Support</a></li>
      </ul>


      <form id="language" action="/" method="get"
            title="Select a language to view the site in">
```

```
    <fieldset>
      <legend>Language</legend>
      <select>
        <option value="en" selected="selected">English</option>
        <option value="fr">Français</option>
        <option value=»es»>Español</option>
      </select>
      <input type=»submit» name=»op» id=»edit-change»
             value=»Change» />
    </fieldset>
  </form>


  <form id=»search» action=»/» method=»get»>
    <fieldset>
      <legend>Search</legend>
      <input type=»text» name=»edit[keys]» id=»edit-keys» />
      <input type=»submit» name=»op» id=»edit-search»
             value=»Search» />
    </fieldset>
  </form>
</div>


<div id=»body»>
  <div class=»teaser»>
    <a href=»#» class=»lead-image»><img src=»files/teaser.jpg»
                                    alt=»Bank on a beach» /></a>


    <p><strong>Lorem ipsum dolor sit amet</strong>, consectetur
       adipisicing elit, sed do eiusmod tempor incididunt ut labore et
       dolore magna aliqua. Ut enim ad minim veniam, quis nostrud
       exercitation ullamco laboris nisi ut aliquip ex ea commodo
       consequat. Duis aute irure dolor in reprehenderit in voluptate
       velit esse cillum dolore eu fugiat nulla pariatur. Excepteur
       sint occaecat cupidatat non proident, sunt in culpa qui officia
       deserunt mollit anim id est laborum.</p>
  </div>
```

```
<div class=»columns»>
  <div class=»column» id=»column-products»>
    <h3><a href=»#»>Products</a></h3>
    <ul>
      <li class=»aircrafts»>
        <a href=»#»>Aircrafts</a>
      </li>
      <li class=»food-beverages»>
        <a href=»#»>Food &amp; Beverages</a>
      </li>
      <li class=»clothing»>
        <a href=»#»>Clothing</a>
      </li>
      <li class=»electronics»>
        <a href=»#»>Electronics</a>
      </li>
      <li class=»telecommunication»>
        <a href=»#»>Telecommunication</a>
      </li>
      <li class=»construction»>
        <a href=»#»>Construction</a>
      </li>
      <li class=»energy-supply»>
        <a href=»#»>Energy supply</a>
      </li>
      <li class=»pharmaceuticals»>
        <a href=»#»>Pharmaceuticals</a>
      </li>
      <li class=»hardware»>
        <a href=»#»>Hardware</a>
      </li>
      <li class=»industrial plants»>
        <a href=»#»>Industrial plants</a>
      </li>
    </ul>
```

```
    <a href=»#» class=»more-link»>See more products…</a>
</div>

<div class=»column» id=»column-news»>
  <h3><a href=»#»>News</a></h3>
  <ul>
    <li>
      <h4>11/23/08: <a href=»#»>Annual business report</a></h4>
      <p>Lorem ipsum dolor sit amet, consectetur adipisicing
         elit, sed do eiusmod tempor incididunt ut labore et
         dolore magna aliqua. Ut enim ad minim veniam…
         <a href=»#» class=»more-link»>read more</a></p>
    </li>
    <li>
      <h4>10/31/08: <a href=»#»>New company branch</a></h4>
      <p>Lorem ipsum dolor sit amet, consectetur adipisicing
         elit, sed do eiusmod tempor incididunt ut labore et
         dolore magna aliqua. Ut enim ad minim veniam…
         <a href=»#» class=»more-link»>read more</a></p>
    </li>
    <li>
      <h4>10/7/08: <a href=»#»>3,208 products launched</a></h4>
      <p>Lorem ipsum dolor sit amet, consectetur adipisicing
         elit, sed do eiusmod tempor incididunt ut labore et
         dolore magna aliqua. Ut enim ad minim veniam…
         <a href=»#» class=»more-link»>read more</a></p>
    </li>
  </ul>
  <a href=»#» class=»more-link»>See previous items…</a>
</div>

<div class=»column» id=»column-misc»>
  <ul>
    <li><a href=»#»><img src=»files/pastries.jpg»
        alt=»Check our large pastry selection!» /></a></li>
```

```
        <li><a href="#"><img src="files/environment.jpg"
          alt=»ACME's environment policy» /></a></li>
      </ul>
    </div>
  </div>
</div>


<div id=»footer»>
  <ul id=»footer-nav»>
    <li id=»footer-privacy»><a href=»#»>Privacy Policy</a></li>
    <li id=»footer-tos»><a href=»#»>Terms of Service</a></li>
    <li id=»footer-feedback»><a href=»#»>Feedback</a></li>
  </ul>

  <p class=»message»>
    Copyright © 1984-2009 ACME Incorporated.
    <a href=»#»>All rights reserved</a>.
  </p>
  </div>
</div>


</body>
</html>
```

index-input.html

The index-input.html file is essentially the same as index.html, except that there's already sample code in the header. The example code adds a default value to the search form, as shown in Chapter 10.

```
$(function() {
  $(function() {
    var searchText = "Enter your search terms";

    var focusSearch = function() {
```

```
        if ($(this).val() == searchText) {
          $(this).val("");
        }
      };

      var blurSearch = function() {
        if (!$(this).val()) {
          $(this).val(searchText);
        }
        else {
          $(this)
            .unbind('focus', focusSearch)
            .unbind('blur', blurSearch);
        }
      };

    $('#edit-keys')
      .val(searchText)
      .focus(focusSearch)
      .blur(blurSearch);
  });
});
```

demo-module

The demo-module folder contains a sample Drupal module. Move this folder to your Drupal installation in sites/all/modules so that you can enable it in the administration section. See Appendix A for instructions on enabling modules. The .info file contains information about the module.

demo.module

The demo.module sample module allows you to add PHP code at various places to test the code explained in Chapter 11. By no means is this a complete example of a Drupal module. Much more documentation on writing modules can be found online at http://drupal.org/node/508 or in the fantastic book *Pro Drupal Development* by John VanDyk, published by APress.

```php
<?php
// $Id$

/**
 * @file
 * This is the file description for demo module.
 *
 * In this more verbose, multiline description, you can specify what
 * this file does exactly. Make sure to wrap your documentation in
 * column 71 so that the file can be displayed nicely in default-sized
 * consoles.
 */

/**
 * Implementation of hook_init().
 */
function demo_init() {

  // Place code that runs on every page here.

}

/**
 * Implementation of hook_menu().
 */
function demo_menu() {
  $items = array();

  $items['demo'] = array(
    'title' => 'Demo module',
    'description' => 'A demo page for testing code.',
    'access callback' => 'user_access',
```

```
    'access arguments' => array('access content'),
    'page callback' => 'demo_page',
  );


  // Insert more menu items here.


  return $items;
}


/**
 * Menu callback; Displays content for 'demo'.
 */
function demo_page() {


  // Insert code that runs only on this page here.


  return 'Lorem ipsum dolor sit amet, consectetur adipisicing elit, ' .
    'sed do eiusmod tempor incididunt ut labore et dolore magna ' .
    'aliqua. Ut enim  ad minim veniam, quis nostrud exercitation ' .
    'ullamco laboris nisi ut aliquip ex ea commodo consequat. Duis ' .
    'aute irure dolor in reprehenderit in voluptate velit esse ' .
    'cillum dolore eu fugiat nulla pariatur. Excepteur sint ' .
    'occaecat cupidatat non proident, sunt in culpa qui officia ' .
    'deserunt mollit anim id est laborum.';
}
```

demo.info

The demo.info file is required so that Drupal will correctly recognize the module. It must be located in the same folder as the .module file. For the various configuration options, see the URLs in the source code.

```
; $Id$
name = Demo
description = "A demonstration module for testing code."
```

```
; Drupal core version this module is for.
core = 6.x


; Package name (see http://drupal.org/node/101009 for a list of names)
; package =


; PHP version requirement
; php = 5.2


; Module dependencies
; dependencies[] = mymodule
; dependencies[] = theirmodule


; For further information about configuration options, see
; http://drupal.org/node/231036 (Drupal 6)
```

template-skeleton

The `template-skeleton` folder contains a skeleton for developing a JavaScript component. This skeleton code is used in Chapter 11 as a basis for developing the horizontal scroller. This `skeleton.js` file is released into public domain. The other files are taken from the Drupal distribution or from the jQuery Web site.

skeleton.js

The `skeleton.js` script file provides a basis on which you can build your own JavaScript components for Drupal. The script is initialized in the `Drupal.behaviors.skeleton` function and creates a new behavior instance for each component found in the HTML source code.

```
/**
 * Initializes the skeleton component.
 */
Drupal.behaviors.skeleton = function(context) {
  $('.skeleton:not(.skeleton-processed)', context).each(function() {
```

```
      // <<< Insert the code to process each skeleton here >>>


  }).addClass('skeleton-processed');
};



/**
 * The skeleton constructor.
 *
 * @param options
 *   You should document all available options here.
 */
Drupal.skeleton = function(options) {
  // Store a reference to this so that anonymous functions can
  // reference it.
  var that = this;

  // Merge in the options object.
  $.extend(this, options);

  // <<< Insert more constructor code here >>>
};


Drupal.skeleton.prototype = {
  /**
   * Method documentation.
   */
  'method': function() {
    // <<< Insert code here >>>
  },

  /**
   * AnotherMethod documentation.
   */
  'anotherMethod': function() {
```

```
    // <<< Insert code here >>>
  }
};
```

skeleton.html

The `skeleton.html` file is a basic HTML file that includes all the required files for developing Drupal JavaScript components. It also includes an HTML dummy of the component you're building. For more information on how this file can be used, check Chapter 11.

```html
<?xml version="1.0"?>
<!DOCTYPE html PUBLIC "-//W3C//DTD XHTML 1.0 Strict//EN"
    "http://www.w3.org/TR/xhtml1/DTD/xhtml1-strict.dtd">

<html xmlns="http://www.w3.org/1999/xhtml" xml:lang="en" lang="en">
<head>
  <meta http-equiv="Content-Type" content="text/html; charset=utf-8"/>
  <title>Skeleton</title>

  <link rel="stylesheet" href="skeleton.css" type="text/css" />

  <script src="jquery-1.2.6.js" type="text/javascript"></script>
  <script src="drupal.js" type="text/javascript"></script>
  <script src="skeleton.js" type="text/javascript"></script>
  <script type="text/javascript"><!--//--><![CDATA[//><!--
    jQuery.extend(Drupal.settings, {
      "basePath": "/"
      // <<< Optionally insert more variables here >>>
    });
  //--><!]]></script>
</head>

<body>
```

```
<p>Lorem ipsum dolor sit amet, consectetur adipisicing elit, sed do

   eiusmod tempor incididunt ut labore et dolore magna aliqua. Ut enim

   ad minim veniam, quis nostrud exercitation ullamco laboris nisi ut

   aliquip ex ea commodo consequat. Duis aute irure dolor in

   reprehenderit in voluptate velit esse cillum dolore eu fugiat nulla

   pariatur. Excepteur sint occaecat cupidatat non proident, sunt in

   culpa qui officia deserunt mollit anim id est laborum.</p>


<div class=»skeleton clear-block»>

  <!-- More HTML code here. -->

</div>


<p>Lorem ipsum dolor sit amet, consectetur adipisicing elit, sed do

   eiusmod tempor incididunt ut labore et dolore magna aliqua. Ut enim

   ad minim veniam, quis nostrud exercitation ullamco laboris nisi ut

   aliquip ex ea commodo consequat. Duis aute irure dolor in

   reprehenderit in voluptate velit esse cillum dolore eu fugiat nulla

   pariatur. Excepteur sint occaecat cupidatat non proident, sunt in

   culpa qui officia deserunt mollit anim id est laborum.</p>


</body>

</html>
```

skeleton.css

The `skeleton.css` file contains the single most important style class from Drupal's default CSS. You'll need it for developing your CSS code for JavaScript components.

```
/* <<< Place your skeleton CSS code here >>> */


/**

 * Markup free clearing
```

```
 * Details: http://www.positioniseverything.net/easyclearing.html
 */
.clear-block:after {
  content: ".";
  display: block;
  height: 0;
  clear: both;
  visibility: hidden;
}


.clear-block {
  display: inline-block;
}


/* Hides from IE-mac \*/
* html .clear-block {
  height: 1%;
}
.clear-block {
  display: block;
}
/* End hide from IE-mac */
```

horizscroll and horizscroll-datasource

The `horizscroll` and `horizscroll-datasource` folders contain two versions of the horizontal scroller developed in Chapter 11. The `horizscroll` folder contains the version without the data source; the companion file contains the version with the data source added. Only the `horizscroll-datasource` file appears here. Library script files are omitted.

horizscroll.js

The `horizscroll.js` file implements the behavior of the horizontal scroller. Check Chapter 11 for a detailed step-by-step explanation on how this has been built.

```
/*

Copyright (c) 2008 Konstantin Käfer

Permission is hereby granted, free of charge, to any person obtaining a copy
of this software and associated documentation files (the "Software"), to deal
in the Software without restriction, including without limitation the rights
to use, copy, modify, merge, publish, distribute, sublicense, and/or sell
copies of the Software, and to permit persons to whom the Software is
furnished to do so, subject to the following conditions:

The above copyright notice and this permission notice shall be included in
all copies or substantial portions of the Software.

THE SOFTWARE IS PROVIDED "AS IS", WITHOUT WARRANTY OF ANY KIND, EXPRESS OR
IMPLIED, INCLUDING BUT NOT LIMITED TO THE WARRANTIES OF MERCHANTABILITY,
FITNESS FOR A PARTICULAR PURPOSE AND NONINFRINGEMENT. IN NO EVENT SHALL THE
AUTHORS OR COPYRIGHT HOLDERS BE LIABLE FOR ANY CLAIM, DAMAGES OR OTHER
LIABILITY, WHETHER IN AN ACTION OF CONTRACT, TORT OR OTHERWISE, ARISING FROM,
OUT OF OR IN CONNECTION WITH THE SOFTWARE OR THE USE OR OTHER DEALINGS IN
THE SOFTWARE.

*/


// Apply the horizontal scroller to all elements with the corresponding class.
Drupal.behaviors.horizScroll = function(context) {
  $('.horizscroll:not(.horizscroll-processed)', context).each(function() {
    new Drupal.horizScroll({ 'root': this, 'datasourceKey': 'imageScroller' });
  }).addClass('horizscroll-processed');
};

/**
 * Adds horizontal scrolling functionality.
```

```
 *
 * Options:
 *  - root: The root of the horizontal scroller HTML structure.
 *
 * HTML structure:
 *     <div class="horizscroll>
 *       <a class="horizscroll-left" href="#"><</a>
 *       <a class="horizscroll-right" href="#">></a>
 *       <div class="horizscroll-container">
 *         <ul class="horizscroll-content">
 *           <li>...</li>
 *           ...
 *         </ul>
 *       </div>
 *     </div>
 *
 * You can change the HTML as long as there are elements with these classes.
 * The direct children of .horizscroll-content are considered as item.
 */
Drupal.horizScroll = function(options) {
  // Store a reference to this so that anonymous functions can reference it.
  var that = this;

  // Merge in the options object.
  $.extend(this, options);

  // Add a default datasource.
  if (!this.datasource) {
    this.datasource = Drupal.horizScroll.settingsDatasource;
  }

  // Store references to all required elements.
  $.each(['left', 'right', 'container', 'content'], function() {
    that[this] = $('.horizscroll-' + this + ':first', that.root);
  });
```

```javascript
  // Possibly initialize items.
  this.initializeItems();


  // We start with the first element in the content area as our target.
  this.target = this.content.find('> :eq(0)');


  // Add callback functions to the left and right buttons.
  $.each({'left': 'prev', 'right': 'next' }, function(key, direction) {
    that[key].click(function() {
      that.scrollToItem(that.findTarget(direction));
    });
  });


  // Initialize the buttons.
  this.updateButtons();
};


Drupal.horizScroll.prototype = {
  // Updates the button status depending on the content position.
  'updateButtons': function() {
    // When the target is the first item, we remove enabled status.
    var leftmost = this.target.is(':first-child');
    this.left[leftmost ? 'removeClass' : 'addClass']('enabled');


    // Another algorithm to determine whether the last item is shown.
    var last = this.content.find('> :last-child');


    // Safari returns 0 sometimes when the image has not yet been loaded.
    var hidden = (last.width() === 0);
    // Otherwise, we check whether the distance from the target to the last
    // item is less or equal to the container width.
    var rightmost = (last.offset().left + last.width() -
                     this.target.offset().left) <= this.container.width();


    this.right[(!hidden && rightmost) ? 'removeClass' : 'addClass']('enabled');
```

```
  },

  // Moves to the passed item and sets it as target.
  'scrollToItem': function(item) {
    // Only proceed when there's an item to scroll to.
    if (item.size()) {
      // Set the item as target because updateButtons relies on this.
      this.target = item;

      // Animate the content frame to the new target position.
      var pos = this.content.offset().left - this.target.offset().left;
      this.content.animate({ 'left': pos });

      // Initialize new items when scrolling.s
      this.initializeItems();

      // Update the buttons. This function is working in a way that does not
      // rely on the current position of the content frame because at this
      // point it's still animating and not yet at the final position.
      this.updateButtons();

    }
  },


  // Calculate the previous or next target item.
  // The direction parameter can either be 'next' or 'prev'.
  'findTarget': function(direction) {
    // We save some information so that it doesn't have to be recalculated
    // in each loop. current will be the target item, next contains the a
    // reference to the next item so that we don't call .next() all the time.
    var width = this.container.width(),
        origin = this.target.offset().left,
        current = this.target[direction](),
        next = current[direction]();
```

```
      // While there is a subsequent item and the distance between the current
      // and the next item is still smaller than the container width, make
      while (next.size() && Math.abs(next.offset().left - origin) <= width) {
        current = next;
        next = current[direction]();
      }

      // Wrap in $() to keep jQuery from storing previous items from the loop.
      return $(current);
    },

    'initializeItems': function() {
      // Pre-calculate values for use in the loop.
      var width = this.container.width();
      var origin = this[this.target ? 'target' : 'content'].offset().left;

      // Find the offset of the current last item. It's possible that there are
      // no items yet, so, make sure this is always a sensible value.
      var last = this.content.find('> :last-child');
      var offset = last.size() ? last.offset().left + last.width() : origin;

      // Keep adding new items until we have enough for the next "page".
      while (Math.abs(offset - origin) < 2 * width) {
        // Fetch the element that comes next. Since the index starts with 0,
        // the number of current items will be the next index.
        var el = this.datasource(this.content.children().size());
        if (el) {
          // Add the new item to the content box and update the offset.
          el = $(el);
          this.content.append(el);
          offset = el.offset().left + el.width();
        }
        else {
          // Stop adding new items when there are no more items in the source.
          break;
```

```
      }
    }
  }
};



Drupal.horizScroll.defaultDatasource = function(index) {
  var el = $('> :eq('+ index +')', this.content);
  if (el.size()) {
    return el.html();
  }
};



Drupal.horizScroll.settingsDatasource = function(index) {
  return Drupal.settings[this.datasourceKey][index];
};
```

horizscroll.html

The horizscroll.html file contains the HTML code that allows the JavaScript code from horizscroll.js to attach its behavior. It also contains all variables for the data source.

```
<?xml version="1.0"?>
<!DOCTYPE html PUBLIC "-//W3C//DTD XHTML 1.0 Strict//EN"
    "http://www.w3.org/TR/xhtml1/DTD/xhtml1-strict.dtd">


<html xmlns="http://www.w3.org/1999/xhtml" xml:lang="en" lang="en">
<head>
  <meta http-equiv="Content-Type" content="text/html; charset=utf-8"/>
  <title>horizscroll</title>
  <link rel="stylesheet" href="horizscroll.css" type="text/css" />
  <script src="jquery.js" type="text/javascript"></script>
  <script src="drupal.js" type="text/javascript"></script>
  <script src="horizscroll.js" type="text/javascript"></script>
```

```
<script type="text/javascript"><!--//--><![CDATA[//><!--
  jQuery.extend(Drupal.settings, {
    „basePath": „/",
    ,imageScroller': [
      ,<li><img src="images/con01.jpg" /></li>',
      ,<li><img src="images/con02.jpg" /></li>',
      '<li><img src="images/con03.jpg" /></li>',
      '<li><img src="images/con04.jpg" /></li>',
      '<li><img src="images/con05.jpg" /></li>',
      '<li><img src="images/con06.jpg" /></li>',
      '<li><img src="images/con07.jpg" /></li>',
      '<li><img src="images/con08.jpg" /></li>',
      '<li><img src="images/con09.jpg" /></li>',
      '<li><img src="images/con10.jpg" /></li>',
      '<li><img src="images/con11.jpg" /></li>',
      '<li><img src="images/con12.jpg" /></li>',
      '<li><img src="images/con13.jpg" /></li>',
      '<li><img src="images/con14.jpg" /></li>',
      '<li><img src="images/con15.jpg" /></li>',
      '<li><img src="images/con16.jpg" /></li>',
      '<li><img src="images/con17.jpg" /></li>',
      '<li><img src="images/con18.jpg" /></li>',
      '<li><img src="images/con19.jpg" /></li>',
      '<li><img src="images/con20.jpg" /></li>',
      '<li><img src="images/con21.jpg" /></li>',
      '<li><img src="images/con22.jpg" /></li>',
      '<li><img src="images/con23.jpg" /></li>',
      '<li><img src="images/con24.jpg" /></li>',
      '<li><img src="images/con25.jpg" /></li>',
      '<li><img src="images/con26.jpg" /></li>'
    ],
  });
  //--><!]]></script>
</head>
```

```
<body>

<p>Lorem ipsum dolor sit amet, consectetur adipisicing elit, sed do
   eiusmod tempor incididunt ut labore et dolore magna aliqua. Ut enim
   ad minim veniam, quis nostrud exercitation ullamco laboris nisi ut
   aliquip ex ea commodo consequat. Duis aute irure dolor in
   reprehenderit in voluptate velit esse cillum dolore eu fugiat nulla
   pariatur. Excepteur sint occaecat cupidatat non proident, sunt in
   culpa qui officia deserunt mollit anim id est laborum.</p>

<div class=»horizscroll clear-block»>
   <a class=»horizscroll-left» href=»#»><</a>
   <a class=»horizscroll-right» href=»#»>></a>
   <div class=»horizscroll-container»>
      <ul class=»horizscroll-content»>
         <li><img src="images/con01.jpg" /></li>
         <li><img src="images/con02.jpg" /></li>
         <li><img src="images/con03.jpg" /></li>
         <!-- further items are loaded from settings -->
      </ul>
   </div>
</div>

<p>Lorem ipsum dolor sit amet, consectetur adipisicing elit, sed do
   eiusmod tempor incididunt ut labore et dolore magna aliqua. Ut enim
   ad minim veniam, quis nostrud exercitation ullamco laboris nisi ut
   aliquip ex ea commodo consequat. Duis aute irure dolor in
   reprehenderit in voluptate velit esse cillum dolore eu fugiat nulla
   pariatur. Excepteur sint occaecat cupidatat non proident, sunt in
   culpa qui officia deserunt mollit anim id est laborum.</p>

</body>
</html>
```

horizscroll.css

The `horizscroll.css` file ensures that the scroller is displayed correctly. It is crucial given that a large part of the functionality is achieved by applying CSS classes.

```css
.horizscroll {
  overflow:hidden;
}


.horizscroll-left, .horizscroll-right {
  float:left;
  color:#000;
  text-decoration:none;
  font-size:60px;
  line-height:61px;
  padding:36px 6px;
  display:none;
  font-family:Arial;
  text-align:center;
  font-weight:normal;
}


.horizscroll-right {
  float:right;
}


.horizscroll-left:hover, .horizscroll-right:hover {
  color:#FFF;
  background:#000;
}


.horizscroll-left:active, .horizscroll-right:active {
  background:#CCC;
  color:#000;
}
```

```
html.js .horizscroll-left, html.js .horizscroll-right {
  display:block;
  visibility:hidden;
}


html.js .horizscroll-left.enabled, html.js .horizscroll-right.enabled {
  visibility:visible;
}


* html .horizscroll-left, * html .horizscroll-right {
  /**
    * IE 6 rounding error: 1px lets the content float to the next line
    * when this is 4%. You might need to tweak this depending on the
    * width of your scroller.
    */
  width:3.95%;
  padding-left:0;
  padding-right:0;
}


* html .horizscroll-container {
  float:left;
  width:92%;
}


.horizscroll-container {
  overflow:auto;
  position:relative;
}


html.js .horizscroll-container {
  overflow:hidden;
}


.horizscroll-content {
```

```
    padding:0;
    margin:0;
    width:32767px;
    position:relative;
    top:0;
    left:0;
}

.horizscroll-content li {
    float:left;
    list-style:none;
    margin:0 5px 0 0;
}

.horizscroll-content li img {
    display:block;
}
```

sparkline

The `sparkline` folder contains an example for using the jQuery plugin "Sparkline," which is available at `http://omnipotent.net/jquery.sparkline/`. For a description of this plugin, see the section "Using Plugins and jQuery UI" in Chapter 11.

sparkline.html

The `sparkline.html` file contains the data based on which the Sparkline plugin creates the visual representation.

```
<?xml version="1.0"?>
<!DOCTYPE html PUBLIC "-//W3C//DTD XHTML 1.0 Strict//EN"
    "http://www.w3.org/TR/xhtml1/DTD/xhtml1-strict.dtd">

<html xmlns="http://www.w3.org/1999/xhtml" xml:lang="en" lang="en">
<head>
```

```
<meta http-equiv="Content-Type" content="text/html; charset=utf-8"/>
<title>sparkline</title>

<link rel="stylesheet" href="sparkline.css" type="text/css" />

<script src="jquery-1.2.6.js" type="text/javascript"></script>
<script src="drupal.js" type="text/javascript"></script>
<script src="sparkline.js" type="text/javascript"></script>
<script src="jquery.sparkline.js" type="text/javascript"></script>
<script type="text/javascript"><!--//--><![CDATA[//><!--
    jQuery.extend(Drupal.settings, {
        „basePath": „/"
        // <<< Optionally insert more variables here >>>
    });
//--><!]]></script>
</head>

<body>

<p>Lorem ipsum dolor sit amet, consectetur adipisicing elit, sed do
   eiusmod tempor incididunt ut labore et dolore magna aliqua. Ut enim
   ad minim veniam, quis nostrud exercitation ullamco laboris nisi ut
   aliquip ex ea commodo consequat. Duis aute irure dolor in
   reprehenderit in voluptate velit esse cillum dolore eu fugiat nulla
   pariatur. Excepteur sint occaecat cupidatat non proident, sunt in
   culpa qui officia deserunt mollit anim id est laborum.</p>

<p>
   1. FC Nürnberg
   <span class=»winlost» style=»vertical-align:middle» title=»ls»>
      -1,0,0,1,1,-1,0,0,1,-1,-1
   </span>
</p>
```

```
<p>Lorem ipsum dolor sit amet, consectetur adipisicing elit, sed do

  eiusmod tempor incididunt ut labore et dolore magna aliqua. Ut enim

  ad minim veniam, quis nostrud exercitation ullamco laboris nisi ut

  aliquip ex ea commodo consequat. Duis aute irure dolor in

  reprehenderit in voluptate velit esse cillum dolore eu fugiat nulla

  pariatur. Excepteur sint occaecat cupidatat non proident, sunt in

  culpa qui officia deserunt mollit anim id est laborum.</p>

</body>

</html>
```

sparkline.js

A tiny JavaScript file, sparkline.js, makes the raw data from the HTML file appear in a nicely formatted manner using a sparkline.

```
/**

 * Initializes the sparkline component.

 */

Drupal.behaviors.winlost = function(context) {

  $('.winlost:not(.winlost-processed)', context)

    .sparkline('html', { type: 'tristate' })

    .addClass('winlost-processed');

};
```

Index

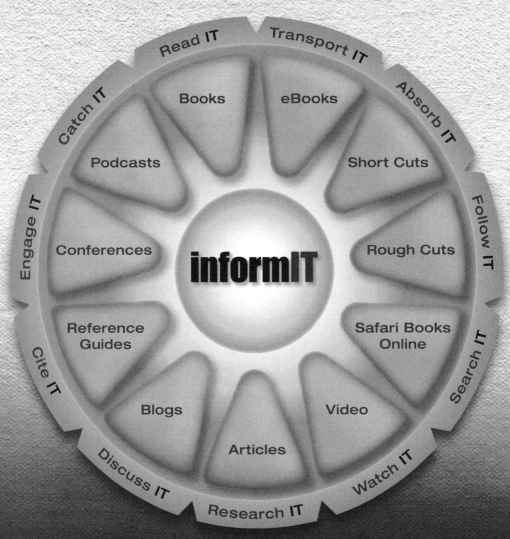

Learn IT at InformIT

Go Beyond the Book

Read IT · Transport IT · Absorb IT · Follow IT · Search IT · Watch IT · Research IT · Discuss IT · Cite IT · Engage IT · Catch IT

- Books
- eBooks
- Short Cuts
- Podcasts
- Rough Cuts
- Conferences
- Safari Books Online
- Reference Guides
- Video
- Blogs
- Articles

informIT

11 WAYS TO LEARN IT at **www.informIT.com/learn**

The online portal of the information technology
publishing imprints of Pearson Education

 Addison · Cisco Press · EXAM/CRAM · IBM · QUE · SAMS

FREE Online Edition

Your purchase of **Front End Drupal** includes access to a free online edition for 45 days through the Safari Books Online subscription service. Nearly every Prentice Hall book is available online through Safari Books Online, along with more than 5,000 other technical books and videos from publishers such as Addison-Wesley Professional, Cisco Press, Exam Cram, IBM Press, O'Reilly, Que, and Sams.

SAFARI BOOKS ONLINE allows you to search for a specific answer, cut and paste code, download chapters, and stay current with emerging technologies.

Activate your FREE Online Edition at www.informit.com/safarifree

> **STEP 1:** Enter the coupon code: NXPXQFA.

> **STEP 2:** New Safari users, complete the brief registration form.
> Safari subscribers, just log in.

If you have difficulty registering on Safari or accessing the online edition, please e-mail customer-service@safaribooksonline.com